DUE

D0088399

CONSTRUCTING

CRIME

Perspectives on Making News and Social Problems

Gary W. Potter
Victor E. Kappeler

Eastern Kentucky University

WAVELAND

PRESS, INC.

Prospect Heights, Illinois

For information about this book, write or call:
Waveland Press, Inc.
P.O. Box 400
Prospect Heights, Illinois 60070
(847) 634-0081

Credits for cartoons:

Calvin & Hobbes cartoon, p. viii, © 1996 by Watterson. Reprinted by permission of Universal Press Syndicate. All Rights reserved.

Non Sequitur cartoons, pp. 25, 112, & 263, © 1997 Washington Post Writers Group. Reprinted with permission.

Cartoon by Don Wright, p. 332, © 1997 Palm Beach Post.

Contents

Part III EFFECTS OF CONSTRUCTING CRIME   263

Preface

If there is one thing U.S. society has an abundance of, it is images and opinions about crime. Pick up and read a newspaper from any city—Chicago, Boston, Detroit, Los Angeles, Houston, or Tampa. Turn on a TV and flip though the channels; stop on anything—news, talk shows, sitcoms, or soap operas. Stop by a cinema and watch any movie—horror, drama, science fiction, or romance. Ask anyone, anyplace, anytime—a student on campus, a professor in the classroom, a banker at the office, a relative at home, or even a stranger on the street. There is no shortage of talk about crime. It is a central theme running through many forms of communication in modern society.

Crime is a staple on many institutional playing fields. It is a focal concern in our schools; it is the subject of sermons in churches; it anchors political platforms; it permeates discussions of the economy; it's a concern of families; and it serves as the foundation for our legal institution. In comparison to these vicarious experiences, our empirical knowledge and experience with crime pales. Most of us have never been the victim of a violent crime, and certainly the majority of the public has never sat down to read a scholarly study of crime. This situation, however, does nothing to mute private and public expressions of opinions. Everyone has an opinion about crime and crime control policy.

In our role as college professors, we often ask students a series of unusual questions on the first day of class. Sometimes we use the language of medicine; other times we adopt the jargon of engineering; and on occasion we drop an example from physics. Simplified, the questions might be posed like this: What do you think about advances in cardiac care? What do you think about the structural quality of this building? or, What do you think about the fact that physicists cannot predict the movement of certain subatomic particles? The response is usually the same (except from the errant physics or health care major)—bright students sit in silence with all expression draining from their faces. As the length of silence grows, gazes begin to be diverted from the inquisitor toward desks or windows. Some students begin to fidget in their seats. Eventually, the uncomfortable silence is broken with yet another series of questions. What do you think about drunk drivers? What are your thoughts on the president's plan to deploy 100,000 new cops on the streets? Should the use of controlled substances be legalized? Expression rushes back to their faces, fidgeting stops, and many lean forward in their seats. The inquisitor has been transformed and is no longer a stranger; a social chord has been struck. The uncomfortable silence is broken in a rush of opinion that has to be diplomatically suppressed to get back to the point of the questions. The purpose, of course, is to demonstrate that while there is a dearth of opinions on many important social and scientific issues, there is no hesitation to express an abundance of opinions about crime and crime control policy.

What explains this sudden break in the silence, the frantic rush to express an opinion, even an uninformed one? To begin to answer this question is to look behind the blue haze projected from television and movie screens; to reconsider the reality imprinted in newspapers and magazines, a reality that changes as easily as print ink rubs off onto our fingers; to listen carefully to the crime stories that are told by friends, professors, bankers, relatives, and passing acquaintances. Crime is intricately woven into the very fabric of society.

In this collection, we explore the processes by which the social reality of crime is constructed. We have pulled together a collection of some of the best studies on the media and crime. Several of the articles included in the anthology are classics while many of the others merely need a bit of time to demonstrate their contribution to our understanding of crime and the media. Several of the newer articles were first published during our tenures as a principal reviewer and the editor of *Justice Quarterly*. We were fortunate to be able to work with the authors of several of these articles from their initial submission to the journal through their publication in this anthology.

In putting together the anthology, we attempted to stay true to its primary objective of bringing together a collection of articles devoted to the construction of crime through the making of news and social problems. We have organized the anthology into three distinct sections that reflect this objective. In the first section, we offer an overview of some of the many issues associated with studying crime and the media. The articles in this section provide a foundation for understanding the concepts employed by researchers who study the media and crime as well as an accounting of the many actors, practices, and techniques involved in the construction of crime. In the section that follows, attention is turned to the making of crime problems. In this section various crime issues and types of crime are considered. The section includes media constructions of crime ranging from drug panics to gang rituals to less mature constructions of crime like road warriors and the "ice" epidemic. In the final section attention is turned to the effects of media constructions of crime. In this section the diversity and complexity of media effects are demonstrated—from the impact they have on police and researchers to the effects turned inward on the media themselves. We close with a brief epilogue that continues the mirroring process, introspectively raising questions about the viability of stripping crime and the media from the broader transformations shaping society.

Gary W. Potter
Victor E. Kappeler
Eastern Kentucky University

Introduction

There is probably no issue that more consistently, over a longer period and with greater emotion, influences public opinion than crime. The results of poll after poll demonstrate that crime—in general or a specific crime issue—captures public attention. Whether the issue is drug-related crime, violent crime, juvenile crime, child abductions, serial killers, youth gangs, or crime against the elderly, a public consensus exists that crime is rampant, dangerous, and threatening to explode. The dangers of crime are seen as immediate, omnipresent, and almost inescapable. For almost three decades in the United States, the fear of crime has been so real that one can almost reach out and touch it. Politicians, law enforcement executives, the private crime industry, and the media cater to the public mood. Their response has been to affirm fear and to offer increasingly draconian solutions in the form of more police, more arrests, longer sentences, more prisons, and more executions. Yet the public's palpable fear grows unabated. Each new crime story, each new crime movie, each new governmental pronouncement on crime increases the public thirst for more crime control, less personal freedom, and greater state-intervention.

In contrast to seemingly tangible public fear, crime facts are far more difficult to assess. The emotional reaction to crime makes the public policy issue of control intensely sensitive. The issue responds to manipulation and pandering so predictably that advertisers and public relations experts would be envious of the responses elicited. Why are crime facts so difficult to determine but crime fear so easy to manipulate? Through what process do rumors, gossip, urban legends, and apochyrphal stories become public "common sense"? Through what mechanisms do isolated and rare incidents weave a tapestry of fear, panic, and hysteria? More importantly, who benefits from the construc-

1

tion of this labyrinth? Those are the questions this book addresses. Whether they can be fully answered is debatable. However, a careful look at crime and crime-related issues can dissect the sometimes cynical and calculated efforts to fashion a web of public fear out of a curtain of gossamer. Public opinion and crime facts demonstrate no congruence. The reality of crime in the United States has been subverted to a constructed reality as ephemeral as swamp gas. The policies and programs emanating from that constructed reality do far more damage than good to public safety and crime control.

Crime Knowledge

What does the public really know about crime and how do they know it? The most reliable crime data available clearly demonstrates that the vast majority of people living in the United States have not been and never will be victims of crime. In fact, over 90% of the U.S. population has no direct experience with crime at all (Barkan, 1997; Kappeler, Blumberg & Potter, 1996). Yet the public remains convinced of the imminent danger—changing their personal habits and lives to accommodate those fears and voting for politicians who promise solutions to the problem. What is the basis for these opinions, fears, and impressions?

In addition to their own experiences, people interpret and internalize the experiences of others. They hear—often second- third- or fourth-hand—about crime incidents involving neighbors, relatives, friends, and friends of friends. This normal process of socialization carries crime "facts" and crime-related experiences from one person to many others like a virus. Crime is a topic of conversation, both public and private. Strong opinions and reactions amplify and extend the content of actual experiences. Lost in the retelling is the relatively isolated aspect of the incidents. Socialization processes, however, have limited utility in explaining the pervasiveness of crime-related concerns. There are other processes at work.

For centuries, the only means of disseminating knowledge from one person to another was orally. Reaching larger audiences was a slow, repetitive process limited by time and place. The printing press relieved some of the restrictions and allowed written messages from one person to many listeners. Although an important revolution for the possibilities it opened, the new technologies have created a maelstrom of information. The mass media can disseminate messages literally with the speed of light and sound. Publishers produce thousands of books about crime—some fictional, some true, some simply crude "pot-boilers." Movies make crime a central theme. Producers know that movies like *Seven*, *Kiss the Girls*, *Usual Suspects*, and *Natural Born Killers* attract large audiences. Television programs also use crime and violence to attract attention. Police programs have been a staple of television programming from *Dragnet* to *NYPD Blue.*

As an outgrowth of the public's fixation on crime, the television industry has constructed a new programming hybrid—a genetic cross between entertainment and the news called reality T.V. By the end of 1993, there were seven national programs representing this new genre: *America's Most Wanted, Top Cops, American Detective, Unsolved Mysteries, Rescue 911, Inside Edition,* and *Hard Copy.* Producers for *American Detective* summarize the content of this genre of programming with six words posted on the production office bulletin board: *death, stab, shoot, strangulation, club, suicide* (Seagal, 1993).

According to research, the mass media are the basic sources of information on crime, criminals, crime control policies, and the criminal justice system for most people (Ericson, Baranek & Chan, 1989; Graber, 1980; Barak, 1994; Warr, 1995). Crime themes are a mother lode for the media. Crime attracts viewers. More viewers mean greater newspaper and magazine circulation, larger television audiences, and consequently larger advertising fees (Barkan, 1997; Chermak, 1994; Gordon & Heath, 1981). The evening news and the reality crime shows focus on dramatic themes to attract viewers: police "hot pursuits"; violent crimes, particularly strange and heinous crimes with innocent and unsuspecting victims; jury trials; and crime alleged to be committed by social deviants like pedophiles, prostitutes, satanists, or cannibals (Lichter & Lichter, 1983).

The adage, "if it bleeds it leads" is a staple of television news industry. In 1993 the three major networks (CBS, NBC, and ABC) ran 1,632 crime stories on their evening newscasts, up from 785 the previous year and from 571 in 1991 (Lichter & Lichter, 1994). In 1993, 329 of those stories focused on murder, compared to 104 in 1992 (Barkan, 1997; Freeman, 1994). Did that obsession with crime and homicide in any way reflect reality? No, it did not. Both victimization rates and crime rates fell between 1992 and 1993. In fact, crime rates have decreased every year since 1991, and victimization surveys indicate that serious crime had been on a perpetual decline since the early 1970s (Freeman, 1994; Maguire & Pastore, 1995; Kappeler et al., 1996). Despite these declines, 88% of the U.S. public in 1994 was convinced that crime rates and crime victimizations were at an all-time high (Barkan, 1997; Jackson, 1994). Politicians reacted to the perception of crime—not the reality—when Congress expanded the federal death penalty, instituted a federal three strikes law, and authorized billions of additional dollars for more police and new prisons.

The Portrayal of Crime in the Mass Media

In addition to devoting a disproportionate amount of coverage to crime, the mass media organize coverage in a way that seriously distorts the reality of crime. First, the media provide a distorted view of how much crime there is in society. The media create a wholly inaccurate image of a society in which violent crime is rampant and in which crime is constantly and immutably on the increase. For example, 33% of all television program time is devoted to shows about crime and the police, and that programming is heavily concentrated during prime time, the period of highest audience participation (Graber, 1980). In addition, 20% of local television news programming, 13% of national news programming, and 25% of newspaper space focuses on crime and law enforcement (Ericson et al., 1989; Surette, 1998). Since the earliest days of television, program time devoted to crime has consistently and persistently increased, with massive increases in prime time coverage starting in 1984 and continuing to today (Beirne & Messerschmidt, 1995).

Second, media coverage of crime seriously distorts public perception of the types of crime being committed and the frequency with which violent crimes occur. The media have a preoccupation with violent crime. In the film *Die Hard II*, 264 people are killed. In *Robocop II*, another 81 victims are claimed. *Another 48 Hours* and *Total Recall* continue the theme of rampant carnage with 20 and 74 violent deaths, respectively (Livingston, 1992). Television entertainment shows are rife with violence. From 1967 to 1987, 80% of all television programs and 90% of children's cartoons had violent themes (Liebert & Sprafkin, 1988).

Researchers looking at ten network and cable channels in 1992 found that a single day's programming portrays 1,846 violent crimes (Barkan, 1997; Lichter & Edmundson, 1992). A study of television programming for the past ten years found that seven out of every ten prime-time programs depicted violent crime and that the level of violence depicted in Saturday morning children's programming had grown dramatically in recent years (Gerbner, 1994). In addition, the news media make crime—particularly violent crime—standard fare. Researchers have demonstrated a consistent and strong bias in the news toward murder, sexual crimes, gangs and violence, and drug-related violence (Beirne & Messerschmidt, 1995; Ericson et al., 1989; Livingston, 1996) A study of crime coverage in New Orleans by Sheley and Ashkins (1981) demonstrated that only 20% of serious index crime reported to the police in that city involved violence. But, 68% of newspaper crime stories and 80% of television crime coverage in New Orleans focused on violent crime. In particular, homicides were featured in 12% of all newspaper crime stories and 50% of all television crime stories, despite the fact that homicide made up only .4 percent of felonies known to the New Orleans police. In the *Chicago Tribune* murder constitutes 26.2% of all stories about crime; however, murder represents only 0.2% of crimes reported to police in Chicago (Graber, 1980). Similarly, a national study conducted by Liska and Baccaglini (1990) surveyed crime stories in major newspapers in twenty-six U.S. cities. In those cities, homicides accounted for .02 percent of all felonies, but homicides were featured in 30 percent of all crime stories.

It is not just homicides which are overrepresented; the less common a crime is, the more coverage it will generate. Sensational and rare crimes which can be fitted into news themes with moralistic messages are particularly popular. Over the years the media have created crime scares by formulating news themes around issues of "white-slavery" in the prostitution industry; sexual psychopaths running rampant in major cities; Communists infiltrating every aspect of U.S. society and in every pumpkin patch relaying vital national security data to the former Soviet Union; satanists engaged in mass murder, child sacrifice, and ritualistic child abuse; serial killers roaming the countryside; and many others. As Philip Jenkins (1996) comments:

> If we relied solely on the evidence of the mass media, we might well believe that every few years, a particular form of immoral or criminal behavior becomes so dangerous as almost to threaten the foundations of society. . . . These panics are important in their own right for what they reveal about social concerns and prejudices—often based on xenophobia and anti-immigrant prejudice. (pp. 67–70)

Mass murders by satanic cults, the predations of roaming serial killers, and organized child abuse in day-care centers are so rare as to be total aberrations. The media choose to ignore common, everyday, typical crime. Nonviolent crimes are 47% of all reported crimes, but only 4 percent of all crime stories in newspapers (Graber, 1980). White-collar crimes such as price-fixing, illegal disposal of toxic waste, and unsafe work conditions get little coverage. In fact the media's consistent pattern of ignoring and de-emphasizing these crimes has created a "collective ignorance" in Western society (Box, 1983).

Media Attention and Citizen Fear of Crime

With such heavy exposure to crime themes in entertainment mediums and through news programming it would appear to be common sense that more media exposure should be directly related to a greater fear of crime (Barkan, 1997). However, unlike media analysts and news anchors, social scientists are constrained by their craft to be more circumspect in their claims. A correlation between media exposure and concerns about crime is easy to demonstrate, but correlation is a long way from causation. Direct relationships are not easy to prove. For example, it is difficult to demonstrate whether greater media exposure causes fear of crime or whether fear of crime causes greater media exposure because people are staying home watching crime on television. As we pointed out earlier, people are exposed to information other than the media which may influence their viewpoints (i.e., rumors, gossip, urban legends). In addition, media research is difficult, complex, and subject to many pitfalls. For example, how does one measure the impact of the media? Is viewing time a measure? Do column inches constitute an index? Does the quality and the impact of language and content take precedence? (Miethe & Lee, 1984; Skogan & Maxfield, 1981; Surette, 1998).

Despite the need for caution and the constraints of science, much evidence indicates that the media do influence the level of fear of crime and contribute to the persistence of crime as a major national issue. For example, a study of public attitudes toward crime in Phoenix was quite revealing (Livingston, 1996; Baker et al., 1983). In this study, the researchers surveyed the residents of Phoenix in both 1979 and 1980. Both surveys found roughly the same levels of crime victimization, but the 1980 survey showed a clear and marked increase in the percentage of residents who thought crime was increasing. Since actual crime incidents could not explain this increase in concern, the researchers turned to the media for clues. They found that during 1980 the local newspapers had intensified their coverage of two crimes: homicides and robberies. That intensification of coverage was congruent with a change in police department leadership and increased dissemination of information about violent crime by the police department. The bureaucratic change in police procedures facilitated media access to certain types of crime data—data emphasizing violent crime. The corresponding increase in media coverage sparked an increase in citizen fear, despite the fact that the reality of crime had not changed. Other studies point to similar media influences. For example, Linda Heath's (1984) research demonstrated that newspaper stories focusing on random violent crimes had the effect of increasing public fear of crime. Liska and Baccaglini (1990) found that newspaper stories about local homicides increased fear of crime. This effect was especially strong for stories appearing in the first fifteen pages of the newspaper.

George Gerbner, a leading media researcher at the Annenberg School of Communications at the University of Pennsylvania, has synthesized these media impacts into a cultivation theory—the "mean world" syndrome. Gerbner argues that the research demonstrates that heavy viewers of television violence, whether in entertainment or news mediums, increasingly develop the feeling that they are living in a state of siege. Gerbner's research shows that heavy television viewers: (1) seriously overestimate the probability that they will be victims of violence; (2) believe their own neighborhoods to be unsafe; (3) rank fear of crime as one of their most compelling personal problems; (4) assume crime rates are going up regardless of whether they really are; (5) support punitive anti-crime measures; and, (6) are more likely to buy guns and anti-crime safety devices (Gerbner, 1994). Other research demonstrates that "heavy viewers . . . exhibit an exaggerated fear of victimization and a perception that people cannot be trusted." (Carlson, 1995: 190).

In addition to increasing public fears, media crime coverage has other, easier to discern and demonstrate impacts on public perceptions and views of crime. Heavy coverage shapes perceptions and directs much public discourse on the crime issue. For example, the media regularly and falsely direct attention to crimes allegedly committed by young, poor, urban males, who are often members of minority groups (Box, 1983; Reiman, 1998). Media coverage directs people's attention to specific crimes and helps to shape those crimes as social problems (i.e., drug use, gangs). Media coverage limits discourse on crime control options to present policies—suggesting that the only options are more laws, more police, longer sentences, and more prisons (Kappeler et al., 1996; Skogan & Maxfield, 1981; Surette, 1998). The impact of media coverage is readily apparent in the creation of crime scares and moral panics.

Moral Panics

The concept of a moral panic was developed by Stanley Cohen (1980). A moral panic occurs when a group or type of activity is perceived as a threat to the stability and well-being of society. The media provide copious details and information (not necessarily accurate); this is followed by attention from law enforcement officials, politicians, and editorial writers who begin to comment on the panic. "Experts" then join the fray and try to explain the panic and offer policy options for dealing with it.

Moral panics direct public attention toward the activity or group and organizes public fear for the well-being of society. The attention amplifies the behavior of the groups under scrutiny. Cohen's study looked at media coverage of the "Mods and Rockers" in the 1960s in Britain (Cohen, 1980). The media seriously exaggerated the behaviors of these groups. More importantly, the media played a key role in taking imprecisely defined social groupings (Cohen's "loose stylistic associations") and redefining them into well-organized youth gangs. The "Mods and Rockers" were transformed by media coverage into folk devils, a stereotyped caricature of reality which became the alleged source of great social danger and harm. Media coverage actually heightened the identification of young people with these two groups, an identification which had been marginal at best. The media intensified both the amount of troubling behavior and the numbers of people engaged in that behavior, thereby becoming a self-fulfilling prophecy. Media attention also exacerbated tensions between these two stylized groups and between young people and their communities in general (Cohen, 1980).

Of course, moral panics did not begin with the "Mods and Rockers." In 1922, future Supreme Court Justice Felix Frankfurter and legal scholar Roscoe Pound took the media to task for creating crime scares. Frankfurter and Pound noted that newspapers in Cleveland had dramatically increased their coverage of crime stories during 1919, even though crimes reported to the police had increased only slightly. They charged that the press was needlessly alarming the public and that the effect was a dangerous tendency for the public to pressure police to ignore due process rights and constitutional protections in their pursuit of criminals (Frankfurter & Pound, 1922)

The "sex fiend" panic of the 1930s and 1940s resulted in the passage of sexual psychopath laws in 28 states. McCaghy and Capron's analysis of the development of these laws reveals a key role played by the media (McCaghy & Capron, 1997). Sex fiend panics typically began with the commission of a sex crime, particularly a crime against a child, accompanied by heavy mass media coverage. This panic included estimates, without any basis in fact, that thousands of sex fiends were at large in the community. These "sex crime waves" were not related to any increase in the actual numbers of reported sex crimes; the panic was artificially induced by media coverage of particularly salacious cases (see Sutherland, 1950). The media advocated such solutions as castration, the outlawing of pornography, and life imprisonment for sex offenders. In the end special sexual psychopath laws were passed which allowed indeterminate confinement for any offender, whether a child molester or an exhibitionist or a fornicator, until the state deemed them to be cured. In fact, in some states the original offense didn't have to be a sex offense—it could be robbery or arson, as long as a psychiatrist could identify sexual dysfunctions in the accused. The irony, of course, was that a violent rapist or child molester could be arrested and released in a few months, and a "masturbator," adulterer, or pickpocket deemed to have a sexual motivation could sit in prison forever.

In the 1980s the same kind of moral panic surfaced with regard to the use of crack (a smokeable form of cocaine hydrochloride). The media—particularly news magazines, television, and newspapers—and the state engaged in a frenzied attempt to create a moral panic in the form of a drug scare as a means of continuing and extending the "War on Drugs" begun in the Reagan administration.

Craig Reinarman and Harry Levine (1989) have carefully researched the media's creation of a drug scare surrounding crack. Reinarman and Levine define a "drug scare" as a historical period in which all manner of social difficulties (such as crime, health problems, the failure of the education system) are blamed on a chemical substance. "Drug scares" are not new. Problems of opiate addiction at the turn of the century were blamed on Chinese immigrants; African Americans were portrayed as "cocaine fiends" during the 1920s; violent behavior resulting from marijuana consumption was linked to Mexican farm laborers in the 1920s and 1930s. The construction of the crack scare was similar in that it linked the use of crack-cocaine to inner-city blacks, Hispanics, and youths. In the 1970s, when the use of expensive cocaine hydrochloride was concentrated among affluent whites, both the media and state focused their attention on heroin, seen as a drug of the inner-city poor. Only when cocaine became available in an inexpensive form, crack, did the scapegoating common to drug scares begin.

The media hype began in 1986, following the spread of crack into poor and working class neighborhoods. *Time* and *Newsweek* ran five cover stories each on crack during 1986. The three major television networks quickly joined the feeding frenzy. NBC did 400 news stories on crack between June and December 1986; in July 1986, all three networks ran 74 drug stories on their nightly newscasts. These stories contained highly inflated estimates of crack use and warnings about the dangers of which far outstripped available evidence.

What is particularly troubling about those news stories is that they were entirely incorrect. Instead of escalating and expanding use of cocaine and crack, research from the National Institute of Drug Abuse showed that the use of all forms of cocaine by youth and young adults had reached its peak four years earlier and had been declining ever since. Every indicator showed that at the height of the media frenzy crack use was relatively rare (Walker, 1998; Beckett, 1994; Orcutt & Turner, 1993). Surveys of high school students demonstrated that experimentation with cocaine and cocaine products had been decreasing steadily since 1980. In fact, the government's own statistics showed that 96% of young people in the United States had never even tried crack. If there had been an epidemic, it was long over.

Officially produced data strongly refuted other claims about crack use. The media reports claimed that crack and cocaine were highly addictive and that crack, in particular, was so addictive that one experience with the drug could enslave a user to addiction for life. However, NIDA estimates showed that of the 22 million people who had used cocaine and cocaine-products, very few of them ever became addicted.

In fact very few of them ever escalated to daily use. NIDA's own estimates indicated that fewer than 3% of cocaine users would ever become "problem" users (Kappeler et al., 1996). The health dangers of cocaine and crack were also widely exaggerated; few users sought medical treatment. Official statistics showed there were 300 tobacco-related deaths and 100 alcohol-related deaths for every cocaine-related death.

The impact of the crack scare was tangible and immediate. New laws were passed increasing mandatory sentences for crack use and sales. Ironically, these laws resulted in a situation where someone arrested for crack faced the prospect of a prison sentence three to eight times longer than a sentence for cocaine hydrochloride, the substance needed to produce crack (Walker, 1998). The drug laws had been turned on their head with wholesalers receiving less severe sanctions than retailers and users.

Reinarman and Levine argue convincingly that the media portrayal of crack use was out of all proportion to reality. They even argue that the intense coverage of crack may have created new markets for the drug and actually threatened the decline in use which had already been underway for almost a decade (Reinarman & Levine. 1989)

One of the most recent moral panics in U.S. society has centered on juveniles. A variety of young people's behavior has been subjected to media analysis, as indicated by this lead for a story in the *Washington Post*: "Unplanned pregnancies. HIV infection and AIDS, other sexually transmitted diseases. Cigarettes, alcohol and drug abuse. Eating disorders. Violence. Suicide. Car crashes" (*Washington Post*, 12/22/92). Headlines and feature articles tell a compelling story of violent teens who are oversexed and sexually reckless, dependent on welfare, and suffering from various psychological abnormalities. Consider this litany of media concerns: "Teens and AIDS" (*Newsweek*, 8/3/92); "Kids, Sex, and Values" (Time, 5/24/93); "Teenage Sex: Just Say Wait" (*U.S. News & World Report*, 7/26/93); "Teen Violence: Wild in the Streets" (*Newsweek*, 8/2/93); "Kids and Guns" (*Newsweek*, 3/9/92; "When Killers Come to Class" (*U.S. News and World Report*, 11/8/93); and, "Big Shots" (*Time*, 8/2/93). Among the issues raised by these articles are teen suicide, teen pregnancy, and teen crime. The content of the media presentations and the reality of each is quite divergent.

For example, the media have consistently repeated the wildly inflated estimate that there are 5,000 to 6,000 teen suicides a year—one every 90 seconds. The source of that estimate is the National Association of Psychiatric Hospitals, an organization representing private businesses which do a land-office business in the forced commitment of teenagers based on vague diagnoses of personality disorders (Males, 1994). In reality, federal estimates place the actual number of teen suicides at an average of 2,050 a year.

With regard to teen pregnancies the media have bandied about the claim that there are 500,000 teen pregnancies every year in the United States. The real number is closer to 280,000 or about half the media estimate. More importantly the standard media representation of teenage mothers being impregnated by teenage fathers as a result of unsafe and wildly hedonistic sexual experimentation is patently wrong. The fact is that 71% of all teenage parents have adult partners over the age of 20.The issue is not "babies having babies," it is "babies" being used by adults (Males, 1994).

Finally, on the issue of teen crime, the Associated Press proclaimed on June 8, 1990 that juvenile crime had increased thirtyfold since 1950. That estimate has been repeated in almost every mass media story on teen crime. These facts are known: (1) the 1950 crime statistics are too incomplete for any comparisons to present crime levels; (2) data comparisons since the 1970s show no increase in juvenile crime in almost three decades. Even more troubling is the misrepresentation of juvenile violence in the media. Magazine stories and newspaper articles have consistently failed to point out that children are victims more often than perpetrators. For example, 83% of murdered children, 50% of murdered teenagers, and 85% of murdered adults are slain by adults. Every year in the United States about 350,000 children and teenagers are the victims of sexual and physical abuse, with the average age of the perpetrator being about 32. For every sexual and violent crime committed by a teenagers, three such crimes are committed by adults against children and teens. The best available estimates tell us that 12 million women in the United States have been raped and that 62% of those rapes occurred before age 18. The average age of the rapist was 27. Finally, estimates suggest that between 60 and 90 percent of all prison inmates, and almost all the individuals presently on death row in the United States were abused as children (Males, 1994). The alleged crime wave by children appears to be more accurately described as the victimization of children.

Finally, not all attempts at creating moral panics are successful. Even unsuccessful crime scares are revealing when placed in context. In 1995, *Time* magazine ran a cover story entitled "Cyberporn" (7/3/95). The cover showed a child at a computer with the word "CYBERPORN" emblazoned across the computer screen. The headline read: "Exclusive: A new study shows how pervasive and wild it really is." In eight pages of text, photographs, and graphics, *Time* alleged that any child could access a harrowing world of sexual depravity simply by turning on a computer and logging onto the Internet. The story claimed that 83.5% of the pictures carried by Usenet news groups were pornographic in nature, citing a study by a principal researcher at Carnegie-Mellon. Subsequent scholarly analysis showed that the actual figure was closer to less than one-half of one percent. In addition, the magazine's principal investigator turned out to have done his research as an assignment for an undergraduate class at Carnegie-Mellon (Cohen & Solomon, 1995). Of course, the truth belatedly revealed did little to curb agitation from the religious right for free speech controls on Internet communication or efforts by both Congress and the Clinton administration to restrict Internet content.

Crime Mythology

False beliefs about crime abound in U.S. society and play a dispro-portionate role in the formulation of government and law enforcement policies. Despite panics about increasing crime emanating from the state and the media, the fact remains that there was no crime wave in the 1980s and 1990s; crime had been falling precipitously for two decades (Kappeler et al., 1996). There was no crack epidemic in the mid-1980s. The crime that does exist is not predominantly violent, and violent crime is not as common or debilitating as the media would lead us to believe. The media, the state, and criminal justice officials create and perpetuate crime myths.

Crime myths focus on unpopular, minority, and deviant groups in society. Drug problems have consistently been laid squarely at the feet of immigrant groups, minority groups, and inner-city residents, wholly displacing the reality of drug use. Problems of opiate addiction in the late 1800s and early 1900s were blamed on immigrant Chinese workers, while the actual problem resulted from the overuse of over-the-counter elixirs by white, middle-aged, rural, Protestant women. The 1980s' cocaine epidemic was blamed on the irresponsible and hedonistic life-styles of inner-city minorities, while the facts were that cocaine was pri-marily a drug of choice of affluent, suburban whites. Law enforcement agencies and the media have combined their efforts to tie serial murder, child abduction, ritualistic child abuse, and child sacrifice and murder to the activities of unpopular religious groups and sexual minorities.

Crime myths come in many forms. For example, in the mid-1970s the media reported that several children had been murdered as the result of the poisoning of their Halloween candy. To this day local televi-sion stations run cautionary stories before each Halloween's "Trick-or-Treat" period. Rather than a wave of poisoning by strangers, careful investigation showed that only two such incidents had occurred, neither of which involved a stranger. One child died from heroin he found in his uncle's house; the other child was poisoned when his father put cyanide in his candy. As with most crime myths, the truth has been

universally ignored and tales of mythical savagery have been perpetu-
ated (Best & Horiuchi, 1985).

In the early 1980s the media and the government helped create a
panic over the issue of child abduction. It was estimated that somewhere
between 1.5 and 2.5 million children were abducted from their homes
every year. Of those children, 50,000 would never be heard from again,
presumably the victims of homicides. Pictures of "missing children"
appeared on milk cartons, billboards, in newspapers, and on television.
Children and parents were cautioned against contacts with strangers.
The police in one town even wanted to etch identification numbers on
school children's teeth so their bodies would be easier to identify (Dunn,
1994). But the child abduction epidemic never happened. About 95% of
those missing children were runaways (most of whom were home within
48 hours) or children abducted by a parent in a custody dispute. The
fact is there are no more than 50 to 150 stranger child abductions a year
in the United States (Kappeler et al., 1996).

From 1983 to 1985 official estimates and media hype fueled a
serial killer panic. Using FBI estimates of unsolved and motiveless homicides, media sources falsely reported that roughly 20% of all homicides,
or about 4,000 murders a year, were the handiwork of serial killers. The
media fed the myth with shocking and untrue confessions from Henry
Lee Lucas, Ted Bundy, and others. Congress and the president reversed
themselves and funded the Violent Criminal Apprehension Program and
a behavioral sciences center for the FBI. When the data was subjected
to careful analysis, scholars determined that at most there were 50 or
60 serial killer victims a year and that serial killers could account for no
more than 2 percent of all homicides (Jenkins, 1996). Despite the creation of a serial killer panic by the media, serial murder remains a rare
and extremely uncommon event.

Starting with the crack panic of the 1980s, both the state and the
media have gone to extraordinary lengths to tie illicit drug use to African
Americans while ignoring heavy drug use among affluent whites. Half of
all television news stories about drugs feature blacks as users or sellers,
while only 32 percent of the stories feature whites (Reed, 1991). This is
out of all proportion to the known patterns of drug use. About 70% of
all drug users are white and about 14% are black. This misrepresentation of race and drug use is reflected in police practices. Blacks represent 48% of all individuals arrested on drug charges, roughly
three-and-a-half times their actual rate of use (Walker, 1998).

The media play a vital role in the construction of crime mythology
(Kappeler et al., 1996). Through selective interviewing the media can,
and often do, fit isolated and rare incidents into what Fishman calls
"news themes" (Fishman, 1978). For example, reporting the details of a
crime involving an elderly victim and then interviewing a police official

in charge of special unit targeting crimes against the elderly creates a news theme—and can eventually create both a "crime wave" and a "crime myth." The use of value laden language also contributes heavily to crime mythology. Youth gang members "prey" upon unsuspecting victims; serial killers "stalk"; child abductors "lurk"; organized criminals are "mafiosi." Such language is common in crime news and substantially changes both the content and the context of crime stories. The media also frequently present misleading data. "Crime clocks" portray an exaggerated threat of crime. Uncritical reproduction of officially produced statistics often organize stories into news themes and deflect alternative interpretations of the data.

An excellent example of such myth-producing techniques occurred in San Francisco in 1994. The *San Francisco Chronicle* ran a front page headline on January 24, 1994 that read, "Teenage Crime Wave in San Francisco—Homicide Arrests Up 87%." Both the language and the substance of the headline were blatantly incorrect. The *Chronicle* based its story on a statistical analysis by the police department which had compared the number of juvenile homicides in 1992 to the number of homicides and attempted homicides in 1993. In actuality, there had been no increase in juvenile homicides at all. The first paragraph in the story made the claim that violent crime committed by juveniles "continues to shoot through the roof" and cited a 77 % increase in juvenile robbery as substantiation. That statistic was based on a police department comparison of arrests in 1992 and referrals to juvenile probation in 1993. Arrests and referrals to probation are entirely different categories having no relation to each other. In fact, arrests had increased only four % over a two-year period (Hoover, 1994).

Another example was the cover story of *U.S. News and World Report* (1/17/1994) entitled "Violence in America." The story began with the statement: "A scary orgy of violent crime is fueling another public call to action." The basic assumption of the story was entirely incorrect. The incidence of violent crime in the United States had not risen in over twenty years, and in fact had fallen in that period. More importantly, the story emphasized a major news theme of recent years—that violent crime was invading safe sanctuaries, particularly the suburbs. The essence of this news theme is the claim that areas that were once relatively safe are now under siege by a wave of violent crime. The article claimed that, "the nature of some of the crime is changing, making some people more vulnerable and bringing the worst kinds of problems into communities that many thought were safe." The truth was far from the rhetoric. In fact, violent crime had been consistently falling in the suburbs. According to National Crime Victimization Survey Data, a suburban resident was 13 % more likely to be a victim of violent crime twenty years ago than today. NCVS data show that crimes such as burglary and robbery have fallen sharply in suburban and rural areas since the 1970s. The story in its entirety was misleading, inaccurate, and inflammatory (Jackson & Naureckas, 1994).

These crime myths are not just curiosities or examples of sloppy work by journalists. They have tangible and serious policy implications. Spurred by crime mythology, politicians clamor for ever tougher sanctions against criminals. Crime myths divert attention away from the social and cultural forces that cause crime to individual pathologies; they reinforce stereotypes of minorities, poor people, and people who are "different." New York City's "crimes against the elderly" crime wave produced more stringent laws, a reorganization of law enforcement, and a reallocation of law enforcement resources (Fishman, 1978). Longitudinal research by Pritchard and Berkowitz (1993) demonstrated a clear impact of press coverage on legislative decisions about crime between 1950 and 1980. Other research has shown that media coverage directly influences prosecutorial decisions in homicide cases (Barkan, 1997; Pritchard, 1986).

Diverting Attention from Serious Social Problems

There is a corollary harm to directing our attention to certain kinds of criminality. Exaggerating the incidence and importance of violent crime, for example, deflects our attention from other serious issues. Consider media portrayals of white-collar crime and crimes against women.

The media pay little substantive attention to corporate crime and other forms of white collar crime (Evans & Lundman, 1987; Randall, 1995). Since the public is far more likely to be seriously harmed by corporate criminals than by violent criminals, this is a major disservice. In addition, ignoring such offenses encourages corporate crime by removing one of the primary modes of deterring that behavior—publicity (Clinard & Yeager, 1980; Fisse & Braithwaite, 1983). The media's neglect of white-collar crime stems from several sources, including: the risk of libel suits; social relationships between media executives and business executives; a pro-business orientation in the media; and the difficulty of adequately investigating and reporting on white-collar crime (Mintz, 1992). In addition, corporations own the major newspapers, television networks, and television stations (Sutherland, 1949). Finally, media revenue comes primarily from advertising purchased by corporations (Sutherland, 1949).

The processes through which the media amplify and exaggerate crime and focus our attention on disadvantaged and relatively powerless groups in society are also use to deflect and diffuse concern over other types of crime. A case in point is the media's treatment of crimes against women, particularly rape and wife battering.

The media frequently distort rape coverage by referring to "careless" behavior by the victim or provocative actions or clothing. The fact is that rape is a violent crime in which carelessness or provocation are clearly anomalies. In the William Kennedy Smith case, media outlets ran stories on the victim's record of accumulating speeding tickets, perhaps suggesting she should have sped away from the alleged rape. The media further distort the rape issue by giving primary coverage to stranger rapes, failing to emphasize the far more common case in which rape is committed by acquaintances, relatives, and "friends." Stories about non-stranger rape frequently repeat and reflect police skepticism about such cases. Acquaintance rape stories often emphasize cases of false reporting, a very rare occurrence. Nonstranger rape case coverage also frequently seeks to humanize the alleged rapist. For example, in 1990 five students from St. John's University were charged with rape. The *New York Daily News* (5/11/90) led its coverage with a story entitled "To Friends, Fab 4." The story quoted the lacrosse coach as saying, "They are the types who give something back to the community" (Flanders, 1991). After a rape at the University of Rhode Island, the *New York Times* led with a story headlined "After Rape Charge, 2 Lives Hurt and 1 Destroyed." The story described the victim and her attacker as equally hurt by the incident. In fact the reporter suggests that "some said the real victim was Mr. Lallymand," the man charged with the rape (Barkan, 1997; Flanders, 1991).

The press gives little coverage to the lives of the victims in these stories, citing conventions protecting the identity of sexual assault victims. However, they are do point out facts related to the victims' drinking prior to the assault and other allegedly mitigating behaviors. They also discuss the alleged attackers, usually humanizing them and suggesting that they acted in confusion or highlighting the unfortunate set of circumstances which led to the rape (Flanders, 1991). The *New York Times* (1991) ran a special report on campus rapes in which a clear sympathy was shown for accused rapists: "Sexual activity that goes too far and becomes abhorrent to the woman is not new among college students . . . But calling it date rape is . . . defining sex between dates or acquaintances without the woman's consent as a form of male assault rather than a form of female error" (Barkan, 1997; Flanders, 1991). The story goes on to talk about the "agony on campus"—the confusion caused by discussions of date rape, not the actual rapes themselves. The story falsely reports that most rapes occur in co-ed dormitories, which are blamed for much of the behavioral confusion. In fact, most campus rapes occur in single-sex fraternity houses. The story then concludes by suggesting that the problem is, at least in part, "the result of mixed signals sent by women."

Similarly, the media distort the issue of battering in a variety of ways. First, battering is a relatively uncovered story in a crime-saturated news environment. When battering is covered it is treated as a bizarre spectacle and news stories make use of euphemistic or evasive language (i.e. marital disputes, domestic disturbance, spouse abuse). Such language obscures the gendered nature of battering and implies the woman may be at fault. Stories on battering often raise the question of why the woman didn't leave her batterer, ignoring the fact that many do try to leave and that many have good reasons not to leave. Battering coverage leaves the clear implication that women are responsible for their own victimization (Barkan, 1997; Devitt, 1992; Devitt & Downey, 1992; Kamen & Rhodes, 1992).

In addition, the media frequently overplay the extremely rare occurrences of women abusing their husbands. Rather than focussing on the common crime of spouse battering, media sources often focus on cases where governors have released women from prison who were convicted of murdering abusive husbands. These stories usually report that women were not living with the husband when they killed him, implying that the danger to the woman had passed. They fail to report this is the most dangerous time for battered women. News stories frequently imply that pardons and releases encourage battered women to commit acts of violence against their abusers (Barkan, 1997; Devitt, 1992; Devitt & Downey, 1992; Kamen & Rhodes, 1992).

Making Sense of Media Representations of Crime

To understand how the media treat the issue of crime and why, a brief look at the role of the media in contemporary society is necessary. Essential to such an analysis are three questions. What functions do the media serve? How do they accomplish those tasks? Who benefits from media actions?

The media comprise only one of several of the many social institutions in complex modern societies. As such, they are both somewhat autonomous and somewhat dependent on other institutions. As one of society's dominant institutions, the media share certain characteristics with other dominant institutions, like the state, corporations, the law enforcement community, and the military. We can therefore assert that the major role of the mass media in U.S. society is the reproduction of a status quo from which they greatly benefit (Alvarado & Boyd-Barrett, 1992; Gurevitch et al., 1982; Lapley & Westlake, 1988; McQuail, 1994; Stevenson, 1995; Strinati, 1995).

The media operate in the same ideological arena as do the educational system, religious institutions, and the family. Ideology is a means of organizing impressions, thoughts, knowledge, and observations into a medium through which we understand, experience, and interpret the world around us. In the ideological arena, the views and interests of competing groups in society are presented and debated. The views and interests of those groups with the greatest political, economic, and social power tend to dominate those debates. That domination becomes even more intense in contemporary society, because economic power is becoming more and more concentrated in fewer and fewer hands. Journalists and other media professionals are trained, educated, and socialized in such a way as to internalize the values and norms of the dominant, mainstream culture. As a result, the media interpret or mediate news, information, and complex issues in a way that is usually consistent with the dominant culture and with the interests of powerful groups. The audience is, of course, free to interpret those reports and stories in whatever manner seems appropriate, but for the most part the media's audience lacks the time, resources, and information to independently construct alternative definitions and frameworks (Alvarado & Boyd-Barrett, 1992; Gurevitch et al., 1982; Hall, 1980; Hall et al., 1978; Lapley & Westlake, 1988; McQuail, 1994; Stevenson, 1995; Strinati, 1995).

The mass media are part of the culture industry which produces tangible products. In general, but not exclusively, the products they produce will reflect the ideas, conceptions, theories, and views of those with power in society. In general, but not exclusively, the products they produce will tend to refute, defuse, or ridicule alternative conceptions of society. This process of advancing some views of the world—and holding back others—reflects the importance of the media to the dissemination of ideology in society. The ideological operations of the mass media in the U.S. contribute to reproducing the dominant ideology of U.S. capitalism (Althusser, 1971; Hall et al., 1978; Marcuse, 1991).

In addition to producing or reproducing ideology, the media also act as "amplifiers." This means that the media tend to present viewpoints which are consistent with those held by powerful groups. They present those viewpoints as the "obvious" or "natural" perspectives, with any alternative or critical view presented as being deviant, different, or even dangerous. The mass media tend to avoid unpopular and unconventional ideas. They repeat views which are widely held and not offensive to audiences, advertisers, or owners. We discussed media reliance on the portrayal of violence in both news and entertainment programming. These portrayals are not just attention grabbing, they serve other purposes as well. They provide legitimacy to the criminal justice system and the police. They build support for more draconian laws and for more state intervention into people's daily activities. They warn us about different ones, outsiders, and the dangers of defying social conventions.

In other words, they reinforce, they amplify, and they extend the existing state of affairs that makes up the dominant culture and the current distribution of power (Althusser, 1971; Alvarado & Boyd-Barrett, 1992; Hall 1980; Hall et al., 1978; Stevenson, 1995).

Of course, the media are only one half of the equation. The audience is the other half. Are audiences passive individuals who absorb ideological propaganda from newspapers, television, movies, and magazines? Of course not. People rely on other experiences and interactions. Social identities are determined by interactions with all kinds of institutions: the family, the school, the state, language, and the media. However, people generally find their sense of identity and their understanding of the reality around them as a result of social identities molded by those institutions—all of which are "ideological state apparatuses" (Althusser, 1971; Lapley & Westlake, 1988). The media have the capacity to concentrate those definitions and interactions in a way that convinces people that the media are presenting a reflection of everyday lives.

Can audiences resist the power of media representations and definitions? Yes. We have seen that some crime scares and moral panics never get off the ground. Ideological state apparatuses are not always successful in defining people's roles and consciousness. While the mass media relay certain ideological images, the audience—if it has the ability, the resources, and the inclination—can remold, adapt, and integrate those messages into an entirely different system of meaning (Althusser, 1971; Berger, 1991; Hall, 1980; Hall et al., 1978; McQuail, 1994).

Mass media (movies, television, news organizations) form a culture industry in modern capitalist societies. They sell their products. The shape and content of those products will be influenced by the economic interests of the organization producing the products. Businesses operating in the culture industry must cater to the needs of advertisers. News shows are set up in standardized formats that cater to the demands of advertising. News must be fitted into the air time and column inches left over after paid advertising is accounted for. As a result, a standard format with news, weather, and sports segments has evolved around the needs of advertisers. They are unlikely to sponsor programs which attack them or which they perceive as the enemy. Because advertisers in essence own the time the news shows occupy, their interests are of great concern and will be given some priority (Berger, 1991; Lapley & Westlake, 1988; Marcuse, 1991; Stevenson, 1995).

In addition, media businesses must maximize their audiences. They do this in several ways. First, they include heavy doses of sex and violence. Second, they appeal to noncontroversial, mainstream views—trying to achieve a nonoffensive middle-ground on most issues. Finally, they treat the news as light entertainment, something not requiring a great deal of thought or attention on the part of the reader or viewer.

In the process, they reduce the danger of alternative interpretations of a story by the audience (Alvarado & Boyd-Barrett, 1992; Berger, 1991; Hall, 1980; Hall et al., 1978; Marcuse, 1991; Strinati, 1995).

As businesses, news media organizations must also respond to the desires of those who own and control them. In the United States twenty-four or so corporations control most of the culture industry (Herman & Chomsky, 1988). Those corporations have no vested interest in radical change or in interpretations of issues which might question the extant configuration of power in society. In addition, the media are increasingly controlled by corporations that are primarily non-media in their orientation. For example, General Electric and Westinghouse, corporations with heavy investments in the production of nuclear weapons and nuclear power, have heavy media holdings. Fewer than 15 corporations control most of the newspaper circulation in the U.S. (Bagdikian, 1987). Time, Inc. accounts for 40 percent of the magazine business. Capital Cities/ABC, CBS, and GE/NBC dominate television broadcasting. This doesn't necessarily mean that all decisions by news organizations are reduced to economic considerations in support of their parent companies. Clearly there is a relative degree of autonomy, and there is a significant difference between control of the news and influencing the content of the news. But the influences of these economic concerns are undeniable (Berger, 1991; Gurevitch et al., 1982; McQuail, 1994).

In general we can safely say that: (1) ownership and economic control of the media are important factors in determining the content of media messages and (2) the media are a powerful influence in shaping public consciousness. The media are something of an irresistible force in modern society. The media are instrumental but not the only players in defining the terms through which we think about the world around us (Marcuse, 1991; Strinati, 1995).

The media play an important role in producing hegemony in society. Hegemony is the predominance of one group's or class's views over the views or interests of other groups or classes. The media projection of this dominant worldview causes most of us to accept the ideology as "common sense." Common sense has been defined as "the way a subordinate class lives its subordination" (Alvarado & Boyd-Barrett, 1992: 51). This kind of common sense is not etched in stone. It has to be redefined and transformed almost daily, and this is the role of the mass media (Hall, 1980). Everyday people are reminded—at work, at play, in social interactions, when buying products, when purchasing food—that there is something unpleasant about not having power, about being subordinate. Maintaining hegemony is a constant, and not always successful, struggle on the part of the powerful. Stuart Hall points out that there is a "preferred reading" of the media's message which buttresses the dominant political, economic, and social relations in society. However, it is not the only interpretation. Some audiences "negotiate" that message and transform it slightly. Others read that message in a very different light and create "oppositional" meanings that are in direct conflict with the views of the powerful.

That is how we should interpret crime news. We must ask questions: Where did that information come from? Who supplied it? Do they have a vested interest in how we react to that information? We must begin to deconstruct the taken-for-granted "common sense" messages of the media. The readings in this volume are roadmaps through that process of deconstruction. It is up to the audience to follow those maps and to redefine "preferred readings."

References

Althusser, L. (1971). Ideology and ideological state apparatuses. In *Lenin and philosophy and other essays*. London: New Left Books.

Alvarado, M., & Boyd-Barrett, O. (Eds.). (1992). *Media education: An introduction*. London, BFI/Open University.

Bagdikian, B. (1987). The 50, 26, 20 . . . corporations that own our media. *Extra!* (Publication of FAIR, Fairness and Accuracy in Reporting). June issue.

Baker, M. H., Nienstedt, B. C., Everett, R. S., & McCleary, R. (1983). The impact of a crime wave: Perceptions, fear, and confidence in the police. *Law & Society Review*, 17, 319–333.

Barak, G. (1994). Media, society, and criminology. In G. Barak (Ed.), *Media, process, and the social construction of crime* (pp. 3–45). New York: Garland Publishing.

Barkan, S. F. (1997). *Criminology: A sociological understanding*. Englewood Cliffs, NJ: Prentice-Hall.

Beckett, K. (1994). Setting the public agenda: "Street crime" and drug use in American politics. *Social Problems*, 41, 425–447.

Beirne, P., & Messerschmidt, J. (1995). *Criminology* (2nd ed). Ft. Worth: Harcourt Brace Jovanovich.

Berger, A. (1991). *Media analysis techniques* (Rev. ed). Newbury Park, CA: Sage.

Best, J., & Horiuchi, G. (1985). The razor and the apple: The social construction of urban legends. *Social Problems*, 32, 488–499.

Box, S. (1983). *Power, crime, and mystification*. New York: Tavistock.

Carlson, J. (1995). *Prime time enforcement*. New York, Praeger.

Chermak, S. (1994). Crime in the news media: A refined understanding of how crime becomes news. In G. Barak (Ed.), *Media, process, and the social construction of crime* (pp. 95–129). New York: Garland Publishing.

Clinard, M. & Yeager, P. (1980). *Corporate crime*. New York: Free Press.

Cohen, J., & Solomon, S. (1995, July 19). How *Time* magazine promoted a cyberhoax. *Media Beat*.

Cohen, S. (1980). *Folk devils and moral panics: The creation of the mods and rockers.* New York: St. Martin's Press.

Devitt, T. (1992). Media circus at Palm Beach rape trial. *EXTRA!* (Publication of FAIR, Fairness and Accuracy in Reporting). Special issue, pp. 9–10, 24.

Devitt, T., & Downey, J. (1992). Battered women take a beating from the press. *EXTRA!* (Publication of FAIR, Fairness and Accuracy in Reporting). Special issue, pp. 14–16.

Dunn, K. (1994, April 10). Crime and embellishment. *Los Angeles Times Magazine,* 24.

Ericson, R., Baranek, P., & Chan, J. (1989). *Negotiating control: A study of news sources.* Toronto: University of Toronto Press.

Evans, S., & Lundman, R. (1987). Newspaper coverage of corporate crime. In M. D. Ermann & R. Lundman (Eds.), *Corporate and governmental deviance: Problems of organizational behavior in contemporary society* (pp. 230–243). New York: Oxford University Press.

Fishman, M. (1978). Crime waves as ideology. In this volume.

Fisse, B., & Braithwaite, J. (1983). *The impact of publicity on corporate offenders.* Albany: State University of New York Press.

Flanders, L. (1991). Rape coverage: Shifting the blame. *EXTRA!* (Publication of FAIR, Fairness and Accuracy in Reporting). March/April issue.

Frankfurter, F., & Pound, R. (1922). *Criminal justice in Cleveland.* Cleveland: The Cleveland Foundation.

Freeman, M. (1994). Networks doubled crime coverage in '93 despite flat violence levels in U.S. society. *Mediaweek, 4,* 4.

Gerbner, G. (1994, July). Television violence: The art of asking the wrong question. *Currents in Modern Thought,* 385–397.

Gordon, M., & Heath, L. (1981). The news business, crime, and fear. In D. Lewis (Ed.), *Reactions to crime.* Beverly Hills: Sage.

Graber, D. (1980). *Crime news and the public.* New York: Praeger.

Gurevitch, M., Bennett, T., Curran, J., & Woollacott, J. (Eds.). (1982). *Culture, society and the media.* London: Methuen.

Hall, S. (1980). Encoding/decoding. In Centre for Contemporary Cultural Studies (Ed.), *Culture, media, language.* London: Hutchinson.

Hall, S., Critcher, C., Jefferson, T., Clarke, J., & Roberts, B. (1978). *Policing the crisis.* London: Macmillan.

Heath, L. (1984). Impact of newspaper crime reports on fear of crime: Multi-methodological investigation. *Journal of Personality and Social Psychology, 47,* 263–276.

Herman, E., & Chomsky, N. (1988). *Manufacturing consent.* New York: Pantheon.

Hoover, K. (1994, February 3). S.F. erred in data on teenage killings. *San Francisco Chronicle.*

Jackson, D. (1994, October 21). Politicians' crime rhetoric. *The Boston Globe,* p. 15.

Jackson, J., & Naureckas, J. (1994). Crime contradictions. *Extra!* (Publication of FAIR, Fairness and Accuracy in Reporting). May/June issue, 10.

Jenkins, P. (1996). Myth and murder: The serial killer panic of 1983–5. In V. Kappeler, M. Blumberg, & G. Potter, *The mythology of crime and crim-*

inal justice (2nd ed.) (pp. 69–91). Prospect Heights, IL: Waveland Press.

Kamen, P., & Rhodes, S. (1992). Reporting on acquaintance rape. *EXTRA!* (Publication of FAIR, Fairness and Accuracy in Reporting). Special issue, 11.

Kappeler, V., Blumberg, M., & Potter, G. (1996). *The mythology of crime and criminal justice* (2nd ed.). Prospect Heights, IL: Waveland.

Lapley, R., & Westlake, M. (1988). *Film theory: An introduction*. Manchester, England: Manchester University Press.

Lichter, R., & Edmundson, E. (1992). *A day in the life of television violence*. Washington, D.C.: Center for Media and Public Affairs.

Lichter, L., & Lichter, R. (1983). *Prime time crime: Criminals and law enforcers in TV entertainment*. Washington, D.C.: Media Institute.

Lichter, R., & Lichter, L. (Eds.). (1994). *Media monitor: 1993—The year in review*, VIII, 1. Washington, D.C.: Center for Media and Public Affairs.

Liebert, R., & Sprafkin, J. (1988). *The early window: Effects of television on children and youth*. New York: Pergamon.

Liska, A., & Baccaglini, W. (1990). Feeling safe by comparison: Crime in the newspapers. *Social Problems*, 37, 360–374.

Livingston, J. (1996). *Crime & criminology* (2nd ed.). Englewood Cliffs, NJ: Prentice-Hall.

Maguire, K., & Pastore, A. (Eds.). (1995). *Sourcebook of criminal justice statistics—1994*. Washington, D.C.: U.S. Department of Justice, Bureau of Justice Statistics.

Males, M. (1994). Bashing youth: Media myths about teenagers. *EXTRA!* (Publication of FAIR, Fairness and Accuracy in Reporting). March/April issue.

Marcuse, H. (1991). *One-dimensional man* (Rev. ed.). Boston: Beacon.

McCaghy, C., & Capron, T. (1997). *Deviant behavior: Crime, conflict and interest groups* (4th ed.). New York: Macmillan.

McQuail, D. (1994). *Mass communication theory* (3rd ed.). London: Sage.

Miethe, T., & Lee, G. (1984). Fear of crime among older people: A reassessment of the predictive power of crime-related factors. *Sociological Quarterly*, 25, 397–415.

Mintz, M. (1992). Why the media cover up corporate crime: A reporter looks back in anger. *Trial*, 28, 72–77.

Orcutt, J., & Turner, J. B. (1993). Shocking numbers and graphic accounts: Quantified images of drug problems in the print media. *Social Problems*, 40, 190–206.

Pritchard, D. (1986). Homicide and bargained justice: The agenda-setting effect of crime news on prosecutions. *Public Opinion Quarterly*, 50, 143–159.

Pritchard, D., & Berkowitz, D. (1993). The limits of agenda setting: The press and political responses to crime in the United States, 1950–1980. *International Journal of Public Opinion Research*, 5, 86–91.

Randall, D. (1995). The portrayal of business malfeasance in the elite and general media. In G. Geis, R. Meier, & L. Salinger (Eds.), *White-collar crime: Classic and contemporary views* (pp. 105–115). New York: Free Press.

Reed, I. (1991, April 9). Tuning out network bias. *The New York Times*, p. A11.

Reiman, J. (1998). *The rich get richer and the poor get prison* (5th ed.). New York: Macmillan.

Reinarman, C., & Levine, H. (1989). Crack in context: Politics and media in the making of a drug scare. *Contemporary Drug Problems*, 16, 535–577.

Seagal, D. (1993, November). Tales from the cutting room floor: The reality of "reality-based" television. *Harper's Magazine*, 51.

Sheley, J., & Ashkins, C. (1981). Crime, crime news, and crime views. *Public Opinion Quarterly*, 45, 492–506.

Skogan, W., & Maxfield, M. (1981). *Coping with crime: Individual and neighborhood reactions*. Beverly Hills, Sage.

Stevenson, N. (1995). *Understanding media cultures: Social theory and mass communication*. London: Sage.

Strinati, D. (1995). *An introduction to theories of popular culture*. London: Routledge.

Surette, R. (1998). *Media, crime, and criminal justice: Images and realities* (2nd ed.). Pacific Grove, CA: Brooks/Cole.

Sutherland, E. (1949). *White collar crime*. New Haven: Yale University Press.

Sutherland, E. (1950). The diffusion of sexual psychopath laws. *American Journal of Sociology*, 56, 142–148.

Walker, S. (1998). *Sense and nonsense about crime and drugs: A policy guide* (4th ed.). Belmont, CA: Wadsworth.

Warr, M. (1995). Public perceptions of crime and punishment. In J. Sheley (Ed.), *Criminology: A contemporary handbook* (pp. 15–31). Belmont, CA: Wadsworth.

Part I

MAKING NEWS

THE BEGINNING OF THE NEWS MEDIA

Enter Moral Panics

Erich Goode and Nachman Ben-Yehuda

The place, Clacton, a small seaside resort community on England's eastern coast, one with an extremely limited range of facilities and amusements for young people. The time, Easter Sunday, 1964. The weather, cold and wet. Hundreds of adolescents and young adults are milling around on the streets and sidewalks, bored and irritated, seeking fun and adventure. A rumor—perhaps true, perhaps false—begins circulating that a bartender refused to serve several young people. A scuffle breaks out on the pavement; factions begin separating out. Youths on motorcycles and scooters roar up and down the street. A starter's pistol is fired into the air. The windows of a dance hall are smashed; some beach huts are destroyed. The damage—perhaps £500 in value, several times that in today's currency. The police, unaccustomed to such rowdiness, overreact by arresting nearly 100 young people, on charges ranging from "abusive behavior" to assaulting a police officer (Cohen, 1972, pp. 29ff).

Media Reaction

While not exactly raw material for a major story on youth violence, the seaside disturbances nonetheless touched off what can only be described as an orgy of sensationalistic news items. On Monday, the day

Source: *Moral Panics: The Social Construction of Deviance.* (Cambridge: Blackwell, 1994), pp. 22–30. Reprinted with permission.

after these events, every national newspaper with the exception of *The Times* ran a lead story on the Clacton disturbances. "Day of Terror by Scooter Groups" screamed the *Daily Telegraph;* claimed the *Daily Express,* "Youngsters Beat Up Town"; the *Daily Mirror* chimed in with, "Wild Ones Invade Seaside." On Tuesday, the press coverage was much the same. Editorials on the subject of youth violence began to appear. The Home Secretary was "urged" to take firm action to deal with the problem. Articles began to appear featuring interviews with Mods and Rockers, the two youth factions, current in Britain at the time, who were involved in the scuffles and the vandalism. The Mods (the term stood for "modernists") tended to be well-dressed, fashion-conscious teenagers and young adults who frequented discos, listened to the music of the Beatles, the Who, and the Rolling Stones, and, if they were on wheels, rode motorscooters. The Rockers tended to be tougher, more politically reactionary, more classically delinquent; they usually stemmed from a working-class background, and often rode motorbikes.

Theories were articulated in the press attempting to explain what was referred to as the mob violence. Accounts of police and court actions were reported; local residents were interviewed concerning the subject, their views widely publicized. The story was deemed so important that much of the press around the world covered the incidents, with major stories appearing in the United States, Canada, Australia, South Africa, and the European continent. *The New York Times* printed a large photograph of two adolescent girls accompanying its story. The Belgian newspapers captioned one photo "West Side Story on English Coast" (pp. 31ff). Youth fights and vandalism at resorts continued to be a major theme in the British press for some three years. Each time a disturbance broke out, much the same exaggerated, sensationalistic stories were repeated. But by the beginning of 1967, young Britishers no longer identified with the Mods or the Rockers, and the youth-violence angle gave way to other issues.

Enter Stanley Cohen

In 1964, Stanley Cohen was a graduate student at the University of London searching for a research topic for his dissertation. A South African who left his homeland for political reasons, a radical who was attracted to the causes and activities of underdogs and eager to critique the doings of the smug and powerful, Cohen found society's reaction to the exuberant activities of rebellious youth both disturbing and intriguing.

To Cohen, a major issue was the "fundamentally inappropriate" reaction by much of society to certain relatively minor events and conditions. The press, especially, had created a horror story practically out of whole cloth. The seriousness of events were exaggerated and distorted—in terms of the number of young people involved, the nature of the violence committed, the amount of damage inflicted, and their impact on the community, not to mention the importance of the events to the society as a whole. Obviously false stories were repeated as true; unconfirmed rumors were taken as fresh evidence of further atrocities (Cohen, 1972, pp. 31ff). During such times of overheated and exaggerated sense of threat, the society generally, including the press and the police, reacted toward the designated behavior and its enactors in a process Cohen referred to as "community sensitization" (1967, p. 280). Once a class of behavior, and a category of deviants, are identified, extremely small deviations from the norm become noticed, commented on, judged, and reacted to. In the case, the Clacton disturbances, minor offenses, or even gatherings which might become offenses, were instantly the focus of press and police attention. The process of sensitization was summed up in a headline at the time which read: "Seaside Resorts Prepare for the Hooligans' Invasion" (1967, p. 281). Moreover, on more than one occasion, the over-zealousness of the police resulted in an escalation of the conflict, where, for instance, by insisting that the crowd "move along," some of "the more labile members" of a crowd were provoked to resist, blows were exchanged, which led to their arrest (1967, p. 281). To Cohen, the sensitization and escalation processes were central to the public's reaction to the Mods and Rockers.

Cohen launched the term *moral panic* as a means of characterizing the reactions of the media, the public, and agents of social control to the youthful disturbances. In a moral panic, Cohen wrote:

> A condition, episode, person or group of persons emerges to become defined as a threat to societal values and interests; its nature is presented in a stylized and stereotypical fashion by the mass media; the moral barricades are manned by editors, bishops, politicians and other right-thinking people; socially accredited experts pronounce their diagnoses and solutions; ways of coping are evolved or . . . resorted to; the condition then disappears, submerges or deteriorates and becomes more visible. Sometimes the subject of the panic is quite novel and at other times it is something which has been in existence long enough, but suddenly appears in the limelight. Sometimes the panic passes over and is forgotten, except in folklore and collective memory; at other times it has more serious and long-lasting repercussions and might produce such changes as those in legal and social policy or even in the way society conceives itself. (1972, p. 9)

Actors in the Drama of the Moral Panic

How is this panic expressed? How did Cohen know he had a panic on his hands after the 1964 Clacton disturbances? Cohen looked at the reaction of five segments of society: the press, the public, agents of social control, or law enforcement, lawmakers and politicians, and action groups.

The Press

The way the press handled the seaside events could be characterized by exaggerated attention, exaggerated events, distortion, and stereotyping (1972, pp. 31–8). As we saw, newspapers "over-reported" the events; the scuffles and minor acts of vandalism that took place were accorded a place in the media far out of proportion to their importance. Not only was the focus of attention exaggerated, but the stories describing the events also exaggerated their seriousness. Phrases such as "riot," "orgy of destruction," scenes being "smeared with blood and violence," "battle," and a "screaming mob," were used regularly. If one boat was overturned, reports claimed that "boats" were overturned. One story claimed that, in one resort, the windows of "all" the dance halls by the beach were smashed, which was true—however, the town only had one dance hall, and some of its windows were smashed by youths (1972, pp. 32–3).

The stories also distorted the events and repeated obviously false stories. One youth told a judge that he would pay his fine with a £75 check. This was repeated as long as four years after the event, usually to show that the rebellious youths were affluent hordes whom "fines couldn't touch." In fact, the youth made this statement as a "pathetic gesture of bravado." He not only did not have the money, he didn't even have a bank account, and had never signed a check in his life (1972, p. 33). But because the tale confirmed a certain public image of the events and who perpetrated them, it was repeated and believed as true. Although myth-making characterizes all societies at all times, during times of the moral panic, the process is especially rapid, and a given myth is especially likely to be believed on relatively little evidence (1972, p. 33).

The youth violence and vandalism stories that ran in the British press between 1964 and 1967 tended to follow a stereotypical pattern. For the most part, they put together a composite picture, containing a number of central elements. It was almost as if a new story could be written simply by stitching these elements together. There was very little interest in what actually happened; what counted is how closely a news account conformed to the stereotype. The youths were depicted as being part of gangs, even though all of the youths involved were part of very loose assemblies rather than tightly structured gangs. The seaside villages were said to have been victims of an "invasion from London," even though many—in all likelihood, most—were local youths or came from nearby towns and villages. Few stories omitted the fact that many of the offenders were on motorscooters or motorbikes, even though the overwhelming majority were on foot. Offenders were said to come from affluent families, even though those on whom data could be gathered lived in extremely modest economic circumstances. They were said to have come to the resorts deliberately to make trouble, even though, in reality, nearly all came merely hoping that there would be some trouble to watch. The offenses described in the press were nearly always violent ones, even though only a tenth of the offenders were charged with violent crimes; even most of the offenses that did take place entailed relatively trivial acts such as petty theft, threatening behavior, and obstruction. The financial loss to local businesses was said to have been drastic. If anything, the reverse was true: more people than usual came to the resorts to check out the action. In short, one indication that a moral panic is taking place is the stereotypical fashion in which the subject is treated in the press (1972, pp. 34–8).

The Public

Cohen's conception of moral panics includes the dimension of public concern. There must be some latent potential on the part of the public to react to a given issue to begin with, some raw material out of which a media campaign about a given issue can be built. The public may hold a more sophisticated view of the issue than the press (1972, pp. 65–70), but if the media is infused with hysteria about a particular issue or condition which does *not* generate public concern, then we do not have a moral panic on our hands. The media's exaggerated attention must touch something of a responsive chord in the general public. The disturbances that attracted so much attention broke out in the 1960s, at a time when much of the adult British public, with the Second World War and the postwar era deprivations still fresh on their minds, saw a younger generation growing up in affluence (they "never had it so good," was a common refrain), responding not with gratitude but with disdain, rebellion, and delinquency. The problem was that the younger generation had been coddled, indulged, treated with kid gloves; the solution—a tougher parental hand, stricter social control, harsher penalties for transgressions, stiffer fines and jail sentences. In short, the events at Clacton and other seaside communities were focused on and reacted to by much of the public as a symbol for some of the larger problems plaguing British society. The events themselves were not so important as what they seemed to represent. But in order to see these disturbances as central, it became necessary to exaggerate and distort their reality.

Law Enforcement

In addition to the press and the general public, the actions of the social (or "societal") control culture demonstrated that a moral panic was taking place in Britain in the mid-1960s over the Mods and Rockers (1972, pp. 85ff). In a moral panic, segments of the society are sensitized to trouble from certain quarters (1972, pp. 77ff); the society is said to be faced with a "clear and present danger" the signs of which it is so sharply attuned to. In no sector is this principle more clearly evident than in public attitudes about what the police and the courts—law enforcement—ought to be doing about the perceived threat. Ties between and among local police forces are established and strengthened, and those between the local and national levels of law enforcement are activated, in order to more effectively deal with the problems faced by the putative threat (1972, p. 86). Cohen calls this process *diffusion*.

Efforts are made by officers to broaden the scope of law enforcement and increase its intensity; punitive and overly zealous actions already taken are justified on the basis of the enormity of the threat the society faces (1972, pp. 86–7). Cohen refers to this as *escalation*. New methods of control are proposed both to legislators and to the police: stiffer sentences, expanded police powers, confiscating motorscooters and motorbikes, banning Mod clothing, cutting long hair on youths, drafting troublemakers into the military, and so on (1972, pp. 88–91). Some police practices, previously rarely used, that were called up to deal with unacceptable Mod and Rocker behavior included: riding suspicious youths out of town or to the railroad station; keeping crowds moving along; confiscating studded belts; keeping certain troublesome locations free of Mods and Rockers; verbally harassing adolescents, particularly in a crowd situation, to "show them up" and "deflate their egos" (1972, p. 95), making immediate (and often wrongful) arrests, and so on (1972, pp. 92–8). The thinking among agents of social control is that "new situations need new remedies"; a national problem called for a drastic solution, and often, this entailed suspending rights and liberties previously enjoyed.

Politicians and Legislators

Members of Parliament (MPs) "took an immediate and considerable interest in disturbances in their own constituencies" (p. 133). Stiffer penalties for youth offenses were called for. Local merchants were assured that "hooliganism" would not threaten their economic interests and would not be repeated. Statements by MPs were issued to the press; "Jail These Wild Ones—Call by MPs," ran one such story. A return to corporal punishment for hooliganism was called for by some. Meetings were held between MPs and local police chiefs, and summaries were sent to the Home Secretary. Suggestions were made by one MP that Britain revive non-military national service, such as construction or mining, as a punishment for hooliganism. A suggestion to raise the minimum driving age from 16 to 19 was introduced in the House of Lords. A Malicious Damage Bill was introduced and debated in the House of Commons only a month after the Clacton incident; in further debate on the Bill two months later, the seaside disturbances became the central imagery dominating the discussion. Though some politicians recognized that the concern was exaggerated, and had a moderating influence on the discussion, the dominant mood among politicians and legislators toward youth crime in the period following the initial incident was angry, self-righteous, vindictive, condemnatory, and punitive. Politicians and other groups aligned themselves against a devil and on the side of angels; the fact is, they picked an "easy target," one that "hardly existed." What counted was not the nature of the target but what side they were on and what they were against (1972, p. 138). Such symbolic alignments represent one defining quality of the moral panic.

Action Groups

At some point, moral panics generate appeals, campaigns, and finally, "fully fledged action groups" (p. 119) which arise to cope with the newly-existing threat. These are "moral entrepreneurs" (Becker, 1963, pp. 147ff) who believe that existing remedies are insufficient. Action groups can be seen as "germinal social movements" (Cohen, 1972, p. 120). Often, participants have something to gain personally from rallying against a problem, but this is not a necessary determinant. The Mods and the Rockers generated two local action groups, one of which proposed that convicted Mods and Rockers be subjected to a penal-style program of discipline and hard labor (1972, p. 121), and the other of which favored the reintroduction of a variety of harsher penalties, including whippings of young offenders with a birch rod (1972, p. 125). These action groups did not grow into social movements, nor did they survive the demise of the Mods and the Rockers.

There are two additional features that characterize moral panics, two developments that inform the observer that a society is in the grip of a moral panic: the creation of *folk devils* (1972, pp. 40ff) and the development of a *disaster mentality* (pp. 144ff).

Folk Devils

A folk devil is the personification of evil. Folk devils permit instant recognition; they are "unambiguously unfavorable symbols" (Turner and Surace, 1956, pp. 16–20; Cohen, 1972, p. 41), that is, stripped of all favorable characteristics and imparted with exclusively negative ones. In such a symbolization process, "images are made much sharper than reality" (Cohen, 1972, p. 43). While all folk devils are created out of some existing and recognizable elements, a full-scale *demonology* takes place by which the members of a new evil category are placed "in the gallery of contemporary folk devils" (p. 44). Once a category has been identified in the media as consisting of troublemakers, the supposed havoc-wreaking behavior of its members reported to the public, and their supposed stereotypical features litanized, the process of creating a new folk devil is complete; from then on, all mention of representatives of the new category revolves around their central, and exclusively negative, features. All moral panics, by their very nature, identify, denounce, and attempt to root out folk devils. A condition that generates such widespread public concern must have had a personal agent responsible for its inception and maintenance. Such evil does not arise by happenstance or out of thin air; there must be a circle of evil individuals who are engaged in undermining society as we know it. In short, folk devils are *deviants*; they are engaged in wrongdoing; their actions are harmful to society; they are selfish and evil; they must be stopped, their actions neutralized. Only an effort of substantial magnitude will permit us to return to normal.

The Disaster Analogy

And lastly, in moral panics, Cohen argues, preparations are taken very much like those taken before, during, and after a disaster, such as a hurricane, a volcano eruption, or an earthquake. As during disasters, in the moral panic, there are predictions of impending doom, a "warning phase," sensitization to cues of danger, coping mechanisms, frequent overreactions, the institutionalization of threat, rumors speculating about what is happening or will happen, false alarms, and, occasionally, mass delusion (1972, pp. 144–8). The perceived threat to, and subsequent reaction by, conventional society to the projected invasion of hordes of deviants and delinquents has many strong parallels with the steps taken before, during, and after a natural disaster.

The Contribution of the Moral Panics Concept

The concept of the moral panic expands our understanding of social structure, social process, and social change. It ties together concepts from a variety of disparate areas—deviance, crime, collective behavior, social problems, and social movements. Moral panics are likely to "clarify [the] normative contours" and "moral boundaries" of the society in which they occur, demonstrate that there are limits to how much diversity can be tolerated in a society. Focusing on moral panics emphasizes the fact that reactions to unconventional behavior do not arise solely as a consequence of a rational and realistic assessment of the concrete damage that the behavior in question is likely to inflict on the society. Without resorting to conspiratorial thinking, an investigation of the moral panic emphasizes that social reaction to a new and seemingly threatening phenomenon arises as a consequence of that phenomenon's real or supposed threat to certain "positions, statuses, interests, ideologies, and values" (Cohen, 1972, p. 191). The cast of characters Cohen located in the moral panic—the media, the general public, the agents of social control, lawmakers and politicians, and action groups—are distressed by a certain perceived threat for a reason. If all panics entailed a public reaction to a specific, clearly identifiable threat, the magnitude of which can be objectively assessed and readily agreed upon, then such reactions would require no explanation. On the other hand, if, as Cohen argues, the reaction is out of proportion to the threat, we are led to ask why it arises; the panic is problematic—it demands an explanation.

Why a moral panic over *this* supposed threat, but not *that*, potentially even more damaging, one? Why does *this* cast of characters become incensed by the threat the behavior supposedly poses, but not *that* cast of characters? Why a moral panic at this time, but not before or after? How and why do moral panics arise? How and why do they die out? What role do interests play in the moral panic? Are the dynamics of the moral panic different during different historical time periods, or different from one society to another? What does the moral panic tell us about how society is constituted, how it works, how it changes over time? Cohen's concept introduces the observer of society to a wide range of questions and potential explorations.

References

Becker, Howard S. 1963. *Outsiders: Studies in the Sociology of Deviance*. New York: Free Press.

Cohen, Stanley. 1967. "Mods, Rockers, and the Rest: Community Reactions to Juvenile Delinquency." *Howard Journal*, 12(2): 121–30.

_____. 1972. *Folk Devils and Moral Panics: The Creation of the Mods and Rockers*. London: MacGibbon & Kee.

Turner, Ralph H., and Samuel J. Surace. 1956. "Zoot-suiters and Mexicans: Symbols in Crowd Behavior." *American Journal of Sociology*, 62(July): 14–20.

2

Media Constructions of Crime

Vincent F. Sacco

Crime, like an economic recession, a lack of affordable housing, or inadequate health care, is experienced as both a private trouble and a public issue: Quite obviously, for victims, a criminal offense and the resulting loss or injury present problems of a highly personal nature. For victims and nonvictims alike, however, the "plague of drugs," the "epidemic of random violence," and other manifestations of the crime problem are matters for intense public discussion and political debate.

While the distinction between private troubles and public issues is an important one, these dimensions are not independent.[1] Citizens' personal troubles with crime provide the building blocks out of which public issues are constructed. On the other hand, the warnings of danger implicit in public pronouncements about the seriousness and pervasiveness of crime problems may be a source of private trouble if they exacerbate the fear of crime among those who have routine exposure to such pronouncements.

Central to the interplay between individuals' private troubles with crime and the social issue of crime are the mass media. The news media, in particular, provide an important forum in which private troubles are selectively gathered up, invested with a broader meaning, and made available for public consumption. The dynamic character of these processes and the consequences that they have for public understanding of crime and its solution invite close scrutiny.

Source: *Annals of the American Academy of Political & Social Science*, 539, May 1995, pp. 141–154. © 1995. Reprinted with permission.

From Private Trouble . . .

Numerous studies of media content have documented the fact that crime reports are a durable news commodity.[2] While news about crime figures prominently in all types of media, important differences exist between print and electronic media, between more elite and more popular media, and between media markets. Because of this variability, estimates of the proportion of total news that is devoted to crime coverage range from 5 to 25 percent.[3]

News about crime is most frequently news about the occurrence or processing of private trouble in the form of specific criminal events. In her study of crime and justice news in Chicago in the late 1970s, Doris Graber found that while attention to crime varied across media, reports of individual crime dominated for all media.[4] With respect to the three newspapers studied, the coverage of individual crimes surpassed the coverage of Congress and the presidency and equaled or surpassed election coverage.

Analyses of media content demonstrate that the news provides a map of the world of criminal events that differs in many ways from the one provided by official crime statistics. Variations in the volume of news about crime seem to bear little relationship to variations in the actual volume of crime between places or over time.[5] Whereas crime statistics indicate that most crime is nonviolent, media reports suggest, in the aggregate, that the opposite is true.[6] While crime news tends to provide only sparse details about victims and offenders, that which is provided is frequently at odds with the official picture. Both offenders and victims, for instance, appear less youthful in media reports than they do in statistical records.[7] In addition, news content does not reflect and frequently even reverses the relationship that, according to much social scientific evidence, exists between minority group membership and criminal offending.[8] With respect to gender, however, both crime statistics and crime news portray offending as predominantly a male activity.[9]

News reports also distort the relationship between crime and legal control. In the news, the police appear to be more effective in apprehending offenders than police data would suggest they are.[10] Moreover, while the activities of the police are prominently featured, the functioning of other actors in the criminal justice system is much less visible.[11] This probably reflects a professional judgment that criminal events are most newsworthy immediately following their occurrence and thus when they are in the early stages of justice system processing, when police activity is prominent.[12]

These images of crime, the criminal, and the victim that appear with patterned regularity in print and broadcast news emerge quite logically from the organizational processes of news production. News stories are most useful to news organizations when they are gathered easily from credible sources; for this reason, policing agencies have become the principal suppliers of these stories.[13] In short, relationships involving news organizations and policing agencies allow the collection of news about common crime to be routinized in a manner that uses the resources of news agencies efficiently.[14] In addition, the public view of the police as apolitical crime experts imbues police-generated crime news with authority and objectivity.

Ease of access to authoritative news is not the only advantage that police-generated crime stories offer, since such stories are consistent with several other professional values that structure the news production process. Much of what we call news consists of reports of specific incidents that have occurred since the publication of the previous day's newspaper or the airing of the previous night's newscast. As discrete incidents that occur at particular times and places, individual crimes conform closely to this requirement of periodicity.

Stories about individual crimes—with their characteristic portrayals of villains and victims—also have dramatic value. The dramatic potential is heightened when the victim or offender is a celebrity, when the incident is of a very serious nature, or when the circumstances of the offense are atypical. In addition, the routine crime story is a rather uncomplicated matter, and it is unnecessary for news workers to assume that readers or viewers require an extensive background in order to appreciate the story. The lack of factual complexity associated with the ordinary individual crime story generally means that it can be easily written and edited by news workers whose professional activities are consistently regulated by rigid deadlines.

The elastic character of the crime news supply offers a further advantage. On any given day, particularly in large metropolitan areas, there is an almost limitless supply of crimes that could be the object of media attention. However, from day to day, or from week to week, the demand of the news agency for crime news may vary due to other events that are seen to demand coverage. Depending on the size of the news hole, crime coverage may be expanded or contracted in compensatory fashion. A study by Sanford Sherizen of crime news in Chicago newspapers found, for instance, that crime reports were often located on the obituary pages so that layout difficulties resulting from the inability to plan these pages could be overcome through the use of crime news filler.[15]

Over the last several years, a number of changes in local and national media environments have altered the nature and extent of crime coverage. The growth of cable stations, for instance, has increased the carrying capacity for news generally and for crime news specifically. More stories can be covered, and those that are judged to be particularly newsworthy can be covered in greater detail. The live television coverage of court proceedings—as in the case of the Menendez brothers, Lorena Bobbit, or O.J. Simpson—has become commonplace. The increasing sophistication of news gathering, surveillance, and home video technologies has meant that it is no longer unusual to capture thefts, robberies, or even homicides on tape. One consequence of the diffusion of these technologies has been to raise to national prominence stories with no real national significance. Crime stories that would have been a purely local affair in an earlier period now attract much wider attention because a videotape of the incident is available for broadcast.

The last two decades have also witnessed a redefinition of what can be considered an appropriate subject for news reporting. Changes in mores relating to public discussion of sex and violence have allowed respectable media outlets to report crimes that would have previously been seen as taboo and to do so at a level of detail that would once have been considered lurid. At the same time, the politicization of crimes such as sexual assault and domestic violence has broadened the range of crime stories that, it can be argued, legitimately require coverage.[16]

Programmatic developments in commercial broadcast media have magnified the impact of these changes. The proliferation of newsmagazines, daytime talk shows, docudramas, and various other forms of infotainment has ushered in a programming cycle that is heavily dependent on crime news and victim accounts. The frequent reliance of many of these programs on dramatic reenactments of real events and their mixing of factual reports with rumor and speculation blurs the basic distinctions that analysts of crime content have traditionally drawn between news and entertainment media.[17]

. . . To Public Issues

Public issues grow up around private troubles when the experiences of individuals are understood as exemplifying a larger social problem, and the news media play a vital role in the construction of such problems.[18] Most notably, professional judgments of newsworthiness and the selective use of news sources allow some groups, rather than others, the opportunity to express a view about what is and what is not a problem and how any such problem should be managed. By implication, the relationships that link the police to news agencies serve law enforcement as well as media interests. The police role as the dominant gatekeeper means that crime news is often police news and that the advancement of a police perspective on crime and its solution is facilitated.[19] It has been argued that this results in the adoption of an uncritical posture with respect to the police view of crime and the measures necessary to control it.[20] More generally, the frame of reference offered by a government bureaucracy or other recognized authority with respect to crime problems may only infrequently be called into question and, as a consequence, competing perspectives may become marginalized.

This tendency may be no less true of in-depth issue coverage than of routine news reporting. Henry Brownstein maintains that during the 1980s, there was relatively little reporting that took issue with the official version of the drug problem constructed by government experts.[21] In a similar way, Philip Jenkins has noted how experts of the Federal Bureau of Investigation were able to present themselves as the authorities on the subject of serial murder and how they made themselves available to journalists who reciprocated with favorable coverage of the agency.[22]

It would be incorrect, however, to suggest that news media are merely the passive conveyors of the claims about problems offered up by government bureaucracies, political candidates, or other self-interested groups, since any such claims must be transformed to meet the requirements of the medium in question. In an analysis of television network news coverage of threats to children, Joel Best argued that "inevitably, network news stories distort the problems they explore,"[23] in large part because news conventions impose severe constraints on how stories are covered. Stories must be told in a few minutes, frequently by reporters who may have little more than a surface familiarity with the complexities of the problem at hand. Moreover, the topic must be viewed as serious enough and as visual enough to be chosen over competing issues. Best found, in the case of child victimization, that the stories used frightening and dramatic examples to typify the problem and that they emphasized the existence of a consensus among knowledgeable experts regarding its scope and seriousness.

In other instances, news media may more actively engage in problem construction. Investigative reporting, or the coverage of an event judged to be especially newsworthy, may contribute to the establishment of a media agenda that finds expression in the reporting of further stories or in more detailed features. A study by David L. Protess and his colleagues revealed how one Chicago newspaper set its own media agenda after an extensive investigative series on rape.[24] The researchers found that while the series did not appear to have a substantial impact on the perceptions of policymakers or the general public, there were significant changes in the extent and depth of rape coverage after the series ended, even though police reports of rape were unchanged. In a related way, during the summer of 1994, the O.J. Simpson case provided an opportunity for sidebar stories relating to the prevalence and causes of domestic violence, the inadequacy of justice system responses, and pending federal and state legislation. Such coverage contextualized the original incident in a way that helped construct the social issue of violence against women at the same time that it legitimated continuing, detailed attention to the original story.

The Content of Crime Problems

Media constructions of crime problems address both the frequency and the substance of private trouble with crime. Rhetoric regarding both of these dimensions serves to impress on readers and viewers the gravity of particular crime problems and the need to confront them in particular ways.

Large numbers of problems provide convincing evidence that problems exist. This is perhaps most evident in the case of crime waves, when it is argued that crime is becoming more frequent. A study by Steven Gorelick, for instance, of an anticrime campaign sponsored by a New York daily newspaper found that crime in the city was frequently described as a "mushrooming cloud," a "floodtide," a "spreading cancer," or in similar terms.[25] Sometimes these claims about the numbers of people affected have greater specificity in that some particular segment of the population is claimed to be experiencing rapidly increasing risks of offending or victimization.[26]

Yet, with respect to many crime waves, it is the belief that crime is increasing, rather than crime itself, that is really on the rise.[27] A study by Mark Fishman of a 1976 New York crime wave against the elderly described how crime waves may be "things of the mind."[28] Fishman found that there was no compelling evidence to indicate that the criminal victimization of the elderly actually increased during the study period. Instead, the crime wave originated in the efforts of journalists to organize individual crime stories around a compelling news theme. The theme of crime against the elderly was elaborated as competing news organizations responded to each other's coverage of the issue. In addition, the police, in their role as gatekeepers of crime news, reacted to the increased media interest by making available more stories that reflected and reinforced the crime-against-the-elderly theme.

A more recent example of a journalistic construction of rapidly rising crime is provided by James D. Orcutt and J. Blake Turner.[29] Their analysis focused on the way in which graphic artists in the national print media transformed survey data, which showed modest yearly changes in drug use, into evidence of a "coke plague." While the numbers were real, their graphical presentation in the weekly periodical under study was misleading. As in the case described by Fishman, the dynamics of competitive journalism created a media feeding frenzy that found news workers "snatching at shocking numbers" and "smothering reports of stable or decreasing use under more ominous headlines."[30]

Claims about statistical frequency are not restricted to reports about how the numbers are increasing, however. With respect to the problem of violence against women, for instance, it is argued that the numbers have always been very high but that the failure to police such incidents, the stigma associated with victimization, and an institutional unwillingness to believe the accounts of victims have resulted in statistical counts that dramatically underestimate the problem. Thus, whether or not the numbers are going up is defined as less salient than the observation that they have always been higher than we have thought.

According to Neil Gilbert, outrageous claims about the prevalence of problems sometimes make their way into news reports in part because of journalists' general inability to evaluate the data supplied to them.[31] Too often, they lack the technical sophistication to critically assess claims about the frequency of crime or victimization in an independent fashion. Instead, they collect and validate information by talking to experts who are expected to offer informed opinions. However, in the case of emergent problems, it is often the problem advocate, interested in advancing a particular point of view, who may be among the first to collect and publicize empirical evidence. As a result, the estimates yielded by advocacy research may be the only ones available at the earliest stages of problem development. Philip Jenkins has argued that the emergence of serial murder as a social issue in the early 1980s was spurred by "epidemic estimates" that placed the number of serial murder victims at between 20 and 25 percent of American homicides.[32] While such numbers continue to circulate through popular and journalistic accounts, more reasoned analysis suggests that the number of serial murder victims is closer to 2 percent of American homicides.

The emergence of crime problems is related not only to claims about the frequency of criminal events but also to claims about their character. Exactly what types of events such incidents are thought to be and who is thought to be typically involved in them matter as much as does the rate at which they are thought to occur.

Any particular social problem can be framed in many ways, and these various frames imply different causal attributions and prospective solutions.[33] Because they are able to legitimate some views and to marginalize others, the news media are an important part of this framing process. Depending on the sources accessed or the type of coverage, rape can be framed as a sex crime or as a crime of violence; the "drug problem" as a product of pushers who hook their victims or as an example of the overreach of criminal law; and violence on the part of youths as a condition necessitating either swift punishment or comprehensive community development.

More generally, when private troubles are constructed as a crime problem of any sort, they are framed in ways that assign primary responsibility for their solution to the criminal justice system. Joel Best has shown how crime problem interpretations of the 1987 freeway shooting incidents in California competed in the relevant news coverage with other interpretations of the incidents.[34] Whereas the crime problem frame implied the need for increased patrols, better investigation, and more effective prosecution, other definitions of the issue—as a gun problem, a traffic problem, or a courtesy problem—suggested other solutions.

In a related way, the social distributional character of victimization is frequently ignored by news coverage that stresses the random character of victimization. While the best social science literature indicates that the risks of crime, like the risks of other misfortunes, are not equally shared, media images often convey a different message. According to Brownstein, for instance, much of the coverage of the drug issue in New York City between 1986 and 1990 emphasized the random character of drug violence even though police statistics indicated that the risks of such violence were extremely low.[35] Themes relating to randomness serve the interests of both news workers and others who seek to frame crime problems. News stories about random crimes have great dramatic value, as the media frenzies that surround serial murders illustrate. Moreover, the advocates to whom news workers have access during the early stages of problem development often stress the random nature of a particular form of victimization since problems must be seen as more urgent when everyone is threatened.

While much routine crime reporting can be understood as maintaining established crime problem frames, new problems are always being discovered as old problem paradigms expand or as novel elements come together with established news themes. The discovery of new problems provides a journalistic opportunity to tell a story that has not been told before, but such stories are told most effectively when they resonate with existing cultural themes. In the 1970s, the problem of crime against the elderly brought together in one package an already familiar concern about crime in the streets and victims' rights with an emerging concern about the aging population.[36] The problem of satanic crime, which received extensive media coverage in the 1980s, combined familiar news themes relating to religious cults, child abuse, and juvenile crime.[37] Media attention to date rape and stalking extends earlier news themes relating to violence against women.

The transition from private troubles to public issues is not always a linear process since media interest in particular crime problems can vary in intensity or decline over time. The 1987 shootings on California freeways never became a well-established problem, despite a strong start.[38] In the case of crimes against the elderly, Fay Lomax Cook and Wesley Skogan observe that while the issue achieved a prominent position on media and other agendas during the early 1970s, by the decade's end, it had declined precipitously.[39] On the other hand, Fishman has argued that as long as police departments are the routine sources of crime news, the media will reinforce a climate of opinion that keeps the attention of the police focused on "crime in the streets." He concludes that while social problems may come and go, "law-and-order news is here to stay."[40]

. . . And Back Again?

There can be little doubt that media consumers have broad and regular exposure to crime news.[41] What are the consequences of this exposure? One potential consequence that has generated considerable interest relates to the deleterious effects that media attention to crime problems may have on audience members' fear of victimization. On the surface, arguments about such effects seem plausible. Public fear of crime is pervasive, and it outstrips measured levels of victimization. By implication, public anxieties would appear to be rooted in vicarious rather than direct experiences, and since messages about crime are so prevalent in the media, it seems reasonable to conclude that much public fear originates in media coverage of crime problems. At issue is whether experience with media treatments of crime as a public issue contributes to fear as a personal trouble. There is a large body of empirical evidence that bears on the relationship between audience exposure to mass media and fear of crime. In the aggregate, however, the findings are equivocal regarding the strength of such a relationship or even whether such a relationship exists.[42]

Some of the inconsistency in this respect is methodological in nature. Considerable variation exists regarding the ways in which crime news, crime news exposure, and fear of crime have been operationalized in the research literature.[43] In addition, since people not only read or watch crime news but also talk about it with friends and neighbors, measured variations in media exposure are not necessarily indicative of exposure to crime news.[44] Nor is it reasonable to assume for research purposes that people are always able to keep clear and report to researchers what is learned in which information channel.[45] Even when such methodological limitations are taken into account, however, the research indicates that the effects of media exposure on fear of crime are less significant than any naive hypothesis would suggest.

Several factors explain this apparent paradox. To begin with, it would be inappropriate to assume that audience members respond passively to the warnings of danger issued by omnipotent news media. Instead, as Paul Williams and Julie Dickinson note, news consumers are actively involved in investing the news with meaning.[46] Audience members bring to the reading and viewing experience their own predispositions, which influence what crime news means for them. These predispositions may include personal experiences with crime or violence,[47] perceptions of the credibility of news media,[48] or the extent of prior concern about personal safety.[49] In the context of cross-sectional research, these predispositions suggest the possibility that the correlation between media usage and fear of crime may be more indicative of selective exposure than of media influence.[50]

While people avidly read and watch crime news, it is unclear that in so doing they extract lessons relating to their own safety. Such lessons, it appears, are more effectively learned in other contexts. The relevant research indicates that the news about crime that travels through interpersonal channels may be more likely to induce fear than is the news that travels through mass channels.[51] To learn about crime by talking to one's neighbors is to learn about victims whose experiences cannot be easily dismissed because they are nameless or faceless or live somewhere else.

By contrast, the typical media crime story is stripped of much of its emotional character and is likely to involve victims about whom the viewer or reader has no personal knowledge. In addition, the average news story may provide readers and viewers with so little information about the victim, the setting in which the crime occurred, or other circumstances of commission that it may be irrelevant to any assessment of personal victimization risks.[52] Most crime news is nonlocal and therefore far removed from judgments that must be made regarding the safety of the immediate environment. Not surprisingly, there is research that suggests that fear is, in fact, related to crime news exposure when local random violent crimes are reported in prominent fashion.[53] Taken together, these findings are consistent with a more general body of research that indicates that people may be less dependent on news media when they seek information about matters close to home.[54]

Overall, it would appear that as crime news relates to matters of personal safety, consumers appear to exercise a healthy dose of skepticism.[55] As Dennis Howitt observes, newspaper readers do not necessarily think that crime rates are going up just because the number of column inches devoted to crime increases.[56] They are more likely to put what is learned from the media in the context of what they learn from other sources, and they may be well aware when media are behaving in a highly sensationalist manner.[57]

Conclusion

If the news business is concerned with the production of crime problems, then the private troubles of criminal offenders and crime victims are the raw materials. These troubles are not simply reported on, however, since they are fundamentally transformed by the news-gathering process. Screened through a law enforcement filter, contextualized by advocacy claims and culturally resonant news themes, and shaped and molded by the conventions and requirements of commercial media, these private troubles become public issues.

While news media coverage of crime may not have a powerful influence on the concern for personal safety, this should not obscure other, perhaps more significant effects. Such effects are not narrowly attitudinal or behavioral but are broadly ideological.

Some critics argue that the police perspective implicit in so much crime news reporting dramatically restricts the parameters of discussion and debate about the problem of crime. As a consequence, the causes of offending are individualized and the relationships that link crime to broader social forces are left largely unexplored.[58] Correspondingly, traditional law-and-order responses are reaffirmed as the most efficient way to manage crime problems. A study of media coverage of attacks against women in Toronto found that explanations of the phenomenon tended to focus attention on the ways in which victims placed themselves in conditions of risk, on offender pathology, and on the need for a more coercive criminal justice response.[59] The authors note that while these terms of reference were not unreasonable, the attention they received left little room for alternative interpretations of the problem, particularly those interpretations that link the victimization of women to structures of gender inequality.

When crime problems are successfully constructed, a consensus emerges regarding what kinds of public issues private troubles represent.[60] Yet the development of such a consensus—regarding what the problems are, who is responsible for them, and how they should be resolved—should not be understood in conspiratorial terms. While both news workers and their sources are interested in offering a convincing and credible construction of reality, for many in the media, the construction of these problems is not a matter of activism but just another day at the office.[61]

As news workers observe and influence each other, and as the line between news and entertainment becomes more confused, public discussion of crime problems reflects and reinforces this consensus, and popular views of these problems begin to assume a taken-for-granted character. Inevitably, but regrettably, the emergence of such a consensus relegates to the margins the search for alternative ways of thinking about crime and its solution.

Notes

[1]   C. Wright Mills, *The Sociological Imagination* (New York: Oxford University Press, 1959), pp. 9–11.

2   See, for example, James Garofalo, "Crime and the Mass Media: A Selective Review of Research," *Journal of Research in Crime and Delinquency*, 18:319–350 (1981); Ray Surette, *Media, Crime and Criminal Justice* (Pacific Grove, CA: Brooks/Cole, 1992); Joseph R. Dominick, "Crime and Law Enforcement in the Mass Media," in *Deviance and Mass Media*, ed. Charles Winick (Beverly Hills, CA: Sage, 1978), pp. 105–128.

3   Surette, Media, *Crime and Criminal Justice*, p. 62.

4   Doris A. Graber, *Crime News and the Public* (New York: Praeger, 1980).

5   F. James Davis, "Crime News in Colorado Newspapers," *American Journal of Sociology*, 57:325–330 (1952); Wesley G. Skogan and Michael G. Maxfield, *Coping with Crime: Individual and Neighborhood Reactions* (Beverly Hills, CA: Sage, 1981).

6   Garofalo, "Crime and the Mass Media"; Skogan and Maxfield, *Coping with Crime*; Philip Schlesinger, Howard Tumber, and Graham Murdock, "The Media of Politics, Crime and Criminal Justice," *British Journal of Sociology*, 42:397–420 (1991).

7   Margaret T. Gordon and Stephanie Riger, *The Female Fear* (New York: Free Press, 1989), p. 70; Roy Edward Lotz, *Crime and the American Press* (New York: Praeger, 1991).

8   Lotz found, for instance, that in newspapers in New York, Miami, and Philadelphia, white offenders outnumbered black offenders by 7 to 1 in those news reports that allowed for the identification of race. Lotz, *Crime and the American Press*, p. 114.

9   M. A. Bortner, "Media Images and Public Attitudes toward Crime and Justice," in *Justice and the Media*, ed. Ray Surette (Springfield, IL: Charles C Thomas, 1984), pp. 15–30.

10   Harry L. Marsh, "A Comparative Analysis of Crime Coverage in Newspapers in the United States and Other Countries from 1960 to 1989: A Review of the Literature," *Journal of Criminal Justice*, 19:67–80 (1991); Bob Roshier, "The Selection of Crime News by the Press," in *The Manufacture of News: Social Problems, Deviance and the Mass Media*, ed. Stanley Cohen and Jock Young (London: Constable, 1973) pp. 28–39.

11   Steven M. Gorelick, "'Join Our War': The Construction of Ideology in a Newspaper Crimefighting Campaign," *Crime and Delinquency*, 35:421–436 (1989).

12   Sanford Sherizen, "Social Creation of Crime News: All the News Fitted to Print," in *Deviance and Mass Media*, ed. Charles Winick (Beverly Hills, CA: Sage, 1978), pp. 203–224.

13   Steve Chibnall, *Law-and-Order News: An Analysis of Crime Reporting in the British Press* (London: Tavistock, 1977); Mark Fishman, "Police News: Constructing an Image of Crime," *Urban Life*, 9:371–394 (1981); Richard V. Ericson, "Patrolling the Facts: Secrecy and Publicity in Police Work," *British Journal of Sociology*, 40:205–226 (1989).

14   In comparison to interpersonal crimes like homicide or robbery, corporate crimes are covered with greater difficulty. Generally, corporate crimes are more complex and more difficult to personalize, and well-established source-reporter relationships do not exist for corporate crime as they do for common crimes. Coverage of corporate, white-collar, and organized crime is more common, however, than is sometimes thought. See, for instance, Donna Randall, "The Portrayal of Business Malfeasance in the Elite and General Public Media," *Social Science Quarterly*, 68:28–93 (1987).

15   Sherizen, "Social Creation of Crime News," p. 221.

[16] Keith Soothill and Sylvia Walby, *Sex Crime in the News* (London: Routledge, 1991), p. 6.

[17] Graeme R. Newman, "Popular Culture and Criminal Justice: A Preliminary Analysis," *Journal of Criminal Justice*, 18:261–274 (1990).

[18] Joel Best, ed., *Images of Issues: Typifying Social Problems* (Hawthorne, NY: Aldine de Gruyter, 1989); Joseph R. Gusfield, "Constructing the Ownership of Social Problems: Fun and Profit in the Welfare State," *Social Problems*, 36:431–441 (1989); Joseph W. Schneider, "Social Problems Theory: The Constructionist View," *Annual Review of Sociology*, 11:209–229 (1985).

[19] Fishman, "Police News"; Ericson, "Patrolling the Facts."

[20] Richard V. Ericson, "Mass Media, Crime, Law and Justice," *British Journal of Sociology*, 31:219–249 (1991); Marjorie S. Zatz, "Chicano Youth Gangs and Crime: The Creation of a Moral Panic," *Contemporary Crises*, 11:129–158 (1987).

[21] Henry H. Brownstein, "The Media and the Construction of Random Drug Violence," *Social Justice*, 18:85–103 (1991).

[22] Philip Jenkins, *Using Murder: The Social Construction of Serial Homicide* (Hawthorne, NY: Aldine de Gruyter, 1994), pp. 212–213.

[23] Joel Best, "Secondary Claims-Making: Claims about Threats to Children on the Network News," *Perspectives on Social Problems*, 1:277 (1989).

[24] David L. Protess et al., "Uncovering Rape: The Watchdog Press and the Limits of Agenda Setting," *Public Opinion Quarterly*, 49:19–37 (1985).

[25] Gorelick, "Join Our War," p. 429.

[26] Much has been made in the popular press about, for instance, crime waves that victimize the elderly. See Fay Lomax Cook and Wesley G. Skogan, "Agenda Setting and the Rise and Fall of Policy Issues: The Case of Criminal Victimization of the Elderly," *Environment and Planning C: Government and Policy*, 8:395–415 (1990).

[27] Mary Holland Baker et al., "The Impact of a Crime Wave: Perceptions, Fear, and Confidence in the Police," *Law and Society Review*, 17:317–334 (1983).

[28] Mark Fishman, "Crime Waves as Ideology," *Social Problems*, 25:531 (1978).

[29] James D. Orcutt and J. Blake Turner, "Shocking Numbers and Graphic Accounts: Quantified Images of Drug Problems in the Print Media," *Social Problems*, 40:190–206 (1993).

[30] Ibid., p. 203.

[31] Neil Gilbert, "Miscounting Social Ills," *Society*, 31:24–25 (1994).

[32] Jenkins, *Using Murder*, p. 22.

[33] Gusfield, "Constructing the Ownership of Social Problems"; Schneider, "Social Problems Theory."

[34] Joel Best, "'Road Warriors' on 'Hair-Trigger Highways': Cultural Resources and the Media's Construction of the 1987 Freeway Shootings Problem," *Sociological Inquiry* 61:327–345 (1991).

[35] Brownstein states, for example, that of the 1051 homicides reported in New York City in 1991, less than 2 percent could be categorized as random. Brownstein, "Media and the Construction of Random Drug Violence," p. 95.

[36] Cook and Skogan, "Agenda Setting and the Rise and Fall of Policy Issues."

[37] Ben M. Crouch and Kelly R. Damphousse, "Newspapers and the Antisatanism Movement: A Content Analysis," *Sociological Spectrum*, 12:1–20 (1992), Philip Jenkins and Daniel Maier-Katkin, "Satanism: Myth and Reality in a Contemporary Moral Panic," *Crime, Law and Social Change*, 17:53–75 (1992).

[38] Best, "'Road Warriors' on 'Hair-Trigger Highways.'"

[39] Cook and Skogan, "Agenda Setting and the Rise and Fall of Policy Issues."

[40] Fishman, "Police News," p. 389.

[41] Garofalo, "Crime and the Mass Media"; Skogan and Maxfield, *Coping with Crime*.

[42] For a range of views, see James M. Carlson, *Prime Time Law Enforcement: Crime Show Viewing and Attitudes toward the Criminal Justice System* (New York: Praeger, 1985) Guy Cumberbatch and Alan Beardsworth, "Criminals, Victims and Mass Communications," in *Victims and Society*, ed. Emilio C. Viano (Washington, DC: Visage Press, 1976) pp. 72–90; Anthony N. Doob and Glen E. Macdonald, "Television Viewing and Fear of Victimization: Is the Relationship Causal?" *Journal of Personality and Social Psychology* 37:170–179 (1979); Garofalo, "Crime and the Mass Media"; George Gerbner et al., "The Demonstration of Power: Violence Profile No. 10," *Journal of Communication*, 10:177–196 (1979); Garrett J. O'Keefe. "Public Views on Crime: Television Exposure and Media Credibility," in *Communication Yearbook* 8, ed. Robert N. Bostrom (Beverly Hills, CA: Sage 1984), pp. 514–535; Richard Sparks, Television and the Drama of Crime (Buckingham, England: Open University Press, 1992); Vincent F. Sacco, "The Effects of Mass Media on Perceptions of Crime: A Reanalysis of the Issues," *Pacific Sociological Review*, 25:475–493 (1982).

[43] Glenn G. Sparks and Robert M. Ogles, "The Difference between Fear of Victimization and the Probability of Being Victimized: Implications for Cultivation," *Journal of Broadcasting and Electronic Media*, 34:351–358 (1990).

[44] Anthony N. Doob, "The Role of Mass Media in Creating Exaggerated Levels of Fear of Being the Victim of a Violent Crime," in *Confronting Social Issues: Applications of Social Psychology*, ed. Peter Stringer (Toronto: Academic Press, 1982), pp. 145–159.

[45] Gordon and Riger, *Female Fear*, p. 85.

[46] Paul Williams and Julie Dickinson, "Fear of Crime: Read All about It: The Relationship between Newspaper Reporting and Fear of Crime," *British Journal of Sociology*, 33:34 (1993).

[47] Philip Schlesinger et al., *Women Viewing Violence* (London: BFI, 1992), p.165.

[48] O'Keefe, "Public Views on Crime."

[49] Sacco, "Effects of Mass Media," p. 483.

[50] Williams and Dickinson, "Fear of Crime," p. 51; Dolf Zillmann and Jacob Wakshlag, "Fear of Victimization and the Appeal of Crime Drama," in *Selective Exposure to Communication*, ed. Dolf Zillmann and Jennings Bryant (Hillsdale, NJ: Lawrence Erlbaum, 1987), pp.141–156.

[51] Skogan and Maxfield, Coping with Crime; Susan J. Smith, "Crime in the News," *British Journal of Criminology*, 24:289–295 (1984); Tom R. Tyler, "Assessing the Risk of Crime Victimization: The Integration of Personal Victimization Experience and Socially Transmitted Information," *Journal of Social Issues*, 40:27–38 (1984).

[52] Gordon and Riger, Female Fear, p. 75; Tyler, Assessing the Risk of Crime Victimization," p. 34.

[53] Linda Heath, "Impact of Newspaper Crime Reports on Fear of Crime: Multimethodological Investigation," *Journal of Personality and Social Psychology*, 47:263–276 (1984); Allen E. Liska and William Baccaglini, "Feeling Safe by Comparison: Crime in the Newspapers," *Social Problems*, 37:360–374 (1990). Interestingly, these studies also suggest that coverage of nonlocal violence may decrease fear among news consumers by allowing them to feel safer by comparison.

[54] Philip Palmgreen and Peter Clarke, "Agenda-Setting with Local and National Issues," *Communication Research*, 4:435–452 (1977).

[55] Jack Katz, "What Makes Crime 'News'?" Media, Culture and Society, 9:60 (1987).

[56] Dennis Howitt, *The Mass Media and Social Problems* (Oxford: Pergamon, 1982), pp. 125–126.

[57] Williams and Dickinson, "Fear of Crime," p. 50.

[58] Gorelick, "'Join Our War'"; Drew Humphries, "Serious Crime, News Coverage and Ideology: A Content Analysis of Crime Coverage in a Metropolitan Newspaper," *Crime and Delinquency*, 27:191–205 (1981).

[59] Sophia E. Voumvakis and Richard V. Ericson, *News Accounts of Attacks On Women: A Comparison of Three Toronto Newspapers* (Toronto: University of Toronto, Centre of Criminology, 1984).

[60] Gusfield, "Constructing the Ownership of Social Problems," pp. 434–436.

[61] Stephen Hilgartner and Charles L. Bosk, "The Rise and Fall of Social Problems: A Public Arenas Model," *American Journal of Sociology*, 94:57 (1988).

3

Crime Waves as Ideology

Mark Fishman

When we speak of a crime wave, we are talking about a kind of social awareness of crime, crime brought to public consciousness. It is something to be remarked upon at the corner grocery store, complained about in a community meeting, and denounced at the mayor's press conference. One cannot be mugged by a crime wave, but one can be scared. And one can put more police on the streets and enact new laws on the basis of fear. Crime waves may be "things of the mind," but they have real consequences.

Crime waves are prime candidates for ideology. This study analyzes a specific crime wave that occurred in New York City in late 1976. This case both illustrates and informs my analysis that the crime waves which periodically appear in the press are constructs of the mass media and contribute to an ideological conception of crime in America.[1]

My use of the term ideology follows Dorothy Smith (1972). All knowledge is knowledge from some point of view, resulting from the use of procedures for knowing a part of the world. Ideological accounts arise from "procedures which people use as a means *not to know*" (1972:3, emphasis mine). Routine news gathering and editing involve "procedures not to know." The business of news is embedded in a configuration of institutions. These include a community of news organizations from which journalists derive a sense of "what's news now," and governmental agencies upon which journalists depend for their raw materials.

Source: *Social Problems*, Vol. 25, No. 5, June 1978, pp. 531–543. © 1978 by The Society for the Study of Social Problems. Reprinted with permission.

Through their interactions and reliance on official sources, news organizations both invoke and reproduce prevailing conceptions of "serious crime."

Crimes against the Elderly

In late 1976, New York City experienced a major crime wave. The city's three daily newspapers and five local television stations reported a surge of violence against elderly people. The crime wave lasted approximately seven weeks, eventually receiving national television and newspaper coverage.

One consequence of this was the public definition of a new type of crime.[2] "Crimes against the elderly" became a typical crime with typical victims, offenders, and circumstances. Reported muggers, murderers, and rapists of the elderly were usually black or Hispanic youths with long juvenile records. They came from ghetto neighborhoods near enclaves of elderly whites who, for various reasons (usually poverty), had not fled the inner city. Using this scenario, journalists reported incident after brutal incident throughout November and December 1976.

The outcry against these crimes was immediate. The Mayor of New York City, who was preparing to run for re-election, criticized the juvenile justice system and the criminal courts. The New York City Police Department gave its Senior Citizens Robbery Unit (S.C.R.U.) manpower to extend plain-clothes operations. Camera crews from local news stations filmed S.C.R.U. officers dressed as old people and arresting muggers. Local police precincts held community meetings to advise the elderly how to protect themselves. New York State legislators introduced bills to make juvenile records available to a judge at the time of sentencing, to deny sixteen- to nineteen-year-olds juvenile status if they victimized an old person, and to mandate prison sentences for crimes of violence against the aged. These proposals were passed in both the State Senate and Assembly, but were eventually vetoed by the Governor on August 19, 1977—nine months after the crime wave had ended.

A May 1977 Harris poll suggested the crime wave also had a nation-wide effect on people's fear of crime. Moreover, it had an effect on the crime categories which the Harris organization used in its surveys; this poll included a new type of crime, crimes against the elderly, not previously present in Harris polls. Harris found that 60 percent of his respondents felt that assaults against elderly people in their home areas had been going up, and that 50 percent of those age fifty or older said they were more uneasy on the streets than they had been one year ago.[3]

It is doubtful that there really was a crime wave or any unusual surge of violence against elderly people. No one really knows, least of all the journalists who reported the crime wave. The police statistics from the N.Y.P.D. do not show a crime wave.[4] In fact, for one type of crime, homicide, the police showed a 19 percent *drop* over the previous year's rate of elderly people murdered. This is significant because the news media began their reporting with coverage of several gruesome murders. (Twenty-eight percent of the stories reported by the three media organizations I surveyed were stories about homicides. In contrast, the police reported that homicides made up less than 1 percent of crimes against the elderly in 1976.)

For other types of crime with elderly victims police statistics showed an increase over the previous year. Crime victimization, however, rose for all age categories in 1976. In some cases, the increases were greater for elderly victims, in others less. Robbery was up 10 percent in the general population, 19 percent for the elderly. Grand larceny was up 29 percent for the general population, 25 percent for the elderly. In short, police statistics substantiate only that there was a continuing increase in victimization of the elderly (as well as of the general population), not that old people were singled out, as never before. Moreover, the homicide rate contradicts the media presentation of a crime wave.

This article, however, is not a study in the disparity between police statistics and crime news. Prior studies of crime news and crime waves (Davis, 1952; Roshier, 1973), as well as anecdotal reports (Steffens, 1931:285–91), have shown the irony of crime waves: although the public is alarmed and politicians respond to media reports of a dramatic increase in crime, such "waves" have no basis in police statistics. This study goes beyond sociological irony to examine *how and why news organizations construct crime waves*. Crime waves are taken to be waves of coverage of some topic in crime. Crime waves as *media waves* may or may not be related to something happening "on the streets" or in the police crime rates. Studying crime waves means studying processes in the mass media.

Method

I collected two kinds of data. First, two student researchers and I conducted participant observation from November 1976 to April 1977 on a New York City local television station, WAVE (a pseudonym). One student was a full-time WAVE journalist who worked as a news writer, program producer, and assignment editor. We focused on how the assignment editor assembled the daily news program by deciding what major stories would be covered for the day and assigning reporters and camera crews to these stories. In addition, we conducted interviews with journalists from WAVE and the New York *Daily News*.

Second, we kept a record of all news relating to crimes against the elderly reported from September 1976 through February 1977 in two newspapers, the New York *Daily News* and the New York *Post*, and on WAVE, which aired a one-hour newscast in the evening. This enabled us to "locate" the New York crime wave, to determine when it began and ended, and to determine the kind of coverage crimes against the elderly received before, during, and after the crime wave period.

The Crime Wave: A View from the Outside

Over the six-month period of observation the *News*, the *Post*, and WAVE presented eighty-nine stories of crimes against the elderly. Fifty-six stories or 63 percent occurred during the crime wave period. The weekly frequencies of news stories from all three media are shown in the appendix. This graph clearly indicates a wave of media reporting that began in the last week of October and trailed off by the second week of December. It shows a sharp, swift rise in coverage for the first two weeks, then a slow, uneven decline for the remaining five weeks.

Examining the individual patterns of coverage for each news organization reveals that prior to the crime wave each organization was reporting approximately one story of crime against the elderly every other week. After the wave, coverage in all three media was sporadic, but heavier than coverage during the prewave period, indicating that the media appear to have been sensitized to the topic.

The three individual crime waves in the *News*, the *Post*, and WAVE show that the marked increase in coverage did not coincide in all three media. The *News* had a sudden increase in the third week of October; WAVE and the *Post* did not increase their coverage until the fourth week of October. Further, in this fourth week the two "latecomers" began their increase *simultaneously*. Prior to their increased coverage, the *Post* and WAVE did not parallel each other. It was only after the *News* began reporting a wave that the others developed a synchronous pattern. This trend suggests that the other media simultaneously responded to the *Daily News'* portrayal of a wave of violence against the elderly.

All three media show different crime wave profiles. WAVE steeply increased coverage to a single peak, then had an equally steep decline (seventeen days rising and sixteen days falling). In contrast, the *Daily News* and the *Post* show bimodal curves. In the *News* there was a swift initial rise (ten days), from which coverage subsided slowly, then it turned upward to a second peak (lower than the first), and finally declined.

The unevenness of the *Daily News*'s wave was echoed in the *Post*. The *Post* participated less actively in the crime wave than did the *News* or WAVE. We might even say that the *Post* did not show a crime wave, except that the period of its heaviest coverage coincided with the crime wave period in the other media. Moreover, the *Post*'s pre- and post-wave patterns were similar to [those of] the other media, and during the crime wave it showed a bimodal wave which paralleled that of the *Daily News*. Thus, the *Post*'s wave seems to have been a weak reflection of the *Daily News*'s curve.

How can we explain these bimodal patterns? The likely reason why the *News* and *Post* reduced their coverage after the first peaks involves a major news event coinciding with this drop: the 1976 Presidential Election of November 2. The elections seem to have crowded out crimes against the elderly from the newspapers, but not from local TV news, since stations like WAVE were not trying to compete with network coverage of the presidential race. Thus, during the slow news period after the elections, the *News* and *Post* seemed to have "rediscovered" the crime wave, which was still present in local TV news.

In other words, it seems the *News*' and the *Post*'s second peak was a response to the continuing crime wave in the television media (assuming other TV stations behaved like WAVE). Just as the initial appearance of the crime wave in the *Daily News* seems to have spurred increased coverage by the *Post* and WAVE, so the continuing coverage of the crime wave on television seems to have "re-awakened" interest in the topic by the *Daily News* and the *Post*. Thus, *the behavior of each news organization during the crime wave seems to have been in response to the other media.*

Seeing Themes in Crime: A View from the Inside

How do individual crimes come to be seen as a crime wave? The answer is found in the methods by which news is organized. News workers make crime waves by seeing "themes" in the news. Crime waves are little more than the continued and heavy coverage of numerous occurrences which journalists report as a single topic (for example, "crimes against the elderly").

News themes are various: "everything Jimmy Carter did today," "the taxi cab strike," "Vietnam," "the disintegrating American family," or "labor disputes." A news theme is a unifying concept. It presents a specific news event, or a number of such events, in terms of some broader concept. For example, the mugging of an eighty-two-year-old Bronx woman can be reported as "the latest *instance* of the continuing trend in crimes against the elderly." A news theme allows journalists to cast an incident as an instance of something.

The Glasgow Media Group (1976:355) provides an interesting example of thematized news events from one British television newscast:

> The week had its share of unrest. Trouble in Glasgow with striking dust-men and ambulance controllers, short time in the car industry, no Sunday Mirror or Sunday People today and a fair amount of general trouble in Fleet Street and a continuing rumble over the matter of two builders pickets jailed for conspiracy.

As the authors point out, disparate incidents are reported together under the single theme of "unrest." Calling these things "unrest" imposes order on the events reported. Audience members are meant to see the events as unified, as instances of a single theme.

Themes give news shows and newspapers a presentational order. Items are presented in groups organized around a theme. Some themes are related to others, making it possible for groups of news stories to be placed near each other. For instance, during the crime wave against the elderly, the first ten minutes of a sixty-minute news program at WAVE was organized around interrelated themes:

1. Police apprehend three youngsters who allegedly mugged an elderly Queens couple.
2. Police and senior citizens meet at a Queens precinct to discuss fighting crimes against the elderly.
3. A feature report on the Senior Citizens Robbery Unit.
4. Police seize guns and drugs intended for warring gangs in the Bronx.
5. Two members of a youth gang are arrested for robbing someone at knife point.
6. R.O.T.C. cadet charged in the stabbing death of another cadet.
7. New York State audit finds the city police have been mishandling $9.1 million of federal funds.
8. New York City and the police union are still working on a new contract, at the same time that some laid-off firemen and subway cops will be rehired.

First, there are small groups of stories, each containing a theme that the stories in the group share in common (the first three stories are about "crimes against the elderly" and the next three about "youth crime"). Second, groups of stories are placed next to other groups, since the different themes of each group share common features (the group of crimes against the elderly and the group of youth crimes both can be seen to be about youthful perpetrators and police responses to them).

Journalists do not create themes merely to show an audience the appearance of order. News themes are very useful in the newswork itself. In particular, editors selecting and organizing the day's stories need themes.[5] Every day, news editors face a glut of "raw materials" (wire service reports, press releases, police crime dispatches) out of which they must fashion relatively few news stories. This task involves a selection process which operates somewhat differently in television and newspaper newsrooms. The essentials of the process are the same: individual news items are identified and sorted according to possible themes.

The chances that any event or incident will be reported increase once it has been associated with a current theme in the news. Crime incidents are rarely reported unless news workers see them related to a past or emerging trend in criminality or law enforcement. A brief description of how the assignment editor at WAVE developed the first segment of the news show just cited illustrates this point. The assignment editor determined the top stories for the day when he noticed that several previously unrelated stories were all part of the same current newsworthy theme: crimes against the elderly. And the discovery of this theme was no coincidence: that day's program was in the midst of the crime wave period.

The assignment editor did not begin his day knowing that crime news, and, in particular, the crimes against the elderly, would receive top billing in the evening's news show. When he started work at 8:45 A.M. he already knew of two stories that he would most likely cover.[6] One was a feature report on the Senior Citizens Robbery Unit fighting crimes against the elderly. This feature, which eventually ran as the third story in the evening newscast, had been taped days before; it was part of a continuing series on S.C.R.U. the station had been airing for the past few weeks. The second story was a feature report on a "food fair" that afternoon in Manhattan. The editor planned to send a reporter and camera crew to cover it, but also wanted to line up, as he put it, "some better stories" for the day.

Ten minutes after he arrived in the newsroom the assignment editor began scanning his news sources for lead stories. He sifted through reams of wire service news that had collected overnight under the wire machines; he scanned the police dispatches of the previous night's and that morning's crime incidents (about ten or twelve) received through a teletype called "the police wire." He also looked to other news media for story ideas: he read the *Daily News* and *New York Times* and he listened to an all-news radio station.

In the *Daily News* he found a small story about rehiring firemen and Transit Authority police who had been laid off. He thought this would be a good story because "this indicates things may be turning around in the city." This incident became newsworthy when the assignment editor could see it as part of a current newsworthy theme (New York's fiscal crisis).

Still, the assignment editor despaired that he had "no real news," that this was "a slow news day." However, around ten A.M. two things happened. First: when scanning the police crime dispatches, the assignment editor found that in the 113th precinct in Queens an elderly couple had been mugged, and that one perpetrator was wounded by police. As he was clipping this dispatch, he heard over the all-news radio that the 112th precinct in Queens, very close to where the mugging occurred, was holding a crime prevention meeting with senior citizens. He now knew what his lead stories for the day would be, and he knew what he had to do to line them up:

1. He would send a reporter out to the 113th precinct to find, and get on film whatever he could about the mugging (interviews with police, perhaps with some witnesses or with the victims themselves; and, if he was lucky, film of any suspects that were apprehended).

2. Then the reporter could go over to the nearby 112th precinct to film the police meeting with senior citizens.

3. These two reports would be followed by the pre-taped feature on S.C.R.U.

4. The story on rehiring firemen and Transit police, as well as a few other brief wire service reports relevant to crime which might come in during the rest of the day, would all follow the above three lead stories in some as yet undetermined order. The story on the "food fair" would be placed further back in the show.

Each story, seen independently, might not have merited attention. But seen together, all of them were made newsworthy by the perception of a common theme. The editor's "discovery" of the theme of crime against the elderly made the day's news come together. He knew how to assign a schedule to his reporter and camera crew; and he knew pretty much what the day's work was going to be.

The selection of news on the basis of themes is one component in the ideological production of crime news. It constitutes a "procedure not to know." This procedure requires that an incident be stripped of the actual content of its occurrence so that it may be relocated in a new, symbolic context: the news theme. Because newsworthiness is based on themes, the attention devoted to an event may exceed its importance, relevance, or timeliness were these qualities determined with reference to some theory of society. In place of any such theoretical understanding of the phenomena they report, newsworkers make incidents meaningful only as *instances of themes*—themes which are generated within the news production process. Thus, something becomes a "serious type of crime" on the basis of what is going on inside newsrooms, not outside them.

From Crime Themes to Crime Waves

Crime themes are potential crime waves. A news organization cannot make a crime wave without the collaboration of other media reporting the same crime theme. Crime waves emerge out of an interaction among news organizations.

The Indefinite Overlapping Character
of News Judgments

All newsworkers depend on other media organizations for their sense of "what's news today." For example, the WAVE assignment editor began his day by reading the morning papers, the *Daily News* and The *New York Times*, and by listening to an all-news radio station. He later read the New York *Post* and watched when other TV stations aired their news. This editor told me that he did not mind using "anything, any source of news. I'm not proud. I'll steal any source of news."

In reality, stories were not stolen wholesale; rather, the other news media provided an important pool of ideas for story assignments. The noon and evening TV news shows rarely were used for this purpose because, by the time these shows were aired, most of the editor's news was set. The news on other stations mainly confirmed the assignment editor's news judgments, since his planned 10 P.M. news, was, with few exceptions, identical to what his competitors were broadcasting. It seems his competitors were doing just what he was doing: reading the *Times* and the *News*, listening to the all-news radio, and taking stories from the same news sources (wire services, police news dispatches, and press releases).[7]

News judgments continuously overlap in space and time. Editors of afternoon and evening media look for, and are oriented by, the news in the morning media. Editors of the morning media derive their sense of news from afternoon and evening media. Since these media may be in different regions and different cities, news judgments spread throughout an indefinite expanse of territory. The wire services and a few nationally-read newspapers, *The New York Times* and *Washington Post*, increase the diffusion of news judgments through the United States.

Moreover, this overlap provides a continuity of news judgments. A specific incident or theme presented in the morning will be covered in the evening, perhaps with fresh incidents, more details, a new development or a "local angle" on the story. The process may repeat itself the next day, reproducing the theme of the previous evening.

The Crime Wave Dynamic

When journalists notice each other reporting the same crime theme, it becomes entrenched in a community of media organizations. Reporters and editors will know that "this kind of crime is news." To use Sack's (1972:333) term, journalists have established a "consistency rule": *every crime incident that can be seen as an instance of the theme will be seen and reported as such.* The rule is used to identify the newsworthiness of certain crimes. Reporters and editors will know, for example, that a certain incident is "another one of those crimes against the elderly" and not just an incident that can be categorized in a variety of ways.

Each use of the consistency rule reestablishes the rule. Any use of the principle invites readers or viewers of the news, including other journalists, to use the same principle. In order to recognize a crime incident as an instance of a theme, readers or viewers must use the same consistency rule which was used to produce that news.

Journalists who have not yet seen a particular crime theme learn to see it simply by watching their competition. They are able, using the consistency rule, to report the same crime theme their competition taught them to see. At this point, when a crime theme is beginning to spread through more and more media organizations, the "reality" of the theme is confirmed for the media organizations who first reported it. They now see others using the theme. Moreover, as the theme persists, news organizations already using the theme will not hesitate to report new instances, because they confirm a past news judgment that "this thing really is a type of crime happening now." Thus, each use of the theme confirms and justifies its prior uses.

If it continues long enough, the process constitutes a crime wave dynamic. All crime waves begin as simple themes but by means of this dynamic can swell into waves. Crime themes constantly appear in the media and few reach the proportions of full-scale crime waves. After all, it only takes one editor with a little imagination to introduce a new theme into the news. Why is it that few crime themes go beyond a few days of coverage by one or two news organizations?

Clearly, something more than the crime wave dynamic is necessary for a theme to grow into a wave: *There must be a continuous supply of crime incidents that can be seen as instances of a theme.* Journalists may be primed to report a wave of crime incidents, but they also must know of enough incidents to report the wave. (During the period of my research, New York City journalists had been frustrated in reporting an expected "mafia war." This theme never persisted long enough for lack of enough incidents. Thus, "mafia war" was a hungry crime theme, starved of enough incidents to make it the crime wave it could have become.) The supply of incidents is crucial in determining the growth of crime waves. What are journalists' sources of crime news?

Perpetrators of crime could be a source, but news workers rarely learn of crimes directly from offenders. The primary source is law enforcement agencies.[8] In the newsroom of WAVE, journalists first learned of crime incidents through three sources:[9] the "police wire," the police radio, and other news organizations (wire service reports, the all-news radio station, and the *Daily News*). The first two of these were direct links to the city police. Crime news is really police news. Thus, *the media's supply of crime incidents is a function of the crime reporting practices of law enforcement agencies.* This reliance on law enforcement agencies constitutes another component of the ideological production of crime news. News workers will not know what the police do not routinely detect or transmit to them. What journalists do know of crime is formulated for them by law enforcement agencies.

The Pool of Potential Crime Waves

The police supply news organizations with an assortment of crime incidents every day. For media organizations in towns and small cities this assortment often consists of *all* crimes known to the police in a twenty-four-hour period. But in large urban areas there are far too many crimes known to the police for any reporter to know them all. Therefore, urban journalists depend on the police to provide a "summary" of these incidents.

In New York City, the daily summary is known as the "police wire." All the city's major media have a teletype that receives crime dispatches from the N.Y.P.D.'s Office of Public Information. In one day, this police wire types out anywhere from twelve to twenty-five messages. The crime items appearing over the police wire constitute a "crime wave pool": a collection of crime incidents known to the media and having the potential of being seen as certain crime themes. Crime themes steadily supplied with instances over the police wire can become crime waves.

While journalists may invent crime themes (I suspect the police suggest and encourage many of them), a crime wave needs enough incidents on the police wire to support it. The police have power to both veto and promote the media's construction of crime waves. The collection of crime incidents the police provide to news organizations may systematically preclude certain themes from becoming waves (the veto power). Moreover, the same collection of incidents may contain enough crime items of a certain type to allow only a restricted class of crime themes to become crime waves (the enabling power).

For three ten-day periods from mid-February to the end of March 1977, a copy of all crime dispatches of the police wire was kept. Over this thirty-day period, 468 individual dispatches (averaging 15.6 per day) were received. Of these, I ignored ninety-seven (21%) which the police and journalists did not consider crime items. (They were mostly traffic advisories and non-suspicious fires.)

The remaining 371 crime dispatches reveal that the police wire provides journalists with a heavy and steady diet of "street crimes." Two-thirds (246 items or 66.3%) of the crime items consisted of: a) robberies and burglaries (85 items or 23% of all crime items), b) unspecified shootings and stabbings (156 items or 42%) and c) a sprinkling of other assaults (five items or 1 percent—mostly rapes).

The remaining one-third of the police wire consisted of a variety of incidents: thirteen bombings; nine police suspended or arrested; six demonstrations requiring police action; five hostage situations; four raids for gambling, pornography, and drugs; three people run over by subway trains; one arson, and one hit-and-run. In addition, this third contained incidents which, I assume, the police considered "strange" and consequently of interest to the media (for example, a bus stolen, the theft of a large amount of poisons, a man threatening to set himself on fire, a person crushed by an elevator, and the discovery of a disembodied head).

The first thing worth noting about the police wire is what it does *not* contain: incidents of price-fixing, consumer fraud, sub-standard housing, unhealthy food, environmental pollution, political bribery and corruption, and the like. None appear in this pool of crime incidents from which crime waves arise, yet all of these may occur enough to constitute a crime wave if the media were to have routine access to knowledge of their occurrence.

One reason why these do not appear over the police wire is that agencies other than the city police enforce the laws governing these kinds of crime. Because police manpower is devoted to street crimes, it is street crime reports that the police wire carries. If journalists are to report other kinds of crime, they must draw on other sources (usually the wire services and other media organizations) which provide instances of such crime only sporadically.

Moreover, in the police wire one is unable to find a number of very common crimes which local police *do* know about but consider "uninteresting" and, thus, not worth transmitting to the media.[10] These included what journalists told me were "too common" to be news: everything from bicycle theft, liquor store stick-ups and rapes, to wife beating, child molesting and other "family matters" not resulting in homicide or hospitalization.

It is likely that a large number of the street crimes reported over the police wire were, in fact, family disputes, crimes against women, and racial conflict. But it was difficult to tell this from the information in the crime dispatches. This is particularly true of the large number of shootings and stabbings, which reporters tended to ignore.

Any descriptive features in a crime dispatch provide important clues to newsworkers looking for themes in crime. From reading the police wire, I was struck by the lack of detail. Victims, if they were identified at all, and if they were persons, not businesses, were identified by sex and age. When more was told, they were described as: 1) "elderly" (for homicides and robberies), 2) policemen (for any assaults), or 3) banks (for robberies). Perpetrators (and in the police wire these were always persons, not businesses) were usually identified by sex and a specific age. When more was said, it was almost always in connection with a "youth gang" or the offender's youth. Victim-offender relationships were rarely mentioned. It was quite difficult to identify cases where the victim and offender knew each other. Thus the police wire gives one the impression most crimes occur between strangers. Finally, the location of a crime was usually provided in terms of a specific address or intersection. But a *type* of location was mentioned only when it could be said the incident occurred in a public or semi-public place, for example, a street, a subway, a schoolyard, or an apartment hallway.

Thus, the kinds of crime items and the descriptions of them in the police wire support only special sorts of crime themes that journalists may report. Crime in public places, crimes between strangers, and crime specific to age are themes that the police wire can and does provide numerous instances of. "Crimes against the elderly" is one theme that has already blossomed into a crime wave with the help of the police wire. But other themes such as "youth gang crime," "subway crime," and "school yard crime" have an excellent chance of becoming new crime waves.

Apparently, the police who transmit crime dispatches to the media select incidents that they think will interest journalists. This criterion of selectivity has two consequences, both keeping the present image of "serious crime" from changing in the news. First, when the police perceive that the media are interested in a certain type of crime (for example, crimes against the elderly), they include instances of it in the police wire whenever they can. Thus, the police bolster emerging crime waves as long as those waves pertain to crimes the police routinely detect (that is, street crime). Second, the police decide what the media are interested in on the basis of what the media have reported before.

The police-supplied incidents that make up the media's crime wave pool all support prevailing notions of "serious crime." The crime wave pool leads the media to reproduce a common image that "real crime" is crime on the streets, crime occurring between strangers, crime which brutalizes the weak and defenseless, and crime perpetrated by vicious youths. Such crimes exist, but this imagery becomes *the only reality of crime* which people will take seriously because it is the only reality impressed upon them in the media. And it is the only reality news-workers are able to report continuously as themes in crime, and periodically, as full-scale crime waves.

The Role of Authorities

I have described the crime wave pool as if it were only composed of crime incidents. This description is only partially true. During the initial phase of crime waves, media organizations mostly report crime incidents as instances of their theme-becoming-a-wave. But as soon as a crime theme looks like it is catching on and becoming a wave, journalists have another kind of news to report: the responses of politicians, police, and other officials.

The first signs of New York's crime wave against the elderly appeared in the last week of October 1976, when the city's media began reporting incidents of crime against old people. There was widespread coverage of three incidents: the murder of two aged sisters in their Bronx apartment, the rape-murder of an eighty-five-year-old Manhattan woman, and the release on fifty dollars bail of a youth who beat an elderly person. After this third incident, the first official response appeared: Mayor Beame called a news conference and, with the Police Commissioner at his side, he vowed to make the city safe for old people by beefing up the police's Senior Citizens Robbery Unit and by working for reforms in the criminal justice system. From this point on, "crimes against the elderly" became a favorite topic for political rhetoric and proposed reforms.

Starting from the very first week of the crime wave, the media could report both crimes against the elderly *and* stories of what authorities were saying and doing about it. The entire wave was bolstered throughout its seven-week course by coverage of official statements, possible reforms of the criminal justice system, legislative debate and action, the formation of new police programs, and community conferences on the problem. These kinds of stories made up 35 percent of the crime-wave-related news published during the period.

Officials and authorities were willing to assume from the outset that the crime wave represented something real or, at least, they were unwilling to express any doubts in public. Thus, by making public statements and taking official action on the basis of this assumption, authorities made the wave look even more real. And they guaranteed that the wave would go on for some time. As official responses to "the problem" trailed off in mid-December, so did the number of crime incidents known to the media from the police wire and other police sources. The wave finally died.

It is clear that officials with a stake in "doing something" about crime have power over crime waves. Whether or not they inspire crime waves, they can attempt to redirect the focus of coverage of a crime wave already being reported. Nowhere is this clearer that in the first four weeks of *Daily News* coverage of the wave of crimes against the elderly. News headlines during the first week emphasized "the problem," citing instance after instance. But in the next three weeks the stories (starting with the Mayor's first press conference) shifted focus to "what is being done about the problem."

Politicians and police use their news-making power to channel the coverage of social problems into a definite direction (Molotch and Lester, 1974): news of the problem becomes news of how the system is working to remedy the situation. Authorities may also use their newsmaking powers to stop certain crime themes from becoming crime waves. There is tentative data indicating that another crime theme, "crimes on the subways," was stopped from becoming a full-scale crime wave by the New York City Transit Authority.

In the third week of February 1977, the *Daily News*, the New York *Post*, and WAVE all suddenly increased their coverage of murders and muggings in subways. In the middle of that week the Police Chief of the Transit Authority told a *Daily News* reporter there was not crime wave and, soon thereafter, three senior Transit officials called a news conference to assert that the subways were safer than the city streets. From that point on, coverage of subway crime steadily decreased to its pre-wave level.

If an unwanted crime should arise, officials can use their newsmaking powers to deny the wave's existence or to redirect crime coverage into a "safe" direction. There is some evidence, however, that crimes against the elderly was not an "unwanted crime wave"—at least for some officials in the New York City Police Department.

The *Daily News* reporter who wrote the feature articles which turned out to be the beginning of the crime wave, told me that he received "considerable help" from the Senior Citizens Robbery Unit, whose job it was to catch muggers and murderers of the elderly (and the same unit that the Mayor expanded early in the crime wave). On October seventh, the reporter first wrote a story on two crimes with elderly victims that appeared over the police wire on the same day. This story was published October 8, two weeks before the wave. At that time, a *Daily News* editor thought it would be a good idea for the reporter to do a series of feature stories on "this kind of crime." (Such features had shown up periodically in other media organizations before.)

While he was first researching these feature stories, the reporter was in frequent contact with S.C.R.U. This police unit let him know they felt beleaguered, understaffed, and that they were fighting a battle that deserved more attention. (According to the reporter, "They proselytized a lot.") After he had written his feature stories, police from S.C.R.U. began calling him whenever they knew of a mugging or murder of an elderly person. This enabled the reporter to follow up his series with reports of specific crime incidents. Finally, it was S.C.R.U. which first told the reporter about the youth who was let out on fifty dollars bail after beating an elderly person. All major media in New York quickly picked up this story after the *News* reported it. At that point, the crime wave had begun.

I do not want to assert that from this brief history of one crime wave all waves are inspired by the police or politicians. It is not that simple. The crime wave against the elderly in New York seems to have resulted from a mixture of happenstance and police assistance. The history of this crime wave, however, does show that officials can and do use their positions to nurture fledgling crime themes first identified by journalists. Equally, they may use their position to deny the reality of crime waves.

Summary and Conclusions

Crime waves begin as crime themes that journalists perceive in the process of organizing and selecting news to be presented to a public. Because journalists depend on one another for their sense of "what's news," a crime theme can spread throughout a community of news organizations. As each news organization sees the theme presented by other organizations, they learn to use the theme and present it in their news.

But for this crime wave dynamic to occur, journalists must be able to associate a crime theme with a continuous supply of incidents that can be seen as instances of the theme. Media organizations know of crime almost exclusively through law enforcement agencies. The media's major source of supply for crime incidents in New York City is the N.Y.P.D.'s police wire. Crime dispatches over this wire are largely reports of street crimes: robberies, burglaries, shootings, stabbings, and other assaults. These constitute a pool of potential crime waves, excluding the possibility of certain themes. Non-street crime themes, if they were to receive massive publicity as crime waves, might challenge prevailing notions of "serious crime" in this society.

Moreover, once crime themes receive heavy coverage in the media, authorities can use their power to make news in an attempt to augment, modify, or deny a burgeoning crime wave. Thus, official sources not only control the supply of raw materials upon which crime news is based, but also the growth of crime waves.

While this study has dealt with the generation of crime waves, the news-making processes it reveals have broad implications. News plays a crucial role in formulating public issues and events, and in directing their subsequent course. Just as the interplay between local politics and local media organizations brought about New York City's crime wave, so the interplay between national elites and national media organizations may well have given rise to a number of social issues now widely accepted as fixtures in the recent American political scene.

Consider Watergate. As a few investigative reporters persisted in digging up news about the illegal activities of the Nixon administration, national elites competed among one another to halt, support, or redefine the growing Watergate news theme. Eventually, special prosecutors and Congressional committees were formed; that is, a bureaucratic apparatus was set up which began to feed the media with fresh instances of the Watergate theme. Once Nixon was deposed, this apparatus was dismantled, and so was the Watergate "news wave."

Watergate, the Bert Lance affair, the "death" of political activism of the 1960s, and many other accepted political "realities" may have been produced by the same ideological machinery that underlies crime waves.

Appendix

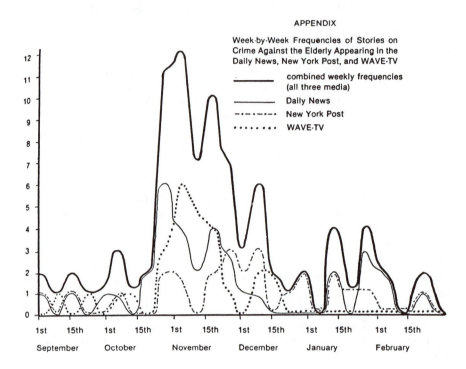

APPENDIX

Week-by-Week Frequencies of Stories on
Crime Against the Elderly Appearing in the
Daily News, New York Post, and WAVE-TV

————————   combined weekly frequencies
(all three media)

————————   Daily News

—·—·—·—·—   New York Post

· · · · · · · ·   WAVE-TV

Notes

[1] This article focuses on the generation of crime waves, not their effects. Thus, I infer that media crime waves contribute to existing images and fears of crime in society. To substantiate this inference would require a study of crime wave effects with a different method from that used here. There is, however, research indicating that people's fears and images of crime derive, in large part, from the news media. See, for example, Davis (1952:330) and Biderman, et al. (1967:128).

[2] While the New York City crime wave represents the first widely publicized formulation of "crimes against the elderly," the issue was not first defined by the New York media. Fredric DuBow (personal communication) has pointed out that the law enforcement establishment had formulated crimes against the elderly as a new type of crime at least two years prior to the crime wave: Since 1974 it was an important funding theme of L.E.A.A.; in 1975 it was the subject of a major conference; and in February 1976 *Police Chief* devoted a special issue to it.

These earlier law enforcement formulations probably led to the creation of the New York Police Department's Senior Citizens Robbery Unit (S.C.R.U.) well before the city's crime wave. As we shall see, S.C.R.U. played a crucial role in directing media attention to crimes against the elderly in the first stages of the crime wave. Thus, it seems that early "professional formulations" led to the establishment of a specialized agency which, in turn, enabled the media publicly to formulate a category for crimes against the elderly.

[3] Reported in the *New York Post*, May 9, 1977.

[4] Thus far I have been unable to obtain a complete, month-by-month set of 1976 N.Y.P.D. crime rates. Therefore, for all but the homicide rate, the figures described below are tentative, based on partial rates for 1976.

[5] The editor's use of news themes is part of the more general tendency of newsworkers to code and categorize news events in order to "routinize their unexpectedness." See Tuchman, 1973.

[6] The assignment editor started with these two stories because his superior in the newsroom had suggested that they be covered.

[7] While my example of overlapping news judgments is drawn from a local television station, the same phenomenon occurs both on newspapers and national network news (Epstein, 1973:150).

[8] The only exception that comes to mind is the coverage of mafia news by specialized reporters on large New York publications: *The New York Times*, the New York *Daily News*, the *New York Post*, the *Wall Street Journal*, and *Newsday*.

[9] There was an occasional fourth source: phone calls from the police.

[10] There were some exceptions. A handful of common crimes did appear over the police wire (e.g., four rapes in a thirty-day observation period). The journalists I observed could not explain why these were there, and they ignored them.

References

Biderman, Albert, Louise Johnson, Jennie McIntyre, and Adrianne Weir
1967   "Report on a pilot study in the District of Columbia on victimization and attitudes toward law enforcement." Washington, DC: U.S. Government Printing Office.

Davis, F. James
1952   "Crime news in Colorado newspapers." American Journal of Sociology 57:325–30.

Epstein, Edward Jay
1973   News from Nowhere. New York: Random House.

Glasgow Media Group
1976   "Bad news." Theory and Society 3:339–64.

Molotch, Harvey and Marilyn Lester
1974   "News as purposive behavior: the strategic use of routine events, accidents, and scandals." American Sociological Review 39:101–12.

Roshier, Bob
1973   "The selection of crime news in the press." Pp. 28–39 in S. Cohen and J. Young (eds.), The Manufacture of News. Beverly Hills: Sage.

Sacks, Harvey
1972   "On the analyzability of stories by children." Pp. 325–45 in J. Gumperz and D. Hymes (eds.), Directions in Sociolinguistics. New York: Holt, Rinehart and Winston.

Smith, Dorothy
1972   "The very ideological practice of sociology." Unpublished paper, Department of Sociology, University of British Columbia.

Steffens, Lincoln
1931   The Autobiography of Lincoln Steffens. New York: Harcourt Brace.

Tuchman, Gaye
1973   "Making news by doing work: routinizing the unexpected." American Journal of Sociology 79:110–31.

4

Fear and Loathing on Reality Television
An Analysis of *America's Most Wanted* and *Unsolved Mysteries*

Gray Cavender and Lisa Bond-Maupin

The media serve to stimulate our interest in crime. Newspapers, for example, detail the exploits of criminals, while television news and crime drama focus on crimes. Although most crime drama is fictional representation, programs like *The F.B.I.* modify actual cases.

Recently, a new type of crime program has been presented to the public. *America's Most Wanted* (AMW) and *Unsolved Mysteries* (UM) present vignettes depicting actual crimes in which theories of crime are dramatized. These dramatizations feature actors, actual photographs or film footage, and interviews conducted with participants and the police. Viewers are urged to call the police or program representatives with information related to the crime, and police officers are on standby in the television studio to take these calls.

AMW and UM represent a hybrid programming format in that a news or public service format is superimposed on entertainment to produce a new television genre, reality programming. But the line between fact and fiction is not so distinct in the media (Williams 1989, p. 5). Even the news represents a social construction of reality in which reporters transform occurrences into news events (Molotch and Lester 1974; Tuchman 1978). On television genres tend to blend together (Gitlin 1985, p. 6). However, such blending of fact and fiction represents

Source: *Sociological Inquiry*, Vol. 63, No. 3, August 1993, pp. 305–317. © 1993 by the University of Texas Press. Reprinted with permission.

a defining characteristic of reality programming inasmuch as these programs are intended to draw the audience into their reality through active participation.

Crime and Danger in the Media

Scholars analyze media crime depictions ranging from the amount of crime news to the demographics of crime drama. The findings of such studies suggest that newspaper coverage bears little relationship to official crime statistics (Davis 1952; Fishman 1978). Although some analysts are not concerned about the divergence of newspaper coverage from official statistics, because such statistics are, like the news, a social construction (Tuchman 1978; Ericson, Baranek, and Chan 1991, p. 54); still others (Graber 1980) argue that newspapers offer a misleading picture of crime and criminals. Newspapers disproportionately report violent crimes, and reporters tend to focus attention on sensational matters such as the capture of a criminal and high status offenders (Graber 1980; Garofalo 1981, pp. 323–25; Humphries 1981, pp. 195–96).

Crime news and fiction go hand in hand because a similar pattern emerges in television drama (Katz 1987). Dramatic criminal plots are featured—usually violence against individuals—and the chase is highlighted (Garofalo 1981, p. 327). Television criminals are predominantly male and disproportionately white, over 30 years of age, and members of a profession (Comstock 1978, pp. 289–93; Pandiani 1978). Television crime is detached from the social context in which it is committed, and non-law-enforcement personnel often solve crimes and capture criminals (Humphries 1981; Lichter and Lichter 1983).

Some research addresses the effects of such depictions on the audience, but the scholarly debate continues unresolved as to whether television affects the public's perception of crime (Gerbner and Gross 1976; Hirsch 1980, 1981). Other researchers suggest that the "meaning" of media crime depictions should be addressed prior to evaluating the effects these depictions have on the public (Gitlin 1979).

The ideological and symbolic dimensions of crime are also present. Television crime drama presents mythic morality plays that privilege a social control orientation (Gitlin 1979, p. 257; Schattenberg 1981), while newspaper coverage reinforces the symbolism of the dominant order (Ericson et al. 1991). Still other researchers analyze the newsworthy effect of such stories (Ericson et al. 1991, pp. 140–48), suggesting that these stories are simple, easily dramatized and personalized, and depict the unexpected. Deviance and control stories meet these criteria. Jack Katz (1987, pp. 50–55) offers four additional criteria for newsworthiness of crime stories: (1) they exemplify human viciousness or audacity, (2) collective integrity is threatened, (3) people who violate moral boundaries are featured, and (4) high status criminals are involved.

Jack Katz's newsworthiness of crime stories criteria parallel the elements of urban legends. Urban legends circulate as true stories, referencing frightening strangers who prey upon unsuspecting victims (Best 1990). Urban legends, such as poisoned Halloween candy, symbolize the strains and unpredictability of modern life (Fine 1980, p. 237; Best 1990, p. 142). Newspaper crime stories produce motifs found in urban legends, expressing the frustrations of a world characterized by the fear of violence (Wachs 1988; Oring 1990).

Crime is an ideal idiom for expressing urban fear and a corresponding sense of danger. Sally Merry (1981, pp. 11–13), for example, identifies three aspects of danger that are linked to crime: a cognitive assessment of cues, harm that transcends the risk of crime, and danger, a cultural construct, learned as part of how the world functions. People who occupy ambiguous and interstitial statuses and roles, such as children, are likely victims (Merry 1981, p. 140). Criminals are beyond normal techniques of social control (Douglas 1966; Merry 1981, pp. 125, 163), and the fear of crime justifies increased control over those who are considered "dangerous" (Merry 1981, p. 220).

Television is especially suited for evoking fear. As a visual medium, television conveys situational cues that elicit fear, such as dark, isolated areas or menacing strangers (Merry 1981; Stanko 1990; Warr 1990). Cinematographic techniques make these cues more realistic (Graber 1990; Kellner 1990). In the following section the image of crime, criminals, victims, police, and the world view presented by AMW and UM are analyzed. This analysis also includes images conveyed through cinematographic techniques and formats.

Method

A content analysis was conducted of AMW and UM programs that aired between January 25 and May 31, 1989. These programs were videotaped and a subsample of 16 episodes was randomly selected: nine half-hour-long AMW episodes and seven hour-long UM episodes. The 16 episodes contain 77 vignettes (48 AMW; 29 UM); the vignette serves as the unit of analysis. In the analysis, all percentages are calculated on these numbers of vignettes.

The protocol used for data collection was focused on three aspects of the programming: (1) *demographics*: types of crime and general information on the crime, criminals, and victims; (2) *characterizations*: specific depictions of crime, criminals, and victims, such as brutality, dangerousness, or a victim's vulnerability; (3) *world view*: relative safety of people and places, the terror and randomness of crime, and what the audience should do about crime.

Information about cinematographic techniques (for example, camera angles and soundtrack) was coded across all three categories. Both programs feature updates about fugitives depicted earlier who are sighted or captured. Such updates were coded with the vignettes in which they originally appeared.

Data and Discussion

There are three parts to the analysis. Part one compares AMW with UM with prior research on crime drama. Part two considers the parallels between AMW and UM's vignettes and urban legends. Part three focuses on the construction and the magnification of the dangers of the modern world depicted in these programs.

Television Crime Drama and Reality Programming

Television depictions differ significantly from official crime statistics. The analysis reveals that AMW and UM's depictions of "real life" crimes and criminals are consistent with crime drama representations.

Television crime is depicted as violent and usually directed against persons. AMW and UM offer a similar view of crime. As shown in table 4.1, in 92 percent of AMW's vignettes ($n = 44$ of 48 vignettes), the crimes depicted also are violent and personal (murder, attempted murder, rape, kidnapping, armed robbery and child molestation). Sixty-two percent of UM's vignettes ($n = 18$) include violence against persons. For both programs, murder is depicted in 52 percent of the vignettes ($n = 40$).

Ninety-one percent of the vignettes ($n = 70$) depict male criminals. Four percent of the vignettes ($n = 3$) feature female criminals, and these are portrayed as accomplices. Criminals are 30 years or older in 56 percent of the vignettes ($n = 43$), and Caucasians are involved in 64 percent of all vignettes ($n = 44$). African Americans ($n = 9$) and Hispanics ($n = 9$) are featured in 12 percent of the vignettes (see table 4.2).

Contrary to television drama, criminals are frequently portrayed as professional criminals. Corporate and political criminals are absent

Table 4.1 Number and Percentage of Vignettes that Depicted Offense Types by Program[a]

	Program Vignettes					
	UM (N = 29)		AMW (N = 48)		Combined UM/AMW (N=77)	
Offense	%	n	%	n	%	n
Murder	41	(12)	58	(28)	52	(40)
Theft/fraud/extortion	21	(6)	8	(4)	13	(10)
Escape	7	(2)	15	(7)	12	(9)
Bank robbery/armed robbery	10	(3)	10	(5)	10	(8)
Illegal arms/terrorism	0		4	(2)	3	(2)
Unexplained death/missing	14	(4)	2	(1)	7	(5)
Rape	3	(1)	6	(3)	5	(4)
Kidnapping	3	(1)	6	(3)	5	(4)
Child molestation	3	(1)	6	(3)	5	(4)
Attempted murder	0		4	(2)	3	(2)
Drug dealing	0		4	(2)	3	(2)
Other[b]	10	(3)	4	(2)	7	(5)

[a]Percentages are based on the total number of vignettes for each program. Note that a vignette may contain depictions of more than one offense type.
[b] The Other category includes bigamy and/or intimidation.

from the vignettes. A motivation for crime is offered in over half of the vignettes (n =42). Greed frequently prompts the crime, especially on UM (n = 11), while emotional motivations, such as jealousy, are prominent on AMW (n = 6). Some crimes are blamed on random violence or mistaken identity (n = 9).

AMW and UM provide a social history, re-enacting past key events in the life of the criminal, and describe their current lives. However, these caricatures tend to reinforce existing stereotypes about criminals.

Citizens play a significant role on both programs. The program hosts credit viewers with captures, while the police are depicted as competent and accessible to the viewers. AMW and UM also provide more information about trial and sentencing than usually appears in crime drama.

Table 4.2 Number and Percentage of Vignettes that Depicted Offender Characteristics by Program[a]

Characteristics	Program Vignettes					
	UM (N = 29)		AMW (N = 48)		Combined UM/AMW (N=77)	
Gender	%	n	%	n	%	n
Male	76	(22)	100	(48)	91	(70)
Female	3	(1)	4	(2)	4	(3)
Unknown/not depicted	21	(6)	0		8	(6)
Age						
20–29	21	(6)	31	(15)	27	(21)
30–39	17	(5)	21	(10)	20	(15)
40–49	21	(6)	31	(15)	27	(21)
50–59	14	(4)	6	(3)	9	(7)
Unknown/not depicted	28	(8)	10	(5)	17	(13)
Ethnicity						
Caucasian	66	(19)	63	(30)	64	(49)
African American	3	(1)	17	(8)	12	(9)
Hispanic	7	(2)	15	(7)	12	(9)
Mixed ethnicity	3	(1)	0		1	(1)
Unknown/not depicted	21	(6)	6	(3)	12	(9)

[a] A vignette may contain depictions of male and female offenders or multiple offenders of the same gender, age, and ethnicity.

AMW and UM as Urban Legends

Fear-evoking cues magnified by sophisticated cinematographic techniques enable AMW and UM to construct entertaining programs that fit the standard format of the television crime genre. The vignettes are symbolic morality plays about good and evil.

As in urban legends, the crime portrayed on AMW and UM symbolizes the dangers and complexities of modern life that threaten the social order. Brutal, violent crimes are featured (for example, UM 2-22-89; AMW 2-12-89), and graphic details are shown, including the number and location of a victim's wounds. For example, one victim is stabbed 30 times through the heart (AMW 2-12-89); another victim is shot "5 times and died of massive bleeding" (AMW 2-5-89).

Cinematographic techniques enhance the affective aspects of crime. In some vignettes, the film speed is reduced to slow motion as a criminal draws a gun and shoots the victim, capturing the muzzle flash (AMW 2-5-89, 2-12-89, 4-9-89). One vignette employs fear cues: the host, emerging from the night on a deserted road, references a common fear of driving on a lonely stretch of highway where one's cries for help would go unheeded (UM 4-12-89).

Described are dimensions or harm that go beyond the risk of victimization. Victims are "embarrassed and devastated" (UM 3-15-89), and their families' and friends' lives are tragically disrupted (UM 1-25-89, 3-15-89, AMW 4-2-89). Dramatic irony intensifies the tragedy. Victims are murdered shortly after achieving an important goal (AMW 3-19-89) or on their birthday (UM 3-15-89). Victims do not merely lose property through theft, they lose "a precious family heirloom that was part of their heritage" (AMW 4-2-89). The narrative, the visual, and the soundtrack combine to communicate a sense of tragedy, e.g., the host notes that a slain policeman is buried with full honors. The vignette shows footage of his funeral as "Taps" is played in the background (AMW 2-5-89). Stories are simple and easily dramatized. Twenty AMW vignettes (42 percent) depict random, purposeless crimes often featured in urban legends, while nineteen UM vignettes (66 percent) offer such a depiction.

Criminals. Like the villains of urban legends, criminals are dangerous people who are beyond social control. Thirty-seven AMW vignettes (77 percent) depict criminals in this manner. Nineteen UM vignettes (66 percent) offer such depictions.

Fugitives are characterized as dangerous (for example, AMW 2-5-89; UM 4-12-89), and the bail bond imposed suggests that these criminals should be incarcerated (AMW 2-5-89). The camera often zooms in on a captured fugitive's handcuffs, providing a visual image of the physical restraints that are required to control these individuals (for example, AMW 2-12-89; UM 3-15-89).

Some criminals are traditional urban legend villains, such as drifters (AMW 3-26-89) and hitchhikers (UM 3-1-89). Other criminals are portrayed as satanists (AMW 4-16-89; UM 3-29-89). AMW and UM also feature criminals who are gang members (AMW 2-12-89) and drug dealers (AMW 2-5-89; 4-16-89).

AMW and UM feature frightening criminals who have ambiguous psychological capacity. One criminal is a "crazed killer, a psycho, a maniac" (UM 3-29-89), while others are characterized as "schizo-phrenic" (AMW 4-2-89) or "emotionally disturbed" (AMW 2-26-89). Both programs feature criminals who "showed no emotion" (for example,

AMW 2-5-89, UM 3-29-89), or who demonstrate "a flamboyant disregard of authority" (AMW 4-12-89).

The programs define criminals through their actions, portraying criminality as a master status, noting such deviance is undifferentiated in that the criminal activity is generalized to other aspects of their lives. For example, one criminal "masqueraded as a construction worker but he was really an escaped murderer" (AMW 2-5-89). Another criminal who "appeared to be a model cop was in reality a child molester" (UM 3-1-89).

The program hosts provide physical descriptions of fugitives in derogatory terms, such as "a scraggly beard" (AMW 4-2-89), or "dirty blonde hair" (AMW 2-26-89). Other deviant behaviors unrelated to the crimes are mentioned, such as dabbling in voodoo (AMW 4-2-89). In one vignette, the host invites the audience to view the physical effects of depravity, using a time-lapse technique on a series of photographs in which the criminal's physical appearance deteriorates (AMW 2-26-89).

Victims. The victims often occupy ambiguous and interstitial roles and statuses and, therefore, are vulnerable to harm. Victims are similar to those of urban legends. Twenty-four AMW (50 percent) and twenty UM vignettes (69 percent) depict such victims. Children are molested and kidnapped (UM 3-1-89, 1-25-89). In this regard, AMW's opening features a visual of an empty playground swing, accompanied by a voice-over of the word "kidnapped."

Women are frequent victims as well. Approximately one-half of the victims whose sex is noted are female, thereby reinforcing the fear of crime and violence that women experience.

AMW and UM offer information about victims designed to achieve viewer empathy. Victims are referred to by their given names, and friends share personal anecdotes. Crimes are re-enacted so as to promote identification with the victim; the camera takes the victim's perspective, reproducing a good/evil dichotomy, with the victim and the audience aligned against the criminal.

The programs focus on the victim's personal and professional worth. In contrast to the criminals, victims are "hard working" individuals (for example, UM 3-15-89; AMW 4-16-89). UM characterizes one victim as a "devoted wife and mother who was active in the community" (UM 3-29-89), and another as "the kind of girl you'd like to have for your daughter" (UM 3-15-89). One vignette featuring wild horses as victims establishes their worth in human terms: "They symbolize the freedom of the American West, and each animal has its own unique personality" (UM 1-25-89).

Modern Danger

Both programs create a sense of modern danger analogous to the fears that urban legends convey. This modern danger is characterized as a world in which no one, no matter how careful, is safe.

Just as urban legends are portrayed as true stories, AMW and UM act as media storytellers of "real life" and the terrible uncertainties of life. The reality program format enhances the sense of modern danger. As entertainment these hybrid programs combine fear cues and cinematographic techniques, and appeal to the conventions of news programming that bolster credibility of reality claims.

An Unsafe World. Good storytellers localize their tales in time and space. AMW and UM program hosts begin their stories with statements like, "27 years ago tonight" (AMW 2-5-89). Exact dates of crimes (UM 1-25-89) and phrases such as "20 days ago" (AMW 3-19-89) provide accessible temporal referents, contributing to reality claims.

Geographic settings are also important. Statements such as "it all started in this house on Chestnut Street" (AMW 2-19-89), or "a quiet blue-collar suburb on the outskirts of Cleveland" (UM 5-31-89) produce an identifiable sense of place. Some locations, such as an unfamiliar area or dark alley, serve as fear cues.

Featured are crimes that occur in safe places, and program hosts draw special attention to such settings. One vignette, set in a conservative Louisiana community, represents, the host notes, an unlikely setting for a crime (UM 3-1-89). In another vignette, "dark forces swirled beneath a small-town facade" (UM 2-22-89). Crimes often violate special places, such as the home. In one dramatization, the camera follows a schizophrenic killer as he observes the sleeping victims (AMW 4-23-89). Another vignette depicts a burglar sneaking through a house while the occupants host a dinner party. Later, a teenage girl showers and her unsuspecting mom works in a bedroom, while the burglar prowls through the house (AMW 4-2-89). When crime occurs in seemingly safe places, a sense of modern danger is enhanced.

Certain predictable people, such as menacing strangers, also serve as fear cures. However, the worst danger portrayed evolves from seemingly trustworthy persons. Likeable and normal people are portrayed as manipulative con artists or crazy (for example, UM 1-25-89; AMW 2-12-89, 4-9-89). In some instances, the unsuspecting criminal occupies a special role, such as a policeman who counsels abused children but who also molests these children (UM 3-1-89), or a sociopathic nurse who kidnaps a newborn baby at gunpoint (UM 1-25-89).

The most terrifying criminals hold a special status with respect to the victim. Examples include the husband who murders his wife while she begs him to spare her life (AMW 2-5-89). Other vignettes depict special criminals who hold an interstitial status, such as the "All American" kid who becomes a drug user and murders his parents (AMW 2-26-89). Such vignettes emphasize the thesis that no place is safe; no person is trustworthy.

Random Terror. One message is that the modern world is filled with danger. Random and terrifying danger lurks everywhere, awaiting the victim and, by implication, the viewer. Powerful, emotionally charged vignettes produce images that reinforce a sense of danger that is commonplace in modern society. Some of the vignettes emphasize the criminal. For example, as the host characterizes the criminal as dangerous, the frame freezes, leaving the criminal's intense stare directed at the audience (AMW 4-9-89). Program hosts urge the audience to remember these visually compelling images, and to be on the lookout for the fugitives.

Victims are also emphasized, many of whom are randomly chosen, innocent individuals who are "arbitrarily targeted" (UM 3-29-89) or murdered by mistake (AMW 4-16-89). On occasion a horror movie format is used in which the foolish character opens a door at the top of the stairs as the audience screams "No." People sense the impending danger and warn victims who rarely heed such warnings. Either victims do not appreciate the extent of the danger (AMW 2-12-89, 4-16-89), or they are engaged in common activities that escalate into sudden violence, such as the woman who became involved in a marital dispute and was murdered (UM 1-25-89).

Equally terrifying are the vignettes in which the victims realize their danger. The camera follows an obviously frightened woman leaving her house. Ominous music complements this fear as she nervously scans the street, searching for some threat. She is careful, but she still disappears (UM 1-25-89).

Other careful victims are murdered by maniacal killers (for example UM 3-29-89), or by satanic blood cults (AMW 4-16-89). Emphasizing victim terror, victims often describe their fear (UM 4-12-89). In other instances the host describes the fear, indicating how it feels for a family to be stalked by a prison escapee bent on revenge (UM 4-12-89).

Situational and fear cues heighten the sense of victim terror and audience frustration. Vignettes feature people who are isolated and alone when victimized (for example, UM 4-12-89). In other instances, people are nearby but do not render assistance to the victim. A woman whose baby has been kidnapped screams for help, but no motorist will stop (UM 1-25-89). Careful, normal, and hard-working people are victimized by base, depraved strangers. They are also victimized by their children, spouses, mates, and friends. In this area, AMW and UM programs extend beyond the content of urban legends, suggesting that modern danger is inescapable.

AMW and UM programs portray a world in which crime is so unpredictable and its consequences so devastating that public safety is at issue. Crime is a metaphor for a world gone berserk, for life out of control. The only recourse viewers have is to call the authorities or the program representative with information that will put criminals behind bars. Program updates attribute captures to viewer tips, and footage of captured fugitives supports these claims.

Modern danger legitimizes public surveillance. Forging a partnership between the police, the media, and the audience, these programs encourage wide dispersal of community social control.

Conclusion

Prior research has shown that television dramatizes stereotype depictions of crime and criminals. In the present study the authors conclude that reality programming presents similar images. Crimes are portrayed as violent and personal, and fugitives are portrayed as dangerous people.

However, the present study diverges from the more traditional media crime approach in that the focus is on program meaning. AMW and UM programs present images common to popular urban legends in that crime is used to symbolize the uncertainties of modern life, that criminals are evil, abnormal people, and victims are portrayed as being vulnerable. Such tales nurture the very fears that produce urban legends.

Using a combination of case selection, cinematographic techniques, and claims, these reality programs depict a sense of modern danger. AMW and UM programs present a world in which anyone can be cast into the role of a criminal or victim. Such an image of reality is frightening because the victims are people with whom viewers can identify.

Reality programs nurture audience participation as one solution to the pervasiveness of crime, supporting the notion that viewers can be empowered in the fight against crime. Viewers are encouraged to watch for fugitives and report them either to the police or the program. Both programs claim that such surveillance leads to the capture of fugitives.

Reality program encouragement of surveillance supports the view that control is dispersing more widely into society. Images of dangerous fugitives who participate in a world characterized by violence and uncertainty justify surveillance and reporting to the police. This world view also supports the claim made by Gitlin (1979) and Schattenberg (1981) that crime drama endorses a control orientation.

In sum, AMW and UM's hybrid news and entertainment format continues the trend toward blurred television genres previously noted by media scholars. The influence of television is so great that it has become an important part of the viewer's reality. Participating in reality programs means the audience is a part of that reality, making that reality almost indistinguishable from any other aspects of life.

References

Best, Joel. 1990. *Threatened Children*. Chicago: University of Chicago Press.

Comstock, George. 1978. *Television and Human Behavior*. New York: Columbia University Press.

Davis, James. 1952. "Crime News in Colorado Newspapers," *American Journal of Sociology* 57:325–30.

Douglas, Mary. 1966. *Purity and Danger: An Analysis of Concepts of Pollution and Taboo*. Hammondsworth: Penguin Books.

Ericson, Richard, Patricia Baranek, and Janet Chan. 1991. *Representing Order: Crime, Law and Justice in the News Media*. Toronto: University of Toronto Press.

Fine, Gary. 1980. "The Kentucky Fried Rat: Legends and Modern Society." *Journal of the Folklore Institute* 17:222–43.

Fishman, Mark. 1978. "Crime Waves As Ideology." *Social Problems* 25:531–43.

Garofalo, James. 1981. "Crime and the Mass Media: A Selective Review of Research." *Journal of Research in Crime and Delinquency* 18:319–49.

Gerbner, George, and Larry Gross. 1976. "Living With Television: The Violence Profile." *Journal of Communication* 26:173–99.

Gitlin, Todd. 1979. "Prime Time Ideology: The Hegemonic Process in Television Entertainment." *Social Problems* 26:251–66.

_____. 1985. "Looking Through the Screen." Pp. 3–8 in *Watching Television*, edited by Todd Gitlin. New York: Pantheon Books.

Graber, Doris. 1980. *Crime News and the Public*. New York: Praeger.

_____. 1990. "Seeing is Remembering How Visuals Contribute to Learning from Television News." *Journal of Communication* 40:134–55.

Hirsch, Paul. 1980. "The 'Scary World' of the Nonviewer and Other Anomalies: A Reanalysis of Gerbner et al.'s Findings on Cultivation Analysis, Part 1." *Communication Research* 7:403–56.

_____. 1981. "The 'Scary World' of the Nonviewer and Other Anomalies: A Reanalysis of Gerbner et al.'s Findings on Cultivation Analysis, Part 2." *Communication Research* 8:3–37.

Humphries, Drew. 1981. "Serious Crime, News Coverage, and Ideology." *Crime and Delinquency* 27:191–205.

Katz, Jack. 1987. "What Makes Crime News?" *Media, Culture and Society* 9:47–75.

Kellner, Douglas. 1990. *Television and the Crisis of Democracy.* Boulder, CO: Westview Press.

Lichter, Linda and Robert Lichter. 1983. *Prime Time Crime.* Washington, DC: The Media Institute.

Merry, Sally. 1981. *Urban Danger: Life in a Neighborhood of Strangers.* Philadelphia: Temple University Press.

Molotch, Harvey, and Marilyn Lester. 1974. "News as Purposive Behavior: On the Strategic Use of Routine Events, Accidents, and Scandals." *American Sociological Review* 39:101–12.

Oring, Elliott. 1990. "Legend, Truth, and News." *Southern Folklore* 47:163–77.

Pandiani, J. 1978. "Crime Time TV: If All We Knew Is What We Saw. . . ." *Contemporary Crises* 2:437–58.

Schattenberg, Gus. 1981. "Social Control Functions of Mass Media Depictions of Crime." *Sociological Inquiry* 51:71–77.

Stanko, Elizabeth. 1990. *Everyday Violence: How Women and Men Experience Sexual and Physical Danger.* London: Pandora.

Tuchman, Gaye. 1978. *Making News: A Study in the Social Construction of Reality.* New York: Free Press.

Wachs, Eleanor. 1988. *Crime-Victim Stories: New York City's Urban Folklore.* Bloomington: Indiana University Press.

Warr, Mark. 1990. "Dangerous Situations: Social Context and Fear of Victimization." *Social Forces* 68:891–907.

Williams, Raymond. 1989. *Raymond Williams on Television: Selected Writings*, edited by A. O'Connor. London: Routledge.

5

State Managers, Intellectuals, and the Media
A Content Analysis of Ideology in Experts' Quotes in Feature Newspaper Articles on Crime

Michael Welch, Melissa Fenwick, and Meredith Roberts

For several decades, scholarly inquiry into the media has revealed key patterns and tendencies in the production of crime news. In particular, scholars have delineated critical stages in the social construction of crime—all of which contribute to the reification of crime news. First, crime is selected from among many available social issues (e.g., education, employment, poverty) and advanced to the status of a *problem* requiring serious policy consideration. Second, the crime *problem* is sufficiently narrowed to include street crime, thereby neglecting other types of lawlessness and harm (e.g., corporate violence). In the final stage, crime is defined as a criminal justice *problem* (Michalowski 1985), and it is this particular image of crime that typically takes the form of crime news (Kappeler, Blumberg, and Potter 1996; Surette 1992; Tunnell 1992; Schoenfeld, Meier, and Griffin 1979).

Operating within the final stage of the social construction of crime, political leaders and law enforcement officials (also known as *state managers*) enjoy the privilege of offering to the media *primary* as well as ideological definitions of crime (Kasinsky 1994:210; Hall et al. 1978). Thus, critics charge that the media serve propaganda functions within the state's ideological machinery (Herman and Chomsky 1988). In particular, it is through the media that state managers *filter* definitions

Source: *Justice Quarterly*, Vol. 15, No. 1, March 1998. © 1998 Academy of Criminal Justice Sciences. Reprinted with permission.

of crime; as a result of this gatekeeping and various other propaganda techniques (Kappeler et al. 1996:24–26), state managers and the media together determine what is *socially thinkable* (e.g., violence committed solely by individual predators instead of corporate offenders). Benefitting from their elevated position within a hierarchy of credibility (Becker 1973, 1967), state managers also promote and legitimize their "law-and-order" crime control agenda (Ericson, Baranek, and Chan 1991, 1989, 1987; Fishman 1978; Hall et al. 1978; Surette 1992; Humphries 1981).

Although crime news exists as a product manufactured by the media, it is significantly shaped by state managers who contribute to its distinct ideological qualities. Fishman (1978:531) reminds us that "all knowledge is knowledge from some point of view." Crime news, therefore, tends to be *ideological* insofar as it represents a worldview of state managers who distort the reality of crime, specifically by disavowing the causal relationship between crime and social conditions (see Marx 1978; Reiman 1995; Sahin 1980).

State managers (e.g., law enforcement officials) have long refined the art of influencing the course and content of crime news (Fishman 1978). Similarly, intellectuals (e.g., professors) have also realized the importance of participating in the construction of crime news. Marking a significant movement in the field, Barak (1994, 1988) introduced the term *newsmaking criminology* to describe a conscious effort by criminologists to engage in the public discourse on crime (see also Fox and Levin 1993; Greek 1994; Henry 1994). "Newsmaking criminology presupposes that there is no such thing as 'objective' news reporting and interpreting: The presentation of crime and violence in the mass media, for example, cannot be disconnected from the prevailing ideologies of the day" (Barak 1994:261).

In this study—the first of its kind—we administered a content analysis of quoted statements offered by different types of experts on crime; namely, state managers (i.e., politicians and criminal justice practitioners) and intellectuals (i.e., professors and nonacademic researchers). In doing so, we examined the ways in which experts' quoted statements convey two principle dimensions of *ideology* of crime: crime *causation* and crime *control*. This investigation is significant because it specifically identifies the sources, forms, and patterns of ideology in crime news, thereby contributing to an understanding of how the media and the state construct misleading depictions of crime and crime policy.

Techniques of Propaganda and Popular Topics in Crime News

An analysis of the social construction of crime news would not be complete without exploring the importance of propaganda as a mechanism facilitating the misrepresentation of crime. Undoubtedly, the elevation of crime to the status of a social problem depends greatly upon the persuasiveness of propaganda: "a technique for influencing social action based on intentional distortions and manipulation of communications" (Kappeler et al. 1996:24). Moreover, it is through numerous propaganda techniques that the media and the state together inject elements of ideology into distorted images of crime. However, these biased versions of crime are not the result of a conspiracy but rather "the unintended consequence of the process by which information is collected, processed, and prepared for dissemination by mass media, government, and interest groups" (Kappeler et al. 1996:22–23; Tunnell 1992; Marsh 1991; Bohm 1986).

Still, it is crucial to emphasize that not all crime news is the product of conscious attempts at propaganda; nevertheless, many distortions of crime are generated by propaganda tactics deeply institutionalized and widely routinized within the media and the government (Kappeler et al. 1996; Kasinsky 1994; Hall et al. 1978). As we explore various examples of propaganda in this and other sections, we should remain mindful of how ideology shapes misleading images of crime at each stage of social construction.

In this study, our sample reveals 47 separate topics represented among 105 feature articles about crime, thus suggesting a diverse range of crime issues. The most common topic was street crime rates/trends ($n=15$); the street crime drop in New York City ($n=8$); youth street crime and juvenile delinquency ($n=8$); and politicians discussing street crime ($n=7$). Furthermore, the remaining articles offered an assortment of issues, including the growth in prison population, "three strikes" laws, firearms, carjacking, genetics, gangs, DNA, stalking, urban violence, women offenders, and the war on drugs.

This sample of crime topics illuminates the process of social construction; first, crime is awarded the status of a social problem requiring massive policy attention; second, the crime problem is distinctly narrowed to include street crime while excluding other forms of lawlessness; and finally, street crime is defined in ways that elicit criminal justice intervention. Conforming to this framework, the most striking characteristic of our sample of topics is its disproportionate emphasis on street crime. Despite 47 different topics, only one of these feature articles went beyond street crime to focus on white-collar offenses. Indeed, the media bias toward street crime (especially offenses committed by *individuals*) to the exclusion of white-collar, corporate, governmental, military, and political crime (especially offenses committed by *groups* and organizations) is abundantly evident.

This particular bias toward street crime suggests that the topics selected for these feature newspaper articles are ideologically filtered or screened. Such a distortion is indicative of a propaganda technique by the which the media manage information through the editorial process; consequently, street crime emerges as the preferred construction of crime. In shoring up the information-management technique, biased language is employed to sensationalize and label certain forms of lawlessness (Kappeler et al. 1996:25). In addition to the frequent and vague use of the term "gang," value-loaded language was also found in references to "stalking" (instead of harassment) and "carjacking" (instead of car theft or robbery). Interestingly, even some law enforcement officials were skeptical of the term "carjacking."

> We don't even like to say "carjacking" . . . It's robbery and it's been going on for a long time. There's a lot of hype going on right now.
>
> > Billy Davis, spokesman for the Chicago Police Department; *New York Times*, December 9, 1992:A-18

Thus, the media together with state managers reproduce an image of public disorder that is overwhelmingly based on street crime, especially offenses committed by low-income individuals. Typically, these constructions of crime are also void of meaningful references to the causal relationship between crime and societal conditions. Consequently, the media contribute to one of the most common forms of propaganda—namely, the creation of criminal stereotypes.

The nature of topics in our sample supports the assertion that crime news is not only commodified for public consumption (Tunnell 1992) but also shaped according to the dominant ideology. A principal aspect of the dominant ideology is its insinuation that street offenses are the most costly, dangerous, and threatening form of crime (see Barlow, Barlow, and Chiricos 1995a, 1995b). Financial losses assessed for different types of offenses, however, contradict the dominant ideology's image of crime. It is estimated that the cost of street crime hovers around $4 billion per year whereas the expense of white-collar and corporate crime exceeds that figure fifty times—reaching $200 billion per year (Mokhiber and Wheat 1995:9; Albrecht, Wernz, and Williams 1995). Further, approximately 24,000 homicides were committed in the United States in, for example, 1995. By contrast, during the same period, more than 56,000 workers died as a result of injuries or diseases caused by unsafe working conditions, totaling more than 300 fatalities per day (Mokhiber and Wheat 1995:9; see also Serrin 1991:80; Welch 1996a, 1996b; Reiman 1995).[1]

Therefore, in publishing messages about certain forms of crime news, the media warn the public of some of the threats to their safety (e.g., street offenses), but neglect—due to ideological constraints—other social harms (e.g., white-collar and corporate offenses) (see also Kappeler et al. 1996:141–63). Again, the framework of social constructionism reminds us of the process by which street crime is selected from many available social harms and defined in ways that legitimize the criminal justice machinery. In facilitating these social constructions, techniques of propaganda serve crucial functions by managing information, thus contributing to stereotypes of criminality (i.e., street crime) (Kappeler et al. 1996:24–25; Tunnell 1992; Bohm 1986; Dickson 1968).

In light of this evidence, our study raises questions about how the media define crime, and just as important to our content analysis, how newspapers *index* topics of crime. Since we examined only those articles listed by the selected newspapers as *features* on crime, our sample was dictated by the newspapers' indexing scheme. As noted, these articles were disproportionately devoted to street offenses; thus, our sample is as much a product (and artifact) of newspaper indexing as it is a reflection of the biases in how the media define crime. In a manner of speaking, we decided to accept the "cards we were dealt" by the newspaper indexing procedure. Regrettably, however, we are aware that many other forms of crime were not indexed into our sample including corporate violence, terrorism, and child sexual abuse, just to name a few.

Research Method

Sample of Feature Articles on Crime

The sample of feature articles in this study was drawn from four major newspapers from 1992 to 1995. These newspapers were selected due to their large circulation, their reputation for offering readers a national coverage of news, and because together they contribute to a sense of geographical representation. A total of 105 feature articles about crime were published in these newspapers between 1992 and 1995; specifically, 42 feature articles were published in the *New York Times*, 24 in the *Washington Post*, 23 in the *Los Angeles Times*, and 16 in the *Chicago Tribune*. It should be noted that the greatest number of feature articles about crime appeared in 1994 ($n=38$) followed by 1993 ($n=31$), 1992 ($n=20$), and 1995 ($n=16$) (refer to table 5.1).

For the purposes of this study, our sample of newspaper articles about crime includes only those articles indexed as *features* and containing at least one quote from a crime expert. Obviously, there are perhaps hundreds of articles about incidents of crime published by each of these newspapers. However, feature articles on crime were targeted

Table 5.1   Number of Feature Articles on Crime Per Year By Newspaper

Newspaper	1992	1993	1994	1995	Totals
NY Times	7	12	15	8	42
Washington Post	7	6	6	5	24
LA Times	3	7	12	1	23
Chicago Tribune	3	6	5	2	16
Totals	20	31	38	16	$N=105$

because they typically offer focused discussions of crime in which experts' quotes are particularly relevant. In this vein, the objective of our research was to examine the content of experts' quotes within the context of feature articles on crime.

Procedure

Two major groups of experts were constructed for this study. The first group of experts—state managers—includes politicians and criminal justice officials and practitioners (i.e., police commissioners, police officers, prosecutors, as well as members of "tough on crime" groups who serve as legislation lobbyists). The rationale for combining politicians and practitioners into one group is based on their roles as state managers; indeed, we also found that the contents of their quotes were consistently similar in terms of ideological statements about crime causation and crime control.

The second group of experts—intellectuals—includes university and college professors as well as nonacademic researchers (e.g., analysts at the Rand Corporation). The rationale for combining professors and nonacademic researchers is based on their roles as intellectuals; additionally, we also confirmed that the contents of their quotes were consistently similar in terms of ideological statements about crime and crime control.

The central purpose of this study is to examine systematically the content of quoted statements offered by experts (as the units of analysis) and to sort them according to two principle dimensions of ideology of crime: crime causation and crime control. Borrowing from Barlow et al. (1995a, 1995b), we relied on three perspectives of crime causation. The first perspective of crime causation in our classification scheme was *utilitarianism*, typically surfacing as references to criminal motives in relation to economic gain. From this viewpoint, the following utilitarian notion of deterrence sheds light on the significance of greater opportunity to commit crime coupled with fewer risks of detection.

Twenty-nine years ago, there was no Medicare, Medicaid and a much smaller pool of (private) health insurance. Doctors were conventionally paid in cash and had greater opportunity to under report income. Today, that's not the case.

> David Levine, Chief Economist for New York-based Stanford C. Bernstein Co., a securities research firm; *Los Angeles Times*, February 13, 1993:A-21

The second perspective of crime causation, *personal pathology*, commonly manifested itself in statements about psychological defects affecting criminals and their inability to control their unlawful behavior. Consider the following item:

Impulsivity, sensation-seeking, and defiance are all stable traits found among juvenile delinquents that can sometimes be seen as early as pre-school.

> Denise Gottfredson, associate professor at the Institute of Criminal Justice and Criminology, University of Maryland at College Park; *New York Times*, July 22, 1993:10

Finally, the perspective that *social factors* cause crime served as our third content category; in sum, this grouping of factors included various microsocial circumstances, social influence, social conflict, and macrosocial conditions.

This is all symbolic. But everybody's avoiding the really tough issues of addressing the fundamental social conditions that are breeding this.

> Stuart A. Scheingold, professor at University of Washington; *New York Times*, October 24, 1993:4

Also drawing from Barlow et al. (1995a, 1995b), we categorized crime control into two types of strategies. The first content category of crime control was designated for *hard control*, including the expansion of law enforcement, "get-tough-on-crime" campaigns, and preventative measures based on deterrence.

This is precisely the type of person three-strikes-and-you're-out was aimed at: career criminals. It's a victory for the people of California because this is a thug who has a record of violence in the past—serious felonies—who believes that it's okay to go out and terrorize little kids.

> Daniel E. Lungren, California State Attorney General; *Washington Post*, March 8, 1995:A-14

The second grouping of crime control intervention was reserved for *soft control*, namely, rehabilitation, decriminalization, gun control, and criminal justice (and social) reform.

Getting in there with programs is more difficult because of this chasm. The issue is not just that people have moved, but the jobs have moved. And for this and other reasons, inner-city residents don't have the resources to deal with these issues.

Donna E. Shalala, Health and Human Services secretary; *Washington Post*, February 12, 1993:A-12

Methodologically, it should be noted that statements critical of hard control were coded as soft control; likewise, statements critical of soft control were sorted into the category of hard control.

In administering a content analysis, we systematically examined each of the experts' quotes to determine whether they conveyed statements about crime causation (as represented by either manifest content or latent content), and, if so, according to which perspective (i.e., utilitarianism, personal pathology, or social factors). Similarly, the quotes also were scrutinized to conclude whether they contained statements about crime control (as indicated by either manifest content or latent content), and, if so, according to which perspective (i.e., hard control or soft control).

Findings

The first task of our content analysis involved identifying and sorting experts' (politicians and practitioners compared to professors and nonacademic researchers) quotes into two principle categories of ideology of crime: crime causation and crime control. Table 5.2 indicates that our sample includes 162 quoted statements about the cause of crime and 132 quoted statements pertaining to crime control (totaling 294 statements overall). What is noteworthy about these findings is that 61 percent (n=92) of the quotes from politicians and criminal justice practitioners deal with crime control, while 39 percent (n=58) are relevant to crime causation. Conversely, 72 percent (n=104) of the quotes from professors and nonacademic researchers pertain to causes of crime, whereas 28 percent (n=40) relate to crime control.

Although the number of statements quoted from each grouping of experts is strikingly balanced (150 statements offered by politicians and practitioners and 144 by professors and nonacademic researchers), the differences between the content of statements—as they reflect an ideology of crime—are marked. That is, politicians and practitioners were quoted along lines of crime control, whereas professors and nonacademic researchers were quoted about the causes of crime. Computations for chi-square test yield statistical significance at the .001 level of probability (refer to table 5.2). Obviously, it is difficult to know whether these differences are the result of fundamental views of ideology of crime (crime causation compared to crime control) or whether these differences stem from how journalists select (or filter and screen) quotes to be used in their feature articles. Given the central importance of this issue in the context of propaganda, we shall return to it later in this section.

Table 5.2   Number of Quoted Statements About Crime Causation and Crime Control by Politicians & Practitioners Compared to Professors & Nonacademic Researchers*

Statements About:	Politicians & Practitioners	Professors & Nonac. Res.	Totals
Crime Causation	58 (39%)	104 (72%)	162 (55%)
Crime Control	92 (61%)	40 (28%)	132 (45%)
Totals	150	144	N=294†

*Quoted statements drawn from 105 feature newspaper articles on crime in the *New York Times*, the *Washington Post*, the *Los Angeles Times*, and the *Chicago Tribune* from 1992 to 1995.

†Computations for chi-square yield statistical significance at .001 level of probability.

Crime Causation

The second task of our content analysis involved identifying and sorting experts' (politicians and practitioners compared to professors and nonacademic researchers) quoted statements into three categories of crime causation: utilitarianism, personal pathology, and social factors. Table 5.3 shows that we located 26 quoted statements about utilitarianism, 33 quoted statements about personal pathology, and 103 quoted statements about social factors (totaling 162 quoted statements about the causes of crime). What is noteworthy about these findings is that more than 46 percent (n=27) of the quoted statements from politicians and practitioners deal with social factors; 38 percent (n=22) embrace utilitarianism; and 15.5 percent (n=9) address personal pathology. Conversely, 73 percent (n=76) of the quoted statements from professors and nonacademic researchers reflect their view that social factors cause crime; 23 percent (n=24) relate to personal pathology; and 4 percent (n=4) pertain to utilitarianism.

In addition to 14 politicians, this pool of practitioners includes 20 law enforcement officials, 6 prosecutors, 2 corrections officials, 1 judge, 1 defense lawyer, 1 probation official, 1 member of the ACLU, 1 state director of criminal justice, 1 director of criminal justice services, 1 coroner, 1 forensic psychologist, 1 criminal justice advocate, and 1 chief economist at a security firm. Additionally, the pool of experts includes 44 men and 8 women.

Table 5.3   Number of Quoted Statements About Crime Causation by Politicians & Practitioners Compared to Professors & Nonacademic Researchers*

	Politicians & Practitioners	Professors & Nonac. Res.	Totals
Causes of Crime:			
Utilitarianism	22	4	26
	(38%)	(4%)	(16%)
Personal Pathology	9	24	33
	(15.5%)	(23%)	(20%)
Social Factors	27	76	103
	(65.5%)	(73%)	(64%)
Totals	58	104	$N=162$†

*Quoted statements drawn from 105 feature newspaper articles on crime in the *New York Times*, the *Washington Post*, the *Los Angeles Times*, and the *Chicago Tribune* from 1992 to 1995.

†Computations for chi-square yield statistical significance at .001 level of probability.

The pool of intellectuals includes 42 professors and 8 nonacademic researchers. Additionally, the pool of intellectuals was made up of 38 men and 12 women.

The differences between the content of statements—as they relate to crime causation—are compelling. That is, professors and nonacademic researchers tend to endorse the view that crime is caused by social factors. Although politicians and practitioners lend some support to this view, as a group they were also more likely to embrace the perspective of utilitarianism. Computations for chi-square test yield statistical significance at the .001 level of probability (refer to table 5.3).

The following quoted statements drawn from the sample illuminate the three perspectives on crime causation: utilitarianism, personal pathology, and social factors.

Utilitarianism. The utilitarian (and deterrence) model of crime was greatly advanced by Cesare Beccaria ([1764] 1981) and Jeremy Bentham ([1789] 1962), who depicted humans as rational, calculative, and motivated by personal (and especially material) gain. Briefly, these classical theorists proposed that crime could be deterred if penalties for crime outweighed the gain of criminal behavior. In this vein, Bentham further developed the utilitarian perspective by referring to these human tendencies as the pleasure/pain principle and hedonistic calculus. In our sample, numerous sources relied on the utilitarian model to describe their view of crime.

> We've even seen altered lottery tickets made to look as if they were winners. People will try just about anything for money.
>
> > Carissa Cragg, document examiner; *Chicago Tribune*, February 28, 1993:8

Not only does the next quote refer to the role of police in deterring crime, but it also suggests a much deeper—and darker—view of society.

> People are gonna do what they're gonna do. They commit crimes when you aren't there. I could be on one street, and there might be something happening on the street directly parallel to it.
>
> > Jurithia Foust, Washington, D.C. police officer; *Washington Post*, September 17, 1993:B-1

In deconstructing a "mean worldview," Surette (1992) and Gerbner et al. (1980, 1979, 1978) point to how the media and state managers depict society as violent and dangerous, consequently compounding attitudes of fear, isolation, and suspicion among citizens. Relying on animal metaphors, the role of police ("sheepdogs") in a "mean world" is to patrol the community and protect the public ("sheep") from the criminal element ("wolves") (Surette 1992:42–44).

In the realm of social constructionism, utilitarian notions of crime in the media rest on the individualistic bias, thus becoming detextualized from the larger social realities of crime causation and social control (Bohm 1986). Indeed, propaganda techniques serve to reinforce the individualistic bias insofar as they contribute to the creation of criminal stereotypes (e.g., offenses committed by low-income individuals) (Kappeler et al. 1996:24).

Personal Pathology. Much like utilitarianism, the perspective of personal pathology as a cause of crime also reinforces the individualistic bias in the social construction of crime (Bohm 1986). Further, the mediated version of personal pathology also promotes criminal stereotypes and, in doing so, contributes to false distinctions between criminals and law-abiding people; for instance, Bohm (1986:200–201) reports that over 90 percent of all Americans have committed some crime for which they could be incarcerated. Personal pathology as a cause of crime stems from early positivism, especially the work of Cesare Lombroso (1876) who proposed that criminals were defective humans. Although the sources of such defects could be genetic, biological, psychological, sociological—or any combination of them—Lombroso's principal assumption was that criminals were pathological, thus different from so-called normal, law-abiding people. With this in mind, several statements from our sample rely on positivism (and even genetic terminology, e.g., "breed") in characterizing some criminals as defective, dangerous, and out of control. One source describes

> . . . a breed of "super-predator" criminal so dangerous that even older inmates working their way through life sentences complain that their youthful counterparts are out of control.
>
>> Professor John J. DiIulio, Princeton University; *Los Angeles Times*, May 2, 1995:E-7

While acknowledging the importance of social factors in crime causation, some statements advocate genetic research in locating individual causes of crime. The following source agrees

> . . . that environmental causes are the "overwhelming" reason for high crime rates in blighted neighborhoods, but she believes that genetics might play a role that should be looked into.
>
>> Diana Fishbein, senior researcher at the Department of Justice, former criminology professor at University of Baltimore; *Washington Post*, September 22, 1995:B-3

In addition to deflecting attention from the social factors in crime causation, the positivistic components of these quotes lend themselves to criminal stereotypes. Further, these remarks are also shaped by another propaganda technique in which opinion is presented as fact (Kappeler et al. 1996:24–25). As a result, such statements promote a degree of fear and terror commonly found in *moral panic*, "a turbulent, excited, or exaggerated response to deviance or a social problem" (Mann 1984:255; Cohen 1972; Hall et al. 1978; Chiricos 1996; Goode and Ben-Yehuda 1995). Although moral panics are projected by the media in a sensationalized, stylized, and stereotypical fashion, as noted, they are also defined as social problems amenable to the criminal justice agenda (Cohen 1972:9; See also Welch et al. 1997).

Social Factors. Social factors causing crime encompass microsociological determinants (e.g., negative family circumstances) and macrosociological and economic conditions (e.g., poverty and unemployment). Consider the following item representative of this perspective of crime causation:

> High-crime areas end up being areas of "disinvestment." These become the areas that need jobs. The cab drivers don't want to go there, the business people don't want to locate there, the tax base erodes. And these are the very areas that require the most services.
>
>> Jerry Abramson, Mayor, Louisville, KY; *Washington Post*, July 5, 1994:A-6

Similarly, the socioeconomic aspect of the drug market and its relationships to violence were also addressed in several references to social factors, for example:

> It's also plausible that the drug market has stabilized and been driven indoors, and that the "private commercialization" causes less fighting over territory.

> Jerome Skolnick, visiting criminology professor, John Jay College of Criminal Justice; *Washington Post*, December 27, 1995:F-2

Several other social factors were the subject of discussion, especially demographics with respect to age:

> Most of the decline that has occurred would have occurred anyway. The baby boom generation, which comprises almost a third of the population is getting older. They are middle-aged, and they are not nearly as aggressive and violent as they were when they were younger.

> Professor James Alan Fox, Northeastern University; *New York Times*, July 23, 1995:4

Crime Control

The third task of our content analysis involved identifying and sorting experts' (politicians and practitioners compared to professors and nonacademic researchers) quoted statements into two broad categories of crime control: hard control and soft control. Table 5.4 shows 132 quoted statements pertaining to crime control. What is worth noting about this particular finding is that 73 percent ($n=67$) of the quotes from politicians and practitioners support hard control strategies, while 27 percent ($n=25$) embrace soft control. Conversely, 75 percent ($n=30$) of the quoted statements offered by professors and nonacademic researchers endorse soft control strategies, whereas 25 percent ($n=10$) favor hard control.

The differences between the nature of the statements—as they relate to crime control—are compelling. While politicians and practitioners endorse strategies of hard control in dealing with crime, professors and nonacademic researchers overwhelmingly support measures of soft control. Computations for chi-square test yield statistical significance at the .001 level of probability (refer to table 5.4).

In addition to 37 politicians, this pool of practitioners includes 15 law enforcement officials, 3 members of the ACLU, 3 criminal justice advocates, 2 prosecutors, 2 corrections officials, 2 judges, 2 defense lawyers, and 1 director of criminal justice services. Additionally, this pool of experts includes 56 men and 12 women.

The pool of intellectuals includes 20 professors and 7 nonacademic researchers. Additionally, the pool of intellectuals includes 25 men and 2 women.

Table 5.4 Number of Quoted Statements About Crime Control by Politicians & Practitioners Compared to Professors & Nonacademic Researchers*

	Politicians & Practitioners	Professors & Nonac. Res.	Totals
Crime Control Strategies:			
Hard Contol	67	10	77
	(73%)	(25%)	(58%)
Soft Control	25	30	55
	(27%)	(75%)	(42%)
Totals	92	40	N=132†

*Quoted statements drawn from 105 feature newspaper articles on crime in the *New York Times*, the *Washington Post*, the *Los Angeles Times*, and the *Chicago Tribune* from 1992 to 1995.
†Computations for chi-square yield statistical significance at .001 level of probability.

Hard Control. Hard control measures range from such deterrent strategies as strengthening and expanding the criminal justice system to contemporary retribution imperatives: "get-tough-on-crime" (and on prisoners) and "three strikes, you're out." From this perspective, the following state manager advocates incapacitation for the purpose of reducing violent crime.

> If you can get these violent criminals to serve more time, you will inevitably reduce the violent crime rate. Anyone who is locked up will not commit a crime.
>
> > Representative Bill McCollum, Florida Republican, Chairman of the House subcommittee on crime; *New York Times*, August 10, 1995:A-14

Returning to classical theory, some experts reiterated the language of Beccaria ([1764] 1981) and Bentham ([1789] 1962) to characterize the nature of punishment as it relates to deterrence. The next passage is firmly rooted in retribution but also contains elements of moral panic underscored with value-loaded language, a common propaganda technique (i.e., the undefined use of the term "gang").

> Punishment has to be swift and certain. When children commit adult crimes, they should be prosecuted as adults. We can't coddle criminals because they are young. We're not just talking about gang members. What we are seeing is total disregard for pain and human life among the young. It's scary, and I predict it will only get worse.

> Jeanine Ferris Pirro, Westchester County [NY] District Attorney;
> *New York Times*, January 30, 1994:15

Interestingly, the following assertion draws on positivist views of criminality; but instead of suggesting rehabilitation in correcting criminal defects, an argument justifying incapacitation is offered. Moreover, the source's presentation of opinion as fact and alarmist use of the terms "new breed" and "predatory street criminal" evidence value-loaded language as a propaganda tactic.

> The new breed of predatory street criminal cannot be deterred. They can only be incapacitated.
>
> > Professor John J. DiIulio, Princeton University; *Los Angeles Times*, May 2, 1995:E-7

Finally, in the realm of promoting a favorable image of law enforcement and their claim of crime deterrence, the following item claims police effectiveness—a prominent theme in criminal justice propaganda. While presenting opinion as fact, such proclamations justify continued investment in the criminal justice system, especially hard control.

> We [the police] are changing behavior in New York City.
>
> > William J. Bratton, New York City Police Commissioner; *New York Times*, November 19, 1995:43

Soft Control. Measures of soft control include efforts to rehabilitate offenders (and drug addicts), decriminalize particular forms of lawlessness (e.g., certain types of drug offenses), impose tighter regulation of gun ownership, and reform the criminal justice system in ways that uphold fairness and reduce discrimination (e.g., addressing racial and socioeconomic biases). Moreover, several statements opposed larger expenditures for hard control strategies (e.g., correctional spending) which flourish at the expense of soft control measures (e.g., social services and education).

> In recent years, the increase in correctional spending for states has been twice that for general fund increases and even larger than in education spending. We have to find new ways to cope with the rate of criminality.
>
> > Jon Felde, studied judiciary issues for the National Conference of State Legislatures; *Washington Post*, June 2, 1994:3

Finally, the following viewpoint is one of many proposals in our sample that endorsed greater restrictions on gun ownership.

> You have to stop and ask: Would you rather have those 6,000 people able to go into a store and buy a gun? [According to Sarah Brady, the Brady bill is] the cornerstone of a serious gun-control policy in America that will eventually include more restrictions.

Sarah Brady, Chairwoman of Handgun Control, Inc.; *New York Times*, August, 15, 1993:4

Discussion

As noted, it is difficult to conclude whether the differences between state managers and intellectuals are the result of fundamental views of crime (i.e., crime causation and crime control) or whether these discrepancies stem from how journalists select quotes in preparing their feature articles. In light of this uncertainty, a number of unanswered questions remain. For instance, while being interviewed by journalists, do politicians and practitioners devote more discussion to crime control while professors and nonacademic researchers reflect more on the causes of crime? Are journalists asking politicians and practitioners more questions that relate to crime control—conversely, asking professors and nonacademic researchers more questions that pertain to crime causation? Or are journalists deliberately filtering the experts' quotes in ways that lead one to the biased viewpoint that politicians and practitioners shall be quoted for statements about crime control while professors and nonacademic researchers are to be sourced for comments concerning the causes of crime?

If such a bias does exist, it might suggest that the media view professors (and nonacademic researchers) as appropriate sources for remarks about crime causation, whereas politicians and practitioners are perceived as suitable sources for comments about crime control. Consequently, it seems that crime control policy is understood by the media as the domain of state managers, while it appears that professors (as well as some nonacademic researchers) remain in—or are consigned by the media to—the "ivory tower." As a result of this marginalization, academics seem to be restricted to offering so-called "theoretical" and "abstract" notions about crime causation; moreover, such ideas about criminological theory are perhaps taken to mean that they have little relation to the "real" world. In fact, many state managers quoted in our sample vehemently ridiculed criminological research while engaging in crass anti-intellectualism.

> I was not hired to be Arizona's chief social theorist. I was not sent here to sit meditating on Freud or on the latest "root causes" of criminal behavior. The criminal law deals not with theories but with thugs.

> Governor Fife Symington, Arizona Republican; *New York Times*, January 24, 1994:B-6

Revealing additional evidence of anti-intellectualism, the law enforcement official attributed to the following statement attacks not only social science in general, but a well-established relationship between aging and declining crime rates in particular.

> When the ball went down in Times Square in 1994, did (the crooks) suddenly age? Or all get locked up? Or kill each other off in that 10 seconds? [he demands, noting that the city's (New York City) youth population was lower in the '80s, when crime was higher.] These excuses are pathetic, worse than sophomoric.
>
> John Maple, NYC Deputy Police Commissioner; *Washington Post*, December 27, 1995:F-2

In the event that this bias exists, the media evidently operate on preconceived notions about the appropriate role of intellectuals (i.e., theorists) vis-a-vis state managers (i.e., policy makers) in the manufacturing of crime news. Moreover, this particular bias may very well be reinforced by various techniques of propaganda, including the masking of opinions through sources and selective interviewing (Kappeler et al. 1996:25–26). With this in mind, it is important to question procedures by which the media determine *who* constitutes a source. Kasinsky (1994:210–11) reminds us: "The dominant sources tend to flood the market. Government sources, including local police departments, the Pentagon, and the State Department, can saturate the media with information or disinformation, because information from these sources is considered official and carries with it the assumption of credibility" (see also Ericson et al. 1989; Chermak 1994). In the same manner, this study finds that print journalists rely heavily on government sources—specifically, law enforcement officials—especially in recommending policies for crime control (refer to tables, 5.2, 5.3, and 5.4).[2]

As far as this study of crime news is concerned, our research design is not entirely without limitations. For methodological purposes, we borrowed categories of crime causation and crime control from Barlow et al. (1995a, 1995b). Although dichotomizing statements about the causes of crime according to utilitarianism, personal pathology, and social factors offers methodological advantages, there are also some drawbacks. Specifically, the social factors category might have been too broad; this category encompasses microsociological determinants (e.g., negative family circumstances), macrosociological and economic conditions (e.g., poverty and unemployment), along with demographics (i.e., age) and the socioeconomic aspects of drug market violence. As a result of collapsing micro- and macrolevels of analysis, a particular problem emerges. Grouping microsociological factors with macrosociological conditions diminishes the saliency of truly critical approaches to crime causation (e.g., the role of capitalism in generating crime). Nevertheless, the presence of genuinely radical voices about crime causation (and crime control) in this sample were nonexistent, thus confirming the suspicion that the media's spectrum of worldviews remains decidedly narrow.

Indeed, the exclusion of radical intellectuals from the social construction of crime news might very well be evidence of a common propaganda technique in the media, namely, selective interviewing (Kappeler et al. 1996:26). Even more to the point, preventing radicals from participating in the public discourse on crime reflects another tactic of propaganda in which journalists mask their own opinions through sources who are selected because their views closely resemble—or do not stray too far from—the media's (Kappeler et al. 1996:25). Tables 5.3 and 5.4 provide evidence of sourcing patterns by enumerating a heavy reliance on politicians and law enforcement officials.

Additionally, the relative independence of the pool of intellectuals could also be called into question insofar as many professors (and nonacademic researchers) fit the description of *de facto* state managers by virtue of having strong funding connections to the state. Further, the presence of *de facto* state managers in this pool may make the intellectuals seem more conservative than they are.

As another methodological limitation, the lack of separation between microsociological factors and macrosociological forces could explain why state managers appear to be more liberal than expected. According to our classification scheme, statements offered by politicians who view crime causation, for instance, from a "family values" standpoint are grouped into a category of social factors which also includes remarks made by professors targeting unemployment as a cause of crime. Not only does this classification procedure blur fundamental distinctions among views of crime causation, it also affects how the respective strategies of crime control are catalogued. In this respect, the categories for crime control may also have been too inclusive—permitting, for example, "family values" strategies to be sorted into the same group of soft control initiatives as economic strategies. Again, this method of coding could explain why state managers appear to be more liberal with respect to crime control than expected.

At the onset of this study, it was presumed that certain views of crime causation would correspond with particular strategies for crime control. Conforming to this logic, utilitarianism coincides with hard control whereas personal pathology and social factors match the ideals of soft control. However, our classification scheme allows sources to equivocate on their beliefs of crime causation and crime control; in fact, politicians were able to lend support to the view that crime is caused by social factors (e.g., negative family circumstances) while simultaneously endorsing punitive measures of crime control (e.g., advocating incarceration) (refer to tables 5.3 and 5.4). This lack of consistency between crime causation and crime control suggests that the media (i.e., journalists) tend to refrain from confronting their sources about apparent incongruities; arguably, this lack of journalistic vigilance facilitates the propaganda process.

Conclusion

Despite its limitations, however, this research sheds light on the roles of the media and the state in the social construction of distorted images of crime which are projected in the form of crime news. To this end, our study shows that the contents of quotes by state managers are significantly more ideological (in both crime causation and crime control) insofar as they neglect the causal connection between social conditions and crime. Additionally, we also find that several state managers repeatedly invoked crime-control mantras which blend elements of political "tough-talk" and "crime-speak" with simplistic views of crime causation. Taken together, these remarks are ideologically self-serving because they reinforce the popular perception that the problem of crime is the sole domain of the criminal justice apparatus, thus excluding other forms of state intervention (e.g., public health services).

> I want to send a message to the violent criminals, that if you commit the crime you do the time.
>
>> Governor Bruce King, New Mexico, Democrat; *New York Times*, January 24, 1994:B-6
>
> We're sending a message—if you commit a crime, you will do the time.
>
>> Governor Ben Nelson, Nebraska, Democrat; *New York Times*, January 24, 1994:B-6
>
> If you've done the crime in this state, you will do the time.
>
>> Governor Mel Carnahan, Missouri, Democrat; *New York Times*, January 24, 1994:B-6

Clearly, these political proclamations about crime share a striking similarity, suggesting that "official" versions of crime are ideologically "prepackaged." Even New Hampshire Governor Stephen Merrill, who conceded that his state was "comparatively free from violence," maneuvered to keep the crime issue in the public mind by insisting, "We will spend more time in 1994 talking about crime, and we should" (*New York Times*, January 24, 1994:B-6).

Overall, the prevailing construction of lawlessness depicted by the media together with state managers is a collage of individual street crimes detextualized from social factors. Surette (1994:148–49) reminds us that "the continuing disparity between the media-constructed reality of crime and justice and the nonmedia reality of crime and justice results in the public receiving an unnecessarily distorted image that supports only one anti-crime policy approach, an expanded and enhanced punitive criminal justice system—an approach lacking evidence of success."

Although macrosociological forces (e.g., politics and economics) significantly shape its content and scope, the social construction of crime news is also subject to meso-level (i.e., organizational) determinants. In this vein, we ought to remain mindful that media (e.g., print and electronic journalism) are formal organizations which administer their tasks in pursuit of institutional goals. Surette (1992:59) insists that "because the market and manipulative models ignore these organizational constraints on the creation of news, they are both inadequate. News is neither a pure picture of society nor a fully controlled propaganda message but instead an organizational product."

In the same manner, the relationship between the media and state managers (serving as primary definers of crime) is structured, in large part, around the organizational needs and routines of journalists. Operating under incessant time restrictions, journalists must rely on institutional resources not only for the purpose of meeting unreasonable deadlines but also to assure the public that information about crime is "officially" confirmed and validated by *credible* sources: law enforcement officials and political leaders (Benedict 1992:10). It should also be emphasized that the relationship between the media and law enforcement agencies is mutually rewarding insofar as police officials help journalists create their product—that is, crime news. According to this *relation of reciprocity*, law enforcement officials not only benefit by serving as primary definers of crime but also gain from publicly promoting their institutional objectives and needs (e.g., financial funding, the hiring of additional employees, and the acquisition of equipment) (Welch, Fenwick, and Roberts 1997; Chermak 1996, 1994; Kasinsky 1994; Hall et al. 1978).

> In short term, the expenditure of money has to increase. We need more and better cops, more prosecutors.
>
> > Eric H. Holder, Jr., U.S. Attorney; *Washington Post*, July 5, 1994:A-6)

> Each one you catch, evidence shows they have committed a host of other crimes. If you take them out of society, these are cost savings never calculated into what we spend on new prisons.
>
> > Bill Jones, Secretary of State, California, former assemblyman and author of the "three strikes law"; *Washington Post*, March 8, 1995:A-14

In sum, the lessons of social constructionism instruct us about the complex process by which crime is not only elevated to the status of a social problem but is distinctly framed in ways that make it amenable to the criminal justice apparatus. Hence, this study contributes to an understanding of this process by illuminating how the state and media collaborate to propagandize distorted images of crime for public consumption.

Finally, social constructionism also teaches us about the significance of a related concept, namely, the *definition of the situation* (also known as the Thomas theorem and the self-fulfilling prophecy). Simply put, what people believe to be real will be real in its consequences (Thomas 1923; Thomas and Znaniecki 1927). Given the power of the media and the state to perceive the world, shape public attitudes and opinions, and manufacture what is socially thinkable (Tunnell 1992; Altheide 1984),[3] we ought not be surprised by the public's willingness to accept ideological views of crime causation (e.g., disavowing the causal relationship between societal conditions and crime) and to lend its support to an expanding criminal justice machinery.

Notes

[1] Reiman (1995), among other scholars, further verifies that white-collar and corporate crime pose greater threats to public safety than street crime: "We have a greater chance of being killed or disabled, for example, by an occupational injury or disease, by unnecessary surgery, by shoddy medical emergency services than by aggravated assault or even homicide (1995:50). In widening the scope of social harm beyond street crime, it should be noted more than 419,000 persons annually die from diseases caused by cigarettes in the United States; similarly, more than two-thirds of homicides and serious assaults involve alcohol (Johnson Foundation, 1993).

[2] Whereas government sources have long been connected to the production of news, professors have recently begun to make inroads into the media. Still, some professors appear in feature articles more frequently than others, thus raising questions about the selection and sourcing of academic experts. It has been suggested that there exists a pool of "usual suspects" consisting of oft-cited academics on whom journalists rely for expert commentary. Although our sample includes a few oft-quoted professors, the dominance of these figures is substantially diminished by the vast number of other professors also quoted in these features. In fact, our sample contained a relatively large quantity of professors, including academics with national reputations as well as those considered regional and local.

In discussing the matter of sourcing with a prominent (crime news) journalist, he stated that he approaches several different professors for each feature; typically, he tries to match a topic with the expertise of the academician. In the past, many journalists relied on their rolodexes for locating experts; today many reporters turn to Lexis/Nexis and other on-line computer services for tracking professors and their expertise (as indicated by published articles and books on a given topic). Nevertheless, professors most likely to be interviewed are those who remain accessible to journalists—especially those who carry pagers, cellular telephones, and return messages promptly (see Fox and Levin 1993; Barak 1994). (Refer to

Welch et al. [1997] for a more elaborate examination of the selection of sources and experts.)

[3] Drawing on the National Crime Survey, Tunnell (1992:295) finds that "96 percent of the respondents reported relying on the news media to learn about crime and criminals, and 49 percent of those surveyed believed that the media gave the right amount of attention to stories about crime." Tunnell also notes: "At that time, more than 50 percent of the news stories were of violent crime, whereas only 6 percent of the actual crimes involved some form of violence. Not surprisingly, 88 percent of those surveyed overestimated the number of crimes they believed involved violence.

References

Abercrombie, N., S. Hill, and B. S. Turner. 1980. *The dominant ideology thesis*. London: Allen and Unwin.

Albrecht, S., G. W. Wernz, and T. L. Williams. 1995. *Fraud: Bringing light to the dark side of business*. Burr Ridge, IL: Irwin Professional Publishers.

Altheide, D. 1984. "TV news and the social construction of justice: Research issues and policy." Pp. 292–304 in *Justice and the Media*, R. Surette, (Ed.). Springfield, IL: Charles C. Thomas.

Barak, G. 1988. "Newsmaking criminology: Reflections on the media, intellectuals, and crime." *Justice Quarterly*, 5:565–87.

Barak, G. 1994. *Media, process, and the social construction of crime*. New York: Garland Publishing.

Barlow, M. H., D. E. Barlow, and T. G. Chiricos. 1995a. "Economic conditions and ideologies of crime in the media: A content analysis of crime news." *Crime & Delinquency*, 41:3–19.

Barlow, M. H., D. E. Barlow, and T. G. Chiricos. 1995b. "Mobilizing support for social control in a declining economy: Exploring ideologies of crime within crime news." *Crime & Delinquency*, 41, 2:191–204.

Beccaria, C. [1764] 1981. *On crimes and punishments*. Translated by Henry Paolucci. Indianapolis: Bobbs-Merrill.

Becker, H. S. 1967. "Who's side are we on?" *Social Problems*, 14:239–47.

Becker, H. S. 1973. *Outsiders: Studies in the sociology of deviance*. New York: The Free Press.

Benedict, H. 1992. *Virgin or vamp: How the Press covers sex crimes*. New York: Oxford University Press.

Bentham, J. [1789] 1962. *An introduction to the principles of morals and legislation*. John Browning, (Ed.). New York: Russell & Russell.

Bohm, R. 1986. "Crime, criminal, and crime control policy myths." *Justice Quarterly*, 3:193–214.

Chermak, S. 1994. "Crime in the news media: A refined understanding of how crimes become news." Pp. 95–130 in *Media, process, and the social construction of crime*, G. Barak, (Ed.). New York: Garland Publishing.

Chermak, S. 1996. "The presentation of drugs in the news media: The news sources involved in social problem construction." An unpublished manuscript. Bloomington: Indiana University.

Chiricos, T. 1996. "Moral panic as ideology: Drugs, violence, race and punishment in America." Pp. 19–48 in *Justice with prejudice: Race and criminal justice in America*, M. Lynch and E. B. Patterson, (Eds.) New York: Harrow and Heston Publishers.

Cohen, S. 1972. *Folk devils and moral panics: The creation of the mods and rockers*. London: MacGibbon & Kee.

Cohen, S. 1985. *Visions of social control: Crime, punishment and classification*. Cambridge: Polity Press.

Cohen, S., and J. Young. 1981. *The manufacture of news*. Newbury Park, CA: Sage Publications.

Dickson, D. 1968. "Bureaucracy and morality: An organizational perspective on a moral crusade." *Social Problems*, 16:143–156.

Ericson, R. V. 1995. *Crime and the media*. Aldershot, VT: Dartmouth.

Ericson, R. V., P. M. Baranek, and J. B. L. Chan. 1987. *Visualizing deviance: A study of news organizations*. Toronto: University of Toronto Press.

Ericson, R. V., P. M. Baranek, and J. B. L. Chan. 1989. *Negotiating control: A study of news sources*. Toronto: University of Toronto Press.

Ericson, R. V., P. M. Baranek, and J. B. L. Chan. 1991. *Representing order: Crime, law, and justice in the news media*. Toronto: University of Toronto Press.

Fishman, M. 1978. "Crime waves as ideology." *Social Problems*, 25:531–43.

Fox, J., and J. Levin. 1993. *How to work with the media*. Newbury Park, CA: Sage.

Gerbner, G., L. Gross, M. Jackson-Beek, S. Jeffries-Fox, and N. Signorielli. 1978. "Cultural indicators: Violence profile no. 9." *Journal of Communication*, 28:176–207.

Gerbner, G., L. Gross, L. Signorielli, M. Morgan, and M. Jackson-Beek. 1979. "The demonstration of power: Violence profile no. 10." *Journal of Communication*, 29:177–96.

Gerbner, G., L. Gross, M. Morgan, and N. Signorielli. 1980. "The mainstreaming of America: Violence profile no. 11." *Journal of Communication*, 30:10–29.

Goode, E., and N. Ben-Yehuda. 1995. *Moral panics: The social construction of deviance*. Oxford: Basil Blackwell.

Gramsci, A. 1971. *Selections from the prison notebooks*. New York: International.

Greek, C. 1994. "Becoming a media criminologist: Is 'newsmaking criminology' possible?" Pp. 265–86 in *Media, process, and the social construction of crime*, G. Barak, (Ed.). New York: Garland Publishing.

Hall, S., C. Critcher, T. Jefferson, J. Clarke, and B. Roberts. 1978. *Policing the crisis: Mugging, the state and law and order*. New York: Holmes and Meiser.

Henry, S. 1994. "Newsmaking criminology as replacement discourse." Pp. 287–318 in *Media, process, and the social construction of crime*, G. Barak, (Ed.). New York: Garland Publishing.

Herman, E. H., and N. Chomsky. 1988. *Manufacturing consent: The political economy of the mass media*. New York: Pantheon.

Hickman, M. 1982. "Crime in the streets—a moral panic: Understanding 'get tough' policies in the criminal justice system." *Southern Journal of Criminal Justice*, 8:7–22.

Humphries, D. 1981. "Serious crime, news coverage, and ideology." *Crime and*

Delinquency. 27:191–205.

Israel, M. 1996. "Should ACJS join Cossa?" *ACJS Today,* XIV, 4:1, 12.

Jenkins, P. 1992. *Intimate enemies: Moral panics in contemporary Great Britain.* New York: Aldine De Gruyter.

Johnson Foundation. 1993. *Substance abuse: The nation's no. 1 health problem.* Princeton, NJ: Johnson Foundation.

Kappeler, V. E., M. Blumberg, and G. W. Potter. 1996. *The mythology of crime and criminal justice* (2d ed.). Prospect Heights, IL: Waveland Press.

Kasinsky, R. G. 1994. "Patrolling the facts: Media, cops, and crime." Pp. 203–236 in *Media, process, and the social construction of crime,* G. Barak, (Ed.). New York: Garland Publishing.

Kidd-Hewitt, D., and R. Osborne. 1995. *Crime and the media: The postmodern spectacle.* East Haven, CT: Pluto Press.

Lombroso, C. 1876. *The criminal man.* Milan: Hoepli.

Mann, M. 1984. *The encyclopedia of sociology.* New York: Continuum.

Marsh, H. L. 1989. "Newspaper crime coverage in the US: 1893–1988." *Criminal Justice Abstracts,* September: 506–14.

Marsh, H. L. 1991. "A comparative analysis of crime coverage in newspapers in the United States and other countries from 1960–1989: A review of the literature." *Journal of Criminal Justice,* 19:67–79.

Marx, K. 1978. "The German Ideology." Pp. 146–200 in *The Marx Engels reader* (2d ed.), R. D. Tucker, (Ed.). New York: Norton.

Michalowski, R. J. 1985. *Order, law, and crime: An introduction to criminology.* New York: Random House.

Mokhiber, R., and A. Wheat 1995. "Shameless: 1995's 10 worst corporations." *Multinational Monitor,* December: 9–16.

Reiman, J. 1995. *The rich get richer and the poor get prison: Ideology, class and criminal justice* (4th ed.). Boston: Allyn and Bacon.

Sahin, H. 1980. "The concept of ideology and mass communication." *Journal of Communication Inquiry,* 61:3–12.

Schoenfeld, A., R. Meier, and R. Griffin. 1979. "Constructing a social problem: The press and the environment." *Social Problems,* 27:38–61.

Serrin, W. 1991. "The wages of work." *The Nation,* January 28:80–82.

Surette, R. 1992. *Media, crime & criminal justice: Images and realities.* Pacific Grove, CA: Brooks/Cole Publishing Company.

Thomas, W. I. 1923. *The unadjusted girl.* Boston: Little, Brown.

Thomas, W. I., and F. Znaniecki. 1927. *The Polish peasant in Europe and America.* Chicago: University of Chicago Press.

Tunnell, K. 1992. "Film at eleven: Recent developments in the commodification of crime." *Sociological Spectrum,* 12:293–313.

Welch, M. 1996a. *Corrections: A critical approach.* New York: McGraw-Hill Book Company.

Welch, M. 1996b. "Critical criminology, social justice, and an alternative view of incarceration." *Critical Criminology: An International Journal* 7:43–58.

Welch, M., M. Fenwick, and M. Roberts. 1997. "Primary definitions of crime and moral panic: A content analysis of experts' quotes in feature newspaper articles on crime." *Journal of Research in Crime and Delinquency,* 34: In Press.

Part II

CONSTRUCTING CRIME PROBLEMS

6

The Gang Initiation Rite as a Motif in Contemporary Crime Discourse

Joel Best and Mary M. Hutchinson

Claims regarding social problems inevitably borrow from the broader culture, interweaving both familiar and original elements to construct particular problems. Thus Gamson and his associates speak of *issue cultures*, in which competing viewpoints are organized in packages of cultural elements, including many drawn from the available culture (Gamson and Lasch 1983; Gamson and Modigliani 1987, 1989). Williams (1995) argues that a social movement must mobilize accessible *cultural resources* to make its cause meaningful both to the movement's members and to those they hope to persuade; Benford (1993) suggests that actors in a movement adapt existing vocabularies of motive. Constructionist analyses of *claimsmaking rhetoric* note that persuasive claims incorporate elements from the broader culture (Best 1990; Gusfield 1981; Ibarra and Kitsuse 1993). Although it is generally agreed that discourse on social problems borrows from its cultural context, most analysts focus on the original, problem-specific elements of claims while neglecting the more familiar elements adapted by claimsmakers from the available cultural repertoire. This emphasis on the original aspects of claims overlooks how the familiar elements shape the construction of social problems.

These familiar elements can take various forms, including (but not limited to) metaphors, motives, exemplars, idioms, catchphrases, social

Source: *Justice Quarterly*, Vol. 13 No. 3, September 1996, pp. 383–404. © 1996 Academy of Criminal Justice Sciences. Reprinted with permission.

types, and motifs. In particular, motifs have received little sociological attention. Folklorists use the term motif to refer to a recurring narrative element; for example, being required to answer a riddle is a common motif in folktales and fairy stories. Although the concept rarely appears in sociological analysis, Ibarra and Kitsuse suggest that it may be useful in analyzing social problems rhetoric:

> Motifs are recurrent thematic elements and figures of speech that encapsulate or highlight some aspect of a social problem. They are . . . a kind of generic vocabulary conventionally used in claims-making, each term or phrase acquiring distinctive connotations in being situated in one kind of context or another. The study of motifs in social problems discourse ought to focus our attention on how morally imbued metaphors and phrases can be intelligibly applied in claims-making. Some examples of motifs: *epidemic, menace, scourge, crisis, blight, casualties, tip of the iceberg, the war on* (drugs, poverty, crime, gangs, etc.), *abuse, hidden costs, scandal.* (Ibarra and Kitsuse 1993:47; authors' emphasis)

Ibarra and Kitsuse, then, equate motifs with metaphors that can be used to characterize many different social problems. Some motifs, however, such as "welfare queen," are specific to discourse about particular problems. When a problem-specific motif recurs in discussions of a particular social problem, it can shape the definition of that problem and its potential solutions.

Many analyses of social problems construction make at least passing reference to particular motifs (e.g., Gusfield [1981] on "the killer drunk" in claims about drunk driving), but we know of no fullscale analysis of a single social-problems motif. In this article we attempt this task: We examine the "gang initiation rite" as a recurring element—a motif—in three forms of contemporary discourse about crime.

Claims that invoke this motif depict joining a delinquent gang as a formal process marked by a ritual of initiation, in which the prospective member usually must commit some deviant act as a condition of membership. We focus, not on this alleged deviance, but on the motif. That is, our interest is in the claims that certain deviant acts occur as part of gang initiations. Whether such acts actually occur in the course of gang initiation rites is not the analytic issue. Rather, we hope to understand how gang initiation rites figure in discourse about crime.

Methods: Examining Three Forms
of Discourse about Crime

Claimsmaking about crime and other social problems occurs in many venues or arenas (Hilgartner and Bosk 1988), and a motif's meaning may vary with the arena.

We compare the imagery of gang initiation rites in contemporary legends (a form of popular discourse), in social scientific research, and in newspaper stories. Gang initiation rites have different meanings in these three forms of discourse; those meanings link contemporary constructions of gangs to their broader cultural context, especially imagery of conspiratorial deviance. After summarizing our methods, we examine how the three forms of discourse use the gang initiation motif; then we discuss the significance of deviant conspiracies in the construction of social problems.

Press Reports

Constructionist researchers often sample the mass media, usually by searching one or more published indexes (e.g., *Reader's Guide to Periodical Literature*, *New York Times Index*, or *Television News Index and Abstracts*). Obviously such analyses depend on the quality of the indexing from which they draw. In attempts to study motifs, however, such indexes are virtually useless; motifs rarely are used as keywords in indexing. Not only is *gang initiation rite* unlikely to be used as an index heading; the motif may not appear in more than a small fraction of the many stories indexed under "gangs," and it may well appear in stories indexed under other headings.[1]

Computerized full-text databases, however, allow researchers to locate even passing references to particular topics. They can search vast collections of material for every use of a particular word or phrase. We used NEXIS, a database that includes press coverage. On September 15, 1995 we searched the MAJPAP and PAPERS files in NEXIS's NEWS library, using the search words *gang initiation* and *rite*. This search identified 114 stories for our analysis.[2]

The use of NEXIS to sample media discourse has limitations. For example, the service is relatively new, so some sources have been part of the database for only a few years; although the service indexes many major newspapers and magazines, coverage is not complete; and slightly different search commands would produce somewhat different samples. Still, it seems reasonable to believe that our search revealed the range of ways in which press reports use the expression *gang initiation rite*.

Popular Discourse

Efforts to learn how the general public talks about social problems present even more daunting obstacles than attempts to sample media coverage. There is no way to identify all popular discourse about crime, no way to systematically sample naturally occurring crime talk. Some social scientists have tried to circumvent these problems by staging discussions about crime problems (Sasson 1995a, 1995b) or by recording individuals' narratives about their personal experiences with crime (Wachs 1988). Such approaches, however, seem ill-suited for analyzing motifs because it would be necessary to examine very large collections of popular discourse to find an adequate sample of even fairly common motifs.

We adopt a different approach: examining contemporary legends that mention gang initiation rites. Contemporary or urban legends are stories, told as true, usually transmitted orally, which often depict dangers in contemporary life (Brunvand 1981; Fine 1992). Folklorists collect and analyze contemporary legends, so we located legends about gang initiation rites by examining recent books and articles by folklorists and by consulting *FOAFTale News*, the newsletter of the International Society for Contemporary Legend Research. In addition, our discussion of contemporary legends draws on newspaper articles that we located in our NEXIS search, which debunk specific reports of gang initiation rites as legends or "urban myths." We focus on two recent legends with wide circulation, but we also identify some less familiar stories that incorporate the motif of the gang initiation rite.

Contemporary legends pose their own analytic problems. Usually it is impossible to know which portions of the population tell, hear, or believe these stories. Legends characteristically occur in a wide range of variant forms. Still, contemporary legends—particularly the two core stories—provide evidence of the general public's perception of gang initiation rites.

Social Science Discourse

Research on gangs by sociologists, criminologists, and other social scientists has a long history. Some of these studies make at least passing reference to initiation practices in gangs. We examined several classic and contemporary studies of gangs; here we compare their discussions of gang initiation rites with the discourse of the press and the public.

Gang Initiation Rites in Contemporary Legends

We begin by examining two contemporary legends concerning gang initiation rites that achieved national currency in the early 1990s. Then we turn to other, apparently less widespread legends. Finally, we identify some general themes in folkloric construction of gang initiation rites.

"The Slasher under the Car"

This contemporary legend circulated nationally after 1984 and peaked in late 1992 ("Ankle Slashers" 1993; Brunvand 1993:134–38; "Close Call" 1993; "Urban Yarn" 1991). The story involves a criminal who crawls under a car and lies in wait until someone returns and begins to open the car door. At this point, the criminal grabs the unsuspecting victim's ankles and begins an assault.

This legend is not new; Brunvand (1993:135) suggests that it may have circulated as early as the 1950s. It takes variant forms. The criminal is often, but not always, said to be a gang member; many versions explain the ankle grabbing as a "gang initiation rite" (e.g., the illustrated version in Fleming and Boyd 1994:18). Usually, but not always, the victim is female, and the setting is a parking lot at that hotbed of contemporary legend violence—the shopping mall. Sometimes the criminal is identified as black or southeast Asian. Often the criminal renders the victim helpless by slicing through her Achilles' tendon with a knife or razor; in other cases, the criminal smashes his victim's ankles with a tire iron, or even plants banana peels and waits under the car for the victim to slip and fall into reach. The ankle grabbing leads to various crimes including rape, purse snatching, robbery, and auto theft; in some versions, when the victim reaches toward her ankles, the gang member grabs her hand and cuts off a finger.

"Lights Out"

A second legend, called "Lights Outs" by folklorists ("Blood" 1993; Brunvand 1995; "Lights Out" 1993), circulated widely in 1993–1994 and involves gang members driving at night. When approaching motorists blink their lights to warn the gang members that their lights aren't on or are on high beam, they are followed by the gang members, who attack and (in most versions) kill them. Almost all versions of this story explain these attacks as part of a gang initiation rite. One faxed version declared "This is the time of year for gang initiations" (Brunvand 1995:32); another stated "police Depts across the nation are being warned that this is 'blood' initiation weekend. Their intent is to have all new bloods nationwide drive around on Saturday and Sunday nights with their lights off" ("Blood" 1993). This story attracted nationwide attention; police departments received many inquiries. Most authorities denied that this story was anything more than a rumor. Our NEXIS search located stories debunking local versions of this legend in 16 major newspapers.

Other Gang Initiation Legends

Although the ankle-grabbing and "Lights Out" stories apparently reached the largest numbers of people, other contemporary legends also involve gang initiations. One common theme in these stories is gang-initiation violence in shopping malls. In "The Castrated Boy," a legend that achieved wide circulation in the 1960s and 1970s, a small boy enters a public restroom—often in a mall—and is castrated by a group of older children or adults from another ethnic group, "often as part of an alleged ritual or initiation ceremony" (Brunvand 1984:88; Carroll 1987; Dorson 1981:228–30). In 1991, a rumor circulated in Wichita, Kansas:

> . . . gangs of black teens were initiating new members by requiring them to grab white children and throw them over a second-level railing to the level below. Lack of public information was blamed on a conspiracy in which police, newspaper editors, and mall owners hushed up the incidents to keep Christmas shopping high and profitable. ("Mall Mayhem" 1992)

A story in the *Chicago Sun-Times* ("Truth is Floored" 1993) debunked this legend about a South Side mall: "Teen thugs are knocking down young female shoppers and slashing them across the cheeks in a gruesome rite-of-passage demonstration."[3] According to a Pittsburgh story, police had been warned that "two juveniles would be shot as part of a gang initiation rite at an undesignated mall" ("Malls on Alert" 1994). As Halloween approached in 1995, a rumor circulating in Sanger, California stated that a gang initiation rite would involve drive-by shootings of trick-or-treaters (Gerald T. Horiuchi, personal communication, November 10, 1995).

Another recently circulated tale is a variant of a well-established contemporary legend, "The Killer in the Backseat" (Brunvand 1981:52–53, 1984:214; 1986:58–59). In this story a woman is warned, usually by a service station attendant or another motorist, that a criminal is hiding in the backseat of her car. Recent tellings of this story often include gang initiations: "The police arrive and arrest a teenager who confesses that, as part of his gang initiation, he must sneak into the cars of two women at gas stations in order to rape and kill them" ("Killer" 1993; also see "New Urban Myth" 1993). A Dallas version specified that the initiates must "rape a white woman" ("Don't Take . . ." 1992).

Occasionally the press speculated that other gang initiation stories might be contemporary legends. In St. Louis, police criticized a radio commentator for describing a gang initiation rite in which "wannabes were driving into crowds of pedestrians . . . just for the fun of seeing them scatter"; the story ran under the heading "Urban Legend Dept." (1994). A San Antonio story that "several teen-age girls willingly had unprotected sex with a male gang member who was HIV-positive as part of a gang initiation rite" was labeled "a public health time bomb," or "maybe . . . just the latest urban myth" ("Gang Rites" 1993).

Themes in Contemporary Legends

Certain clear similarities run through the contemporary legends that mention gang initiations. Virtually all of the legendary initiations demand that initiates commit acts of serious, even deadly violence against strangers who are chosen virtually at random. Frequently the victims are women or children, some of society's most vulnerable members. The violence often seems pointless; its only purpose is to fulfill the requirements of the initiation rite. In many cases the gang members are identified as members of ethnic minorities; their victims, implicitly if not explicitly, belong to the white majority. In short, popular discourse, at least in the form of contemporary legends, views gang initiation rites as serious threats to the social order, a cause of unpredictable violence in which deviant gang members attack innocent, respectable citizens. In these stories, the motif of gang initiation provides a motive: "Why kill another driver for blinking headlights?" "Because the initiation rite demands it." The motif makes sense of the senseless.

Although contemporary legends usually are believed to be true by those who tell and hear them, they are considered false as soon as they are labeled "just" rumors or legends.[4] That is, someone (believing the tale to be true) might warn a friend about ankle grabbers at the local mall, but the friend might respond that the story is "just a rumor" (and therefore false). Thus the newspaper stories cited above acknowledged that many people believed these stories about gang initiations, but declared that these particular stories were legends, not true reports. (As we observe below, newspapers have treated other stories about gang initiation rites as true.)

Gang Initiations in the Social Science Literature

The notion of the gang initiation rite is familiar to sociologists and criminologists. Spergel notes:

> According to gang lore, gang initiations have ranged from drinking a large quantity of alcohol to using or selling drugs, fighting other members or running a gauntlet, stealing from a store, and doing a chit" (e.g., shooting a member of an opposing gang). Females may be required to have sex with a male core gang member, or fight a leader or core member of the female gang. (1995:91)

Whereas "gang lore" identifies a wide range of initiation practices, ethnographers' reports on gangs describe a much narrower range of practices, very different from the random violence associated with gang initiations in contemporary legends.

Researchers consistently report that gangs require prospective members to demonstrate toughness and commitment to the gang before they can join. Toughness is a key virtue for gang members; they must be prepared to defend themselves and their territory against rivals (Jankowski 1991; Miller 1958). Most often, gangs initiate new members by making them demonstrate an ability and willingness to fight:

> Although initiation ceremonies are not universal features, many fighting groups of ghetto adolescents have found them attractive over the years. In contemporary Mexican-American barrios, they commonly take the form of brief, casually arranged episodes of submission to group fist pounding. On the East Coast among white ethnics in the fifties and among Puerto Ricans in the sixties, initiation procedures were described as formalized, elaborate, painful, and terrifying. They are rarely mentioned in the ethnographies of black urban gangs of the sixties [but see Keiser, cited below]. When they are performed, initiation rituals most directly work like a metaphysical immigration ceremony, granting membership in an ontologically higher order. (Katz 1988:134)

Similar accounts can be found in a wide array of ethnographic reports of gangs (Jankowski 1991:12, 50; New York City Youth Board 1960:50), including case studies of Hispanic gangs (Horowitz 1983:98–99; J. Moore 1991:49; Padilla 1993:182; Vigil 1993:105), African-American gangs (Hagedorn 1988:90–91; Keiser 1969:21; Shakur 1993:9), suburban gangs (Monti) 1994:68), female gangs (Campbell 1984:25; J. Moore 1991:49), and motorcycle gangs (Wolf 1991:110–14). Such accounts also appear in training materials about gangs, prepared for law enforcement and social welfare professionals:

> There are a variety of ways to become a member of a gang. The most common is through an initiation process of being "jumped in" or "courted in." This means you may have to physically fight two or more members of the gang for approximately 15–60 seconds. If you fight well, show that you are not afraid, and can defend the honor of the gang, you are accepted as a member. (Operation Safe Streets 1995:37; also see Carondelet Management Institute N.D.:4)

The practice of requiring initiates to fight experienced members may have emerged sometime after World War II. Most of the earlier accounts of gangs do not mention initiation through ritualized fighting; instead an informant in Thrasher's (1927:28) classic study reported: "We took in only two new members . . . but for them we devised a special initiation, copying some of our stunts from the 'Penrod and Sam' stories by Tarkington."[5]

Although some ethnographies discuss initiation rites, the researchers often observe that not all gang members go through these rituals:

Seven of those we interviewed answered that initiation rites included an act of some sort of "fighting," and two said the new member had to "rip off" something in order to become a member. All others (36) said either that there was no initiation procedure or that it varied with circumstances. (Hagedorn 1988:90. For similarly qualified statements, see Campbell 1984; Jankowski 1991; Keiser 1969; J. Moore 1991; New York City Youth Board 1960; Operation Safe Streets 1995)

In none of the ethnographic accounts do gangs demand that initiates commit crimes of random violence against nongang members. One of Hagedorn's (1988:91) informants specifically denied this possibility: "Nothing like, OK, we wanna see how bad you are—go rob the next corner store you see. Nothing like that." Although some observers charge that gay bashing is a skinhead initiation rite, Hamm's (1993:138) "most unequivocal finding" was that all his interview subjects "denied taking part in an initiation rite of violence." Yablonsky (1970:193) reports, "There is a mythology built up around initiation rites, such as the requirement that a potential member steal something or assault someone, but these entrance demands are seldom fulfilled or really expected to take place."

Themes in the Social Science Literature

Social scientists, then, depict gang initiation rites very differently than contemporary legends. Although random, often lethal violence against nonmembers is a central theme in contemporary legends, virtually all of the violence described by social scientists occurs within the gang as ritualized fighting between initiates and experienced gang members. Serious injuries can occur, but they are uncommon; the point of the ritual is to test—not to harm—the prospective member. In short, the reports of researchers who claim firsthand knowledge of gangs and their initiation rites differ markedly from the accounts in contemporary legends. These legends clearly are not grounded in a reading of ethnographers' accounts.

Gang Initiation Rites in Newspaper Coverage

Most of the 114 newspaper stories that mentioned gang initiation rites fall into one of three distinct categories. First, 29 stories (25 percent) debunk contemporary legends with gang initiation themes. As noted above, these tales tend to feature elaborate but senseless violence: "Lights Out," ankle grabbing, rapists hiding in the backseat, and so on.

Second, the NEXIS search revealed 22 reports (19 percent) of mundane "beat-downs" or "jump-ins"—the violent tests of character described by social scientists in which initiates must fight experienced members. In Seattle, two police officers making a training film on gangs were criticized after they videotaped (with the gang's permission) an initiation rite:

> Between six and eight gang members took turns punching and kicking a youth at a playground . . . as part of a gang initiation rite. . . . Sources say . . . the beating lasted less than one minute, no weapon was used, and the youth suffered only minor bruises and some swelling . . . the officers reportedly heard the youth consent to being beat up. The teenager was struck several times on his arms, legs, and torso. . . . ("County Police" 1992; also see "Ganging Up" 1987)

These fights sometimes had serious consequences. One news story involved a boy killed during an initiation ("Boy was Kicked" 1990). In a notorious Houston case, two young women were raped and murdered when they came upon several gang members who had held an initiation rite earlier in the evening ("Blacks N Whites" 1993). For the most part, however, newspaper accounts of initiation rites pitting initiates against experienced members resembled the descriptions in the social science literature.[6]

In the third and largest category of newspaper articles, 47 stories (41 percent) linked gang initiations to murder, assaults, and other crimes against nongang members.[7] These stories generally lacked the detailed reporting found in stories about initiation by fighting; only six cited gang members' claims that the violence was part of a gang initiation. In contrast, 22 stories in this category speculated that crimes were part of gang initiations:

> Right-wing groups like Skinheads and junior Klan groups . . . might require initiates to attack gay and homeless people. . . . ("Gang Beat-Downs" 1994)

> Police assume Adams [shot in a drive-by] was victim of a gang initiation rite. . . . Adams, the father of two young sons, said he is not considering moving to the suburbs. (Such random violence can happen anywhere in America.) Instead, he and his wife, Carol, are seriously thinking about moving to the southwest coast of Ireland. ("Staunch Advocate" 1994)

The remaining 19 stories in this category attributed crimes to gang initiations. Often they cited a source but did not explain the basis for the attribution:

> A teenage gang in New York City is forcing each of its new recruits to shoot one person in the leg as an initiation rite, the New York Post has reported. . . . The newspaper said members of the gang had denied the accusations. ("Gang Initiation" 1990)

> The FOLKS, the Crips and La Raza in Chamblee have made auto theft an initiation rite, police said. Those gangs, police say, have targeted suburban malls. ("Where Are You Safe?" 1994)

Many of the stories in this category concerned unsolved crimes or general types of crime, and accounted for their occurrence by referring to possible gang initiation rites. Often they attributed this explanation to the police.[8] These articles also mentioned random violence, and cited gang initiation rites as an explanation.

Themes in Newspaper Coverage

Press coverage mentions gang initiation rites in diverse contexts. Some press reports focus on ritual fights between initiates and experienced members; often these fights become newsworthy only when someone—typically an initiate or a passerby—suffers a serious injury. Other press reports debunk contemporary legends; usually these involve extravagant forms of violence against strangers, as in the "Lights Out" tale. The largest number of stories, however, attributes shootings, stabbings, arson, and other acts of "senseless," "random" violence to gang initiation rites.[9] Although the violence in these stories tends to be more mundane and less dramatic than the melodramatic violence in contemporary legends, the two forms of discourse share the view that gang initiation rites involve unprovoked attacks against strangers. In other words, the accounts of gang initiation rites promoted by contemporary legends can be regarded as melodramatic versions of press reports that routinely attribute violence to gang initiations.

Conspiracies of Deviants

In his discussion of ritual in preindustrial social movements, Hobsbawm notes

> . . . the heightened ceremony which surrounded the initiation of a man into a special group of his fellows, one designated to demonstrate its utter difference from other groups and to bind him to it by the strongest conceivable links. It combined awe, the element of testing the candidate and that of instructing him in the mysteries of the group, and naturally culminated in some form of most solemn declaration—normally an oath—and some ceremony symbolizing adoption into the group. (1959:154)

Simmel (1950) observed the centrality of initiation rituals in secret societies; ethnographers have described rites of passage and other initiation rites in a wide array of cultures; and theorists have interpreted initiation as a psychological and cultural process (Eliade 1958; La Fontaine 1985). Such analyses typically focus on the meaning of rituals for the participants, both the initiates and those who do the initiating.

The interpretation of recent discourse on gang initiation requires a rather different approach. Popular treatments of gang initiation rites in legends and in the press invoke standard themes found in discussions of other initiations: secret ceremonies that admit individuals into a select group; ritual symbolism, sometimes including blood, oaths, renaming, and the like; and trials or tests that demonstrate the individual's commitment to the new identity. The very term *initiation rite* evokes anthropological imagery; it suggests scientific objectivity but has other connotations as well. It hints that gang members might be characterized by various invidious terms for the anthropologist's subjects—*primitives, savages,* and the like. In these ways, claims about gang initiations borrow from generally available understandings of the nature of initiation rituals. As Simmel (1950:360) suggests, "Through the symbolism of the ritual, which excites a whole range of vaguely delimited feelings beyond all particular, rational interests, the secret society synthesizes those interests into a total claim upon the individual." According to legends and press reports about gang initiations, the rituals require prospective gang members to commit terrible crimes; in doing so, the initiates not only demonstrate their capacity for and commitment to the gang's criminality, but also take an irrevocable step into deviance.

Our analysis focuses not on the putative rituals, but rather on these accounts of gang initiation rites—particularly the discourse of the press and the public. We begin by indicating parallels between claims about gang initiation rites and accounts of other conspiracies of deviants; then we offer an interpretation of stories about initiation into deviant conspiracies.

Initiations into Other Deviant Conspiracies

Accounts of conspiracies of deviants often include descriptions of initiation rituals. Frequently these rituals require initiates to commit or join in the commission of serious acts of deviance, as in these examples:

Satanism. Contemporary claims about a powerful satanic blood cult engaged in tens of thousands of human sacrifices as well as other crimes emphasize cult rituals, including rituals of initiation:

> First a blood relative or trusted friend inducts a child. Secret ceremonies instill a ritualistic fear of evil, accompanied by robed and hooded figures, naked women on altars, hypnotic chants, goblets of animal blood, bottles of human flesh preserved in formaldehyde, and orgies between adults and children and children and animals. The eating of feces, drinking of urine, sacrifices of babies, and taking of pictures for pornographic purposes are other elements. . . . (Larson 1989:122)

These accounts, especially when they depict the initiation of small children, contrast the initiate's innocence with the awful practices required by the rites (Richardson, Best, and Bromley 1991).

La Cosa Nostra. In his testimony to Senate investigators, Joseph Valachi described his own initiation into a Cosa Nostra organized crime family: a ritual involving swearing oaths before a gun, a knife, and flame, blood brotherhood, and adoption by a godfather (U.S. Senate 1963:180–84). Although Valachi denied witnessing other such ceremonies, he insisted that all members went through the same initiation rite (p.210). His testimony influenced popular and academic conceptions of organized crime groups as tightly organized, formal criminal organizations with powerful holds on their members (Smith 1975).

Other deviant conspiracies. Many other accounts portray initiation rituals as thresholds to deviant conspiracies. First-century Romans believed that Christians initiated new members in rituals involving sacrificing and eating infants (Ellis 1983). Claims of ritualized child sacrifice by Jews (the "Blood Libel"), witches and other heretics, and other supposed deviant conspiracies have long histories (Dunces 1991; R. Moore 1987). The moral panic about the criminal "Mohocks" in eighteenth-century London featured claims about their initiation rituals (Statt 1995). Other accounts describe initiation rituals among criminals, pirates, and other deviants (Hobsbawm 1959).

Initiation and Conspiracy

The imagery of conspiratorial deviance emphasizes secrecy, power, purpose, and difference. In contrast to the standard image of deviance as rule breaking by individuals or small groups of accomplices, claims about conspiracy locate deviance in a larger context:

> Conspiracy implies that members of a confession, party, or ethnicity (Jews, Freemasons, communists, pacifists, etc.) are united by an indissoluble secret bond. The object of such an alliance is to foment upheaval in society, pervert societal values, aggravate crises, promote defeat, and so on. The conspiracy mentality divides people, things, and actions into two classes. One is pure, the other impure. These classes are not only distinct, but antagonistic. They are polar opposites: everything social, national, and so forth, versus what is antisocial or antinational, as the case may be. On the one hand, everything normal, lawful, that is, native; on the other hand, everything abnormal, unlawful, and hence, alien. The opposing groups belong to two distinct universes: a region of daylight and clarity versus an opaque and nocturnal milieu. (Moscovici 1987:154)

Most theories of conspiratorial deviants hold that outsiders—especially members of ethnic or religious minorities—band together in the cause of deviance.[10] This conspiratorial alliance is hidden from view, and the secrecy conceals the web connecting apparently unrelated acts of deviance. Dedicated to advancing the deviant cause, the conspirators are a powerful yet invisible social force. Such imagery gives rhetorical power to claims about conspiratorial deviance. It suggests that deviant acts should be understood as part of a large, powerful, insidious campaign. Thus any deviant act, no matter how mundane it may seem, can be defined as evidence of a major threat to societal well-being.

Descriptions of deviant conspirators' initiation rites emphasize the gulf between the deviance and respectability. In joining the conspiracy, individuals commit themselves to the deviant cause. The transformation from respectability to deviance is made manifest in the initiation ritual, which usually requires initiates to commit some sort of serious deviant act, thereby demonstrating commitment to deviance and binding the new members to the deviant group.

Ethnographers and historians often dispute conspiratorial interpretations of deviance. Researchers studying organized crime, for instance, criticize Valachi-inspired descriptions of nationally coordinated organized crime for exaggerating the bureaucratization, centralization, and power of organized crime families (Haller 1990; Ianni 1972; Reuter 1983; Smith 1975). Similarly, ethnographies of satanists find no evidence of a powerful, conspiratorial blood cult (Bainbridge 1991; Ellis 1991; Lowney 1995). Proponents of conspiracy claims, however, do not consider such findings compelling: After all, a successful conspiracy would conceal its true workings from naive researchers, or even would enlist researchers as conspirators.

Understanding Claims about Gang Initiation Rites

Contemporary discourse about gang initiation rituals resembles other accounts of conspiratorial deviance. The motif of the gang initiation rite has parallels in claims about initiations into deviant cults and criminal organizations. What accounts for this pattern? How should we interpret contemporary claims linking gang initiation rites to random violence against respectable strangers?

Fear of crime has become a central theme in contemporary American culture. The press, popular culture, and everyday conversation emphasize the threat of crime, especially the risk of random attacks by strangers. This theme runs through claims about serial murder, hate crimes, violence against women, carjacking, sexual predators, freeway shootings, stalking, kids and guns, and other recently constructed crime problems. Claimsmakers promote notions that even very serious crimes are commonplace and virtually patternless—that everyone is at risk of victimization from these threats.

Of course, much social scientific research demonstrates that the risks of victimization are not distributed evenly throughout society. The urban poor, in particular, are far more likely than others to be victimized. Such findings usually lead social scientists to explain crime in terms of inequities in the social structure, but these explanations are relatively unpopular in the society at large. Popular discourse tends to focus not on the victims' poverty but on their respectability and innocence. Thus, typical accounts of criminal violence juxtapose deviant offenders (often portrayed as evil, exploitative, depraved, or irrational) with respectable victims (portrayed as innocent and powerless).

Since the mid-1980s, gangs have played a featured role in discourse about crime because of several interrelated developments, each inspiring claimsmaking campaigns: press coverage of rivalry between large "supergangs," especially confederations of black gangs (e.g., the Crips and the Bloods in Los Angeles; People and Folks in Chicago); the emergence of crack in the ghetto and gangs' involvement in its distribution; the spread of more—and more powerful—firearms among youths; the emergence of what are perceived as new forms of gang-related violence (e.g., drive-by shootings); the rise of popular-culture forms dramatizing inner-city violence (e.g., gangster rap music); and the dramatic rise in adolescent homicide deaths, particularly among African-Americans. Some researchers dispute claims about large, powerful, tightly organized supergangs,[11] but the public, the press, and policy makers attribute much contemporary crime to such conspiratorial groups (Jackson 1993).

In this cultural context, the gang initiation rite makes sense. The motif provides a reason for irrational, random crimes. We don't need to wonder why a respectable citizen is shot or why a car is stolen from a mall; such hard-to-explain crimes, which may seem pointless, can be attributed to gang initiation rites, in which criminal conspiracies require initiates to commit terrible, otherwise senseless crimes. Moreover, the initiation rite is the entryway into gang membership. Presumably gangs that require such crimes of their initiates do so because they are conspiracies dedicated to disorder. Having passed the initiation test, gang members will no doubt be willing and ready to commit other acts of random violence.

Studies of criminal violence commonly reveal that homicide, rape, and robbery have relatively mundane interactional causes; the offenders' motives hardly seem to measure up to the consequences of their acts. Popular discourse rectifies this discrepancy by giving terrible actions terrible motivations. One way to do this is to define the deviant as different in kind; thus varieties of insanity are said to motivate the "serial killer," the "sexual predator," and the "copycat criminal." Another way is to locate the deviant act within a larger conspiracy. Thus a belief in gang initiation rites helps to make acts of random violence explicable.

Motif, Meaning, and Cultural Resources

We began this analysis by contrasting references to gang initiation rites in contemporary legends, in press coverage, and in social science research: Social scientists report that gangs sometimes initiate members by testing their fighting abilities, whereas legends attribute horrific, melodramatic crimes to initiates, and the press uses gang initiations to explain crimes of unknown motivation. We then argued that initiation rites often figure in claims about deviant conspiracies, and noted how contemporary developments have fostered concerns about conspiratorial gangs. This motif constructs society as a locus for disorder, but in doing so, offers an explanation for that disorder.

Our analysis, then, uses a contemporary motif—the gang initiation rite—to link individual events described in legends and press reports to a centuries-old conception of conspiratorial deviance. The initiation of deviant conspirators is a familiar element in the cultural repertoire or "toolkit" (Swidler 1986), an element long used to construct many social problems including (most recently) gang violence. Our analysis reveals how discourse on social problems—even very specific talk about particular events—is embedded in a broader cultural context. Thus a given shooting may be explained by drawing on the familiar, currently popular motif of the gang initiation rite, which in turn evokes traditional imagery of conspiratorial deviance. That imagery gives meaning to the motif, which in turn explains the shooting.

The motif of the gang initiation rite is not new; it has a complex history. Evidence from both folklore and ethnography reveals that it was used in discourse about gangs during the 1960s, if not a decade earlier. It is impossible to know exactly when people first used the expression *gang initiation rite*, to trace its precise evolution, or to know how—or whether—popular discourse, ethnography, and media coverage influenced one another's use of the motif. This motif apparently became prominent in the early 1990s; its visibility seems to be tied to a diverse set of concerns about inequality, racial tensions (particularly middle-class whites' fears about the black underclass), urban unrest, random violence, drugs, assault weapons, and media violence, as well as gangs. Each of these issues became the subject of considerable claims-making; each was defined as troubling; each demanded explanation. The image of powerful, conspiratorial gangs helped to explain these problems in a way that focused blame on evildoers, rather than, say, on structural inequities. In this view, gangs were much more than a symptom of ghetto problems; they were a major cause of those problems. The gang initiation rite provided dramatic evidence of the moral gulf between this conspiracy of deviants and respectable society, just as the image of this gulf in turn fostered melodramatic portrayals of gangs in the press and in popular culture. Thus the various contemporary claims about gangs, including references to gang initiation rites, reinforced one another and reaffirmed the gang's threat to respectability.

In no sense is the gang initiation rite motif unique. All talk about social problems borrows from the broader culture, and can be understood only within that cultural and historical context. Moreover, motifs and other claimsmaking elements do not exist in isolation. Although we have chosen to focus on the motif of the gang initiation rite, we recognize that one motif does not a social problem make. Discourse about gang initiation rites commonly incorporates other cultural elements such as ideas about random violence, waves or trends in crime, and rebellious youths. Each of these elements lies embedded in its own cultural context—in understandings about deviance, morality, social order, and so on. These links need not be made explicit; when experienced members of the culture make sense of a particular legend or news report about a gang initiation rite, they draw on their broader understandings of the nature of deviance and social problems. Thus the construction of "new" crimes and other social problems inevitably incorporates familiar cultural elements, while the very familiarity of those elements discourages critical evaluation.

History offers many examples of warnings about conspiracies of deviants; such warnings evoked concerns that later analysts judged to be exaggerated or distorted. In retrospect, witches, Reds, mafiosi, dope peddlers, and white slavers often appear to be less organized, less powerful, and less threatening than claimsmakers imagined, just as the great juvenile gang menace of the 1950s became the stuff of nostalgic musicals. It is easy to debunk nearly forgotten claims, but more difficult to think critically about constructions of contemporary problems. Nonetheless, the familiar, taken-for-granted imagery in today's claims about social problems is consequential, and it demands our attention.

Studies of social problems construction have devoted considerable attention to organizational matters: claimsmakers' interests, mobilizing resources, achieving ownership of problems, and the like. Cultural analyses have focused mostly on rhetoric—overt efforts to persuade. The cultural context of claimsmaking in general, and particularly the role of familiar cultural elements such as motifs, has been largely ignored. Yet the motif of the gang initiation rite suggests that claimsmaking inevitably draws on familiar cultural resources in ways that shape the construction of social problems and, in turn, social policy. Constructionism reminds us that social problems take form through the language of claims. We must ask how this language, including even the most familiar motifs, shapes what we know—or fear.

Notes

¹ In the 1980s, indexing services began using computers to index newspapers and periodicals. These computerized indices relied on the Library of Congress (LC) subject headings that most U.S. libraries use to categorize books. Although LC subject headings can be subdivided, they are generally broad, formal categories, and do not include information at the level of motifs. There is an LC heading for *gangs*, but *gang initiation rites* is not an LC subheading and thus is not used as a heading in most indices.

² The search identified 169 stories, but we eliminated 55 of these from our analysis. Among these were four stories from newspapers published outside the U.S. and Canada. We also decided to include only one story about each incident, for example, although 16 stories discussed the 1993 rape-murders of two Houston teenagers, we included only one of these stories in our sample.

³ This account does not give a detailed description of the cheek slashing, but the tale may be a variant of an English legend involving members of a gang (the "Chelsea Smilers") who cut their victims' "mouths at the sides in a grotesque smile." The report of the English legend does not mention initiation rites, however (Roud 1989).

⁴ In general, legend scholars consider the factual truth of legends irrelevant. A legend is a story that is repeated widely by individuals; in the course of transmission, most legends are altered, usually by the claim that the events occurred locally. In some cases a particular incident might have provided the basis for what became a legend, but that initial truth has been lost in the hundreds of variants that evolved.

⁵ Booth Tarkington's humorous Penrod stories featured preadolescent middle-class boys: In *Penrod and Sam*, the boys establish a secret society—not a gang—with a "'nishiation" ritual featuring blindfolds, secret oaths, and paddling (Tarkington 1916).

⁶ A few news stories described female initiates choosing or being compelled to have sex with male gang members: "There's a choice you can make as a woman if you want to join a gang. . . . You can either be beaten in, or you can choose to have sex with up to 20 members of the gang" ("Rapes" 1994). The ethnographic accounts do not describe this practice, although Spergel (1995) mentions it as part of "gang lore," and Hopper and Moore (1990:372–73) report that outlaw motorcycle gangs sometimes require male initiates to supply a woman who will have sex with the gang's members.

⁷ Two additional categories accounted for the 16 remaining stories: five stories (4 percent) attributed violence to gang initiation rites, but it was not clear whether the victim was an initiate (i.e., in a beat-down) or someone outside the gang; the remaining 11 stories (10 percent) did not address gang violence and formed a residual category.

⁸ Such news reports sometimes resemble contemporary legends. For example, the *Durham (NC) Herald-Sun* ran a front-page story headlined "Police: Gang Rapes Women for Initiation" (1993). This story began: "Durham police believe a gang of teen-agers in Northern Durham has developed a brutal rite of initiation—new

members must kidnap and rape a white woman." One week later, a follow-up story explained that some rapes had been committed, but gave no evidence of gang involvement ("Police Chief" 1993). (These stories were not part of our NEXIS sample; we are indebted to Bill Ellis for calling them to our attention.)

9   The following section on initiation rites appears in a popular handbook on gangs published by the National Counseling Resource Center, "a not-for-profit organization started to combat many of the destructive beliefs and behaviors (e.g., gangs, Satanism, etc.) which are plaguing our nation and world.") This list illustrates how these different images can be conflated:

1. Many are "*beat in*" to the group. . . . These beatings are usually very severe.
2. Some are asked to do a "*Drive-by*" killing. . . .
3. Commit a *crime* (e.g., steal, rape, extortion, assault, arson, auto theft, etc.)
4. *Spray paint over enemy graffiti.* . . .
5. Those who grow up with a gang or in gang turf may have *no initiation ceremony.*
6. *Shoot someone in uniform.*
7. *Rob a home with the occupants there.*
8. *Girls* are initated in a variety [sic] ways:
   a. "*Raped in*" or "*sexed in*" by a predetermined number of guys in the gang, . . . [or] have sex with someone who has AIDS. . . .
   b. They may be "*beat in*" by other girls in the set. . . .
   c. Others are asked to *beat up their mother* [sic] as a way of showing allegiance to the gang. (Larson and Amstutz 1995:42; authors' emphasis).

10   Although claims about conspiratorial gangs fit this model, other popular discourse depicts crime as a product of conspiracies by elites. For example, Turner (1993) and Sasson (1995b) examine how some African-Americans blame conspiracies of government and business elites for street crime, crack, AIDS, and other ghetto problems.

11   The analytic problems identified by researchers include: defining gangs and distinguishing among various types of gangs; assessing the degree to which gangs feature hierarchies of authority, centralized decision making, and other characteristics of formal organizations; determining the nature and strength of ties among gangs; and deciding which deviant acts committed by gang members should be considered "gang-related." In general, ethnographic research (cited above) tends to find gang activities less structured, less rationalized, and less centralized than do descriptions in the press or in popular discourse.

References

"Ankle Slashers at the Mall." 1993. *FOAFTale News* 29:10–11.

Bainbridge, W. S. 1991. "Social Construction from Within: Satan's Process." Pp. 297–310 in *The Satanism Scare*, edited by J. T. Richardson, J. Best, and D. G. Bromley. Hawthorne, NY: Aldine.

Benford, R. D. 1993. "'You Could Be the Hundredth Monkey': Collective Action Frames and Vocabularies of Motive within the Nuclear Disarmament Movement." *Sociological Quarterly* 34:195–216.

Best, J. 1990. *Threatened Children.* Chicago: University of Chicago Press.

"Blacks N Whites Gang Probably Formed Recently, Police Believe." 1993. *Houston Chronicle* July 1, p. A25.

"Blood Initiation Weekend." 1993. *FOAFTale News* 31:6.

"Boy Was Kicked to Death in Gang's Test, Police Say." 1990. *Orlando Sentinel*, November 22, p. A20.

Brunvand, J. H. 1981. *The Vanishing Hitchhiker.* New York: Norton.

_____. 1984. *The Choking Doberman.* New York: Norton.

_____. 1986. *The Mexican Pet.* New York: Norton.

_____. 1993. *The Baby Train.* New York: Norton.

_____. 1995. "'Lights Out': A Faxlore Phenomenon." *Skeptical Inquirer* 19 (March): 32–37.

Campbell, A. 1984. *The Girls in the Gang.* New York: Basil Blackwell.

Carroll, M. P. 1987. "'The Castrated Boy': Another Contribution to the Psychoanalytic Study of Urban Legends." *Folklore* 91:216–25.

Carondelet Management Institute. *N.D. Gangs.* Tucson: Carondelet Health Care.

"Close Call Heightens Fear of Crime." 1993. *Arizona Republic*, October 17, p. F3.

"County Police 'Documentary'." 1992. *Seattle Times*, April 21, p. D1.

"Don't Take Fearful Tale on Faith." 1992. *Dallas Morning News*, December 18, p. 29A.

Dorson, R. M. 1981. *Land of the Millrats.* Cambridge: Harvard University Press.

Dundes, A. ed. 1991. *The Blood Libel Legend.* Madison: University of Wisconsin Press.

Eliade, M. 1958. *Rites and Symbols of Initiation.* New York: Harper & Row.

Ellis, B. 1983. "De Legendis Urbis: Modern Legends in Ancient Rome." *Journal of American Folklore* 96:200–208.

_____. 1991. "Legend-Trips and Satanism: Adolescents' Ostensive Traditions as 'Cult' Activity." Pp. 279–95 in *The Satanism Scare*, edited by J. T. Richardson, J. Best, and D. G. Bromley. Hawthorne, NY: Aldine.

Fine, G.A. 1992. *Manufacturing Tales.* Knoxville: University of Tennessee Press.

Fleming, R. L. and R. F. Boyd Jr. 1994. *The Big Book of Urban Legends.* New York: Paradox Press.

Gamson W. A. and K. E. Lasch. 1983. The Political Culture of Social Welfare Policy. Pp. 397–415 in *Evaluating the Welfare State*, edited by S. E. Spiro and E. Yuchtman-Yaar. New York: Academic Press.

Gamson, W.A. and A. Modigliani. 1987. "The Changing Culture of Affirmative Action." *Research in Political Sociology* 3:137–77.

_____. 1989. "Media Discourse and Public Opinion on Nuclear Power." *American Journal of Sociology* 95:1–37.

"Gang Beat-downs Called Common Initiation Rite." 1994. *Atlanta Journal and Constitution*, March 25, p. F1.

"Gang Initiation Requires Shooting Folks in the Leg." 1990. *Orlando Sentinel*, April 29, p. A18.

"Gang Rites, AIDS and Unprotected Sex." 1993. *Houston Chronicle*, May 2, p. A26.

"Ganging Up." 1987. *Los Angeles Times*, November 30, p. Il1.

Gusfield, J. R. 1981. *The Culture of Public Problems: Drinking-Driving and the Symbolic Order.* Chicago: University of Chicago Press.

Hagedorn, J. 1988. *People and Folks: Gangs, Crime and the Underclass in a Rustbelt City.* Chicago: Lake View Press.

Haller, M. H. 1990. "Illegal Enterprise." *Criminology* 28:207–35.

Hamm, M. S. 1993. *American Skinheads: The Criminology and Control of Hate Crime.* Westport, CT: Praeger.

Hilgartner, S. and C. L. Bosk. 1988. "The Rise and Fall of Social Problems." *American Journal of Sociology* 94:53–78.

Hobsbawm, E.J. 1959. *Primitive Rebels: Studies in Archaic Forms of Social Movement in the 19th and 20th Centuries.* New York: Norton.

Hopper, C. B. and J. Moore. 1990. "Women in Outlaw Motorcycle Gangs." *Journal of Contemporary Ethnography* 18:363–87.

Horowitz, R. 1983. *Honor and the American Dream.* New Brunswick, NJ: Rutgers University Press.

Ianni, F. A. J. 1972. *A Family Business.* New York: Russell Sage Foundation.

Ibarra, P. R. and J. I. Kitsuse. 1993. "Vernacular Constituents of Moral Discourse." Pp. 25–58 in *Reconsidering Social Constructionism,* edited by J. A. Holstein and G. Miller. Hawthorne, NY: Aldine.

Jackson, P. 1993. "Moral Panic and the Response to Gangs in California." Pp. 257–75 in *Gangs: The Origins and Impact of Contemporary Youth Gangs in the United States,* edited by S. Cummings and D. J. Monti. Albany: SUNY Press.

Jankowski, M. S. 1991. *Islands in the Street: Gangs and American Urban Society.* Berkeley: University of California Press.

Katz, J. 1988. *Seductions of Crime.* New York: Basic Books.

Keiser, R. L. 1969. *The Vice Lords.* New York: Holt, Rinehart and Winston.

La Fontaine, J. 1985. *Initiation.* New York: Penguin.

Larson, B. and W. Amstutz. 1995. *Youth Violence and Gangs.* Rochester, MN: National Counseling Resource Center.

Larson B. 1989. *Satanism: The Seduction of America's Youth.* Nashville: Thomas Nelson.

"'Lights Out' Gang Initation." 1993. *FOAFTale News* 31:5–6.

Lowney, K. 1995. "Teenage Satanism as Oppositional Youth Subculture." *Journal of Contemporary Ethnography* 23:453–84.

"Mall Mayhem in Wichita." 1992. *FOAFTale News* 25:11–12.

"Malls on Alert After Rumor of Gang Rite." 1994. *Pittsburgh Post-Gazette,* March 20, p. W1.

Miller, W. B. 1958. "Lower Class Culture as a Generating Milieu of Gang Delinquency." *Journal of Social Issues* 14:5–19.

Monti, D. J. 1994. *Wannabe: Gangs in Suburbs and Schools.* Cambridge, MA: Blackwell.

Moore, J. W. 1991. *Going Down to the Barrio.* Philadelphia: Temple University Press.

Moore, R. I. 1987. *The Formation of a Persecuting Society.* New York: Basil Blackwell.

Moscovici, S. 1987. "The Conspiracy Mentality." Pp. 151–69 in *Changing Conceptions of Conspiracy,* edited by C. F. Graumann and S. Moscovici. New York: Springer-Verlag.

"New 'Urban Myth' Surfaces in Valley." 1993. *Arizona Republic,* October 2, p. A1.

New York City Youth Board. 1960. *Reaching the Fighting Gang*. New York: New York City Youth Board.

Operation Safe Streets. 1995. "L.A. Style: A Street Gang Manual of the Los Angeles County Sheriff's Department." Pp. 34–45 in *The Modern Gang Reader*, edited by M. W. Klein, C. L. Maxson, and J. Miller. Los Angeles: Roxbury.

Padilla, F. 1993. "The Working Gang." Pp. 173–92 in *Gangs: The Origins and Impact of Contemporary Youth Gangs in the United States*, edited by S. Cummings and D. J. Monti. Albany: SUNY Press.

"Police Chief Apologizes for Handling of Rape Warning." 1993. *Durham (NC) Herald-Sun*, January 12, p. A1.

"Police: Gang Rapes Women for Initiation." 1993. *Durham (NC) Herald-Sun*, January 5, p. Al.

"Rapes a Gang Ritual, Police Say." 1994. *Rocky Mountain News*, August 29, p. 5A

Reuter, P. 1983. *Disorganized Crime*. Cambridge, MA: MIT Press.

Richardson, J. T., J. Best, and D. G. Bromley, eds. 1991. *The Satanism Scare*. Hawthorns, NY: Aldine.

Roud, S. 1989 "Chelsea Smilers: Interim Report on a Gang-Violence Rumor." *FOAFTale News* 15:1–2.

Sasson, T. 1995a. *Crime Talk: How Citizens Construct a Social Problem*. Hawthorne, NY: Aldine.

_____. 1995b. "African American Conspiracy Theories and the Social Construction of Crime." *Sociological Inquiry* 65:265–85

Shakur, S. 1993. *Monster: The Autobiography of an L.A. Gang Member*. New York: Atlantic Monthly Press.

Simmel, G. 1950. "The Secret Society." Pp. 345–76 in *The Sociology of Georg Simmel*, edited and translated by K. H. Wolff. New York: Free Press

Smith, D.C., Jr. 1975. *The Mafia Mystique*. New York: Basic Books.

Spergel, I.A. 1995. *The Youth Gang Problem: A Community Approach*. New York: Oxford University Press.

Statt, D. 1995. "The Case of the Mohocks: Rake Violence in Augustan London." *Social History* 20:179–99.

"Staunch Advocate of Urban Living Having Second Thoughts after Drive-by Attack." 1994. *Atlanta Journal and Constitution*, March 15, p. D1.

Swidler, A. 1986. "Culture in Action." *American Sociological Review* 51:273–86

Tarkington, B. 1916. *Penrod and Sam*. New York: Doubleday, Page. Chicago: University of Chicago Press.

The Killer in the Backseat." 1993. *FOOAF Tale News* 33:5–6.

Thrasher, F.M. 1927. *The Gang*. Chicago: University of Chicago Press.

"Truth Is Floored by Urban Rumor." 1993. *Chicago Sun-Times*, January 31, p. 11.

Turner, P. A. 1993. *I Heard It through the Grapevine: Rumor in African-American Culture*. Berkeley: University of California Press.

U.S. Senate. 1963. "Organized Crime and Illicit Traffic in Narcotics." Hearings by the Permanent Subcommittee on Investigations, Committee on Government Operations, Part 1. October 1–2.

"Urban Legend Dept." 1994. *St. Louis Post-Dispatch*, October 30, p. CL1.

"Urban Yarn of 'Mall Slasher' Just Won't Die." 1991. *Chicago Tribune* October 11, p. CL1.

Vigil, D. 1993. "The Established Gang." Pp. 95–112 in *Gangs: The Origins and Impact of Contemporary Youth Gangs in the United States*, edited by S. Cummings and D. J. Monti. Albany: SUNY Press.

Wachs, E. 1988. Crime.Victim Stories. Bloomington: Indiana University Press.

"Where Are You Safe?" 1994. *Atlanta Journal and Constitution*, November 15, p. B6.

Williams, R.H. 1995. "Constructing the Public Good: Social Movements and Cultural Resources." *Social Problems* 42:124–44.

Wolf, D.R. 1991. *The Rebels: A Brotherhood of Outlaw Bikers*. Toronto: University of Toronto Press.

Yablonsky, L. 1970. *The Violent Gang*. Rev. ed. Baltimore: Penguin.

7

"The Ice Age"
The Social Construction of a Drug Panic

Philip Jenkins

Research in illicit drugs has often emphasized the disparity between the perceived threat of a substance and the actual social harm involved. A distinguished literature deals with successive drug "panics," which have focused on marijuana in the 1930s, amphetamines in the 1950s, glue sniffing in the 1960s, and crack cocaine in the 1980s (Brecher 1972; Musto 1973; Reinarman and Levine 1989; Goode 1984; 310–34). This is not to argue that any of these substances is harmless or (necessarily) socially acceptable, but in each case, the extravagant claims permit us to employ the term panic.

Drug scares generally follow broadly similar patterns in which it is suggested, for example, that the drug in question is currently enjoying an explosive growth in popularity; that it is extremely addictive, and that even occasional use can cause severe physical addiction; and that it is destructive to the user or to others, threatening health or encouraging bizarre and violent behavior. Such claims are buttressed in a number of ways, including the use of exemplary cases and the parading of what appear to be objective statistics and scientific studies; the latter often turn out to be rather questionable on further examination. In addition, claims makers usually demonstrate a certain historical amnesia, often rediscovering problems which in fact are well-established while failing to note how thoroughly earlier panics were discredited.

Source: *Justice Quarterly*, Vol. 11, No. 1, March 1994, pp. 7–31. © 1994 Academy of Criminal Justice Sciences. Reprinted with permission.

Social scientists have explained such periodic waves of concern in various ways. Many emphasize the role of political or bureaucratic interest groups seeking to enhance their claims on resources and status. Others stress the role of factors in the broader society, such as ethnic or generational tension and hostility, which come to be symbolized by the drug in question. In this sense it is almost irrelevant whether the claims presented by the rhetoric of a "panic" are well-founded or wholly spurious: the panic itself is valuable in itself for what it suggests about the perceptions of a society as a whole, and specifically of policy makers and legislators. The incident thus has great significance for understanding the social contruction of crime and deviance.

Some claims are widely accepted and have the effect of remolding law and public policy: the crack issue has done so in the last decade (Reinarman and Levine 1989). Other issues, however, are more ephemeral, and the claims appear to enjoy far less success. In recent years we have witnessed a dramatic example of such a short-lived panic in the public reaction to the alleged boom in the use of the drug "ice," or smokable methamphetamine. During 1989 and early 1990, it was widely claimed that this substance was becoming enormously popular in certain regions, and that it had the potential to "sweep the nation" in a few months or years. Dramatic statistics were offered to support these claims; it was suggested that ice was uniquely dangerous in combining extremely addictive qualities with the advantages of cheapness, easy access, and domestic manufacture. The media panic about ice found its focus in Congressional hearings during October 1989 and January 1990. The stage seemed to be set for a repetition of the crack "explosion" of 1986.

This concern about ice was not sustained, however, and media references to the topic diminished sharply within a few months. Outside a few cities and regions, the issue either has ceased to exist or is dormant. The incident thus offers an unusual opportunity to trace the creation of a drug panic from its inception to its eclipse. In understanding the phenomenon, we must emphasize that "ice" originated as a very localized event, confined largely to Hawaii, and that the words epidemic and explosion arose from partisan and bureaucratic rivalries within that state. The projection of this local concern onto the national stage was made possible by a number of factors, including the existence of specialized agencies and investigative bodies focusing on drug issues, and the intensification of public expectations and fears following the crack scare. I suggest that all these elements still exist and are likely to lead in future to other ephemeral drug panics. The "ice" incident is likely to be repeated in various forms.

The Methamphetamine Industry

Methamphetamine is a stimulant of the central nervous system which, as a street drug, is often known as "speed" or "crank" (Graham 1976; Grinspoon 1975; *Methamphetamine Abuse* 1989; Miller and Kozel 1991). The illegal manufacture of methamphetamines began in the early 1960s, and networks of clandestine laboratories emerged to produce several synthetic drugs. During the 1970s, such laboratories tended increasingly to shift their production towards methamphetamine and away from other synthetics such as PCP (Jenkins 1992b). Between 1981 and 1984, methamphetamine producers represented half of all laboratory seizures; by 1988 they exceeded 80 percent (*U.S. Congress: Laboratories* 1980; *U.S. Congress: Re-emergence* 1990:25, 90–91).

The attractions of the industry were obvious. The manufacturing process required little expertise; several cheap "hands-on" manuals were available to provide detailed instruction. A laboratory could make as much as five to 10 pounds of methamphetamine in a week, and the pure substance usually was "cut" repeatedly for street sale. The annual production of a laboratory thus might be worth several million dollars (Jenkins 1992b). In 1989 a Dallas police officer remarked, "We think the profit is much greater when we look at methamphetamine production, as compared to heroin or cocaine. We know that an investment of $3000 to $4000 in chemicals, in glassware, can turn a profit of $25,000 to $30,000." (*U.S. Congress: Re-Emergence* 1990:39).

One appeal of methamphetamine was that the substance was manufactured in the United States and did not need the sophisticated importation and distribution networks required for heroin or cocaine. Laboratories needed no elaborate facilities or natural resources beyond an ample supply of electricity, and distribution demanded little more than convenient access to the interstate highway network (Skeers 1992; Weingarten 1989; Witkin 1989).

During the 1980s, methamphetamine manufacture tended to become strongly regionalized. In the late 1970s and early 1980s, the Philadelphia area was said to be "the speed capital of the world," with networks of hundreds of laboratories in the southern and eastern parts of the state (Jenkins 1992b; *U.S. Congress: Profile* 1983). By the mid-1980s, the city of Eugene, Oregon was believed to enjoy a similar role in manufacturing; other law enforcement sources emphasized the importance of San Diego and the San Francisco Bay area (*Organized Crime in California* 1989:55, Wiedrich 1987). In 1987 and 1988 more than 300 methamphetamine laboratories were seized in the San Diego area alone. Centers of methamphetamine use included Denver, Portland (Oregon), Dallas, and Phoenix; some problems also were observed in Los Angeles, San Francisco, and Seattle (*Arrestee Drug Use* 1990:6;

U.S. Congress: Re-Emergence 1990:37, 46). Though it is hard to assess the extent of methamphetamine use, there appears to be substantial demand in many parts of the nation (Isikoff 1989; Miller and Kożel 1991; Morgan 1992; *Methamphetamine* 1989).

The Emergence of Ice

Like other drugs, methamphetamine can be taken in various ways: either injected, smoked, or ingested orally. The dominant mode of use tends to reflect the tastes and traditions of local subcultures. In view of the highly regional nature of manufacture and distribution, suppliers do not find it difficult to accommodate these local tastes, and it is natural to find wide disparities in patterns of use. Fashions that emerge in one city or region can become dominant in that area without making much impact elsewhere. In short, there is no such thing as a national market in methamphetamines.

During the 1980s, a vogue for smokable crystal methamphetamine developed in Hawaii and some western states under the common nickname *ice* (Cho 1990; Pennell 1990). A similar, though somewhat less pure, product called *glass* also made its appearance in California. The manufacturing process has been described as follows:

> Two basic methods are used to produce crystal meth. The first and most common method is the reaction of phenyl-2-propanone (P2P or phenylacetone) and methylamine. The second method uses ephedrine as a precursor. The second method uses a simple formula and does not require the use of controlled precursors. It is known as the ephedrine/red phosphorus method and requires the use of a hydrogenator. It takes two to four days to make a batch of ice. . . .

> In Honolulu, crystal meth is most commonly smoked with a glass pipe, the bowl of which becomes coated with a milky white, brownish or black residue, depending on the form of crystal meth used. A gram of ice sells for $250 to $400 in Honolulu right now, with a 1/10 gram paper going for $50 to $75. It is inexpensive to produce, so the profit margin is tremendous. (*U.S. Congress: Re-Emergence* 1990:74-75).

The drug itself had long been known and used in this crystal form, but apparently the specific process used to make the extremely pure ice was not yet in use in the United States itself. Instead the substance, like the fashion for its use, had been imported from the Pacific Rim. Amphetamines, specifically methamphetamines, had long been popular in Japan and other east Asian countries. In that region, illicit markets were supplied by sizable narcotic networks with roots in organized crime among both Chinese triads and Japanese *yakuza* (Delfs 1991). During the 1970s and 1980s, such networks had collaborated in a variety of activities, including product counterfeiting and trafficking in guns and prostitutes in addition to narcotics; we have much evidence of cooperative endeavors, based (for example) in Taiwan or South Korea (Buruma and McBeth 1984–85; Posner 1988). For methamphetamines, the *yakuza* had developed manufacturing facilities in South Korea; these supplied much of East Asia, though the triads also were active in Hong Kong (Kaplan and Dubro 1986:198–200; *U.S. Congress: Re-Emergence* 1990:11, 99). Entrepreneurs and distributors might be nationals of any of a dozen Asian countries.

Though illegal, the amphetamine drug "family" was stigmatized far less severely than opiates, cocaine, or even marijuana. Most estimates place the number of regular amphetamine (*shabu*) users in Japan at more than half a million. In the 1980s, smokable methamphetamine became the drug of choice among upwardly mobile urban dwellers in several Pacific Rim nations, especially Taiwan, South Korea, and the Philippines (Delfs 1991; McBeth 1989; Savadove 1991).

Therefore it is not surprising to find a similar habit developing in Hawaii, which has so many cultural and economic affinities with the Pacific Rim, and in which Japanese organized crime had developed a strong foothold. In fact, Kaplan and Dubro's (1986) study of the *yakuza* calls Hawaii the "forty-eighth Prefecture," an annex to the 47 administrative units of the Japanese home islands. *Yakuza*-supplied amphetamines were identified in the state during the 1970s, and Korean-manufactured methamphetamines appeared in the following decade (Shoenberger 1989). Beginning in 1987, island authorities had described an "ice problem," linked in part to Filipino youth gangs and Korean groups (*U.S. Congress: Re-Emergence* 1990:5).

Discovering a Problem

By 1989, law enforcement agencies were finding evidence of localized use of smokable methamphetamine, originally in Hawaii and subsequently in and around San Diego. The perceived "wave" of new activity was epitomized by a series of federal drug raids on 20 laboratories in southern California during March, and by a series of smaller raids over the next year (Ford 1990; Reza 1989). Concern about the drug in Hawaii was given a new focus in March 1989 by the arrest of a substantial ice-importation ring headed by one Paciano Guerrero (*U.S. Congress: Drug Crisis* 1990:74–75; *U.S. Congress: Re-Emergence* 1990:70–72).

It might be thought that the perceived boom in the smokable drug reflected strictly local conditions, unlikely to be replicated in other areas. Even in Hawaii, the problem was confined largely to Oahu (*U.S. Congress: Drug Crisis* 1990:56, 205, 215). Now, however, there began a media campaign to emphasize the perils of the "new" drug, and the danger that this would soon be reflected across the nation. A headline in the *Los Angeles Times*, for example, read "Potent Form of Speed Could Be Drug of 90s" (Corwin 1989). *The Economist* noted that ice could make crack seem almost benign ("Drugs: Ice Overdose" 1989). Rep. Charles Rangel coined the alliterative description "the narcotics nemesis of the nineties" (*U.S. Congress: Re-Emergence* 1990:59).

The theme was taken up by all the major regional newspapers and national newsmagazines, as well as more specialized publications serving the medical and pharmaceutical communities (Cho 1990; "Illicit Methamphetamine" 1991; Zurer 1989). Between September and December 1989, major stories appeared in the *New York Times* (Bishop 1989), *The Washington Post* (Thompson 1989), *The Atlanta Constitution* (Curriden 1989), *The Economist* ("Drugs; Ice Overdose" 1989), *The Boston Globe* (Howe 1989; Tabor 1989), *The Chicago Tribune* (Weingarten 1989), *The Christian Science Monitor* (Larmer 1989), and *Newsweek* (Lerner 1989). The tone of the coverage was epitomized by the *New York Times* headline "Fear Grows Over Effects of a New Smokable Drug" (Bishop 1989). This story was printed on the front page; equal prominence was given to ice related stories on the front pages of the *Los Angeles Times* (Corwin 1989) and *The Chicago Tribune* (Weingarten 1989). In October the *Los Angeles Times* presented a series of four stories on ice within a nine-day period (Corwin 1989; Essoyan 1989; Shoenberger 1989; Zamichow 1989). Clearly, pronouncements about the new drug were finding a ready and enthusiastic market in the mass media.

The jeremiads about ice were heard most frequently in the last quarter of 1989, though a few stories appeared in early 1990, and television news shows such as *60 Minutes* sustained the focus on methamphetamines in general for a few months more ("Meth" 1990). The height of the panic, however, can be identified clearly between about September 1989 and February 1990 (See table 1 for a chronology of media accounts).

The peak of public concern can be associated with Congressional hearings on this topic; Rep. Rangel's Subcommittee on Narcotics Abuse and Control held a session titled "The Re-Emergence of Methamphetamine" in October. A follow-up session, the "Drug Crisis in Hawaii," was held in Honolulu the following January (*U.S. Congress: Re-Emergence* 1990; *U.S. Congress: Drug Crisis* 1990. For criticisms of the latter session as a Congressional junket, see Anderson and Van Atta 1990). Taken together with the media accounts, the hearings became the chief vehicle for the burgeoning panic about ice. Here it will be useful to analyze the language and rhetoric employed to present the new phenomenon as a major problem.

Table 7.1 Chronology of Media Accounts, 1989–1991

1989

Sept. 16	*New York Times*	(Bishop 1989)
Oct. 1	*Boston Globe*	(Howe 1989)
Oct. 8	*Los Angeles Times*	(Shoenberger 1989)
Oct. 14	*Los Angeles Times*	(Essoyan 1989)
Oct. 16	*Los Angeles Times*	(Essoyan 1989)
Oct. 16	*Los Angeles Times*	(Zamichow 1989)
Oct. 24	Congressional hearings, *The Re-Emergence of Methamphetamine*	
Nov. 6	*Chemical and Engineering News*	(Zurer 1989)
Nov. 21	Washington Post	(Thompson 1989)
Nov. 27	*Newsweek*	(Lerner 1989)
Nov. 30	*Atlanta Constitution*	(Curriden 1989)
Dec. 2	*The Economist*	("Drugs: Ice Overdose" 1989)
Dec. 8	*Boston Globe*	(Tabor 1989)
Dec. 8	*Christian Science Monitor*	(Larmer 1989)
Dec. 18	*Jet*	(Carthane 1989)

1990

Jan. 13	Congressional hearings, on *The Drug Crisis in Hawaii*	
Feb. 8	*Rolling Stone*	(Sager 1990)
February	*Good Housekeeping*	(Holland 1990)
April 22	CBS news program *60 Minutes* broadcasts story on methamphetamine trafficking ("Meth" 1990).	
May 23	*Journal of the American Medical Association*	(Cotton 1990)
Aug. 10	*Science*	(Cho 1990)

1991

March 6	*Journal of the American Medical Association*	(Hong, Matsuyama, and Nur 1991)
May 9	*Washington Post*	(Holley, Venant, and Essoyan 1991)
June 30	*Emergency Medicine*	("Illicit Methamphetamine" 1991)

The Rhetoric of Ice

Certain themes and expressions recur with striking regularity. Ice was new, potent, and dangerous, and had acquired high prestige as the new "in" drug. Taken together, these features meant that the use of ice apparently was about to expand rapidly and to create a national menace at least comparable to crack cocaine.

The experience of Hawaii was recounted often, as in a *Boston Globe* story titled "Ice in an Island Paradise" (Tabor 1989). The use of ice, in the words of a Congressional report, "has escalated in such leaps and bounds that we have not been able to keep pace" (*U.S. Congress: Re-Emergence* 1990:2). Generally such accounts suggested that what such areas were experiencing today would be the fate of the whole country in a few months or years. Honolulu police chief Douglas Gibb told the story of a New York City Korean gang that had flown some members to Honolulu to attack some local Samoans. "The whole purpose . . . was to come into town to establish a connection for ice, a line for ice to take back to New York" (*U.S. Congress: Re-Emergence* 1990:8). "It is probably only a matter of time until other parts of the country start to see crystal meth and its attendant problems . . . we fully expect the Ice Age to spread east from Hawaii" (p. 77).

The idea that ice was gradually penetrating areas of the mainland gave a local angle to media reporting of the drug in cities such as Atlanta (Curriden 1989), Boston (Howe 1989), and Philadelphia (Durso 1992). In the Congressional hearings, this was a frequent theme. One subcommittee member noted, "We have got ice in Virginia . . . it is for sure coming our way and we had better get ready for it" (*U.S. Congress: Re-Emergence* 1990:19). Another member stated, "Reports are already filtering in of ice use in New York and Washington DC" (*U.S. Congress: Drug Crisis* 1990:3). A lengthy investigative account in *Rolling Stone* quoted law enforcement officials, who believed that the Hawaii "epidemic" soon would sweep the mainland and that the drug would surpass both heroin and cocaine, marking a new and still more deadly era in drug abuse (Sager 1990).

One paradox was that ice, by its nature, negated some of the obvious advantages of methamphetamine: as an imported drug for example, it encountered the obstacles and expense involved in crossing national borders. The witnesses at the hearings, however, emphasized repeatedly that it would only be a matter of time before domestic manufacturers learned to reproduce Asian techniques; at that point, ice would begin to conquer the American "speed" market. In the words of a Dallas police official, "We have cooks, we have numerous cooks scattered throughout the country, literally thousands of persons who are qualified to make methamphetamine. So, we have the processes in place to make ice. I think we also have a ready consumer market out there, individuals who want the drug. I have no doubt that ice will come to the United States" (*U.S. Congress: Re-Emergence* 1990:39–40).

Particularly evocative was the word *epidemic* which was employed in most of the accounts, with its implications of plague, disease, and uncontrollable spread (compare Reinarman and Levine 1989). During the Congressional hearings, U.S. Attorney Daniel Bent described Hawaii ice use as already an "epidemic" (*U.S. Congress: Re-Emergence* 1990:5). When a DEA spokesman was quoted as having denied the validity of the "epidemic," he was taken to task by members of the committee, especially Florida Rep. Tom Lewis, who described the opinion as "irresponsible" and "lackadaisical" (p. 17). "Epidemic" was a politically valuable concept that would not be abandoned easily.

Other significant terms included *deluge, plague,* and *crisis*. Congressman Rangel remarked that Honolulu police were "deluged" by ice (*U.S. Congress: Re-Emergence* 1990:1). Sociologist Elliott Currie spoke of "this hidden methamphetamine plague" (p. 44). The word *crisis* was much used, generally in the context of an "emerging" crisis, to suggest that what had gone before was trivial compared to what would come in the future (p. 61). As has been noted, the January hearings of the Narcotics Subcommittee were devoted explicitly to the drug crisis in Hawaii.

The term *ice* offered great potential for writers, suggesting as it did the phrase *ice age* and thus implying that the drug somehow could dominate American society so strongly that it could give its name to an era. The phrase *The Ice Age* was employed both by Douglas Gibb and Hawaii Rep. Daniel Akaka in the Congressional hearings (*U.S. Congress: Re-Emergence* 1990:3, 77). It was used subsequently for major investigative accounts in *Rolling Stone* in 1990 and in the *Washington Post* in 1991 (Holley, Venant, and Essoyan 1991; Sager 1990; compare LaBianca 1992). "Ice" also suggested "chilling" in the metaphorical sense of "extremely frightening;" it was used in this sense by several journalists. In late 1989, for example, the *Atlanta Constitution* carried the headline "Police Chilled By New In-Drug: Ice" (Curriden 1989). Within two weeks, the *Christian Science Monitor* warned similarly, "Ice Chills US AntiDrug Officials" (Larmer 1989).

In addition, these arguments were stated by individuals and agencies with great expertise in the field. Every news story was buttressed by the opinions of prominent and credible law enforcement officials, police, and prosecutors from California and Hawaii, together with academics and other experts. In the Congressional hearings, major witnesses included Daniel Bent, the U.S. Attorney for Hawaii; Douglas Gibb, the police chief of Honolulu; and David Westrate of the DEA; all were prestigious and experienced officials. Other presentations were made by reputable doctors and academics. The potential "ice epidemic" thus appeared both plausible and threatening.

Ice and Cocaine

One potent element of the attack on ice involved the analogy with cocaine. In seeking to portray a new problem as serious or dangerous, one well-known rhetorical device is to stigmatize that problem by associating it with another, already familiar issue, thus placing it into an existing context. Problem construction is a cumulative or incremental process in which each issue is built, to some extent, on its predecessors. As Best remarks.

> As an acknowledged subject for concern, a well established social problem becomes a resource, a foundation upon which other claims may be built. Rather than struggling to bring recognition to a new problem, claimants may find it easier to expand an existing problem's domain. These new claims take the form (new problem) X is really a type of (established problem) Y (1990:65–66).

Issue (X) therefore demands the array of responses and reactions that already have been judged appropriate for Problem (Y). This is the process described by Hall et al. (1978:223) as "convergence:"

> [C]onvergence occurs when two or more activities are linked in the process of signification so as to implicitly or explicitly draw parallels between them. Thus the image of "student hooliganism" links student protest to the separate problem of hooliganism—whose stereotypical characteristics are already part of socially available knowledge. . . . In both cases, the net effect is amplification, not in the real events being described but in their threat potential for society (1978:223).

By 1989 cocaine, especially crack cocaine, had been invested with an enormous amount of "threat potential," suggested, for example, by the "drug war" rhetoric, which was then at its height. President Bush had made the "drug war" a major part of his domestic policy; his commitment to drug eradication was symbolized by the appointment of William Bennett as "drug czar." During 1989, American activism against international drug traffickers contributed to the near-civil war in Colombia, beginning in August, and to the invasion of Panama in December. Media coverage in the latter part of the year featured almost daily news of violence and conflict associated with these incidents. In September, President Bush made a nationally televised address on drug control strategy, in which he stated, "All of us agree that the gravest domestic threat facing our nation today is drugs . . . our most serious problem today is cocaine and in particular crack." Producing a sample of crack, which he said had been purchased close to the White House, the president continued, "It's as innocent looking as candy, but it is turning our cities into battle zones, and it is murdering our children. Let there be no mistake, this stuff is poison" ("Text" 1989). President Bush argued that the drug control budget for the coming year should be raised by more than one-third from the 1989 figure, to $8 billion.

If crack was indeed "the gravest domestic threat," then it was a highly effective strategy to suggest that ice was associated somehow with the better-known drug. Superficial parallels also existed. It could be suggested, for example, that crack was an especially virulent and addictive form of powder cocaine, while ice bore a similar relationship to "regular" methamphetamine. Also, the two substances were similar in general appearance and means of ingestion. The ice threat was amplified by its association with crack, an association pursued most vigorously on the Narcotics Subcommittee by Rep. Akaka. From the viewpoint of the media, the analogy with crack made ice an attractive subject because its dangers and thus its social significance could be comprehended easily; thus the drug would be likely to excite public concern and fear.

Ice was said to cause as much social damage as cocaine, in terms of overdoses and emergency room admissions (Gross 1988; "Illicit Methamphetamine" 1991). Rep. Akaka stated that in Hawaii, ice contributed to the problems that elsewhere were linked to crack: "ice-addicted babies, gang activities, turf battles and hospital emergency cases of overdoses . . . this drug has the capacity to drag our country even deeper into the dark abyss created by crack" (*U.S. Congress: Re-Emergence* 1990:3). "It doesn't make any difference whether it is ice, crack, crank, cocaine. We are losing kids. We are corrupting our police departments. We are corrupting our political arena. We are breaking up families" (p. 17).

U.S. Attorney Daniel Bent stated that ice was "presenting the same problems to Hawaii as crack cocaine has in areas of the Continental United States in terms of its popularity, availability, addiction potential and destructiveness" (*U.S. Congress: Re-Emergence* 1990:64). It was alleged to stimulate violent behavior even more sharply than did crack; Hawaii, it was said, was seeing the birth of a generation of "crystal meth babies" (*U.S. Congress: Drug Crisis* 1990:2, 226–33; *U.S. Congress: Re-Emergence* 1990:66, 76; for the idea of the "crack baby," however, see Jacobs 1991). Such remarks made the two drugs appear all but indistinguishable; in fact, Rep. Akaka even asked a witness, "Can you explain to me the differences between crack, crank, ice and croak . . . ?" (*U.S. Congress: Re-Emergence* 1990:54).

In some ways, ice could be made to appear even more dangerous than crack. First, it was superior to crack because of its lower cost and its longer-lasting high. The effects were reported to last from four to 14 hours, as opposed to a few minutes for crack (Carthane 1989; Holley et al. 1991). Also, ice did not necessarily have to be imported from over-seas (though it was imported currently); therefore it did not encounter the stringent restrictions imposed by Customs and the Coast Guard as part of the current "war on drugs." In addition, ice lacked the features that might safeguard individuals from experimenting with other sub-stances. It did not require injection, as did heroin, and did not yet have the destructive associations of crack cocaine. By 1989, crack had acquired undesirable connotations that deterred many people from using it: it was associated with cultures of violence and extreme urban poverty, and was linked especially with racial minorities.

In contrast, methamphetamine generally was linked to hard work. Insofar as it had any racial overtones, it tended to be favored by white users (*Methamphetamine* 1989; Miller and Kozel 1991). Nationally, said the congressional account, "the typical methamphetamine user is a white male 22 to 26 years of age, who is employed in a blue-collar job. The most frequently cited occupations are in construction trades and the trucking industry" (*U.S. Congress: Re-Emergence* 1990:87). In the San Diego region, "abusing populations are predominantly white, lower middle income, high school educated, young adults ranging in age from 18–35 years" (p. 111). A Texas police officer stated, "The persons who we most often encounter in Dallas, the users we most often encounter are primarily Caucasian, primarily lower income" (p. 39).

Ice users tended to fit a similar profile. In Hawaii, ice was "popular in the workplace, particularly among blue collar workers, people who do mechanical tasks, and it has also spread into office workplaces as well . . . (it is) the drug of choice for on the job use in Honolulu. . . . It is generally in the blue collar community and the service community" (*U.S. Congress: Re-Emergence* 1990:6–7–9). In short, ice could appeal to white or Asian middle-class people; teenagers especially were at risk. The title of a *Good Housekeeping* article described ice as "a New Drug Nice Kids Can Get Hooked On" (Holland 1990). Women also were believed to be particularly vulnerable: "In Honolulu, most ice users range in age from the late teens to the early thirties. The drug is popular with young women, perhaps because users tend to lose weight" (*U.S. Congress: Re-Emergence* 1990:75).

It was suggested that ice might be able to wreak havoc in all sec-tions of society, not merely in the inner cities. Rep. Rangel thus was tap-ping into potent fears when he wrote, "[W]e shudder to think of what would happen in this country if the devastation of the crack crisis were doubled or even tripled by adding on a whole new layer of illicit drug abuse" (*U.S. Congress: Re-Emergence* 1990:59). This rhetoric was even more powerful in the context of current developments in the "drug war" at home and overseas.

Whatever Became of Ice?

"Ice" thus was attracting quite fervent interest. One might suggest that it had the potential to attract the same kind of fear as crack. The recent precedent of crack cocaine provided a set of stereotyped images and rhetoric on which ice could build readily, with the added "bonus" that ice threatened to reproduce these disturbing images outside the African-American urban community. Ice (it appeared) could cause the same kind of havoc as crack in geographical, social, and ethnic settings still untouched by ice or any other "hard" drug. It would not be difficult to imagine that the new problem could thrive through the use of ethnic and xenophobic stereotypes: the substance was imported from Asia and had Japanese connotations. *Yakuza* drug dealers might easily acquire the stigma that had adhered earlier to gangsters from immigrant ethnic groups such as Jews and Italians.

In addition, it has been argued that intense media attention to a particular drug might tend to incite interest in the substance, and to lead to experimentation. Prophecies of an "epidemic" thus might be self-fulfilling in that they could unwittingly generate the problem that activists were seeking to avoid (MacDonald and Estep 1985; compare Young 1971). In the 1960s this kind of imitation caused glue sniffing to spread at "incredible speed . . . the enemies of glue-sniffing popularized the custom all by themselves" (Brecher 1972:326, 332). In the 1980s it was suggested that media portrayals of the effects of crack cocaine might have excited interest among users of powdered cocaine. With these precedents in mind, observers of ice warned that ice was being "beautifully advertised by the media" to cocaine users (Cotton 1990). The *Journal of the American Medical Association* warned, "News articles describing (ice) as like 'ten orgasms pronto' are working like paid ads. . . . If the media says it's an epidemic, drug adventurers say everybody's using it so I've got to try it" (Cotton, 1990).

The ice danger, however, did not materialize as a national crisis, and the prospective "plague" faded rapidly in early 1990. Media accounts became far less frequent from February onwards, and virtually none appeared between August 1990 and spring 1991 (see table 1). In part this silence reflected the new concern of the media with political affairs in Iraq and the Persian Gulf, but the ice panic had been declining sharply for several months before the August invasion of Kuwait. The rather sudden eclipse of the ice problem requires explanation.

Some observers had been skeptical even during the height of the panic, and witnesses at the October hearings faced criticism for their use of the term *epidemic*. The evidence presented also contained clear contradictions—for example, in the damage caused by ice. Early reports of the testimony quoted Chief Gibb's statements that "since 1985, there

have been 32 deaths in Honolulu attributed to ice," including eight homicides and seven suicides (*U.S. Congress: Re-Emergence* 1990:76).
Gibb, however, also stated that "32 people were confirmed to have crystal methamphetamine in their system at the time of deaths," which does
not necessarily establish a causal link between the drug and the fatality
(pp. 7–8). Hawaii's Governor Waihee placed the number of deaths at 36,
of whom "three died as a direct result, and 32 had traces of the drug in
their systems" (p. 80). It was embarrassing when Gibb was publicly challenged on his statistics; as a result, the early claims about the impact of
the drug, even in Hawaii, were reduced substantially. Thus it was even
more difficult to claim that ice presented a potential national menace.

During the October hearings, one DEA spokesman commented, "I
can confirm there is a drug out there called ice, which is certainly bad
news. But D.E.A. agents are not looking for it yet. . . . It will take a while
for ice to proliferate. When we get reports from police departments that
ice has gotten to be at the epidemic state, such as crack did in 1985, then
we will move in" (*U.S. Congress: Re-Emergence* 1990:17). Such a drug
"explosion" seemed remote, however. In early 1990, testing of arrestees
confirmed considerable amphetamine use in San Diego, Portland, Phoenix, and San Jose, but the figures did not appear to be growing.

Moreover, ice as such had made few inroads among the arrestees,
though a substantial majority knew the substance by reputation: the
media were cited overwhelmingly as the main source. Even in San Diego,
almost 70 percent of those who knew about ice based their knowledge
on media accounts rather than on information provided by friends or
dealers. Nationwide the proportion who admitted ever having used ice
nowhere exceeded 3 percent (though no community in Hawaii was
included in the survey) (*Arrestee Drug Use* 1990:6; Pennell 1990). This
picture was confirmed by other survey data. Among male hustlers and
sex workers in San Francisco, for example, ice had made very limited
inroads, even among heavy users of methamphetamine. Moreover, the
number of habitual ice users in such groups remained negligible
(Lauderback and Waldorf 1992).

Largely on the basis of such data and of the reexamination of the
drug's impact in Hawaii itself, law enforcement and DEA officials soon
were saying that the danger of ice had been substantially overstated.
Media rhetoric subsided within a few months of the Congressional hearings. Ice continues to be popular in some regions, but the language of
epidemic no longer seems realistic—if it ever did.

The Construction of the Ice Danger

In retrospect it seems certain that the menace of ice was considerably overstated, and we might well ask how such a misperception could

emerge. A considerable literature exists on the origins of such scares and perceived social problems; some of the explanations suggested by that literature seem relevant here. Many researchers, for example, follow some form of what is generally known as the "moral entrepreneur" theory. The classic discussion of this term comes from Becker, who emphasized the role of a particular individual in the formulation of American narcotics policy in the 1930s:

> Wherever rules are created and applied we should be alive to the possible presence of an enterprising individual or group. Their activities can properly be called "moral enterprise" for what they are enterprising about is the creation of a new fragment of the moral constitution of society, its code of right and wrong (1963:145).

Such entrepreneurs might have diverse motives. In the case of a drug panic, for example, we might find activism by an interest group or a bureaucratic agency that was seeking to portray a serious social danger in order to focus public attention on issues falling within its scope of activity. This effort would permit the agency to expand its influence and resources, and might allow local authorities and law enforcement agencies to justify requests for federal funding and other support. In such circumstances, we often find a cyclical pattern in which greater concern causes more resources to be devoted to a problem; the result is more detection and more vigorous prosecution of the activity in question. This process in turn generates statistical evidence that can be used to intensify public concern, and thus to argue for still more resources. "Epidemics" thus can be self-sustaining.

Such bureaucratic concerns may have played some role in the case of ice. One recurrent theme of the hearings was the need to strengthen still further the numbers and resources of the DEA (*U.S. Congress: Re-Emergerce* 1990:8–9). This agency had grown in numbers from 1,900 in 1980 to 2,900 in 1989. Currently it was requesting 160 new agents, chiefly for international enforcement in Latin America and the Pacific Rim (34–35). An ice panic therefore served the interests of the DEA, but it certainly cannot serve as a full explanation. As we have seen, the DEA was strongly critical of the exaggerated claims made for ice, and during 1990 was instrumental in damping down the nascent panic. In January, for example, the head of the Honolulu office wrote that ice was still confined largely to Hawaii and "very limited West Coast areas;" otherwise, he reported, "we know of no ice samples (having) been analyzed elsewhere in the United States" (*U.S. Congress: Drug Crisis* 1990:76).

Instead of examining national groups and controversies, it would be more profitable to consider the needs of the political and bureaucratic interests in Hawaii that sponsored most of the extravagant claims about ice and first identified an "epidemic." For example, the major claims makers heard by the Congressional committees included two of the leading figures in the state's law enforcement bureaucracy, police chief Douglas Gibb and U.S. Attorney Daniel Bent. The evidence offered by these two witnesses accounted for more than one-third of the total testimony presented during the October hearings, and both men emphasized the "epidemic" quality of the ice threat. As in the case of the DEA, an ice panic would enhance the reputation of local police agencies as well as increasing their access to resources. In addition, the powerful office of U.S. Attorney often provides any incumbent with the opportunity to win prestige and visibility that can be translated subsequently into a wider political career. This is not to suggest that either individual was insincere in his claims about the ice problem, but both had clear bureaucratic interests in formulating the issue in a particular way.

Electoral politics also played a role in shaping official claims and statements. At the opening of the 1989 hearings, which did so much to put ice on the map of American social problems, Congressman Rangel emphasized that the impetus for concern came chiefly from the Hawaii Congressional delegation of Representatives Daniel Akaka and Patricia Saiki. Both in fact had a strong vested interest in appearing to be active and interested in drug issues, and in adopting hard-line antidrug stances. Therefore they stood to benefit from making ice seem as perilous and as threatening as possible; both can be viewed as classical moral entrepreneurs.

This political context can be observed if we describe recent developments in Hawaii, traditionally one of the most loyally Democratic states in the nation (Smith and Pratt 1992). In the 1980s, for example, both of the Democratic U.S. senators could count regularly on receiving 70 to 80 percent of the votes cast, and the powerful governor's office remained firmly in Democratic hands throughout these years (Benenson 1991). Republicans were placed extremely poorly; they won offices chiefly when Democratic factions were split, as when Republican Patricia Saiki won the First Congressional District. By 1989 she had retained this position in two elections, but with progressively slimmer majorities. Democrat Daniel Akaka had remained firmly in control of the Second District in every contest since 1976.

Saiki's presence as a Republican representative therefore might appear anomalous, but the Republicans had one major point of potential strength, namely in the general area of law and order. Throughout the decade, Democratic authorities had been involved in a series of scandals; these had exposed alleged links between organized crime and the labor unions, which play so crucial a role in Hawaii Democratic politics. These incidents reached a climax in 1984 with the investigation by Charles F. Marsland, the Republican Honolulu city/county prosecutor, into a series of gangland murders that included the killing of Marsland's own son. Marsland targeted a prominent political ally of Democratic

Governor George Ariyoshi as the alleged "godfather" of organized crime in the state (Turner 1984a, 1984b). The ensuing scandals and lawsuits did not destroy Democratic power. In fact, the next governor, elected in 1986, was a close associate of Ariyoshi, but the incident suggested one area in which Democrats were politically vulnerable: Daniel Akaka himself had been an Ariyoshi protegé. In addition, he is of native Hawaiian descent, and thus could potentially be associated with Larry Mehau, the ethnically Hawaiian "godfather."

In the following years, Saiki and Akaka emerged as powerful figures in Hawaii politics, and they clashed on crime-related issues. In the U.S. Congress, Saiki voted for a measure to extend the death penalty to major drug dealers, which Akaka opposed. The rivalry between the two was especially significant in 1989, when it became increasingly likely that soon they would be vying for a U.S. Senate seat in Hawaii. The junior senator's position currently was held by Spark Matsunaga, a very popular figure first elected in 1972, but a series of health crises beginning in 1984 made it unlikely that Matsunaga would run again in 1990, even if he completed his current term.

Therefore it was likely that within a year, Saiki would challenge Akaka for the hitherto solidly Democratic Senate seat, but the balance in this apparently unequal match could be tipped in a number of ways. One would be the ethnic factor. As noted above, Akaka is a native Hawaiian. The strongest faction in his Democratic party, however, is Japanese-American, a group to which Saiki could be expected to appeal. In addition, it would be natural to portray the relatively liberal Akaka as soft on crime and drugs, and possibly not sufficiently vigorous in the war on local organized crime. As a result, it was important for Akaka to rebut such charges; his membership on the House Subcommittee on Narcotic Abuse provided an ideal opportunity.

Both representatives therefore needed to appear strong on drug issues, and ideally both needed national media credentials as antidrug crusaders. Local ethnic and partisan alignments, however, circumscribed the kinds of rhetoric that would be appropriate in such a campaign. Although organized crime in general could be denounced, it is significant that none of the ice rhetoric focused on the specifically Japanese component of drug manufacture and distribution or on the role of the *yakuza* described so frequently by other law enforcement agencies and investigators. One might suggest that the nature of the forthcoming Hawaii elections made such accusations too sensitive to be presented at that time, for fear of perpetrating ethnic slurs against one of the most influential communities in the islands.

In fact, both Akaka and Saiki succeeded in gaining significant political capital from the ice issue. Saiki earned credit for having brought the problem to national attention and for requesting increased resources, but Akaka also shared the credit, and was not portrayed as soft on the crime issue in any sense. Akaka first used the term *ice age* in the hearings, and drew some of the starkest analogies between ice and crack. Both confirmed their role as standard-bearers of their respective parties. When Senator Matsunaga died a few months later, in April 1990, Akaka was the natural choice to fill the unexpired portion of his term. Both he and Saiki easily won their parties' nominations for the November election ("Hawaiian Politics" 1990). That contest normally would have been a Democratic walkover, but Saiki had established her prestige so firmly that she made it a close race, and lost only narrowly to Akaka. He thereby became the first native Hawaiian to be represented in the U.S. Senate (Saiki went on to head the federal Small Business Administration) (Reinhold 1990; Richburg 1990).

Domestic politics in Hawaii thus made it likely that the state representatives would seek to focus on a crime or drug problem of local significance. It was by no means apparent, however, that these issues would come to wider attention, especially when conditions and controversies in Hawaii so rarely attract the attention of the national media. The opportunity was provided by Akaka's service on the House Narcotics Subcommittee, where he was aided by another representative with a strong record in drug issues and a long career as a "moral entrepreneur." This was a Pennsylvania representative named Lawrence Coughlin, from the thirteenth district in suburban Montgomery County, outside Philadelphia. Coughlin, the ranking Republican on the Narcotics Subcommittee, was instrumental in bringing Akaka's views to Rangel's attention. His advocacy was significant in showing that ice was causing concern far outside Hawaii, and legitimately could be presented as a national issue.

Other agendas, however, may have been at work here as well. Coughlin's interest in methamphetamine issues dated back at least to the late 1970s, when he had been one of the most active supporters of the theory that Philadelphia was the "speed capital of the world" (Jenkins 1992a, b). To illustrate this questionable assertion, Coughlin had publicized stories from local Montgomery County newspapers as if they represented conditions throughout the state or the nation, and in effect had generated a mythology about the prevalence of speed in southeastern Pennsylvania. In 1980, largely at Coughlin's behest, the Narcotics Select Committee had been persuaded to hold special hearings in Philadelphia, where local issues and investigations received national attention (*U.S. Congress: Laboratories* 1980). The campaign to link Philadelphia with speed was so successful that it became the focus of the popular 1985 film *Witness*, whose plot concerns a huge shipment of the precursor chemical P2P. Coughlin thus emerges as a long-standing protagonist of a "speed menace." As a result, it is scarcely surprising to see the limited experience of Hawaii extrapolated to the entire nation in the 1989–1990 hearings, just as had happened with conditions in Philadelphia in 1980.

Transforming Local Issues into National Problems

In studying social problems, one critical theme is the relationship between local and national perceptions, and the way in which some (but by no means all) local phenomena come to be regarded as issues of far wider significance. The panic about ice serves to remind us that drug problems are extremely localized, and that in crime, as in so much else, it is difficult to generalize about the American experience. Drug problems rarely strike the nation in a regular or homogeneous way. Much has been written about the "crack epidemic" that swept the United States in the mid–1980s, but we must always remember that this phenomenon was highly localized. The "epidemic" initially was centered in the major cities of the east and west coasts, but scarcely penetrated large sections of the midwest until the early 1990s. This situation has many possible explanations—the strength of local traditions and subcultures, patterns of law enforcement vagaries of manufacture and supply, the interests of criminal groups—but the point is that a "panic" might be well under way in one area years before it is felt elsewhere, and it is by no means inevitable that it ever will move beyond the original region (for the localized nature of drug cultures, see, for example, Weisheit 1992).

On the other hand, certain extraneous factors demand that a local problem should be viewed in a national context, and that policy responses should be developed accordingly. One important element in this regard is the mass media, which had come, during the 1980s, to treat drug-related stories as events of major significance. Newspapers assigned journalists to cover such stories as their sole or major responsibility; thus the papers had a vested interest in the constant generation of newsworthy items in this area. One way to achieve this goal was to focus on local concerns or incidents, but to project them as if they were of wider, even national significance. A notorious example appeared in 1986 in the CBS television documentary *48 Hours on Crack Street*. This program presented the (then) essentially New York City problem of crack cocaine as if it were already a national epidemic, with vials littering the streets and parks of virtually every community across the country (Reinarman and Levine 1989). Though largely spurious, this account had enormous influence in generating fears of a national crack epidemic.

In the early 1980s, before the advent of crack, the media often presented the localized PCP problem in Washington, DC in such a way as to suggest that it soon would become a national crisis. (Such "extrapolations" are not confined to drug issues: witness the suggestions, at about that time, that Los Angeles's distinctive gang problems were spreading to cities throughout the nation.) Once the media present à problem in this way, Congressional hearings permit the issue to be discussed in another national forum, with the certainty that national news coverage will reinforce perceptions of a widespread crisis.

This process of "nationalization" gives rich opportunities to local activists, moral entrepreneurs, or claims makers who wish to draw attention to a particular issue, and who do so by presenting it as more dangerous or more important than it may be in fact. One natural way to do this is to suggest that a local issue either is national in scope or has a strong potential to become so in the very near future: in short, that it is about to "sweep the nation." This process enhances the importance of local campaigns; it also offers the local moral entrepreneurs the opportunity to acquire the status of national leaders and experts, should their analysis be accepted. This enhancement, in turn, can reinforce the position of local figures in their home areas.

The panic about ice is a model example of this process. The use of the drug was a local phenomenon; the national concern about the drug in 1989 derived chiefly from Hawaii's elected officials and law enforcement agencies with a definite political agenda. For two specific reasons, they were relatively successful in projecting their concerns. First, the recent experience of crack made it easy for them to represent ice, in effect, as part of the same problem; this process is known by the rhetorical term *convergence*. The ice phenomenon occurred at precisely the right time, when the rhetoric about crack was still fresh in the public mind and when the "drug war" was reaching a crescendo. It is difficult to imagine that the ice issue would have arisen at all if public expectations had not been conditioned by these recent precedents.

Second, the intense public focus on drug issues during the 1980s had created bureaucracies and political frameworks able to publicize information and opinion about drugs. These groups, such as the DEA, the NIDA, and the Narcotics Subcommittee itself, had excellent media ties and could be relied on to provide newsworthy stories about crime and drug abuse. In the case of the Congressional committee, it is inevitable that members of any political organization charged with investigating drug problems will attempt to attract as much publicity as possible by presenting themselves as concerned, active, well-informed guardians of the public good. There are few better opportunities to do so than by recognizing a problem at an early stage to prevent it reaching crisis proportions. The case of Hawaii offered the committee members the chance to investigate and combat a drug problem in a proactive, farsighted way.

No significant risk was involved in this strategy. If an "ice epidemic" occurred, the committee earned credit for having predicted it and for urging preemptive action; if it faded away, the committee could claim that its forethought had prevented a drug crisis. Conversely, there was much to be lost by cautious or skeptical reactions to an incipient crisis. If the predicted menace actually materialized, an agency or an administration stood to attract most of the blame for the ensuing problems.

None of the factors that produced the ice panic has changed significantly since 1989, or is likely to change significantly in the near future. Therefore it is probable that local drug fads will be presented once again as potential crises, likely to spread rapidly across the entire country. Social scientists must recognize and publicize the social and political factors that generate such misleading expectations.

References

Anderson, J. and D. Van Atta (1990) "Big Plane Junket for Hill Spouses." *Washington Post*, January 10, p. 3.

Arrestee Drug Use (1990) National Institute of Justice, Research in Action. Washington, DC: U.S. Government Printing Office.

Becker, H. (1963) *Outsiders*. New York: Free Press.

Benenson, B. (1991) "Democrats Reassert Primacy in Hawaii Politics." *Congressional Quarterly*, October 12.

Best, J. (1990) *Threatened Children*. Chicago: University of Chicago Press.

Bishop, K. (1989) "Fear Grows over Effects of a New Smokable Drug." *New York Times*, September 16, p. 4A.

Brecher, E. M. (1972) *Licit and Illicit Drugs*. Boston: Little, Brown.

Buruma, I. and J. McBeth (1984–85) "An East Side Story. . . ." *Far Eastern Economic Review*, 27 December/3 January, p. 15.

Carthane, A. (1989) "Will New Drug 'Ice' Freeze Hope in Black Communities?" *Jet*, December 18.

Cho, A. K. (1990) "Ice: A New Dosage Form of an Old Drug." *Science* (249): 631–34.

Corwin, M. (1989) "Potent Form of Speed Could Be Drug of 90s." *Los Angeles Times*, October 8, p. 1A.

Cotton, P. (1990) "Medium Isn't Accurate Ice Age Message." *Journal of the American Medical Association* (263): 2717.

Curriden, M. (1989) "Police Chilled by New In Drug: Ice." *Atlanta Constitution*, November 30, p. 1.

Delfs, R. (1991) "Cocaine Surge." Far Eastern Economic Review, November 21, p. 7.

"Drugs: Ice Overdose" (1989) *Economist*, December 2, pp. 29–30.

Durso, C. (1992) "Powerful Drug 'Ice' Is Found at Lab." *Philadelphia Inquirer*, August 14, p. 1B.

Essoyan, S. (1989) "Use of Highly Addictive 'Ice' Growing in Hawaii." *Los Angeles Times*, October 16, p. 3A.

Ford, A. (1990) "Federal, Local Police Raid House in San Diego." *Los Angeles Times* July 26, p. 7A.

Goode, E. (1984) *Drugs in American Society.* 2nd ed. New York: Knopf.

Graham, J. M. (1976) "Amphetamine Politics on Capital Hill." In W. J. Chambliss and M. Mankoff (eds.), *Whose Law? What Order?*, pp. 107–22. New York: Wiley.

Grinspoon, L. (1975) *The Speed Culture: Amphetamine Use and Abuse in America.* Cambridge, MA: Harvard University Press.

Gross, J. (1988) "Speed's Gain in Use Could Rival Crack." *New York Times,* November 27, p. A9.

Hall, S., Critcher, C., Jefferson, T., Clarke, J. and Roberts, B. (1978) *Policing the Crisis.* London: Macmillan.

"Hawaiian Politics: Ethnic Pineapple Salad" (1990) *Economist,* October 20, p. 32.

Holland, L. (1990) "All about Ice: New Drug Nice Kids Can Get Hooked On." *Good Housekeeping,* February, pp. 215–16.

Holley, D., E. Vernant, and S. Essoyan (1991) "The Ice Age." *Washington Post,* May 9, p. 1A.

Hong, R., E. Matsuyama, and K. Nur (1991) "Cardiomyopathy Associated with the Smoking of Crystal Methamphetamine." *Journal of the American Medical Association* (265):1152–54.

Howe, P. J. (1989) "Ice Worse Than Crack, Officials Warn." *Boston Globe,* October 1, p. 2.

"Illicit Methamphetamine: Street Drug on the Rise" (1991) *Emergency Medicine,* June 30, pp. 13–17.

Isikoff, M. (1989) "Rural Drug Users Spur Comeback of Crank." *Washington Post,* February 20, p. 3A.

Jacobs, J. (1991) "Debunking the Crack Baby Myths." *Centre Daily Times,* State College, PA, August 11, p. 6A.

Jenkins, Philip (1992a) "Narcotics Trafficking and the American Mafia: the Myth of Internal Prohibition." *Crime, Law and Social Change* 18: 303–18.

Jenkins, Philip (1992b) "The Speed Capital of the World: Organizing the Methamphetamine Industry in Philadelphia 1970–1990." *Criminal Justice Policy Review* 6(1): 17–39.

Kaplan, D. E. and A. Dubro (1986) *Yakuza.* Reading, MA: Addison-Wesley.

LaBianca, D. A. (1992) "The Drug Scene's New Ice Age." *USA Today,* January, pp. 54–56.

Larmer, B. (1989) "Ice Chills US Anti-Drug Officials." *Christian Science Monitor,* December 8, p. 7.

Lauderback, D. and D. Waldorf (1992) "Whatever Happened to Ice?" Paper presented at meetings of the American Society of Criminology, New Orleans.

Lerner, M. L. (1989) "The Fire of Ice." *Newsweek,* November 27, p. 26.

MacDonald, P. T. and R. Estep (1985) "Prime Time Drug Depictions." *Contemporary Drug Problems* 12(3):419–38.

McBeth, J. (1989) "The Junkie Culture: Supercharged Speed is Scourge of Manila's Smart Set." *Far Eastern Economic Review,* November 23, pp. 23–25.

"Meth" (1990) Report broadcast on *60 Minutes,* April 22.

Methamphetamine Abuse in the United States. (1989) Rockville, MD: U.S.

Department of Health and Human Services.

Miller, M. A. and N. J. Kozel (1991) *Methamphetamine Abuse: Epidemiological Issues and Implications*. Rockville, MD: U.S. Department of Health and Human Services.

Morgan, J. P. (1992) "Amphetamine and Methamphetamine during the 1990s." *Pediatrics in Review* 13(9): 330–36.

Musto, D. (1973) *The American Disease: Origins of Narcotic Control*. New Haven: Yale University Press.

Organized Crime in California: Annual Report to the California Legislature. (1989) State of California: Department of Justice.

Pennell, S. (1990) "Ice: DUF Interview Results from San Diego." *NIJ Reports* 221:12–13.

Posner, G. L. (1988) *Warlords of Crime*. New York: McGraw-Hill.

Reinarman, C. and H. G. Levine (1989) "The Crack Attack: Politics and Media in America's Latest Drug Scare." In Joel Best (ed.), *Images of Issues*, pp. 115–37. Hawthorne, NY: Aldine.

Reinhold, R. (1990) "Seaway Race Tests Democratic Hold." *New York Times*. November 1, p. 9B.

Reza, H. G. (1989) "Raids Shut 23 Drug Labs." *Los Angeles Times*, March 20.

Richburg, K. B. (1990) "For Hawaii Democrats, Anxiety Over Safe Seats." *Washington Post*, November 1, p. 7A.

Sager, M. (1990) "The Ice Age." *Rolling Stone*, February 8, pp. 53–57.

Savadove, B. (1991) "High Society: Growing Drug Abuse Reflects Economic Changes." *Far Eastern Economic Review*, September 12, pp. 45–46.

Shoenberger, K. (1989) "South Korea Seen as Major Source of Ice Narcotic." *Los Angeles Times*, October 14, p. 9A.

Skeers, V. M. (1992) "Illegal Methamphetamine Drug Laboratories." *Journal of Environmental Health* 55(3):6–9.

Smith, Z. A. and R. C. Pratt, eds. (1992) *Politics and Public Policy in Hawaii*. Albany: SUNY Press.

Tabor, M. (1989) "Ice in an Island Paradise." *Boston Globe*, December 8, p. 7.

"Text of President's Speech on Drug Control Strategy" (1989) *New York Times*, September 6, p. 4A.

Thompson L. (1989) "Ice: New Smokable Form of Speed." *Washington Post*, November 21, p. 2.

Turner, W. (1984a) "Hawaii Criminal's Pledge to Talk Seen as Door to Underworld." *New York Times*, July 24, p. 11A.

_____ (1984b) "Inquiry on Murders in Hawaii Brings Governor and Prosecutor into Conflict." *New York Times*, August 28, p. 7A.

U.S. Congress: Drug Crisis (1990) *Drug Crisis in Hawaii: Hearing before the Select Committee on Narcotics Abuse and Control, House of Representatives, 101st Congress, Second Session, January 13, 1990*. Washington, DC: U.S. Government Printing Office.

U.S. Congress: Laboratories (1980) *Illicit Methamphetamine Laboratories in the Pennsylvania /New Jersey/Delaware Area: Hearing before the Select Committee on Narcotics Abuse and Control, U.S. House of Representatives, 96th Congress, Second Session, July 7, 1980*. Washington, DC: U.S. Government Printing Office.

U.S. Congress: Profile (1983) *Profile of Organized Crime: Mid-Atlantic Region:*

Hearings before the Permanent Subcommittee on Investigations of the Committee on Governmental Affairs, United States Senate, 98th Congress, First Session, February 15, 23, and 24, 1983. Washington, DC: U.S. Government Printing Office.

U.S. Congress: Re-Emergence (1990) *The Re-Emergence of Methamphetamine: Hearings before the Subcommittee on Narcotics Abuse and Control, U.S. House of Representatives, 101st Congress, First Session, October 24, 1989.* Washington, DC: U.S. Government Printing Office.

U.S. Congress: Small Business (1988). *Impact of Clandestine Drug Laboratories on Small Business: Hearings before the Subcommittee on Regulation and Business Opportunities of the Committee on Small Business, U.S. House of Representatives, 100th Congress, Second Session. Eugene, Oregon, May 13, 1988.* Washington, DC: U.S. Government Printing Office.

Weingarten, P. (1989) "Profits, Perils, Higher for Today's Bootleggers." *Chicago Tribune,* September 14, p. 16.

Weisheit, R. A. (1992) *Domestic Marijuana: A Neglected Industry.* Westport, CT: Greenwood.

Wiedrich, B. (1987) "San Diego Has Become National Center for Manufacture of Methamphetamine." *Chicago Tribune,* April 20, p. 11.

Witkin, G. (1989) "The New Midnight Dumpers." *U.S. News and World Report,* January 9, p. 23.

Young, J. (1971) "Drugs and the Media." *Drugs and Society* 2(1): 14–18.

Zamichow, N. (1989) "Navy Hopes Drug Test Will Detect, Deter Meth Users." *Los Angeles Times,* October 16, p. 6A.

Zurer, P. S. (1989) "Federal Officials Plot Strategy to Stop Methamphetamine Spread." *Chemical and Engineering News,* November 6, pp. 13–16.

8

The Presentation of Drugs in the News Media
The News Sources Involved in the Construction of Social Problems

Steven Chermak

Politicians and criminal justice officials have both a financial and an ideological stake in the way social problems are presented to the public. The issue of drugs, for example, tends to fade in and out of political priority (Peyrot 1984). Most recently, political interest in drugs escalated steadily through the 1980s. Drug enforcement was part of Ronald Reagan's crime control agenda, culminating in his declaration in 1986 that America needed yet another war on drugs (Jensen, Gerber, and Babcock 1991). George Bush retained Reagan's concern for drugs, developing a national drug control strategy, appointing the nation's first drug czar, and using the military to aid interdiction efforts.

The principal response advocated by both presidents, reflecting their political ideology, was to increase criminal justice and military enforcement efforts. Police departments cracked down on sellers, using undercover and "buy-and-bust" operations to increase the number of arrests. Courts cleared their dockets or created special drug courts to process the large influx of drug offenders. Penalties for drug offenses increased, with concomitant growth in prison populations. Moreover, the distinction between the police and the military in fighting the war on drugs eroded (Kraska 1993, 1994). Kraska (1993:161), for example, discusses how the formerly figurative "drug-war metaphor" has become

Source: *Justice Quarterly*, Vol. 14 No. 4, December 1997, pp. 687–718. ©1997 Academy of Criminal Justice Sciences. Reprinted with permission.

more literal with the significant involvement of the military in foreign and domestic drug-control efforts.

It is significant that the rise and fall of drugs as an important political issue has not coincided with changes in the reported incidence of drug use (Beckett 1994; Jensen et al. 1991; Reinarman and Levine 1995). Beckett (1994:442) discovered that public concern about drugs was affected only by shifts in the level of state-initiated activities. Similarly, Jensen et al. (1991) found that the enactment of federal drug legislation was not related to objective conditions of drug use, but to politicians' efforts to promote drugs as a social problem.

For several reasons, the news media are an effective resource available to claimsmakers when they seek support for policy preferences. First, news images are important because the public's exposure to the political process is limited (Edelman 1964; Kessel 1975). According to McCombs and Shaw (1991:17), "the information in the mass media becomes the only contact many have with politics." Second, media coverage is a cost-efficient way to garner support for a policy position because the public relies heavily on the news media (Graber 1980; Skogan and Maxfield 1981; Tunnell 1992). Third, the news media are an important agent of social control. Claimsmakers need public support to survive, compete, and thrive in the "social problems marketplace" (Best 1990:15), although predicting public preferences is difficult. Because "public perceptions are malleable," influenced by forces such as the mass media (Tittle 1994:32), social control agents are motivated to participate as news sources to transmit their beliefs and values, and also to legitimize themselves with the public.

An event that is presented to the public is shaped by a reporter's perception of it because it is rarely observed directly (Kappeler, Blumberg, and Potter 1996). Reporters rely on authoritative sources, such as political and criminal justice officials, to construct the event (Berkowitz 1987; Berkowitz and Beach 1993; Brown et al. 1987; Chermak 1995; Gans 1979; Sigal 1973). Sigal (1973:123) found that government officials accounted for approximately half of the sources cited in articles published in the *New York Times* and the *Washington Post*. Similarly, Chermak (1995:89) found that law enforcement and court officials accounted for more than half of the sources cited in crime stories.

"Although most research agrees with these findings, there are two general explanations for the dominance of official sources in news stories. First, several researchers argue in support of a conflict or structuralist perspective. This explanation emphasizes how the reliance on state officials is determined by macro-level forces. The structuralist perspective assumes that the media are an important symbolic mechanism used in the construction of ideology (Binder 1993; Sacco 1995). It is argued that the ideological power of the media results from their control over consumers' views of the world. Events are framed into standard modes of communication. These frames, according to Binder (1993:754–55), "help receivers make sense of social occurrences because they organize events into recognizable patterns." Consumers rely on this framing of events when deciphering reality; thus alternative viewpoints are eliminated from consideration (Beckett 1994; Binder 1993; Gamson et al. 1992; Gitlin 1980; Sacco 1995).

This macro-level focus deals specifically with questions of power and how power is expressed and distributed in society. It is important to understand the sources involved in the construction of crime because social problems can be framed in many different ways. For our analysis, the key aspect is how the reliance on government claimsmakers allows these sources to make claims and to characterize problems so as to legitimize existing social, cultural, and political relations. Political and economic elites have preferential access to the media because of their hierarchic position in society; they use this access to define the social order, maintain cultural boundaries, and reaffirm the status quo (Hall et al. 1978; Herman and Chomsky 1988).

Second, other researchers explain the reliance on these sources from an organizational perspective. Although news content may support a specific ideology, researchers argue that this is not done intentionally (Berkowitz 1987; Berkowitz and Beach 1993). Instead this reliance results from organizational and economic needs (Benedict 1992; Fishman 1980; Gans 1979; Tuchman 1978). News organizations are structured bureaucratically and rely on decentralized news beats to create news efficiently. Sources able to provide information in an efficient and newsworthy manner receive the opportunity to influence public discourse on crime and social control. Representatives from bureaucratic organizations understand the routine channels of news discourse and make themselves available to reporters. Researchers with this perspective, however, concede that the relied-upon sources do not completely control news images: News personnel accept only images consistent with their own organizational needs and media formats (Ericson, Baranek, and Chan 1987, 1989, and 1991).

Katherine Beckett's (1995) study examining the impact of sources on the presentation of drugs in the media contributes to these theoretical viewpoints and illustrates the importance of examining the presentation of sources in various types of story. In a sample of "hard" and "soft" (editorials, cartoons, opinion columns) drug stories, Beckett linked the sources cited to the "framing" of the issue. She found that the sources' ability to influence the presentation of drugs varied according to the type of story examined. First, she found that state officials affected the issue frames presented in the "hard" news stories and that the frequent presence of these frames resulted in a narrow perspective on the drug issue, supporting conservative "law and order" themes. Second, she found that a wider range of issue frames was presented in the "soft" items, supporting the conclusion that such a range results from state officials' exclusion from stories. These stories are media-generated, and the news personnel producing them are not constrained by the information provided by sources.

Other research examining relations between reporters and sources has rarely considered how these interactions evolve by type of story. Some researchers acknowledge, however, that sources other than routine crime authorities can procure media coverage, thus affecting news content and public attention to social problems (Best 1990; Gitlin 1980; Jenness 1993; Schlesinger and Tumber 1994). Joel Best's (1990) study of crimes against children documents the influence that outsider claimsmakers, such as activists and moral entrepreneurs, can exert on public and political attention to social problems by securing media coverage. Similarly, Valerie Jenness (1993) demonstrated how a group of outsider claimsmakers was able to reshape the "symbolic landscape" of prostitution and challenge the way traditional experts constructed this social problem.

The news process evolves according to the importance of the story. Chermak (1995) found that most stories are routine occurrences produced quickly in order to fill the space or time needs of a news organization. Chermak also found, however, that stories receiving significant amounts of attention are produced differently. Several reporters work on various aspects of these stories, four or five stories are presented to the public when the event is initiated, and the news media follow these stories closely over time (Chermak 1995:28–410.)

Similarly, Mark Fishman (1978:531) discussed how the news media can construct "crime waves," thus contributing to an ideological conception of crime. He found that incidents which could be attached to an ongoing theme of violence against the elderly were more likely to be published and received more attention in the news. Momentum increased as other media organizations tried to capitalize on this theme. Fishman also found that political and criminal justice officials contributed to the construction of this crime wave by taking action that received media coverage, shifting media attention to "how the system [was] working to remedy the situation" (p. 541).

In an analysis of criminal justice case processing, Friedman and Percival (1981:237) identified this "handful of cases at the apex of the system" as "celebrated." Criminal justice officials respond to different cases in different ways, and possess great discretion in deciding the importance of a case (Walker 1989:24–25). Because of the publicity received by these celebrated cases, they can affect public perception of the criminal justice system (Walker 1989:25). In applying this notion to media coverage, Surette (1989) calls the celebrated case a "media trial." Such trials have an impact far beyond their number, Surette argues, "because many viewers believe that the news and its portraits are real and accurate, the image of justice that media trials project has serious implications for public understanding of basic judicial concepts and support for the legitimacy of the entire criminal justice system" (p. 293).

The claimsmakers' involvement in celebrated cases, in contrast to their participation in typical cases, is an important aspect of social constructionism. Although celebrated cases are rare, they provide high-ranking officials with an opportunity to define the "hierarchy of credibility" in society and to reaffirm their position as a "primary definer" of an issue (Fishman 1980; Johnson 1995). Moreover, these cases can be "powerful teachers and preachers of conventional morality" (Friedman and Percival 1981:259). In documenting the sources that participate in celebrated news stories, we clarify how the relationship that results from the production of ordinary stories gives political and criminal justice officials strategic access to media personnel when opportunities arise to institutionalize their authoritative position.

In this article we examine how reporters and sources construct social problems in the news media. Specifically, we examine the sources cited in routine crime stories, in stories linked to a highly visible policy issue, and in stories examining celebrated cases relevant to policy issues. We document the news sources cited in these three types of story to determine whether the relationship between reporters and sources evolves as a story increases in importance. By examining the sources used by news organizations to define what is important about a topic of substantial interest, and then comparing the results with those for other crime stories, we understand more clearly how official sources define social problems in the news.

To illustrate the construction of social problems, we examine the problem of drug abuse, documenting the "primary definers" of the drug problem during a period when it was a high-priority news topic. Schlesinger and Tumber (1994:2) note that "only very recently have questions begun to be asked in a consistent and focused fashion about the tactics and strategies pursued by sources seeking media attention," and researchers on this topic have used only one of two research methodologies. First, most studies employ content analysis, counting and nonofficial sources (Berkowitz 1987; Berkowitz and Beach 1993; Brown et al. 1987; Sigal 1973). Second, other studies examine the relationship between reporters and sources by observing the news production process (Fishman 1978; Gans 1979; Tuchman 1978). Most research fails to link these two research methodologies, although each has limitations when used alone (Ericson et al. 1987). In this study we combine content and observational analysis to precisely document the sources involved in news production and to explain why, and how, political and criminal justice officials are involved in the representation of social problems in the news.

We believe that the theories traditionally used to explain the heavy reliance on official sources for news construction are not in conflict, but operate at different levels of understanding. Considered in this way, these theories are seen to complement one another; this suggests that an integrated theory may be more appropriate for understanding these officials' involvement in news construction. We argue that the relationship between sources and news personnel can evolve, and that it is influenced by the type of story in question. Most stories support the convergence of the bureaucratic goals held by news and source organizations: To make the production of crime news manageable, news media routinize their task by positioning themselves so as to gain easy access to sources that can supply crime news (Berkowitz and Beach 1993; Chibnall 1977; Fishman 1980; Gans 1979; Tuchman 1978). This reliance, in turn, provides these sources with the opportunity to shape the crime images presented in the news, although the information provided must be consistent with the media organization's time, resource, and format concerns (Ericson et al. 1987, 1989, 1991). In keeping with the organizational perspective, we hypothesize that criminal justice officials will dominate coverage of all types of routine crime story.

In addition, in the organizational process used to produce crime stories, news reporting is structured to support existing political, social, and legal systems. Issues that are thematically important or can be linked to celebrated cases provide strong opportunities to reaffirm the status quo. We hypothesize that a different class of social control agents will be used as sources in all drug stories and in celebrated drug cases. Because government claimsmakers have established access to media organizations, they can use specific stories as opportunities to legitimize their position as an important voice of the "deviance-defining elite" and to promote and frame a social problem. We hypothesize that high-ranking officials will be involved more frequently in typical drug cases and in celebrated cases, and will use these types of story to argue in support of a policy position because of the attention received. Drug abuse is a well-established, "recurring" social problem with potential for policy innovation and change (see Best 1990; Scheingold 1984). We examine the involvement of sources in incidents, policies, and celebrated stories about drugs to document whether the organizational constraints of news production place government claimsmakers in a position to use social problems for their strategic advantage.

Research Methodology

To examine the information on drug crimes available to the public, it is important to use various research methodologies. Here we employ content analysis of print and electronic news media to examine how drug crimes, policies, and sources are presented to the public; we also use observational and interview data to understand the origins of these news stories, the motivations of news sources, and the underlying intentions of the parties involved in news production.

We used content analysis to examine the presentation of drug-related crime in newspapers and on television. Content data were collected from six print and three broadcast media organizations, selected by geographic location and city size. We selected news organizations by generating a list of cities that had at least one local newspaper with a circulation greater than 50,000 *(Gale Directory* 1990). We matched the cities according to population size and number of index offenses for 1990, then stratified them into medium, large, and extra-large categories. The media from two cities in each category were selected to represent as many regions of the country and as much variation in crime rate as possible.[1] We examined content from one newspaper in each of the six cities (two medium, two large, two extra-large) and one television station in three of the cities (one medium, one large, one extra-large).

We coded 36 days of newspaper content from six print organizations: the *Albany* (New York) *Times-Union,* the Buffalo *News,* the *Cleveland Plain Dealer,* the *San Francisco Chronicle,* the *Dallas Times Herald,* and the *Detroit News.* Newspaper stories were coded for every fifth day of the first six months of 1990. In addition, we coded the *Cleveland Plain Dealer* for 18 days over a three-month period in 1991. These 18 days were coded for two reasons: First, the additional coding strengthens the reliability of comparisons between newspaper and television samples. Second, it allows for a comparison with the results from the 1990 newspaper sample.

Television content was coded from local evening broadcasts in Albany, Cleveland, and Dallas for an eight-week span from May to July 1991. We recorded and viewed a total of 168 broadcasts in their entirety. Crime stories were transcribed and then content-coded.[2]

We conducted a theme analysis of content, using a combination of coding rules from other research that examined crime content (Ericson et al. 1991; Graber 1980). Source variables, such as who was cited in a news story and that person's position in an organization, were added to the codebook to document precisely how news media present sources. We coded more than 2,500 crime stories.

The second methodology used in this study is ethnography. Ethnographic observation of the crime news production process was conducted in 1991 at one newspaper and one television station in a large metropolitan city; we spent approximately 150 hours in each news agency. These observations help to overcome the limitations of content analysis and demonstrate how decision making in news and source organizations contributes to the way the news is represented to the public.

The newspaper observed, which we will call the *Midwest Tribune*, is a large organization with a daily circulation of about 500,000. Police and court reporters produce most of the crime stories presented in the *Tribune*. Reporters working the police beat, located on the first floor of police headquarters, are responsible for producing stories about any crimes reported to the police. Court reporters are responsible for producing crime stories after an arrest is made and the defendant is arraigned. We made most of our observations on these two beats, but we also spent time with general assignment reporters and editors to broaden our understanding of news production.

Observations were also conducted at a television station in the same city, which we call the Midwest Nightly. All of the Midwest Nightly reporters are general assignment reporters, any of whom could be assigned to cover a given crime story. Reporters are assigned to stories at an afternoon editorial meeting; after these meetings, we asked reporters if we could follow their coverage of a particular story or shadow them as they made their daily routine checks.

We supplemented the ethnographic findings with 40 interviews. In addition to asking specific questions about the production process, we conducted structured, open-ended interviews for a broader perspective on how each media organization produced stories on crime: These included 20 long interviews with crime beat reporters and editors working for the organizations we observed, 15 interviews with news personnel from other organizations, and five interviews with criminal justice and victim sources. These interviews help to increase the generalizability of the observational findings.

Findings

The findings are presented in three sections. First, we establish the heightened attention given to drug crimes during the sample period, and compare the presentation of drugs as incident and policy stories with other types of crime story. Second, we examine the sources cited in typical drug stories, and compare the results with the presentation of sources in all crime stories. Although officials were the most common source cited in all types of story, we found several interesting differences when examining drug stories. Finally, we examine local and national celebrated incidents. These results help to document the importance of such cases in the construction of social problems.

The Importance of Drugs as Incident and Policy Stories

Nearly 75 percent of the crime stories presented were specific incident stories ($N = 1,982$). A law violation is noted, and the reporter discusses who was involved and what occurred. Table 8.1 lists the 12 types of crime most frequently cited in print and in electronic news media. At least one of these 12 offenses was presented in 70 percent of all the crime incident stories. As in other content studies, these results show that serious violent crimes are presented frequently (Chermak 1995; Ericson et al. 1991; Graber 1980).

Table 8.1   The 12 Crimes Most Frequently Presented in Print and Electronic Media[a]

	Lead Crime	Crimes Combined	Newspaper Results[b]	Television Results[c]
Murder	28.1%	24.6%	28.3%	27.3%
Drugs	11.1	9.4	11.8	8.2
Rape	4.7	5.0	3.7	8.5
Fraud	3.8	3.7	4.0	2.8
Assault	3.7	3.5	3.7	3.6
Robbery	3.5	4.4	3.8	2.3
Shooting[c]	3.0	2.2	2.5	4.6
Burglary	2.4	2.6	2.6	1.5
Kidnapping	2.2	2.2	1.9	3.4
Extortion	2.2	2.6	2.5	.8
Manslaughter	2.1	1.8	2.3	1.5
Larceny	2.1	2.0	2.4	1.0
	$N = 1,890$	$N = 3,712$	$N = 1,502$	$N = 388$

[a]We coded up to three crimes to document the crimes that news media present as most significant. If more than three crimes were mentioned, we coded the first three crimes presented in a story, using order of presentation as our best indicator of significance. The first column in table 8.1 presents the results of the first crime mentioned in a specific incident story. The second column in table 8.1 presents multiple crime results combined into a single category.
[b]According to presentation of the lead crime.
[c]Not specific as to charges filed.

Drug crimes were the subject of the second most frequently cited incident story, accounting for over 11 percent of the stories. Approximately 12 percent of the incident stories in newspapers and over 8 percent of the incident stories in television news focused on drug crimes. These results differ significantly from the findings of research conducted before 1980. Graber (1980:39) found that drug offenses were the tenth most frequently cited crime in the *Chicago Tribune*; they represented less than 1 percent of the total number of offenses when examined as a single-topic category and less than 2 percent when studied as a three-topic category (1980:22). Drugs also were important in policy stories: Changes in the criminal law, usually consisting of proposed sentencing modifications, accounted for nearly 30 percent of the 138 policy stories presented. Drugs were the topic of the second most frequently presented policy story (approximately 16 percent). These results support the conclusion that drugs become more newsworthy in 1990, and presented officials with a social problem of strong public interest (see Jerin and Fields 1995).

The activities of the reporters observed and interviewed here are consistent with these content findings. Early in our observations of the *Midwest Tribune*, for example, we shadowed a reporter recently assigned to the police beat. One of the first steps in his daily news production routine was to peruse the police blotter to select potential stories. He had unrestricted access to these reports, but the pile was more than one inch thick. When we asked him what he was looking for in these reports, he emphasized that violence, crimes with young victims, and drug crimes received priority because they had the potential to win a significant amount of news space. Drugs, he explained, had the potential to evolve into an important news story, especially when large amounts of drugs or cash were confiscated. He ignored most other crimes because they rarely had the potential to be newsworthy.

On the basis of our observations of the *Tribune*, court reporters also considered drug crimes newsworthy and adjusted their newsgathering routines to increase exposure to known drug offenses. As in the news selection techniques used on the police beat, reporters relied on court documents such as motion papers, court calendars, and appellate decisions. Court reporters also established access to returned search warrants to search for drug news. These documents included a detailed inventory of the evidence seized by police officers after the execution of a warrant. Court reporters invested time to peruse these documents because of the potential for payoff in the form of a front-page story.

Reporters learned the news value of specific types of crime by interacting with their superiors. These interactions helped reporters to develop and internalize an understanding of the crimes that should receive attention in their daily work routines. Reporters contacted their superiors early in the day to discuss story selection options. As they developed their stories, they frequently consulted the editors for suggestions on story frames and contacts with sources. These editors then reviewed stories before publication; frequently they changed the structure of a story or altered the presentation. This finding is consistent with that of others who have emphasized that the hierarchical structure of the newsroom has an important effect on news content (Benedict 1992; Ericson et al. 1987).

Similarly, the managing editor of the Midwest Nightly played a particularly important role in determining the stories to be included in the evening's broadcast. His first task every morning was to generate a list of story ideas. Later in the day, the news director, producers, assignment editors, and reporters attended an editorial meeting to decide which of the stories selected by the managing editor would be produced for the evening broadcast. Moreover, he had already made the initial contacts for the potential lead stories, and told reporters when specific sources would be available for an interview.

Sources Cited in Crime and Drug Stories

Table 8.2 presents the sources cited in specific crime incident stories.[3] Police and court officials account for over 50 percent of the source attributions in all such stories.[4] These results are consistent with other research examining the presentation of crime (Chermak 1995; Sherizen 1978), specific crime topics (Best 1990; Johnson 1995), and other news topics (Sigal 1973).

Our ethnographic results suggest that news organizations rely on police and court officials primarily because this method is most efficient for the organization. Criminal justice organizations provide reporters with access to organizational documents, and supply accommodating sources. The reliance on these sources increased the ability of the *Tribune* and Nightly to fulfill daily crime story quotas.[5] Newspapers utilize decentralized police and court beats to produce crime stories, and allow reporters to interact with official sources. Police beat reporters from the *Tribune* rarely left police headquarters, where they had access to blotter reports, arrest logs, and public relations personnel. Similarly, the court beat was in the courthouse, where reporters had access to various court documents and members of the courtroom workgroup. In general, television stations do not have enough employees to permanently assign reporters to police headquarters or the courthouse, although television reporters speak with these sources by telephone.

Table 8.2 Sources Used in Specific Incident Stories

Sources	All Crimes	Murder	Drugs	Rape	Fraud	Assault	Robbery	Shooting	Burglary	Kidnapping	Extortion	Manslaughter	Larceny
Police	27.7%	29.1%	26.3%	35.6%	20.7%	54.8%	44.3%	58.9%	50.0%	40.9%	11.7%	13.2%	33.8%
Court	22.9	22.6	31.6	26.0	36.2	14.4	17.9	1.4	12.5	9.1	41.6	28.3	26.5
Defendant[a]	9.5	12.5	8.8	11.0	13.8	4.8	2.1	2.8	5.6	7.6	11.7	13.2	1.5
Victim[b]	8.3	6.5	1.0	11.7	6.0	8.7	11.5	12.3	12.5	13.7	5.2	9.4	16.2
Politician	3.8	1.9	6.4	.0	3.4	1.0	2.1	1.4	2.8	.0	3.9	1.9	2.9
Witness	3.7	4.8	2.7	4.8	2.6	2.9	3.6	5.5	1.4	1.5	2.6	9.4	1.5
Citizen	3.4	3.5	1.3	1.4	3.4	1.9	2.9	2.7	1.4	1.5	2.6	3.8	4.4
Documents	3.4	3.1	5.7	2.7	6.0	1.0	2.1	.0	1.4	1.5	3.9	3.8	2.9
Media	2.0	1.3	1.3	1.4	1.7	.0	1.4	.0	.0	6.1	2.6	7.5	1.5
Experts	2.0	1.7	.7	.0	.9	.0	.7	.0	.0	1.5	.0	.0	.0
Corrections	.8	.9	.0	.7	.0	1.9	1.4	.0	.0	1.5	.0	.0	.0
Other[c]	5.3	4.3	.7	.7	.0	1.0	2.1	4.1	4.2	3.0	.0	3.8	.0
Not Specific[d]	7.0	7.1	10.8	3.4	5.2	5.8	7.9	8.2	4.2	9.1	9.1	5.7	7.4
	N=5,038	N=776	N=297	N=146	N=116	N=140	N=140	N=73	N=72	N=66	N=77	N=53	N=68

N = Number of sources that commented on the crime incident.

[a]Category includes attributions to defendants and acquaintances of defendants.

[b]Category includes attributions to victims and acquaintances of victims.

[c]Includes attributions to school and church officials.

[d]Coded as not specific when attribution was "sources say," "officials say," or "authorities say."

Reporters supplemented the information provided in official reports with two or three contacts with police or court personnel; these individuals were presented to the public as authorities on an incident. Police reporters had frequent contact with a departmental spokesperson; court beat reporters relied primarily on attorneys from the prosecutor's office. These representatives were willing to provide information and answer questions, thus contributing to the completion of a story.

A day we spent with a police beat reporter illustrates how reliance on police sources increases efficiency of news production. We shadowed "Carl Sanders" on a day when the other police beat reporter called in sick. Although Sanders was annoyed by his partner's absence, he easily produced three crime stories because of his access to police sources and documents. After making his morning calls to sources that might provide breaking news (e.g., police districts, suburban departments, airport security), he examined the blotter reports and asked the departmental spokesperson for reports about four crime incidents: an assault in which the victim's skull was fractured, the robbery of an elderly man, the robbery of a teacher, and the burglary of a county administrative building. We met with the spokesperson, who provided Sanders with the reports for the assault and the burglary, but he also mentioned a shooting that had just occurred. Sanders produced the stories on the assault and the burglary as "local briefs," using verbatim the facts provided in the police reports. In addition, he was able to interview a sergeant and a detective by telephone to ask about the shooting. He tried to contact the victim and the victim's family, but they were unavailable for comment. Sanders produced a third story, about 12 column inches long, from the report and the information provided from the two police sources.

Access to police and court sources and documents increases news efficiency, but this reliance allows sources to protect themselves or to provide information to reporters in a way that benefits themselves. For example, reporters had only limited access to organizational documents. Police reporters did not know whether the blotter reports provided to them included every crime incident, but they did know that only partial information about an incident was included in the reports made available. From the name, age, sex, and type of crime included in these summary reports, reporters determined whether an incident had news potential. They had to request the complete report from an organizational representative, who then decided whether it would be released. Court reporters had unimpeded access to court hearings, but could report only what resulted from informal decision-making processes such as plea negotiations. Some sources refused to cooperate with news personnel. When we interviewed a news director from a television station in a large city he commented, "Sometimes [sources are willing to cooperate], sometimes they're not. It depends what their interests are in a particular story. There are many instances where the police cooperate with us so they get a story out."

Reporters rarely questioned the veracity of the information provided by officials and did not criticize the activities of the source organization. They were more concerned about keeping access to sources and organizational documents than about the reliability of information provided by officials. Loss of access to information affected not only the reporters' decision-making processes but also reporter-editor relationships, decisions about story assignments, and the images presented to the public.

Reporters' concern that sources might obstruct the flow of information was not unfounded. One reporter we interviewed had recently completed an investigative reporting series that criticized a local police department. After the stories were aired, he was denied access to organizational documents and had difficulty finding a police representative who would provide comment on camera. His investigative series also damaged the relationship of this police department with other persons employed by the same news organization.

Table 8.2 also presents the sources cited in the large number of typical drug stories. The reliance on police and court sources in drug stories is greater than in all other types of crime story, accounting for nearly 58 percent of the information. This heavy use of police and court sources reflects how official sources fulfill organizational needs in the construction of crime news.

Moreover, the fact that drugs are "victimless" crimes narrows the range of sources and perspectives provided in drug stories. When reporters construct crime stories involving victims, they frequently attempt to contact victims or family members for an emotional quotation. This emotion is sometimes directed at officials because of their handling of a case. Reporters rarely have access to victims in drug stories; victims accounted for only 1 percent of the source attributions. Defendants, who could provide alternative perspectives on drug incidents, are difficult to contact; reporters rarely considered them an important source.

Other sources are excluded from drug stories because they cannot meet the immediate needs of story production or provide responses consistent with expected frames. For example, experts such as criminologists and sociologists are rarely cited in crime stories; they accounted for only 2 percent of the source attributions in all crime stories and were cited even less frequently in drug stories (see table 8.2). Reporters are not likely to have easy access to such sources, and it is unlikely that these sources would state the information in a way that is consistent with the format needs of the news organization.

Politicians are not generally considered standard sources for comment on specific incidents. They accounted for only 3.8 percent of the sources cited when the sources from all crime stories were considered, and were involved even less when almost all of the specific crime categories were examined. These sources are rarely used because their involvement is beyond reporters' daily routines. Politicians, however, accounted for 6.4 percent of the source attributions in drug crimes in early 1990; this, in turn, encouraged politicians to make themselves available for routine coverage of drug incidents.

In several instances, when we observed activities at the *Tribune* and Nightly, politicians used an event such as an arrest or a trial to comment on the effectiveness of current drug policy. Some of these incidents received enormous amounts of attention (see "Sources Used in Celebrated Crime Stories"). Moreover, politicians used isolated incidents as opportunities to publicize policy efforts. When several individuals were arrested for selling drugs, the mayor held a press conference to discuss the incident and link the event to drug crackdown initiatives.

Table 8.3 displays the results of the sources cited in all types and specific types of policy story. Although politicians are rarely used as authorities in specific incident stories, they are the most frequent source cited in all types of policy story combined and in most individual categories. For example, politicians accounted for 26.6 percent of the source attributions in all policy stories, 45.9 percent in death penalty stories, 37.5 percent in stories about changes in the criminal law, and 20.3 percent in drug policy stories.

The media use political, police, or court officials to evaluate the quality of current responses to crime and to recommend specific changes in policy. Nearly 60 percent of the attributions in all types of policy story were sources serving in some official capacity. The explanation for such reliance—consistent with the organizational explanation for the news production of specific incident stories—is that they are available and willing to participate as news sources. Moreover, these sources involve themselves in the production of policy news stories because of the possibility of generating support for their own position. These sources promote specific policy issues by requesting coverage, and then frame what is discussed by participating as news sources.

To further illustrate officials' involvement in news construction, we examined the specific types of police and court sources used in incident and policy stories about crime and drugs. We expected that the upper echelons of the police hierarchy would take an active role in defining what was important about crime, drugs, and crime policy. In addition, we thought that the political members of the courtroom workgroup (prosecutors and judges) would take a more active role in policy news

Table 8.3 Sources Used in Policy Stories

Sources	All Policy Stories	Criminal Law Changes	Drugs	Victim	Death Penalty	Police	Guns	Courts	Corrections	Other
Police	11.4%	5.1%	7.8%	16.7%	5.4%	42.1%	36.4%	.0%	.0%	4.8%
Court	24.9	32.3	28.1	23.3	13.5	7.9	.0	52.9	23.5	23.8
Defendant[a]	3.6	1.0	1.6	.0	.0	.0	.0	23.5	.0	4.8
Victim[b]	6.6	4.0	.0	23.3	10.8	5.3	.0	.0	.0	23.8
Politician	26.6	33.3	20.3	16.7	45.9	18.4	54.5	5.9	11.8	23.8
Witness	.0	.0	.0	.0	.0	.0	.0	.0	.0	.0
Citizen	3.3	2.0	.0	.0	5.4	5.3	.0	.0	17.6	9.5
Documents	4.8	4.0	7.8	10.0	.0	.0	.0	11.8	.0	9.5
Media	1.5	1.0	.0	.0	8.1	2.6	.0	.0	.0	.0
Experts	3.3	5.0	7.8	.0	2.7	.0	.0	.0	.0	.0
Corrections	3.0	2.0	1.6	.0	5.4	.0	.0	.0	29.4	.0
Other[c]	3.6	1.0	7.8	3.3	2.7	2.6	9.1	.0	11.8	.0
Not Specific[d]	7.5	9.1	9.4	6.7	.0	15.8	.0	5.9	5.9	.0
	N=334	N=99	N=64	N=30	N=37	N=38	N=11	N=17	N=17	N=21

N = Number of sources

[a]Category includes attributions to defendants and acquaintances of defendants.

[b]Category includes attributions to victims and acquaintances of victims.

[c]Includes attributions to school and church officials.

[d]Coded as not specific when attribution was "sources say," "officials say," or "authorities say."

production than would other court sources. The results support both expectations.

When police sources are cited, the dominance of police chiefs, captains, and lieutenants is persuasive. Members of the command staff account for most of the information provided by police organizations; they are cited in at least 20 percent of the police attributions in all types of crime incident story. The upper levels of the police hierarchy accounted for 20.6 percent of the source attributions in drug incident stories. Police chiefs accounted for more than 13 percent of the source attributions in policy stories. We discussed source interactions with a television reporter, who emphasized his reliance on police officials in power:

> I get most of my information by talking with people in charge. Every once in a while, I get a call from somebody who is not of officer rank, with a "tip." I then call the people in charge. They ask, "Where did you get that information?" Primarily the routine daily calls go to those in charge.

The highest ranks of the police involve themselves in the news production process to increase their control of the images of police departments. The bureaucratic structure of police organizations guarantees that only a limited number of sources—individuals with policy-making power—will have the most access to internal organizational information and can choose the information that is funneled to media personnel.

The division of labor in police organizations also "fosters unique accounting strategies" (Cavender, Jurik, and Cohen 1993:153). Information, reports, and statistical data about departments typically are released through spokespersons. These public relations employees, trained by the department in image building, work closely with other officials to represent the department's position favorably; they nurture their relationship with reporters to ensure that this image is presented prominently. *Tribune* police reporters interacted daily with the spokesperson in his office, and *Nightly* reporters contacted him by telephone when they needed sound bites. The spokesperson was willing to be questioned by reporters to influence the type of coverage presented about the police department.

Prosecutors accounted for at least 25 percent of the court source attributions across all categories of incident crime. When all crime stories were examined, prosecutors accounted for 32.6 percent of the court source attributions, defense attorneys for 24.7 percent, and judges for 12.9 percent. Similarly, prosecutors and judges dominate court source attributions in policy stories. Judges accounted for more than 37 percent of the attributions to court sources in policy stories. This high percentage is impressive because judges are involved in the routine coverage of news only when they allow reporters to record courtroom comments. Judges were cited frequently in all types of policy stories, including more than 40 percent of the court source attributions in drug policy stories. (Most judges are elected officials, who can benefit from positive news coverage.) Prosecutors accounted for 34.1 percent of the remaining court attributions in drug policy stories, but defense attorneys for only 12.1 percent.

Sources Used in Celebrated Crime Stories

The findings on the types of sources presented in crime and drug stories indicate the possibility that officials use specific types of story to define the parameters of social problems. An additional method for examining sources' involvement in construction of social problems is to consider the authorities cited in celebrated drug cases. News space is not a luxury; stories thought to be most attractive to news consumers receive disproportionately large amounts of space. Because celebrated stories are rare events, compared with the traditional, routine "who, what, and where" crime story, the news organization expends valuable resources to cover all angles of these stories and constantly brings news consumers up to date. Because of the space and significance given to celebrated crime stories, they are also important for sources interested in generating public support for policy initiatives. We examine sources' involvement in celebrated cases using two lines of inquiry. First we discuss several local celebrated cases, combining the content and the observational results. Then we examine sources' involvement in two national celebrated cases.

While examining the media content and making observations, we were exposed to several celebrated local cases linked to the heightened interest in drugs. These local events received great amounts of space, were presented on the front page, often with a banner headline, and were revisited constantly as they progressed through the criminal justice system. Moreover, media personnel often were able to link these local scandals to a national drug story, such as a policy proposal or the arrest of a national figure. For example, a story about a federal investigation that resulted in the arrests of five Buffalo police officers was juxtaposed with a story about President Bush's involvement in a Latin American drug summit (Herbeck 1990).

One way to study sources' involvement in the presentation of local celebrated cases is to examine the officials cited in different-sized stories. The size of a story (in column inches or in amount of time) can be used as a proxy for its importance. These data are rather crude, but they indicate that routine sources, such as police and court officials, were presented disproportionately in stories of all sizes. Moreover, these quantitative results show that as the size of a story increased, so did the involvement of high-ranking police officials and politicians.

We suspect that the percentage of source attributions to these officials significantly underrepresents the officials' involvement in construction of social problems. One limitation of examining sources' involvement in quantitative terms is that each attribution to a source is given equal value. This methodology overlooks the possibility that one source may influence the discourse of others or that an official contributes to the framing of social problems by leaking information to officials or other sources. This limitation can be addressed, however, by relying on other methodologies.

Three types of drug story received large amounts of space in the media organizations we examined: the arrest of a large number of individuals involved in a single incident, an innocent victim caught in the crossfire of a drug turf war, and the arrest or trial of a high-profile defendant such as a police officer. Officials linked these celebrated events to an issue, and framed them as supporting their drug policy position or used them to request additional funding. Local celebrated events were explained within a similar framework, regardless of the medium or the media organization considered.

Officials used the first two types of local celebrated incident to advocate a law-and-order response to drugs; they cited them as illustrating the need for additional resources to crack down on drug dealers or as examples of successful efforts. In agreement with the national response to the drug problem, local politicians across the country declared their own localized version of a war on drugs. When a significant arrest occurred or when a bystander was killed, the incident provided an opportunity to seek support for a policy position or to advocate the creation of a task force or special unit.

An example from our observations at the *Tribune* illustrates how politicians used their access to reporters and criminal justice personnel as an opportunity to comment on drug policy. A spokesperson from a suburban police department contacted one of the reporters about a press conference that had been called to announce a major drug bust. A man had been stopped for speeding, but the officer making the stop found a box of cash and a gun in the back seat, and (upon further investigation), a large amount of drugs in the trunk. At the press conference, attended by the mayor and the police chief, the drugs, gun, and cash were displayed for photographers and television news crews. The case was discussed in detail by several police representatives, but the story was always framed within the suburb's efforts to crack down on drugs. The mayor was quoted several times in the story.

In the third and last type of local celebrated event, political and criminal justice officials use their status as standard sources to respond to a scandal (see Cavender et al. 1993). In another incident that occurred during our observations at the *Tribune*, when we arrived at the court beat early one morning, we were told that 30 police officers had been arrested and were being arraigned on drug and gambling charges. At the federal courthouse, we encountered about 25 reporters and 10 videographers in the hallway outside the courtroom, waiting for people to exit. We spent the day with one of several *Tribune* reporters who were assigned to attend the arraignments and two press conferences about this case.

Officials speaking at both press conferences focused on positive attributes of the police department, reassuring the public that the department's position in the community's social control structure was not fundamentally flawed. At the first conference the mayor stated his support for the department and focused on its accomplishments. He also stressed his disdain for the behavior of these officers.

The second news conference was held at the offices of the FBI. Comments were made by the agent in charge of the investigation, the police chief, the director of public safety, and a U.S. attorney. In this second news conference, the police chief's initial comments framed how the newspaper and television organizations presented the incident to the public, and affected how other officials discussed it. In his opening statements, the chief stated that he no longer considered the arrested officers worthy of employment. He also claimed that they were not representative of the department. Most of the questions posed to the panel focused on his statement, allowing him to clarify his position and to discuss the department's efforts to respond to corruption. Moreover, the chief's initial comments provided the lead article in the next morning's newspaper.

The editorial staff coordinated the efforts of the reporters assigned to cover this case. Four stories detailed the investigation and how the combined efforts of the police department and the FBI resulted in the arrests. The primary minority voice presented was a union official; when asked to respond to the chief's statement, he reminded reporters that the officers had not yet been convicted.

Buffalo's police department responded similarly when five of their officers were arrested on drug charges. At the news conference announcing the arrests, a U.S. attorney said that the police commissioner requested the investigation. Moreover, the agent in charge of the sting operation was quoted as saying, "What we found was not a widespread drug problem in the department, but a very, very serious problem involving a fairly small group of officers" (Herbeck 1990).

To conclude this discussion, we present the content results from two national events. Each case is unique, but the results illustrate how relationships between officials and reporters, and access to the "symbolic landscape," provided opportunities to demonize drug use and gain policy support (see Kraska 1993). One case was used to advocate a crackdown on drug crimes; the other illustrates efforts to respond to scandal on the national level.

In the first case, General Manuel Noriega was indicted for federal drug trafficking charges in February 1988, two months after George Bush began his presidency. On December 19, 1989, when almost two years of political and military pressure had failed to remove Noriega from power, the United States invaded Panama and legitimized the invasion by claiming that it was needed to bring Noriega to trial. Noriega evaded capture for 10 days by seeking refuge in the Vatican embassy, but eventually surrendered and was brought to the United States on January 4, 1990.

The second celebrated case involved Marion Barry. In his third term as mayor of Washington, DC, Barry was arrested and indicted by a federal grand jury on 11 drug and 3 perjury charges. The arrest was made in the Vista Hotel on January 18, 1990 as the result of a drug sting operation set up by federal drug agents. The evidence implicating Barry included videotape of Barry smoking crack from a crack pipe. Barry's case received news attention throughout the sample period, including stories about his arrest, the pretrial motions, and the prosecution witnesses' opening statements and testimony.

Twenty-eight stories about Noriega and 37 stories about Barry fell on the sampled content days, accounting for nearly 30 percent of the drug stories presented. Moreover, the stories about these two cases were generally larger than the other crime and drug stories presented. The stories about Noriega's case averaged over 16 column inches and the stories about Barry averaged over 15 column inches, whereas all stories of specific incidents averaged just over 12 column inches and all other drug stories averaged under 12 column inches.

The incident and defendant sources cited in the stories about these two celebrated cases are presented in table 8.4. These findings differ dramatically from those on the sources cited in routine crime stories: For example, political sources accounted for 16 percent of the source incident information and 15 percent of the defendant information in the Noriega stories. The presentation of Noriega's case in the news was unique in that it involved high-ranking officials, including President Bush, because of the events leading up to Noriega's arrest. Administration officials, Justice Department spokespersons, State Department officials, White House Press Secretary Marlin Fitzwater, senators, and President Bush were among the politicians quoted in the stories about Noriega that framed the discourse about his case.

These sources used Noriega's arrest to justify current drug policy and to win public approval for a law-and-order response to drug enforcement. In August and September 1989, four months before Noriega's arrest, President Bush had made drugs his primary domestic

Table 8.4 Sources Cited in Celebrated Crime Stories

| Sources | High-Profile | | | |
| | Noriega | | Barry | |
	Incident	Defendant	Incident	Defendant
Police	1.1	.0	6.5	2.0
Court	56.4	35.0	19.4	10.0
Defendant[a]	3.2	5.0	33.3	48.0
Victim[b]	.0	.0	.0	.0
Politician	16.0	15.0	1.1	6.0
Witness/Jurors	.0	.5	5.4	4.0
Citizen	1.1	20.0	9.7	6.0
Documents	1.1	.0	2.2	4.0
Media	1.1	.0	2.2	6.0
Experts	2.1	5.0	1.1	6.0
Corrections	.0	.0	.0	.0
Other[c]	1.1	5.0	.0	.0
Not Specific[d]	13.8	10.0	19.4	6.0
	$N=94$	$N=20$	$N=93$	$N=50$

N = Number of sources
[a]Category includes attributions to defendants and acquaintances of defendants.
[b]Category includes attributions to victims and acquaintances of victims.
[c]Includes attributions to school and church officials.
[d]Coded as not specific when attribution was "sources say," "officials say," or "authorities say."

policy issue and had announced his program to fight them. The President then used the capture of Noriega to generate public support; he reacted immediately to Noriega's surrender and linked his arrest to the need to crack down on drug dealers: "His apprehension and return to the United States should send a clear signal that the United States is serious in its determination that those charged with promoting the distribution of drugs cannot escape the scrutiny of justice" (Rosenthal 1990:A1). Senator Dole expressed similar sentiments: "Noriega's arrest was good news for our war on drugs" (p. Al). Two months after Noriega's arrest, as approval ratings for President Bush soared, administration officials declared that the U.S. was succeeding in the war on drugs, and cited the arrest as evidence ("U.S. Cites Progress" 1990).

The source results for the Barry stories are very different. Although Barry's case involved a prosecutor with political motivations and high-profile defense attorneys who knew how to benefit from news coverage, Barry himself was the most frequently cited source in stories about his case.[6] One-third of the source incident attributions and nearly one-half of the defendant attributions were direct quotes from Barry or his acquaintances. Barry alone accounted for 25.8 percent of the total source incident attributions about his case.

We believe that Barry was used frequently as a news source for two reasons. First, he had enormous media savvy, which he had developed as a politician in a city where competition for news space is fierce. Barry used his access to the news media, orchestrating news events after his arrest to influence public opinion about his case. He apologized for his actions to the city's children, voluntarily entered drug treatment, announced that he had become a born-again Christian, lashed out at the FBI for endangering his life by allowing him to smoke crack, and reacted to the prosecution's case on the courthouse steps. Second, it could be argued that these two celebrated cases were in direct competition for the daily headlines, and clearly the Noriega case provided a better opportunity for generating support for national drug control policy. The Barry case was less politically appealing and created considerable risk for officials identified with his arrest. Questions of entrapment and racism were important themes in the news about his case.

Our research has identified two complementary processes involved in the representation of social problems in the news media. We will show how these processes can be explained by integrating the bureaucratic perspective of news production with the structuralist perspective. We conclude by elaborating on this integrated theoretical perspective and applying it to the presentation of drugs by the media.

Most crime news is produced through a process that satisfies organizations' bureaucratic goals. Media organizations present several crime stories daily: According to our research, print media present nine crime stories a day, on average, and electronic media four crime stories per day. The heavy demand for crime stories, coupled with the unpredictability of news, generates the need to simplify news production (Tuchman 1978). Efficiency is increased by placing reporters near sources, thus increasing their exposure to documents and to individuals willing to impart their official knowledge of crime. The research results presented here show that police and court sources are cited frequently in all types of crime, drug, and policy stories.

The reliance on these sources affects how crime, and criminal justice organizations, are presented in the news. Sources are willing to expose their organizations to media scrutiny in exchange for the opportunity to influence public opinion by framing issues within a narrow range of discourse. As sources they are given an accepted public forum to define what is important about crime policy. For example, the structured hierarchy of police organizations limits outsiders' access to organizational information and increases the organization's control over the dissemination of information. Police organizations use the upper echelons of the department in the news production process to ensure that the images provided are consistent with the department's goals. Reporters, however, do not blindly accept what the organizations say, but use the information selectively. The resulting images are the product of the interplay between reporters and officials.

The relationship that evolves from source organizations' structured involvement in the routine coverage of news is beneficial to those organizations because it provides strategic access to the media; it allows them to determine and support the traditional frames of events. The organizational features that produce crime stories, including the decentralized beat structure, the developed routines, and the reliance on official sources, all structure news media reporting so as to legitimize the system. This research has illustrated several important characteristics of media constructionism which ensure that the representation of crime supports the status quo.

First, media personnel are not likely to criticize the activities of the source organization because they treat as factual the information provided by official sources (see Fishman 1980). Moreover, the officials' ability to deny access or withhold information from reporters significantly shapes the reporters' decision-making process. Reporters are unlikely to criticize official sources because they fear losing access to information. Helen Benedict's (1992:10) study examining how the media cover sex crimes illustrates how "the habitual hurry and pressure under which reporters work render them particularly susceptible to manipulation." This manipulation is most likely to occur when public and political interest in a problem area is substantial, such as when specific issues or types of crime attract heightened media attention. In such cases, sources have the opportunity to expand the organization's power and to reaffirm their position as agents of social control. Celebrated cases provide officials with opportunities to bring attention to a social problem and to recommend policy initiatives.

Second, the reliance on these officials causes events to be framed in ways that reaffirm standard approaches to crime. Reporters are not likely to question officials' "bureaucratic accounts" because sources provide information consistent with their expectations (Fishman 1980; Gitlin 1980). By interacting with other reporters and with supervisors, reporters learn the established frames that help to legitimize accepted practices. These frames are reinforced by the way stories are reconstructed, where stories are placed, and how much attention is given to a specific crime incident. Moreover, even though officials or a specific individual may not receive attribution in every story about an issue they can still affect its presentation because others are forced to respond to the way officials expect issues to be framed.

Third, news organizations are structured so as to ensure exposure to a limited range of viewpoints. Media routines for the production of crime stories expose reporters primarily to high-ranking political and criminal justice officials. These sources are particularly highly motivated to manage the portrayal of crime news. For example, high-ranking members of the police hierarchy—either the police chief or the public relations spokesperson—dominated the representation of the police in the news. Other sources, such as experts, victims, and defendants, were rarely contacted by reporters because of their inaccessibility and their inability to provide information within expected frames. Also, experts were rarely cited in celebrated cases. Although both the Noriega and the Barry case presented legal, moral, and political issues of interest to experts, most of the information cited in these stories was provided by politically affiliated sources.

Politicians, police chiefs, prosecutors, and judges participate as news sources when new or recurring social problems arise, because they receive attention and the opportunity to promote themselves or the institution they represent. These powerful sources are expected to comment on important social problems because of their position in an organization and in society: They are "recognized socially to be in a position to know" (Ericson et al. 1989:4). Tittle (1994:50) discussed how [elites] almost always find it necessary to create some sense in others that the elites deserve to be in powerful positions because they do, or have done, something good for the collectivity."

Moreover, a source's initial involvement in a celebrated case encourages continued involvement by others. The public, noticing the amount of space given to celebrated events, assumes that the issue and the person commenting on the issue are important. News consumers develop psychological relationships with these sources, increasing the sources' credibility and the expectation that they should continue to provide comment about the same and similar events (Reese, Grant, and Danielian 1994). The media access accorded to officials and the expectation of continued involvement allow officials to determine the scope of the debate and ultimately the interpretation and control of the topic (see Hall et al. 1978). Additional and contradictory stories about a topic might be presented; they will be framed according to what has been established, however, and the privileged access enjoyed by officials gives them an opportunity to respond.

Media coverage of drug cases illustrates clearly how the media routines that result from organizational needs allow politicians and law enforcement officials to accomplish system-legitimizing goals. Drugs are a well-established social problem; according to Best (1990:13), "most well-established social problems are owned by well-established claims-makers."

Drug abuse is a social problem that rises and falls in political priority. When it is popular, sources realize the potential to obtain organizational or individual benefits by defining themselves as authorities on the issue. Drugs historically have been used to further law-and-order approaches to crime. In the 1980s, politicians, including Presidents Reagan and Bush, paid an enormous amount of attention to drugs and defined the drug crisis in a particular way (Beckett 1994, 1995; Brownstein 1995; Kappeler et al. 1996; Reinarman and Levine 1995). Drugs have been framed as a criminal justice problem, with the implication that a law enforcement solution is the most effective.

Police and court officials accounted for a disproportionate amount of the information provided in incident and policy stories about drugs. The reports' reliance on these sources for drug stories is consistent with their frequent involvement in all types of crime story. In addition, politicians were involved in the social construction of this problem: We found that political officials increased their involvement in stories about drug crimes in general, in stories that received a large amount of space, and in stories about the celebrated arrest of Manuel Noriega.

The reliance on these news sources, coupled with the sources' understanding of standard media operating procedures, provided them with opportunities to determine how the drug issue would be framed for public consumption. Kappeler et al. (1996:9) discuss how drug wars exemplify the way crime myths are created, supported, and maintained. Drugs are an easy political target and offer an opportunity for bureaucratic expansion. Thus the crisis response that typically accompanies the heightened attention to the issue can be easily predicted. Politicians pander to popular fear, frame the issue in the "most unyielding terms," and call for more law and more order—the safest political response (Kappeler et al. 1996:167). The message conveyed is the need for another war on drugs, with a crackdown on buyers and sellers regardless of the amount involved. Officials use dramatic examples, such as random acts of drug violence, to typify the problem and to establish consistency in the preferred response. Moreover, when a high-profile event occurs, officials can use it to reaffirm the accepted frames.

Alternative approaches such as drug treatment or drug education programs are much less likely to be presented and supported in the news, in the current political environment. Although a cadre of law enforcement officials, politicians, and economists have argued in support of drug legalization, this has not been presented as a viable alternative in the news media. Legalization was discussed in approximately 30 percent of the drug policy stories presented during the sample period. Legalization, however, was presented only in contrast to the preferred criminal justice response. The great majority of stories, including the celebrated events, were framed in language consistent with a need for law enforcement crackdowns, increased sentences, and zero toler-ance.

The particularly important point about the ideological power of the news media is that these frames helped to support and reproduce elite interests. For example, the heightened attention resulted in policy initi-atives. Public opinion about the seriousness of the problem peaked in 1990, at about the time when we conducted the content analysis. In 1985 a Gallup Poll survey showed that only 2 percent of respondents men-tioned drug abuse as the single most important problem facing the coun-try. In 1990, 38 percent of the respondents cited it as the leading problem (Gallup 1990). Such attention provides the opportunity to implement policy that addresses the problem in response to the way it was framed in the news media.

The sources involved in defining the drug crisis have made sub-stantial financial and political gains. For example, the federal drug bud-get has quintupled since 1981 (Gardiner and McKinney 1991). According to a national report on drug statistics, the federal drug control budget was nearly 43 dollars per capita in 1991; in 1981 it had been less than 7 dollars. Over half of the available money ($28.24 per capita) was used for law enforcement; the rest was distributed between treat-ment ($6.91), prevention ($5.85), and research ($1.78) (U.S. Depart-ment of Justice 1992:128).

Moreover, treating drugs strictly as a problem of the criminal jus-tice system, and advocating a response involving more arrests and longer sentences, had disproportionate effects on different social and racial groups. Amy Binder (1993:755) describes how the representation of events by the media is ideological—when officials in powerful institu-tional positions support frames that reinforce unequal social relations. According to research, drug wars have been designed to affect certain groups disproportionately (Currie 1993; Kappeler et al. 1996: Tonry 1995). Reinarman and Levine (1995:147), in examining crack cocaine, illustrate vividly how "drug scares typically link a scapegoated drug to a troubling subordinate group—working-class immigrants, racial, or eth-nic minorities, or rebellious youth." They conclude: "Crack was a god-send to the Right. They used it and the drug issue as an ideological fig leaf to place over the unsightly urban ills that had increased markedly under Reagan administration social and economic policies" (p. 170).

Our latest drug war was fought primarily in the inner cities, drug use was associated with the lower classes, and drug policy affected black communities disproportionately (Currie 1993; Tonry 1995). Research-ers argue that the policy makers who designed our approach to drugs knew it would affect various groups differently. According to Michael Tonry (1995:123), "the War on Drugs and the set of harsh crime-control policies in which it was enmeshed were launched to achieve political, not policy, objectives, and it is the adoption for political purposes of policies with foreseeable disparate impacts, the use of disadvantaged black Americans as a means to the achievement of politicians' electoral ends, that must in the end be justified, and cannot." Officials attempted to justify the policy response to drugs, and to generate support for their position, by being involved in the social construction of the drug problem.

We conclude that news sources involve themselves in the news production process to further their own social control agendas. In our integrated theory of news production, we assume that the two processes identified are closely linked, and that the negotiations between reporters and sources determine what is presented about social problems in the news. Media organizations rely on official sources to fulfill daily production objectives. These routine stories are irrelevant in terms of their impact on public opinion, and the established news production process ensures that they rarely harm news sources. When public interest is focused on a specific social problem or a celebrated case that can be linked to a policy issue, high-ranking officials use their access to the news production process to frame social problems and to *increase the likelihood* that public opinion will coincide with their own beliefs. Other social problems might present different sources with opportunities to gain support and legitimacy.

Future research should examine how sources use specific types of stories to promote issue frames, how the relationship between reporter and source evolves by type of story, and whether this relationship varies by type of organization. With such knowledge we could comprehend more clearly the involvement of sources in the news production process and the social control functions of the news media.

Notes

[1] Medium-sized cities are those with 100,000 to 400,000 inhabitants and 5,000 to 50,000 index offenses per year; large cities are those with 400,000 to 800,000 inhabitants and 50,000 to 90,000 index offenses; extra-large cities have 800,000 to 1,500,000 inhabitants and register 90,000 to 150,000 index offenses.

[2] Each of the news organizations considered here has an interest in attracting a local audience; therefore this is a study of local media organizations. One would expect that the national officials' predominance is underestimated because local news presents only wire reports that contain comments from these officials.

[3] Nearly 60% of the stories contained fewer than five cited sources. When a story included a large number of sources, we collected data on as many as nine sources cited; as many as three sources providing comment on the incident, three on the defendant, and three on the victim. In this article we discuss findings on source incidents. Only information that was attributed directly to a source was coded. If more than three sources provided information, we coded the first, third, and fifth sources. We chose the sources at the beginning of stories because we thought

these sources represented those whom news organizations deemed the most important voices on a topic; we also wanted to capture as many of the voices cited in crime stories as possible.

4   These results are consistent across each news organization in the sample. Police and court sources accounted for 57% of the attributions in the *Albany Times Herald*, 56.1% in the *Buffalo News*, 53.6% in the *Cleveland Plain Dealer*, 48.1% in the *San Francisco Chronicle*, 48.7% in the *Dallas Times Herald*, and 48.3% in the *Detroit News*.

5   No specific amount of space is set aside for crime stories; events either increase or decrease the importance of crime. We argue that crime is an important news topic in general. The content results show that approximately 11% of all news stories were related to crime, the fourth most likely category to be presented. Production of these stories requires a substantial investment of organizational resources.

6   Although Mayor Barry was a politician at the time of his arrest, we coded his source results in the defendant category because of his role as a defendant.

References

Beckett, K. 1994. "Setting the Public Agenda: 'Street Crime' and Drug Use in American Politics." *Social Problems* 41:425–47.

_____. 1995. "Media Depictions of Drug Abuse: The Impact of Official Sources." *Research in Political Sociology* 7:161–82.

Benedict, H. 1992. *Virgin or Vamp: How the Press Covers Sex Crimes*. New York: Oxford University Press.

Berkowitz, D. 1987. "TV News Sources and News Channels: A Study in Agenda-Building." *Journalism Quarterly* 64:508–13.

Berkowitz, D. and D. W. Beach. 1993. "News Sources and News Context: The Effect of Routine News, Conflict, and Proximity." *Journalism Quarterly* 70:4–12.

Best, J. 1990. *Threatened Children: Rhetoric and Concern about Child-Victims*. Chicago: University of Chicago Press.

Binder, A. 1993. "Constructing Racial Rhetoric: Media Depictions of Harm in Heavy Metal and Rap Music." *American Sociological Review* 58:753–67.

Brown, J. K., C. R. Bybee, S. T. Wearden, and D. M. Straughan. 1987. "Invisible Power: Newspaper News Sources and the Limits of Diversity." *Journalism Quarterly* 64(2):45–54.

Brownstein, H. 1995. "The Media and the Construction of Random Drug Violence." Pp. 45–65 in *Cultural Criminology*, edited by J. Ferrell and C. R. Sanders. Boston: Northeastern University Press.

Cavender, G., N. C. Jurik, and A. K. Cohen. 1993. "The Baffling Case of the Smoking Gun: The Social Ecology of Political Accounts in the Iran-Contra Affair." *Social Problems* 40:152–66.

Chermak, S. M. 1995. *Victims in the News: Crime and the American News Media*. Boulder: Westview.

Chibnall, S. 1977. *Law and Order News*. London: Tavistock.

Currie, E. 1993. *Reckoning: Drugs, the Cities, and the American Future.* New York: Hill and Wang.

Edelman, M. 1964. *The Symbolic Uses of Politics.* Urbana: University of Illinois Press.

Ericson, R. V., P. M. Baranek, and J. B. L. Chan. 1987. *Visualizing Deviance: A Study of News Organization.* Toronto: University of Toronto Press.

_____. 1989. *Negotiating Control: A Study of News Sources.* Toronto: University of Toronto Press.

_____. 1991. *Representing Order: Crime, Law, and Justice in the News Media.* Toronto: University of Toronto Press.

Fishman, M. 1978. "Crime Waves as Ideology." *Social Problems* 25:531–43.

_____. 1980. *Manufacturing the News.* Austin: University of Texas Press.

Friedman, L. M. and R. V. Percival. 1981. *The Roots of Justice: Crime and Punishment in Alameda County, California 1870–1910.* Chapel Hill: University of North Carolina Press.

Gale Directory of Publications and Broadcast Media. 1990. New York: Gale Research.

Gallup, G. G. 1990. *The Gallup Poll Monthly,* No. 298. Princeton, NJ: Gallup.

Gamson, W., D. Croteau, W. Hoynes, and T. Sasson. 1992. "Media Images and the Social Construction of Reality." *Annual Review of Sociology* 18:373–93.

Gans, H. J. 1979. *Deciding What's News: A Study of CBS Evening News, Newsweek and Time.* New York: Pantheon.

Gardiner, G. S. and R. N. McKinney. 1991. "The Great American War on Drugs: Another Failure of Tough-Guy Management." *Journal of Drug Issues* 21:605–16.

Gitlin, T. 1980. *The Whole World Is Watching: Mass Media in the Making & Unmaking of the New Left.* Los Angeles: University of California Press.

Graber, D. 1980. *Crime News and the Public.* New York: Praeger.

Hall, S., C. Critcher, T. Jefferson, and B. Roberts. 1978. *Policing the Crisis.* London: Macmillan.

Herbeck, D. 1990. "Drug Probe Nets 5 City Officers: U.S. Undercover Investigation Yields Charges of Cocaine Dealing." *Buffalo News,* February 15, p. Al.

Herman, E. and N. Chomsky. 1988. *Manufacturing Consent: The Political Economy of the Mass Media.* New York: Pantheon.

Jenness, V. 1993. *Making It Work: The Prostitutes' Movement in Perspective.* New York: Aldine.

Jensen, E. L., J. Gerber, and G. M. Babcock. 1991. "The New War on Drugs: Grass Roots Movement or Political Construction?" *Journal of Drug Issues* 21:651–67.

Jerin, R. A. and C. B. Fields. 1995. "Murder and Mayhem in *USA Today*: A Quantitative Analysis of the National Reporting of States' News." Pp. 187–202 in *Media, Process and the Social Construction of Crime: Studies of Newsmaking Criminology,* edited by G. Barak. New York: Garland.

Johnson, J. M. 1995. "Horror Stories and the Construction of Child Abuse." pp. 17–31 in *Images of Issues: Typifying Contemporary Social Problems,* edited by J. Best. New York: Aldine.

Kappeler, V. E., M. Blumberg, and G. W. Potter. 1996. *The Mythology of Crime and Criminal Justice*. 2nd ed. Prospect Heights, IL: Waveland.

Kessel, J. H. 1975. *The Domestic Presidency: Decision-Making in the White House*. North Scituate, MA: Duxbury.

Kraska, P. B. 1993. "Militarizing the Drug War: A Sign of the Times." Pp. 159–206 in *Altered States of Mind: Critical Observations of the Drug War*, edited by P. B. Kraska. New York: Garland.

_____. 1994. "The Police and Military in the Post-Cold War Era: Streamlining the State's Use of Force Entities in the Drug War." *Police Forum* 4(1):1–8.

McCombs, M. E. and D. L. Shaw. 1991. "The Agenda Setting Function of Mass Media." Pp. 17–26 in *Agenda Setting: Readings on Media, Public Opinion, and Policy Making*, edited by D. L. Protess and M. McCombs. Hillsdale, NJ: Erlbaum.

Peyrot, M. 1984. "Cycles of Social Problem Development: The Case of Drug Abuse." *Sociological Quarterly* 25:83–96.

Reese, S. D., Grant, A., and Danielian. L. H. 1994. "The Structure of News Sources on Television. A Network Analysis of CBS News," "Nightline," "MacNeil-Lehrer," and "This Week with David Brinkley." *Journal of Communication*, 44(2):84–107.

Reinarman, C. and H. G. Levine. 1995. "The Crack Attack: America's Latest Drug Scare, 1986–1992." Pp. 147–90 in *Images of Issues: Typifying Contemporary Social Problems*, edited by J. Best. New York: Aldine.

Rosenthal, A. 1990. "Noriega Gives Himself Up to U.S. Military: Is Flown to Florida to Face Drug Charges." *New York Times*, January 4, p. Al.

Sacco, V. F. 1995. "Media Constructions of Crime." *The Annals of the American Academy of Political and Social Science*, 539:141–54.

Scheingold, S. A. 1984. *The Politics of Law and Order: Street Crime and Public Policy*. New York: Longman.

Schlesinger, P. and H. Tumber. 1994. *Reporting Crime: The Media Politics of Criminal Justice*. Oxford: Clarendon.

Sherizen, S. 1978. "Social Creation of Crime News: All the News Fitted to Print." Pp. 203–24 in *Deviance and Mass Media*, edited by C. Winick. Beverly Hills: Sage.

Sigal, L. V. 1973. *Reporters and Officials*. Lexington, MA: Heath.

Skogan, W. G. and M. G. Maxfield. 1981. *Coping with Crime: Individual and Neighborhood Reactions*. Beverly Hills: Sage.

Surette, R. 1989. "Media Trials." *Journal of Criminal Justice* 17:293–308.

Television and Cable Factbook. 1991. Washington, DC: Warren.

Tittle, C. R. 1994. "The Theoretical Bases for Inequality in Formal Social Control." Pp. 21–52 in *Inequality, Crime, & Social Control*, edited by G. Bridges and M. Myers. Boulder: Westview.

Tonry, M. 1995. *Malign Neglect: Race, Crime, and Punishment in America*. New York: Oxford University Press.

Tuchman, G. 1978. *Making News: A Study in the Construction of Reality*. New York: Free Press.

Tunnell, K. D. 1992. "Film at Eleven: Recent Developments in the Commodification of Crime." *Sociological Spectrum* 12:293–313.

"U.S. Cites Progress in Latin American Drug War." 1990. Reuters Wire Service, March 6.

U.S. Department of Justice. 1992. *Drugs, Crime, and the Justice System: A National Report from the Bureau of Justice Statistics.* Washington, DC: U.S. Government Printing Office.

Walker, S. 1989. *Sense and Nonsense about Crime: A Policy Guide.* 2nd ed. Pacific Grove, CA: Brooks/Cole.

9

The Social Construction of an Alcohol Problem
The Case of Mothers against Drunk Drivers and Social Control in the 1980s

Craig Reinarman

Social problems have careers that ebb and flow independent of the "objective" incidence of the behaviors thought to constitute them. This is nowhere more amply illustrated than in the history of alcohol issues. I offer here a description of the rise and impact of Mothers Against Drunk Drivers—the latest in a long line of social movements that have contended over the definition of alcohol problems—and an interpretation of why this movement managed to make drinking-driving into a major public problem in the conservative ethos of the 1980s.

The anti-drunk driving movement did not spring from any rise in the incidence or prevalence of drinking-driving or in accidents thought to be related to it. In fact, the rate of road accidents in the United States remains lower than in most other Western industrial democracies. It is widely believed that people who drink and drive end up in accidents in which there is tragic and costly loss of life, limb, and property.[1] However, none of the organizations or leaders of the movement against drinking-driving have even suggested that their efforts were prompted by some sudden rash of drinking-driving accidents. On the contrary, all claim that their work arose from the fact that the injustices attributed to drinking-driving have long been a problem and have never been

Source: *Theory and Society,* 1988, Vol. 17, pp. 91–120. © 1988 Kluwer Academic Publishers. Reprinted with permission.

treated seriously by legislatures and courts. Indeed, in the late 1960s and early 1970s, the federal government promoted and funded a variety of drinking-driving countermeasures, and arrests did rise in several states. However, despite a steady stream of accidents and the best efforts of both local civic groups across the country and the National Highway Traffic Safety Administration (NHTSA), it was not until 1981 that a *movement* against drunk driving arose and succeeded in putting the issue in the public policy spotlight.[2]

Thus, the thematic questions addressed in this article: If the carnage along U.S. highways thought to be causally related to drinking-driving has long been part of our culture—and always an unacceptable one—while a national movement against this has never before existed, why all this fuss *now*? How was a problem long held to be merely an unfortunate fact of modern life—or, in Joseph Gusfield's phrase, a "folk crime" (an offense routinely committed by many a "good citizen")—reconstituted into a focal point of public outrage? And why should this occur in the early 1980s?

By making this sort of question central, I am placing my analysis of MADD squarely within the social constructionist tradition in the study of social problems. This tradition has focused on the claims-making activities and structuring practices that, whether or not "objective" human suffering exists or is rising, constitute the *sine qua non* of a social problem.[3] Such an analytic stance draws attention to the role of interest groups and social movements that contend for ownership of a problem and the power to define and give public prominence to it.

The MADD case raises the issue of the *viability* of claims made by social movement organizations about putative conditions being problems.[4] I suggest that the viability of a claim that a problem exists depends upon the *interaction* of at least two factors—the credibility of the claims-makers and the historical context in which such claims become utterable and resonate with the dominant discourse. In the case of MADD, the credibility of those who have lost children to drunk drivers has, quite rightly in my view, never been questioned. But the fact that thousands of such victims and their family members have been heretofore mute is intriguing. After describing the rise and impact of MADD, I shall argue that its foci and tactics succeeded when they did largely (although not merely) because they were in harmony with the morality, policy ideologies, and social-control strategies of the Reagan administration and a renascent right. First, however, it is useful to review briefly the history of earlier constructions of alcohol problems.

The modern understanding of alcohol as a dangerous and problematic substance was first articulated at the end of the eighteenth and the beginning of the nineteenth century in the United States. In the colonial era alcohol consumption was virtually universal and drunkenness common practice. Even the Puritans deemed alcohol "the Good Creature of God." The radical shift in problem definition and public discourse by which the "liquor problem" was constituted began with the writings of Dr. Benjamin Rush. Over the first three decades of the nineteenth century, Rush and a variety of other medical, religious, and business leaders established the anti-alcohol or "temperance" movement and redefined alcohol from the Good Creature to a destructive, demonic, and addictive substance. Temperance authorities scapegoated alcoholic beverages, blaming drink for most of the ills in American society at the dawn of industrialization—poverty, business failure, broken homes, madness, immorality, and crime. The emerging temperance ideology held that alcohol was *inherently* addicting, and that it weakened the moral and mental as well as the physical constitution of drinkers. By the 1830s, such a view spread downward from elites to the middle classes, and later to women in particular, who saw solutions to the alcohol problem as central to a broader moral reformation. As would be the case with MADD a century later, temperance groups frequently held that "mothers and children" were "the innocent victims" of alcohol.[5]

In the twentieth century a new wave of prohibitionist agitation developed in response to new economic and political conditions, although it continued to scapegoat alcoholic beverages for most social ills and to hold out abstention as the only hope. Prohibitionists took on the liquor industry and the saloon in an attempt to use the power of state to eliminate alcohol completely and thus help impose a new order on an increasingly conflict-ridden society. Levine captures this well:

> In the 19th century, the American middle class thought itself hegemonic; temperance was aimed at bringing the lower classes and outsiders into the middle class society and culture. In the 20th century, however, the middle class of small businessmen and entrepreneurs felt increasingly overwhelmed and displaced by the growing corporate, industrial society. Enormous corporations called "trusts" seemed more and more to control America. Further, the undeniable presence of a permanent industrial working class was shattering the dream of America as the land where everyone could achieve middle class success. . . . The old middle class of small businessmen, and the new middle class of professionals and technical experts, as well as representatives of the corporations, all shared the concern with finding new ways of maintaining social, political, and economic order. The growth of middle class support for legislative and Constitutional prohibition should be understood, paradoxically, both as attacks on the symbols of corporate capitalist society, and also as part of a larger . . . "search for order". . . .

> To the old 19th century fear of the barroom as the breeding ground of immorality and personal ruin, was added the almost total identification of it as alien and subversive; the saloon was unmiddle class and unAmerican. Saloons were now not only immoral, they were also political evils, where unions were organized, where urban political machines purchased

votes, and where anarchists and communists found recruits. The obliter-
ation of the saloon, it was argued, was a precondition for the management of America in the 20th century.[6]

For both material and ideological reasons, the captains of industry had
by 1915 thrown their decisive weight behind Prohibition. Business
leaders held that in addition to a more productive labor force, prohibition would reduce industrial accidents and workers' compensation
costs. Also, because workers would be unable to spend their wages on
whiskey, their disposable income would rise such that there would be
fewer wage demands, unions, and strikes. Moreover, without alcohol
there would be less poverty, disease, madness, and crime, and therefore
less need for taxes to support institutions and services. Perhaps as
important to a corporate elite then under fire for their avarice was the
legitimation to be gained by expressing concern about the nation's social
problems—particularly when booze rather than business was construed as culprit. As historian Andrew Sinclair put it, "prohibition
became a sort of moral mask for big business."[7] As I will suggest later,
this kind of link to business, at least to the alcohol industry, is also critical in understanding MADD.

Little more than a decade would pass before the onset of the
Depression, when much of the corporate elite made an about face and
began to push for Repeal. As Levine shows, leading figures among the
corporate rich wanted taxes on alcohol restored in order to reduce both
business and personal tax burdens. Further, many of them began to fear
that widespread violations of Prohibition were delegitimating other
forms of law as well, including property law. Ironically, many of the same
economic arguments used in support of Prohibition were later invoked
to justify its repeal. Former Prohibitionist John D. Rockefeller, Jr. was
only the most prominent of corporate leaders to argue that a legalized,
healthy liquor industry would mean a desperately needed increase in
employment and tax revenues that could help pull the nation out of the
Depression.[8] In a scant dozen years, spirits were transformed from the
source to the solution of economic woes, from panapathogen to panacea.

At the height of the Great Depression, Repeal set the stage for the
redefinition of alcohol problems with which we are most familiar, the
alcoholism-as-addictive-disease paradigm. This model of alcohol problems was invented (some might say reinvented, as it borrows heavily
from temperance ideology) by the founders of Alcoholics Anonymous
(AA) in 1935. It had been clear to most Americans since the end of the
nineteenth century that the case for alcohol being inherently addicting
was weak. Most drinkers, after all, never became drunks, and the notion
that chronic drunkenness was at least in part due to individual character was always part of popular understanding. Yet, throughout the conflict over Prohibition the "alcohol problem" had been seen as just that—a

problem having to do with the substance itself. AA set in motion a process that soon succeeded in radically transforming the definition of the problem. In the broadest sense, the alcohol problem was, in Gusfield's phrase, reprivatized—the evil shifted from the bottle to the person. AA maintained that people who drank compulsively had a disease, like an allergy to alcohol. This shift did not signify a complete break with temperance thought; the disease still was said to be progressive, its defining symptom a "loss of control" over drinking, its cure abstinence. However, AA and the emerging alcoholism movement established a new discourse about alcohol problems: the individual drinker became the locus of "the alcohol problem," and, equally significant, the range of public problems held to be alcohol-related shrank in proportion to the growing influence of the disease model.[9]

AA and the alcoholism movement rapidly gained important adherents who helped establish the disease concept as the dominant paradigm in both social policy and public discourse. By the close of World War II, Yale had established a Center on Alcohol and a Summer School in Alcohol Studies. The scientists associated with these institutions spread a new, medical rather than moral conception of alcohol problems. With their focus on the plight of the individual alcoholic, they steered an ideological course around all of the public, i.e., social and political, dimensions of alcohol that were so central to and problematic for the earlier temperance and Prohibition movements. Indeed, they held that only by dropping alcohol's political baggage could they overcome the moral obstacles to "scientific" *treatment* for problem drinkers. At the close of World War II, the activist core of the alcoholism movement also established what is now called the National Council on Alcoholism with the express purpose of spreading their new conception of alcoholism.[10] Throughout the post-war period and up to the present, the alcoholism movement has succeeded in maintaining the disease model as the dominant frame through which alcohol problems are viewed in American culture and policy circles alike. As the welfare state grew, this model became ensconced in public agencies at all levels of government, focusing funding, scholarship, and public attention on the disease of alcoholism rather than a range of alcohol problems. In contrast to the morality plays of earlier epochs, on this new "scientific" stage few villains were visible—only victims of a disease in need of treatment.

There are now two generations in the United States who have no personal memory of the "failed" (Herbert Hoover called it "noble in intention") experiment that was Prohibition. They have grown up in a culture in which both drinking and the discourse of disease are taken for granted. If mass-circulation periodicals are any guide, however, there has been more interest in alcohol problems in the past five years than at any time in the past fifty. In its New Year's Eve edition of 1984, *News-*

week's cover story, "Alcohol on the Rocks," cited "the new prohibition-ists" and "the country's new Temperance movement" as having arisen from the anti-drunk-driving movement. Although a shift toward drink-ing lighter-alcohol beverages had begun in the late 1970s as the baby boom generation became more health conscious, and despite the fact that the scholarly literature in alcohol studies had begun to focus on a range of drinking problems at about the same time, the anti-drink-ing-driving movement became the centerpiece of the media's attention to the so-called new temperance.

Following *Newsweek*, *Business Week* (2/25/85) offered a similar cover story called "The Sobering of America," and, not to be outdone, *Fortune* contributed to this emerging news theme by following with "America's New Abstinence" (3/18/85). In April 1985, *Newsweek*'s "On Campus" edition featured "A New Prohibition" as its lead, and told of "a new era of campus prohibition" springing "from the nationwide crusade against drunken driving." The next month, *Time*'s cover, "Cocktails 1985: America's New Drinking Habits" (5/20/85), referred repeatedly to "the new temperance" in the same terms.[11] These were only the most prominent of hundreds of news articles on alcohol issues, most center-ing on the movement against drunk driving, particularly the largest, most prominent and powerful organization in that movement, Mothers Against Drunk Driving (MADD).

A Brief History of MADD

In May of 1980, 13-year-old Cari Lightner was walking along a bicy-cle path in the central valley town of Fair Oaks, California, a suburb of Sacramento. She was struck and killed by a hit-and-run driver who was later found to have been intoxicated. He was, moreover, both on proba-tion for previous Driving Under the Influence (DUI) convictions and out on bail for another hit-and-run DUI offense a few days before hitting Lightner. In discovering these facts and following the defendant through the criminal justice process, Cari's mother, Candy Lightner, a part-time real estate agent, grew increasingly outraged at what she perceived as the extraordinary leniency with which DUI offenses were routinely handled. She began channelling her grief and anger into efforts to get tougher DUI laws passed by the California legislature.[12]

Most of her initial inquiries were met with indifference by policy makers who tended not to define DUI as a politically "hot" issue. Ms. Lightner has often remarked publicly that prior to her daughter's death she had been apolitical—neither registered to vote nor able to distin-guish Democrat from Republican. After being shocked by the legal leniency with which her daughter's killer was treated and repeatedly rebuffed by representatives, her eyes were opened to ways political. With the aid of a few sympathetic legislators, she was given a crash course in lobbying. She began holding dramatic press conferences, giving tearful and angry testimony before legislative committees, and organizing what was to become Mothers Against Drunk Drivers.

MADD was incorporated as a non-profit organization in August 1980. Lightner worked tirelessly, full-time on building the organization, and invested her daughter's insurance settlement and her own savings to get it off the ground. She enlisted the help of the executive director of the District Attorneys Association, a few legislative aides who were interested in the issue and skilled at political work, and a few friends and dedicated volunteers. The fledgling group pushed then-Governor Jerry Brown to set up a state task force on drunk driving. Like most legislators, he hesitated initially on the grounds that there was not sufficient citizen interest, and assumed that people tended to feel "There but for the grace of God go I." The governor soon sensed, however, that potential support existed (and little if any opposition), so he set up a task force and appointed Lightner to it.

A MADD board of directors was formed from the nucleus of early activists, and they got a small grant from the American Council on Alcohol Problems for a brochure. Next the board wrote a grant proposal and received $65,000 from the National Highway Traffic Safety Administration to organize more MADD chapters. This was quickly followed by an unstipulated $100,000 grant from the Levy Foundation, a principal benefactor of which was an insurance company heir who also had lost a daughter to a drinking driver. By 1982 MADD had begun to employ a direct-mail solicitation firm with experience in mailings to Christian constituencies. With growing media coverage and the power of computerized, direct-mail solicitations, "the money just literally started pouring in," according to an original board member.

From the beginning MADD billed itself as "The Voice of the Victim," a victim's rights organization concerned with advocating for and counseling bereaved relatives, preparing them for a trying adjudication process in which "the rights are with the defendant," and ostentatiously monitoring courtrooms in the hope of insuring more convictions and stiffer sentencing of drinking-drivers.[13] Although the victim remained the focus at local chapters, the strategy of the national organization grew increasingly media oriented. Lightner's preoccupation quickly became the maximization of media attention to what she called the "dirty little secret" of drinking-driving: that 250,000 American lives had been lost in "alcohol-related auto crashes" in the past decade, "70 Americans a day, one every 23 minutes"; that drunk driving was "the leading cause of death for 16–24 year olds," 360 of whom are injured in drunk-driving accidents daily; that a million crippling or serious injuries occur in the

United States annually due to drinking drivers; that all this costs more than $5 billion per year; that on an average weekend night one of ten drivers on the road is intoxicated; and, importantly, that of every 2,000 drinking drivers on the road, only one will get arrested, and the chances of even that one getting any "serious" penalty are "mathematically insignificant."[14] Unlike some other groups such as the Center for Science in the Public Interest, whose strategy was to work against the alcohol industry's massive promotion of drinking in general, MADD focused exclusively on the sins of the drinking driver.

In the past, without a visible moral entrepreneur to give a human voice to these figures, drinking-driving tended to be treated matter-of-factly as episodic, unconnected accidents. But with the rise of MADD, the media seemed willing to oblige in recounting such compelling statistics from a dramatic spokesperson such as Lightner. She appeared in front of all manner of legislative committees, on all national and dozens of local television talk shows, and was written about in literally thousands of newspaper and magazine articles. Virtually all this coverage was explicitly supportive, although one media observer offered a more critical interpretation of why, now, the media found this old issue so appealing:

> Television began this groundswell by giving airtime to MADD's painful [Congressional] Hill testimony. . . . It did so not merely because of its perceived importance—important but complex and boring testimony is given all the time without a dream of TV coverage—but because it was emotional, sentimental. No sane news director will pass up a grieving, sobbing mother; it is the basic image of tragedy on which TV thrives. . . . It was the beginning of an orgy of attention. In their search for safe issues on which to take a 10-second position, TV editorial directors pounced on drunk driving as if it were an end-zone fumble. They called repeatedly, almost weekly for "stiffer penalties." . . . It was a heaven-sent: instantly graspable and without opposition. . . . At the same time, the National Association of Broadcasters organized a massive public service campaign on the problem. . . . Broadcasters aren't stupid; the motivation behind all this attention was forestalling any efforts to ban [alcohol beverage] ads.[15]

The efforts of Lightner and the national MADD led to explosive growth of the organization. Only a year after it began, the organization had generated income of nearly a half-million dollars and sprouted eleven new chapters in four states. A year later, in 1982, seventy chapters were in operation. By 1985 MADD had over 600,000 members and donors, 360 chapters in all fifty states, and a budget approaching $10 million administered by a full-time professional staff of at least twenty.[16] Throughout 1985, not a week would go by without a MADD story in most major newspapers and magazines.

The media-based organizing strategy of MADD and the media's fascination with Lightner and her organization led to a symbiosis that put floodlights on the issue. Newspaper coverage of drinking and driving grew from a handful of articles in 1978 and 1979 to several hundred articles in both 1983 and 1984. In a 1984 national poll, MADD got 85 percent name recognition—double the percentage of people who could name their congressional representative. A *Washington Post* columnist could claim, without fear of contradiction, that "1984 was the year of the Anti-drunk-driving Campaign," while *Time*'s "Man of the Year" edition cited MADD President Lightner as one of "Seven Who Succeeded" because "MADD is getting just about all the laws it wants." Under the magnifying glass of the media, MADD had effectively made drinking-driving into a "hot" issue.[17]

Perhaps the most substantive impact of the movement was on law and public policy. Under pressure from MADD, Reagan appointed a Presidential Commission on drunk driving (and, like Gov. Brown, appointed Lightner). It recommended legislation to force states to raise the minimum drinking age to 21. A bill to this effect was originally proposed by congressional Democrats in early 1985. But despite a strong endorsement for the anti-drunk driving movement in the 1984 Republican Presidential Platform and his own Commission's recommendation, Reagan opposed the age 21 measure until three weeks before signing it. The *New York Times* noted that "almost everyone involved was stunned by the swift, overwhelming Congressional approval" (81 to 16 in the Senate), and that "the statistics were alarming but had theretofore failed to provoke action." According to this and many other accounts, MADD's dramatic testimony in favor of the bill—echoed by other important groups like the American Medical Association, the Parent Teachers Association, the National Council on Alcoholism, insurance industry lobbies, and the National Safety Council—led Reagan's advisors to argue that drinking-driving had been made into a "sleeping giant" of an "apple pie issue" that he could not afford to oppose. Some conservatives still threatened to block the bill on the grounds that it was yet another mode of "social engineering" and an "unwarranted federal intervention into states' rights," but the President began to sense a natural conservative issue and changed direction. The *Times* gave this account of his reversal: "At first President Reagan criticized the legislation . . . as just another instance of Washington wanting to meddle in the states' affairs. But by last week he sounded like a life-long advocate. . . . Looking on were representatives of such groups as MADD, which had lobbied for the legislation for years." In what can be seen as a well-crafted piece of ideological work, the President turned to smile at Candy Lightner, pen in hand, and announced to the assembled press, "The [drunk driving] problem is bigger than the states . . . [so] we have no misgivings about this judicious use of federal power."[18]

Less noticed but equally striking was the passage of more than 230 new anti-drunk driving laws at the local level. In virtually every state and city, MADD was acknowledged as the leading force behind the new statutes. All fifty states toughened their laws against drinking and driving between 1981 and 1985, and the number of states requiring mandatory jail sentences for first offenders convicted of DUI doubled in the same period. Other states sharply raised fines, began to suspend licenses, curtailed judicial discretion with minimum sentence requirements, or enacted "per se" standards that make driving with certain blood-alcohol content (BAC) levels criminal offenses in and of themselves. More broadly, under the momentum of the MADD movement, an additional one hundred alcohol control statutes were passed between 1981 and 1984, including server liability laws and bans on happy hours.[19]

The Context of Success

Both social movement theory[20] and the social constructionist approach to social problems suggest that the existence of compelling troubles or substantial human suffering may be necessary but not sufficient conditions for the emergency of a successful movement for public action. The history of alcohol problems in general and the long latency of the drinking-driving problem in particular suggest the need for an analysis of the special resonance of MADD in the early 1980s. I will argue in what follows that the remarkable rise of MADD must be understood as a product of the interaction between the strategic focus of claims by this moral-entrepreneurial movement and a historical context marked by a peculiar conjuncture of trends favorable to those claims in both the alcohol arena and the larger political culture.

In the late 1970s health consciousness spread across America. Whether this fitness fetish derives from the greater need to exercise in a service economy that reduces the need for physical exertion while increasing tension, from some deeper narcissism, or from the mere demographic ascendancy of the 1960s generation who popularized health foods, few would deny that hordes of runners are visible everywhere and that the health spa and aerobics industries have enjoyed meteoric growth. Bound up with such developments are changes in what we eat and drink: less red meat and more fish and poultry, fewer spirits and more white wine and "lite" beer. It is also worth noting that this health craze seemed particularly marked among the middle and upper-middle class (it is often referred to as a "yuppie" phenomenon) and that these groups are most likely to vote and otherwise participate in political life. Insofar as this makes them the sort of people about whom legislators (and advertisers) worry, trends in their values and behaviors can be seen as influential.

The alcohol industry has adjusted adroitly to such trends by stepping up its marketing of low-alcohol beverages. Yet, distillers, brewers, and vintners perceived more ominous possibilities in all this that were not so amenable to shifts in product lines and advertising strategies. In addition to declining per capita consumption of alcohol and all the media attention to "the new temperance" and "neo-Prohibitionism," the fiscal crisis and growing budget deficits led many legislators to call for increased taxes on alcohol. This strategy is often advocated by many public health specialists as a means of both reducing alcohol abuse and raising revenues needed to pay for alcohol treatment. Still more threatening to the industry, the Center for Science in the Public Interest (CSPI) launched a national campaign to ban all alcohol advertising in the electronic media (Stop Marketing Alcohol on Radio and Television, or SMART), which had gained endorsements and momentum by 1985. In the context of such developments the alcohol industry began to see the movement against drinking and driving as the lesser of evils.

While other anti-drunk-driving organizations refused industry support, MADD accepted a variety of financial contributions from alcohol interests. Anheuser-Busch and Miller Brewing, for example, both contributed money to the national anti-drunk driving movement. One of MADD's original board members proposed that, as a matter of principle, they refuse to accept money from the alcohol industry. He was out-voted on the basis of Lightner's argument that it is not alcohol itself that causes death and injury but rather irresponsible users and abusers of alcohol. She remained steadfast in her opposition to the idea that widespread promotion of alcohol consumption was in any way related to drinking-driving. Moreover, after Lightner purged the original board of all her adversaries, she appointed to it representatives of the alcohol and broadcasting industries. Unlike many of the lesser known anti-drunk-driving organizations, MADD has not advocated increases in alcohol taxes as a means of reducing consumption or financing prevention and treatment, and it sent a memo to its local chapters stating the official MADD policy against participation in the SMART petition drive. In a position paper, national MADD took the position of taking no position on the debate over regulation of alcohol advertising, save that of urging the industry to "police itself." Further, MADD supported the alcohol and broadcasting industries in their attempt to stave off demands that networks broadcast "counter-messages" to alcohol commercials.[21]

In a context marked by "neo-temperance" sentiments, declining alcohol consumption, and increasing pressure for higher alcohol taxes and tighter controls over alcohol advertising, the advantages of MADD's narrow focus on the drunk driver—on the individual deviant—was not lost on alcohol producers. Indeed, both the alcohol and broadcasting industries "courted" MADD. As the *Wall Street Journal* put it, "In an effort to blunt criticisms of its products and restrict the debate to alcohol *abuse*, the industry has lent its financial support to those combatting drunk-driving." This way, the "new prohibitionism" would not, as one alcohol industry executive put it, "dismember" the beverage alcohol business "one bite at a time."[22] In fairness it must be said that the alcohol industry was never the main source of funding for MADD; nor can it be proven that industry contributions softened MADD's stance. What can be noted, however, is the *affinity* between MADD's strategy of rhetorically locating the source of the problem in individual-level deviant behavior and the alcohol industry's strategies for deflecting attention away from the full range of problems related to consumption of their products in general. One consequence of this affinity was that a potentially powerful form of corporate opposition to MADD was not only neutralized but turned to the organization's financial and ideological advantage.

Other developments on the government side of the alcohol arena also made for fertile soil for the growth of MADD. Although the disease paradigm had been part of state and local government alcohol programs for most of the post-war period, the alcoholism movement first established a national institutional beachhead in the welfare state in the early 1970s—the National Institute of Alcohol Abuse and Alcoholism (NIAAA). By the late 1970s a growing network of state and local alcohol agencies, treatment programs, research centers, and alcohol professionals was funded by NIAAA. They constituted an active, institutionalized constituency, which arguably had created cultural space for and was ready to echo the cry of an anti-drunk-driving movement.[23] More specifically, this network of institutions was by 1980 edging away from the intellectual hegemony of the disease concept toward a "disaggregative" approach to alcohol problems. In this framework a *range* of alcohol-related problems is held to exist, rather than one in which all such problems are conceived as either so many manifestations of an underlying "disease" entity called alcoholism or as the less important, poorer relatives of the disease.

Robin Room's historical analysis of the disease concept notes that "In the last few years, . . . an 'alcohol problems' approach has gained considerable ground in alcohol policy statements [which entails] the abandonment of the assumption of entitivity" underlying the alcoholism-as-disease-entity paradigm. This shift may be seen, for example, in recent policy statements contained in a 1979 report to Congress ("Alcohol problems in the general population do not seem to form a coherent pattern. The problems are too diffuse to be described as part of a single concept of alcohol addiction . . ."). A 1980 World Health Organization Expert Committee Report said much the same thing ("Until recently, there has been a widespread tendency to conceptualize the whole gamut of alcohol problems as manifestations of an underlying entity, alcoholism. . . . Alcohol dependence constitutes only a small part of the total of alcohol-related problems.")[24]

Bound up with these developments is the emergency of a "public health" perspective on alcohol that takes a *preventative* approach to alcohol-related problems.[25] Examples of this include the recent increases in federal funding for prevention education, the sponsorship of national prevention research centers, and the SMART campaign against deceptive alcohol advertising in electronic media. In a related development, the private National Council on Alcoholism experienced an internal rift over what many staff felt was an alcohol industry-induced, excessively narrow focus on the disease and its treatment at the expense of other alcohol problems and solutions. In the end, NCA moved to limit industry involvement on its board and to broaden its perspective toward a general public health view. Such arguable liberal, at least partly progressive developments in the scientific and public policy sides of the alcohol arena seem to have given intellectual elbow room to those calling attention to non-disease alcohol problems such as drinking-driving.

The second set of historical developments that has aided the rise of MADD concerns changes in the broader political arena. Here I shall refer to the political culture of Reaganism and suggest that MADD's claims were ideologically harmonious with the policy rhetoric of the Right. Like the Temperance and Prohibition movements of the nineteenth and early twentieth centuries, neither MADD nor the anti-drunk-driving movement in general are politically monolithic or ideologically homogeneous.[26] It is possible, however, to glimpse MADD's underlying conservatism by contrasting its politics with those of the "Stop Marketing Alcohol on Radio and Television" campaign (SMART). The origins of SMART lie in the consumer movement for *corporate* accountability and responsibility. SMART leaders speak of the "total social costs" of alcohol production and consumption; they explicitly confront corporate power and influence; they propose solutions aimed at the *structural* sources of alcohol-related problems.[27] Their rhetoric evokes notions of *collective* responsibility and social justice, and implies regulatory-state solutions when corporations and industries resist or ignore moral appeals for the public good.

MADD's origins, on the other hand, lie in victims' rights movements, which seek retribution from criminals. MADD's Lightner chose an organization name that ends with "drunk drivers" rather than "driving" and yields an acronym symbolizing moral anger; MADD members repeatedly rail against the "Killer Drunk"; they complain of the neglect of drinking-driving as "America's most frequently committed violent crime," the "only socially acceptable form of homicide."[28] MADD's organizing strategy is explicitly one of personal vilification, and it assiduously avoids attention to corporate interests and structural sources of alcohol problems in favor of a rhetoric of *individual* responsibility, the private moral *choice* of drinkers, and solutions based upon *self*-regulation by both drinkers and the alcohol, advertising, and broadcast industries.[29]

From the MADD perspective, then, the *aperture of attribution* for all the suffering and social costs that they claim are caused by drinking-driving is constricted; only the lone deviant comes into focus. Such constriction, I submit, largely explains industry support for the movement. It tacitly legitimatizes the continued production, promotion, and consumption of alcohol products that are vulnerable to the more structural critique of SMART and other groups. Some forty years ago in the pages of *American Sociological Review*, Alfred McClung Lee offered an analysis of the politics of Prohibition that parallels this point:

> Large contributors to political movements and campaigns found that the Drys offered a more attractive issue than did those who stressed issues more fundamental to the control of our economic and political institutions. The "era of the muckrakers" of about 1901 to 1912 . . . struck many business leaders in particular as having an unsettling tendency. The Prohibitionists merely attacked Booze, the Saloon, the Whisky Trust, and the Brewers, but Lincoln Steffens, Ray Stannard Baker, Upton Sinclair, and others went after the political bosses, the public utilities, patent medicines, advertising, and even capitalism itself. Let the reformers have Booze and the Saloon. Let that keep them busy![30]

MADD's self-image as "the voice of the victim" also lends itself to a narrow and conservative focus. The organization has drawn upon the victims' rights groups that were first given national recognition in the law-and-order campaign of the Nixon administration. Both victims' rights groups and MADD bemoan the injustices victims suffer at the hands of defendants whom they see as overly protected by Miranda rights and other impediments to retribution, which are also anathema to the Reagan/Meese Justice Department. Both MADD and its law-and-order, victims' rights predecessors call for less judicial discretion and an end to plea-bargaining so as to ensure longer sentences. Newspaper accounts of MADD often cite, for example, the "national punishment mentality" in the "very punitive era" of the 1980s as a factor in the organization's rise.[31]

Each of these major facets of MADD's orientation—its individualist focus, its systematic inattention to structural/corporate sources of problems, and its narrow retributive prescriptions—is in ideological harmony with and gains legitimacy from the policies and the rhetoric of Reagan and the New Right. There is also some preliminary evidence on the social base of the movement that supports such an interpretation. Although a substantial number of MADD activists (e.g., chapter officers) are either victims of drinking-driving accidents or members of families with victims, the rate of MADD chapter formation across states and regions of the United States is strongly correlated with standard survey measures of politico-religious conservatism. Moreover, the National Association of Evangelicals pushed for stiffer punishments for drinking-driving and was instrumental in getting a plank to that effect put into the 1984 Republican Presidential Campaign Platform. New Right fundraisers also have targeted people who strongly oppose drinking-driving as people who look to them for leadership.[32]

Of course, neither the shifts in the alcohol arena nor those in political culture can be construed as *causal* in any rigorous, theoretical sense. However, they do suggest that a thorough, textured account of the rise of MADD cannot rest upon the mere existence of drinking-driving accidents and an effective social-movement organization; the former has long existed and it is the effectiveness of the latter that needs to be explained. Rather, this form of anti-drunk-driving movement took off when it did in large part because of its *elective affinity* with a political context dominated by Reaganism and the Right, and also, ironically, with a subtle shift toward what I would construe as more liberal, public health perspectives in the alcohol arena.

Weber's concept of elective affinity seems especially valuable here. His most well-known use of it was to conceptualize the relation between Calvinism and other Puritan sects and the spread of capitalist social organization and accumulation. Weber argued that although the "spirit of capitalism" and the accumulation of "worldly goods" flowed quite naturally from Puritan religious principles designed to ensure the "salvation of the soul," the material results that stemmed from such "purely religious motives" were "unforeseen and even unwished-for." He explicitly rejected both the idea that the Reformation could be deduced "as a necessary historical result" of the rise of capitalism, as well as the converse notion "that the spirit of capitalism [. . .] could only have arisen as the result of certain effects of the Reformation." What he attempted to demonstrate instead were the ways in which the Puritan ethic had *taken part* in the qualitative formation and the quantitative expansion of the spirit of capitalism.[33] Whatever subsequent scholars have made of the specifics of Weber's case, the theoretical and conceptual utility of "elective affinity" has endured. I believe it most closely captures the more or less fortuitous, mutually-informing relation between MADD and elements of the new conservative era in which it grew.

Clearly most people stand firmly against the loss of life, limb, and property at the hands of drivers who have been drinking. But MADD's claims draw much of their support from and resonate strongly among the core constituencies of renascent conservatism. Thus, I would argue that the rather remarkable fortunes of this movement cannot be understood apart from their emergence in an epoch about which it safely could be said, "The notion is gaining that intervention in other people's lives is more legitimate." For the Right, as its leaders proudly profess, is as anxious to intervene in most private moral spheres as it is loath to do so in public economic ones. MADD's approach to drinking-driving fits snugly within this ideological mold. [34]

What MADD Has Wrought, and What It Means

Although changes in the alcohol arena contributed to the emergency of MADD and the anti-drunk-driving movement, it is also true that MADD and the movement have in turn altered the alcohol arena. First and most obvious, both the quantity and quality of anti-drinking-driving weapons have increased. The following measures are all parts of the MADD agenda and most have been enacted in many states: computerized criminal and driving record retrieval systems for police cars; citizen reporting systems; elimination of plea bargaining for DUI offenses; reduction of the blood-alcohol-content standard from .10% to .08% or even .05%, with implied consent from all licensed drivers for BAC testing and "per se" license suspensions on the scene for any who meet that standard; mandatory jail sentences and higher minimum fines; pre-sentence probation investigations of driving records and alcohol-problem assessments, reclassification of alcohol-related injury and death accidents to felonies; "dram shop" (server) liability laws; roadblocks or highway "sobriety checkpoints" to stop vehicles randomly; and a nationwide minimum drinking age of 21.[35] Together such measures open up to surveillance new areas of the private sphere for more and more people, and invite concern about the erosion of civil liberties.

Less obvious are the changes wrought by the movement in the treatment of alcohol problems. In many jurisdictions fee-paying drunk drivers have replaced public inebriates, alcoholics, and other problem drinkers in both public and private treatment programs. With arrests rising and stiffer sentences, fines, and drinking-driver education becoming increasingly mandatory, a brisk business in the treatment of drinking drivers has developed. It is not clear where the old clients of the alcohol treatment system are going instead, if anywhere. This shift in clientele also seems to entail a subtle but important shift in treatment ideology. It had been axiomatic in the alcohol treatment field that alcoholics must "hit bottom," "be ready," and frequently volunteer for treatment if it was to be effective. Now phrases like "constructive coercion," "breaking down denial," and "tough love" have crept into the argot of alcohol treatment professionals, and clients more frequently enter treatment under court sentencing.[36]

The new laws enacted at the behest of the movement have provided treatment programs with a new funding base as well as a new class of clients. Convicted drinking drivers are now assessed fines (often allocated in part to treatment programs) and required to attend treatment programs that charge fees. These developments have fed other treatment trends that began prior to MADD.

The growth of what may fairly be called a treatment industry began in the early 1970s. First, in response to the fiscal crisis many counties began "contracting out" or "privatizing" treatment programs that had previously been public social-service functions. Some states adopted the quasi-partnership role of organizing the efficient distribution of state-referred clients and ensuring "sufficient marketing of provider services . . . [to] demonstrate market demand."[37] Second, during the same period NIAAA and other treatment interests succeeded in getting alcohol and drug problems defined as diseases for purposes of health-insurance coverage. These so-called third-party payments added to the pool of financial resources on which the new treatment industry could draw.[38] Third, in response to rapid growth and high profit margins in the health care industry, many hospitals expanded. This additional bedspace became excess plant capacity, however, when Medicare reforms and other cost-containment measures of the early 1980s reduced many hospital stays. With occupancy rates down and profits squeezed, many corporate hospital chains either started marketing their own alcohol and drug treatment programs or sold franchises for "chemical dependency units" to national companies specializing in this service. All of these supply-side trends created a new growth industry in alcohol and drug treatment.[39] The anti-drunk driver movement has now provided an additional market segment and a new funding base that has furthered the growth of private, for-profit treatment—for a different, more well-heeled clientele with different alcohol problems, for whom treatment is not voluntary and traditional treatment ideology is not designed.

MADD's success also has implications for the criminal justice system. Higher arrest rates, mandatory jail sentences, prohibitions on plea bargaining, and other features of the new laws are putting added stress on courts and jails. A recent National Institute of Justice study, for example, warns that the movement's impact has led to the need for more judges, jail cells, and probation reports, and that such strains should be considered before enacting additional "mandatory confinement" laws.[40] Additional problems are likely to result as more middle-class defendants are caught in the new, wider drunk-driving nets. They are more likely to pay private attorneys and demand jury trials to avoid jail and license revocation. The *Wall Street Journal* reported that under the new laws, defending drinking drivers has become "a booming and lucrative legal speciality," and the "fastest growing area of the law." Such cases are taken more often by senior attorneys (who charge "three to ten times more") because the "stakes are higher." These lawyers are attempting to "put the breathalyzer on trial"; to use physicians who will testify that because alcoholism is a "debilitating disease" the criminal status of drinking-driving is dubious; and to question the constitutionality of arrests on the grounds that people too drunk to drive are incapable of understanding their Miranda rights.[41] While the ultimate success of such strategies and their impact on conviction rates and drinking-driving cannot be known at this writing, it is clear that stiffer penalties have evoked stiffer resistance, that average adjudication times will probably increase, that there will be new legal challenges to drinking-driving statutes and arrest procedures.

Beyond these relatively concrete effects of MADD on the alcohol arena and the criminal justice system, the movement may well have other, more profound implications for problem definition that are less amenable to empirical description and interpretation. First, there is MADD's role in the ongoing construction of alcohol problems. In the post-World War II period the disease concept became the dominant paradigm in alcohol treatment and policy—dominant but not completely hegemonic. Robin Room has argued persuasively that at least in popular culture and public opinion, the notion that problem drinkers of all sorts had a disease about which they had "no choice" (and, implicitly, therefore, reduced responsibility for their actions) has always coexisted with earlier notions about free choice and moral culpability. We have had, that is, something like a dialectic of ambivalence wherein "both choice and compulsion" are juggled, the one or the other invoked as the micro-political exigencies of the situation require. Orcutt suggests that this ideological amalgam of medical and moral frames may be emblematic of a "transitional" stage in the broader historical trend away from moral and toward medical views.[42] This is a useful insight, but just as opiate addiction was effectively demedicalized by pressure from the federal Bureau of Narcotics and Dangerous Drugs, so MADD has further complicated the trend toward medicalization of deviance by again drawing out those ostensibly dormant antagonisms to a pure alcoholism-as-disease paradigm. The movement has successfully claimed that drinking drivers are, first and foremost, "violent criminals" in need of punishment rather than merely victims of a disease in need of treatment. Thus, the march of medicalization may be less inexorable and more circuitous than many have believed. Just as the old moralistic frame was politically supplanted by the scientific alcoholism movement forty years ago, the medicalization of at least some alcohol problems has now become vulnerable to the vicissitudes of politics—this time the retributionism of MADD as it echoes harmoniously with the calls of the New Right for harsher social control.[43]

Such a conceptual-ideological shift carries with it some potentially important implications for public discourse and public policy. To the extent that MADD has captured popular imaginations on drinking-driving issues, and insofar as the alcohol industry continues to counter the myriad threats posed by the so-called New Temperance with support for the anti-drunk-driving movement, then the "evils of drink" will continue to be situated squarely *in the person* rather than *in the bottle*.[44] Thus, another facet of MADD's impact will be to limit discussion of alternative or structural conceptions of alcohol-related problems and the policies that might be brought to bear upon them. In this new delimited discourse, we will hear less and less, for example, about safer automotive design, the lives saved by seat belt laws, the auto industry's success in forestalling air bags, cuts in funding for public transportation, and the dubious advisability of tacitly subsidizing alcoholic drinks by making them tax-deductible "business expenses."[45] Perhaps most important, the rise of MADD has helped to eclipse competing claims about the social costs of unregulated cultural promotion of *drinking-as-intrinsic-to-social-life*. By this I mean the expansion through alcohol advertising the number of spheres and practices in which alcohol is depicted as a natural accoutrement—and this in a society organized around the automobile as the principle mode of transport from one sphere to another.

At the most general level, MADD and the anti-drunk-driving movement it spawned have resurrected a drama that *reaffirms a particular symbolic order*. As Joseph Gusfield renders it,

> The laws against driving under the influence of alcohol constitute a moral drama which states the public definition of moral conduct in American life. In differentiating the drinking driver from the traffic offender these laws create an identity for the moral person and a counteridentity of deviance and guilt. The law in this area symbolizes a public commitment to the centrality of work, safety, and individual responsibility in American society. It supports and enhances a view of a "generalized other," of a "society" committed to the legitimacy of a style of living in which alcohol is a symbol of risk and danger and its control a mark of morality and social responsibility. The modern world has not been the first to discover the joys of inebriety. It is, however, unique in defining these also as woes that call for public actions.[46]

This conflict between the moral safety of self-control and the dangerous immorality of self-indulgence was increasingly camouflaged in the post-World War II years. The combination of the Repeal of Prohibition and the narrowing of alcohol problems to the disease concept normalized drinking in American society. Repeal made drinking acceptable while the success of the alcoholism movement meant that people with alcohol problems had a disease and thus were to be helped and redeemed through science rather than punished and stigmatized.[47] Now that the anti-drunk-driving movement has created a public problem where once there were only tragic "accidents," they have helped define a discourse in which there is, as Gusfield puts it, "the re-emergence of the perception of alcohol problems as those produced by people who make trouble rather than those from troubled people."[48]

Neither the reaffirmation of this symbolic order nor the new discourse that reduces social problems to individual immorality is the handiwork of MADD alone. On the contrary, as suggested above, MADD is but a part of similar and more sweeping shifts in political culture and public policy in the 1980s. While these shifts differ in each sphere of life and realm of public policy, taken together they seem to center on the *re-regulation of pleasure and the constriction of personal liberty.* In the past few years drugs, sex, and rock and roll have all been defined as *dangerous*, and those who indulge in such problematic practices have been subjected to greater surveillance.[49] I am speaking here of more than mass urinalysis testing, the promotion of chastity as public policy, and attempts to censor rock music lyrics. The new minimum drinking age law, for example, central to MADD's legislative agenda, limited the liberties of youth, albeit "for their own good." It is at least arguable that this law is part of a wider network of control measures enacted in the Reagan era, which include greater discipline in school, the renewed use of corporal punishment, adult trials for juvenile offenders, drug searches, dress codes, curfew laws, and "squeal rules" that inhibit the flow of birth control and abortion information to young people. At the risk of oversimplification, I suggest that the 1980s constitute an epoch in which corporation, state, church, and family are all reasserting authority over individual desires, and in the process attempting to reimpose a real or imagined moral *ancien régime* in which social control takes precedence over social welfare as the organizing axis of both ideology and policy.

The kind of relation I have tried to sketch between MADD and its context is neither a simple nor a novel one. Alcohol problems have never been merely problems having to do with alcohol. It is as if battles against alcohol in American history have been the cultural equivalent of the civil conflicts of Third World countries that provide terrain for the proxy wars of distant superpowers. I have tried to show that the movement against drinking-driving, too, is about more than just its stated object, serious though that object is. The problem that remains is how this might be theorized fruitfully. Clearly the moral/symbolic facets of social movements and social problems cannot neatly be reduced to any material/economic core. MADD in some senses did suit the interests of the alcohol, advertising, and broadcasting industries who were facing what they saw as a broader threat, and the movement both aided and was aided by broader conservative currents. Yet, unrelated and arguable progressive shifts in the alcohol arena also abetted MADD. Further, the conflict over drinking-driving has always been largely moral and symbolic in nature, cutting across social classes and having very different implications for different fractions of capital (alcohol, advertising, and autos, versus insurance), different aspects of the state (alcohol treatment versus criminal justice), and different strands of conservative ideology (libertarian versus law and order). Nor does it seem to be the case that MADD designed its focus to fit with the new conservatism or the affected business interests. There is nothing in MADD's organizational history to suggest that its strategies were anything but the instinctual consequence of a bereaved and angry American mother bent on rectifying injustice who then developed a lucrative career as a moral entrepreneur. Yet, although MADD's birth seems quite autonomous, its particular power in adolescence surely owes much to the political and economic circumstances of its development.

Notes

1   Although they are beyond the scope of this article, it should be noted that there are many questions about both the extent of alcohol-related accidents and the extent of alcohol's role in accidents so categorized; serious doubts exist about the validity of commonly used figures on the number of injuries and fatalities said to be "caused" by drinking-driving. These methodological and measurement problems are well covered, e.g., in J. Gusfield, *The Culture of Public Problems* (Chicago, University of Chicago Press, 1981); D. S. Reed, "Reducing the Costs of Drinking and Driving," in M. Moore and D. Gerstein, editors, *Alcohol and Public Policy: Beyond the Shadow of Prohibition* (Washington, DC: National Academy Press, 1981); H. L. Ross, *Deterring the Drinking Driver: Legal Policy and Social Control* (Lexington, MA: D. C. Heath, 1982); "Social Control Through Deterrence," *Annual Review of Sociology* 10 (1984): 22; and L. Lanza-Kaduce and D. M. Bishop, "Legal Fictions and Criminology: The Jurisprudence of Drunk Driving," *Journal of Criminal Law and Criminology* 77 (1986): 358–78.

2   Ross, *Deterring the Drinking Driver*, T. Cameron, "The Impact of Drinking-Driving Countermeasures," *Contemporary Drug Problems* 8 (1979): 495–565; "Trends in Alcohol Problems in California, 1950–1979," in N. Giesbrecht et al., editors, *Consequences of Drinking: Trends in Alcohol Problem Statistics in Seven Countries* (Toronto: Addiction Research Foundation, 1983).

3   From the social constructionist perspective, the thing-to-be-explained, or explananadum, is the crusade against what is known as drunk driving, not the behavior itself. The lineage and theoretical contours of this tradition may be traced in the following: R. Fuller and R. Myers, "The Natural History of a Social Problem," *American Sociological Review* 6 (1941): 320–28; E. Sutherland, "The Diffusion of Sexual Psychopath Laws," *American Journal of Sociology* 56 (1950): 142–48; H. S. Becker, *Outsiders* (New York: Free Press, 1963); *Social Problems: A Modern Approach* (New York: Wiley, 1966); M. Foucault, *Madness and Civilization* (New York: Random House, 1965); T. S. Kuhn, *The Structure of Scientific Revolutions* (Chicago: University of Chicago Press), 1970, 2nd ed.); H. Blumer, "Social Problems as Collective Behavior," *Social Problems* 18 (1971): 298–306;

J. Kitsuse and M. Spector, "Toward a Sociology of Social Problems: Social Conditions, Value Judgments, and Social Problems," *Social Problems* 20 (1973): 407–19; M. Spector and J. Kitsuse, "Social Problems: A Reformulation," *Social Problems* 21 (1973): 145–59; *Constructing Social Problems* (Menlo Park, CA: Cummings, 1977); A. L. Mauss, *Social Problems as Social Movements* (Philadelphia: Lippincott, 1975); P. Conrad and J. Schneider, *Deviance and Medicalization* (St. Louis: C. V. Mosby, 1980); J. Schneider, "Social Problems Theory: The Constructionist View," *Annual Review of Sociology* 11 (1985): 209–29. An insightful review of the intellectual cousin of this tradition in psychology is in K. Gergen, "The Social Constructionist Movement in Modern Psychology," *American Psychologist* 40 (1985): 226–75. Works in this tradition specifically on alcohol problems include: J. R. Seeley, "The W.H.O. Definition of Alcoholism," *Quarterly Journal of Studies on Alcohol* 20 (1959): 352–56; J. R. Seeley, "Alcoholism is a Disease: Implications for Social Policy," in D. J. Pittman and C. R. Snyder, editors, *Society, Culture, and Drinking Patterns* (New York: Wiley, 1962); C. MacAndrews and R. Edgerton, *Drunken Comportment* (Chicago: Aldine, 1969); R. L. Chauncey, "New Careers for Moral Entrepreneurs: Teenage Drinking," *Journal of Drug Issues,* 10 (1980): 48–70.

4   On the viability of claims-making, see Spector and Kitsuse, *Constructing Social Problems.*

5   This draws heavily upon the key works of Gusfield and Levine. See J. Gusfield, *Symbolic Crusade: Status Politics and the American Temperance Movement* (Urbana: University of Illinois Press, 1963); H. G. Levine, "The Discovery of Addiction: Changing Conceptions of Habitual Drunkenness in American History," *Journal of Studies on Alcohol* 39 (1978): 143–67; "Temperance and Women in 19th Century United States," *Research Advances in Alcohol and Drug Problems* 15 (1980): 26–67; "The Good Creature of God and the Demon Rum: Colonial and 19th Century American Ideas about Alcohol, Accidents, and Crime," in R. Room and G. Collins, editors, *Alcohol and Disinhibition* (Washington, DC: National Institute on Alcohol Abuse and Alcoholism, 1983); "The Alcohol Problem in America: From Temperance to Alcoholism," *British Journal of Addiction* 79 (1984): 109–19. For a useful, class-rooted revisionist interpretation of Gusfield's classic study of temperance as symbolic conflict, see J. J. Rumbarger, *The Social Origins and Function of the Political Temperance Movement in the Reconstruction of American Society, 1825–1917.* Ph.D. dissertation, University of Pennsylvania, 1968 (forthcoming in revised form, State University of New York Press). Note, too, that while women played crucial roles in the temperance movement and were often cast as the victims, the movement was dominated by men.

6   Levine, "The Alcohol Problem in America," 113. See also Gusfield, *Symbolic Crusade*; and J. H. Timberlake, *Prohibition and the Progressive Movement 1900–1920* (Cambridge: Harvard University Press, 1963).

7   A. Sinclair, *Era of Excess: A Social History of the Prohibition Movement* (New York: Harper, 1965), 107; see also Timberlake, *Prohibition and the Progressive Movement*; and A. McClung Lee, "Techniques of Social Reform: An Analysis of the New Prohibition Drive," *American Sociological Review* 9 (1944): 65–77.

8   Levine, "The Alcohol Problem in America."

9   Ibid.; and Levine, "The Discovery of Addiction."

10   R. Room, Governing Images of Alcohol and Drug Problems, Ph.D. Dissertation, University of California, Berkeley (1978); "Sociological Aspects of the Disease Concept of Alcoholism," *Research Advances in Alcohol and Drug Problems* 7 (1983): 47–91; C. Wiener, *The Politics of Alcoholism: Building an Arena Around*

a Social Problem (New Brunswick, NJ: Transaction, 1971); Levine, "The Alcohol Problem in America"; J. Schneider, "Deviant Drinking as Disease: Alcoholism as a Social Accomplishment," *Social Problems* 25 (1978): 361–72.

11 See also J. Gusfield, *The Culture of Public Problems: Drinking-Driving and the Symbolic Order* (Chicago: University of Chicago Press, 1981); "Alcohol Problems—An Interactionist View," in J. P. von Wartburg, P. Magnenat, R. Miller, and S. Wyss, editors, *Currents in Alcohol Research and the Prevention of Alcohol Problems* (Berne, Switzerland: Hans Huber, 1985).

12 This historical sketch of MADD is based upon three types of data: First, an archive of journalistic accounts of the organization's founding, growth, and trials and tribulations, which is housed in the library of the Alcohol Research Group at Berkeley, the most important of which are cited directly (Note: there were no journal articles on MADD as of late 1985); second, depth interviews with founding members of the MADD Board of Directors and selected local chapter officers and members from the San Francisco Bay Area; and third, MADD literature, publications, newsletters, and selected board meeting minutes. Although the sketch should not be taken as exhaustive or definitive, it is based upon all information available. Note, too, that since these data were originally compiled and reviewed, MADD founder, president, board chair, and chief executive officer, Candy Lightner, was removed from two of those official posts by the new MADD Board in a power struggle. See R. D. McFadden, "Founder of Anti-Drunken Drive Group Loses 2 Posts," *New York Times* (10/4/85).

13 J. Vejnoska, "Citizen Activist Groups Affecting Policy on Drinking and Driving," *Alcohol Health and Research World* Fall (1987); Mothers Against Drunk Drivers, "M.A.D.D." [brochure], n.d.

14 Mothers Against Drunk Drivers, "A Summary of Statistics Related to the National Drunk Driving Problem" (Hurst, Texas: MADD, 1984); "Research on Teens: Drinking, Drugs, and Driving" (Hurst, Texas: MADD, 1984). Although MADD collected an impressive array of statistics on which to base their claims, the empirical certainty of their figures is still subject to dispute—although, perhaps surprisingly, no more so than the drinking-driving statistics used by most public health professionals when documenting the horrors of drinking-driving accidents. It is clear that the commonly cited figures on deaths due to drinking-driving are organizationally constructed and rhetorical in character, and that the precise role of alcohol in auto accidents remains unknown; cf. Gusfield, *The Culture of Public Problems*; Ross, *Deterring the Drinking Driver*, and Lanza-Kaduce and Bishop, "Legal Fictions and Criminology."

15 C. P. Freund, "Less Filling, Tastes Great," *City Paper* [Washington, DC], Feb. 1–8, 1985, 1. On the attention given to MADD, see C. Lightner, "MADD at the Court," *Judges' Journal* 23 (1984): 36–39; Insurance Information Institute, *International Symposium on Alcohol and Driving: Conference Report* (Washington, DC: American Insurance Association, 1982); John McCarthy has graphed a 500 percent increase in newspaper coverage of the drinking-driving issue since MADD began; see his "The Causes and Consequences of the Citizens' Movement Against Drunk Driving" [proposal to National Science Foundation] (Washington, DC: Catholic University Center for the Study of Youth Development, 1984). Also note that the Center for Science in the Public Interest was making considerable headway by 1984 in its SMART campaign (Stop Marketing Alcohol on Radio and Television), which was adamantly opposed by the National Association of Broadcasters, the Advertising Council, various liquor lobbyists such as the Distilled Spirits Council, and brewers' associations and vintner groups. See *The*

Alcoholism Report, volume XIII, Number 3 (1984): 1 [Minneapolis: The Johnson Institute].

16 Figures on membership, budget, and growth were taken from the following sources: T. Akeman, "Lightner Settles $7,900 Personal Debt to MADD," *Sacramento Bee* (Jan. 1, 1983); "MADD to Add Big D—Moving to Dallas." *Sacramento Bee* (Mar. 29, 1983); Vejnoska, "Citizen Activist Groups"; Lightner, "MADD at the Court"; *Time*, "Man of the Year" (Jan. 7, 1985), 77; Council of Better Business Bureaus, "Philanthropic Advisory Service Report: Mothers Against Drunk Drivers," Sept. 24, 1984; and McFadden, "Founder of Anti-Drunken Driver Group Loses 2 Posts."

17 Regarding newspaper coverage, see McCarthy, "The Causes and Consequences of the Citizens' Movement Against Drunk Driving"; S. Cunningham, "Still MADD, but More Strategic," *American Psychological Association Monitor* 15 (1984); M. Jordan, "Drinking and Driving Mar Merrymaking," *Washington Post* (Dec. 31, 1984); *Time*, "Man of the Year." On the curious courtship between media and movements, see T. Gitlin, *The Whole World is Watching: Mass Media in the Making and Unmaking of the New Left* (Berkeley, University of California Press, 1980).

18 M. Tolchin, "States Face Carrot or a Stick on the Drinking Age," *New York Times* (July 1, 1984); "Law is Signed to Nudge States on Drinking Age," *New York Times* (July 22, 1985). The law provides that states that do not increase the minimum drinking age to 21 will lose 5 percent of their federal highway funds each year; all but six states had complied as of this writing (April 1987). I have borrowed the notion of "ideological work" from the insightful study by Bennett M. Berger, *The Survival of a Counterculture: Ideological Work and Everyday Life Among Rural Communards* (Berkeley: University of California Press, 1981).

19 *Time*, "Man of the Year"; *Newsweek*, "Alcohol on the Rocks" (Dec. 31, 1984); *Wall Street Journal*, "Industry Headache—Americans Drink Less, And Makers of Alcohol Feel a Little Woozy: Concerns of Drunk Driving, Health, and Sales to Youths Force Producers to Adapt" (March 14, 1984); *U.S. News and World Report*, "War on Alcohol Abuse Spreads to New Fronts" (Dec. 24, 1984); S. P. Sherman, "America's New Abstinence," *Fortune* (Mar. 18, 1985); M. J. Weiss, "The Crusade Against Drunk Driving," *Ladies Home Journal* (Feb. 1985). MADD was mentioned by name in all these accounts as the leading moral entrepreneur (the term is Howard Becker's [Outsiders]) behind this landslide of legislation. There were other anti-drinking-driving organizations that began a full two years prior to MADD, but none achieved MADD's visibility, size, or stature. By stressing the central role played by MADD here I do not wish to minimize other dynamics—electoral, organizational, or cultural. It is clear, however, that MADD generated the national and local publicity that made it nearly impossible for elected officials and state agencies not to respond. Frances Fox Piven and Richard Cloward have outlined a similar theoretical perspective on political change initiated from the grass roots; see their *Poor People's Movements* (New York: Vintage, 1977), 14–18 et passim.

20 Both McCarthy and Zald's resource mobilization perspective, which focuses on the capacities for movement organizations to mobilize human and financial resources, and Smelser's notion of "structural conduciveness" suggest the importance of historical context. See J. McCarthy and M. Zald, "Resource Mobilization and Social Movements—A Partial Theory," *American Journal of Sociology* 82 (1976), 1212–1241; N. Smelser, *Theory of Collective Behaviour* (New York: Macmillan, 1963).

21 MADD, *Newsletter* [national edition], Spring, 1982; "Mothers Against Drunk Drivers Position Paper on Alcohol Advertising," Hurst, Texas, 1985; *Advertising Age*, "Lightner Urges Ad Self-Rule" (Apr. 22, 1985); *Wall Street Journal*, "Crusaders Against Drunk Driving Split Over Whether to Fight Alcohol Broadly" (Nov. 6, 1985).

22 *Wall Street Journal*, "Industry Headache"; *Wall Street Journal*, "Crusaders Against Drunk Driving Split." The National Association of Broadcasters labeled the threat to alcohol-beverage advertising posed by CSPI and their SMART campaign "our number one priority." According to a CSPI representative, the alcohol industry has responded to the threat by casting aspersions on CSPI and public health officials, and by attempting to enhance "alcohol advertisers' public image" by sponsoring public service announcements against drinking-driving. Both quotes from *The Alcoholism Report*, volume XIII, number 3 (1984): 1.

23 R. L. Chauncey, "New Careers for Moral Entrepreneurs"; P. Morgan, "The State as Mediator: Alcohol Problem Management in the Post-War Period," *Contemporary Drug Problems* 9 (1980): 107–22; C. Wiener, *The Politics of Alcoholism*; R. Room, "Sociological Aspects of the Disease Concept."

24 Cited in Room, "Sociological Aspects of the Disease Concept," 62. See also R. Room, "Alcohol as Cause: Empirical Links and Social Definitions," in J. P. von Wartburg, P. Magnenat, R. Miller, and S. Wyss, editors, *Currents in Alcohol Research and the Prevention of Alcohol Problems*; Moore and Gerstein, editors, *Alcohol and Public Policy*; and the useful precursors from J. R. Seeley, "The W.H.O. Definition of Alcoholism," and "Alcoholism is a Disease."

25 See, for example, L. Wallack, "Drinking and Driving: Toward a Broader Understanding of the Role of Mass Media," *Journal of Public Health Policy*, 5 (1984): 471–96; R. Room, "Alcohol Control and Public Health," *Annual Review of Public Health*, 5(1984): 292–317. Cf. H. G. Levine, "What Is an Alcohol-Related Problem?", *Journal of Drug Issues* 14 (1984): 45–60. It should be noted that this public-health perspective was not necessarily invented de novo in the late 1970s. It may have been in some small way a recrudescence of a strand of temperance rhetoric that held that Prohibition was a preventative public-health measure (James Baumohl, personal communication, 1987), although I know of no evidence that current public-health professionals in the alcohol field knowingly draw upon or consider themselves part of a temperance tradition.

26 On the progressive facets of temperance politics, cf. Gusfield, *Symbolic Crusade*; Timberlake, *Prohibition and the Progressive Movement*; Blocker, *Retreat From Reform*. On the political beliefs and policy preferences of MADD activists, see S. Weed, "Local Chapter Leadership Study for MADD," mimeo (Arlington, University of Texas Center for Social Research, 1985); "Grass-Roots Activism and the Drunk-Driving Issue: A Survey of MADD Chapters," paper presented at the Annual Meeting of the *American Sociological Association*, Washington, DC, 1985.

27 M. Jacobson and R. Collins, "Ads Glamorize Alcohol, Hide Dangers," *New York Times* (Apr. 21, 1985).

28 MADD, "Fact Sheet," n.d.

29 One example of this tendency toward personal vilification was shown in a recent magazine article about MADD. Its lead (a tacit typification that could not have been better suited if created by a novelist) was about a "19 year old sailor" who, drunk *and* drugged, killed two innocents and had to be "hauled to the police station in a drunken rage" while he "cursed" his victims for "having wrecked his car." The article concludes with a quote from a local movement activist: "What he did

was no accident. When a person drinks, drives, and kills people, he's a murderer." Weiss, "The Crusade Against Drunk Driving."

30 Lee, "Techniques of Social Reform." It should be noted in passing here that although I found no evidence of direct support of MADD from the auto industry, it is quite clear that the movement's focus on the deviant drinking driver benefits the auto industry insofar as questions about automotive safety design and manufacture are not raised. Moreover, the auto industry was implicated by the National Highway Traffic Safety Administration in their push against drinking-driving in the late 1960s; see Gusfield, *The Culture of Public Problems*, chapters 2–3.

31 For example, D. Cohn, "Reformers of a New Breed Pour It on Against Alcohol," *Los Angeles Times* (Aug. 26, 1984).

32 On membership characteristics, see Weed, "Local Chapter Leadership Study for MADD"; and his "Grass-Roots Activism and the Drunk-Driver Issue"; and S. Ungerleider and S. A. Bloch, "Developing Grass Roots Support for Drinking Driving Countermeasures: A Review of Mothers Against Drunk Drivers," *Journal of Traffic Safety Education* (April, 1987): 20–22. On the relation between political and religious conservatism and MADD chapter formation, see F. J. Ritchey and L. L. Daniels, "Regional Variations in Support of the Anti-Drunk Driver Movement," paper presented at the annual meeting of the *Southern Sociological Society*, Atlanta, 1983. With regard to the role of evangelicals and the Republican party platform, see "Battling Drunk Driving," *Christianity Today* 26 (1982): 50–53. Further, the dean of New Right fundraising, Richard Viguerie, wrote in *Conservative Digest* that "people who feel strongly about drunk driving" are a key New Right constituency (cited in Ritchey and Daniels).

33 Max Weber, *The Protestant Ethic and the Spirit of Capitalism* (New York: Scribners, 1958), 90–92, emphasis added. The concept of elective affinity was used explicitly in "Die Wirtschaftsethick der Weltreligionen," *Archiv für Sozialforschung* 41 (1915), translated and edited by H. Gerth and C. W. Mills as "The Social Psychology of the World Religions," in their *From Max Weber* (New York: Oxford University Press, 1946), 284. The utility of the notion is that it does justice to influence without implying strict causality. In this sense it shares some features with the concept of "relative autonomy" as used in neo-Marxian writings.

34 The quotation is from *Business Week*, "The Sobering of America" (Feb. 25, 1985). The implication that state intervention in "private" spheres is a right-wing phenomenon is, of course, overly simple. Clearly the left far more than the right favors intervention against, e.g., "domestic tyrants" who physically abuse their wives or children, just as there are right-wing libertarians who oppose such intervention. Moreover, I am certain that moral outrage against drinking drivers is shared by people from all ideological camps. My point, however, is that the New Right seems to like to attribute all manner of social problems to individual deviance that is held to be the product of mere moral volition, and that MADD's "theory" of drinking-driving offers just such attributional advantages.

35 MADD, "National Newsletter," Hurst, Texas (Spring, 1985), 9; *Alcoholism Report*, XI, No. 16, Minneapolis: Johnson Institute (June 16, 1983), 4.

36 C. Weisner, "The Transformation of Alcohol Treatment: Access to Care and the Response to Drinking-Driving," *Journal of Public Health Policy* 7 (1986): 78–92; C. Weisner and R. Room, "Financing and Ideology in Alcohol Treatment," *Social Problems* 32 (1985): 167–84; R. Speiglman, "Issues in the Rise of Compulsion in California's Drinking Driver Treatment System," in M. R. Valverius, editor, *Punishment and/or Treatment for Driving Under the Influence of Alcohol and Other*

Drugs (Stockholm, Sweden: International Committee on Alcohol, Drugs, and Traffic Safety, 1985).

37 For example, see California Department of Drug and Alcohol Programs, *Alcohol Program Certification and Third-Party Payments*, ADP 82–113 (Sacramento, CA: Health and Welfare Agency, 1982).

38 C. Holden, "Alcoholism and the Medical Cost Crunch," *Science* 235 (1987): 1132–1133.

39 See also C. Reinarman, D. Waldorf, and S. Murphy, "Scapegoating and Social Control in the Construction of Public Problems: Cocaine in the Workplace," *Research in Law, Deviance, and Social Control* 9 (1987).

40 National Institute of Justice, *Jailing Drunk Drivers: Impact on the Criminal Justice System* (Washington, DC: U.S. Government Printing Office, 1985). See also W. L. Hepperle and D. Klein, "An Analysis of the Impact of the 1982 Drunk Driving Legislation on the Alameda County Municipal Courts" (Alameda County, CA: Office of Court Services, 1985).

41 *Wall Street Journal*, "Lawyers Are Finding Ways to Circumvent Stricter Statutes Against Drunken Driving" (Nov. 2, 1984), 33.

42 Room, "Sociological Aspects of the Disease Concept." Regarding "choice and compulsion," see R. Roizen, "Barriers to Alcoholism Treatment: Report Submitted to NIAAA," paper #F145, Alcohol Research Group, Berkeley, CA (1977). J. D. Orcutt, "Ideological Variations in the Structure of Deviant Types: A Multivariate Comparison of Alcoholism and Heroin Addiction," *Social Forces* 55 (1976): 419–39. On the ambivalent character of beliefs and the coexistence of multiple belief systems, see M. Edelman, Political Language (New York: Academic Press, 1977); Berger, *The Survival of a Counterculture*; and C. Reinarman, *American States of Mind: Political Beliefs and Behavior Among Private and Public Workers* (New Haven, CT: Yale University Press, 1987).

43 Professor James Baumohl of McGill University pointed out (personal communication, 1985) that the notion that there has been a transition per se from moral to medical models is in need of complication. While science, particularly medicine, has dominated discourse about alcohol problems since the 1940s, moralism did not so much go away as make an accommodation with the disease model (much as liberal theologians, in accepting science, kept on preaching, and, indeed, argued that science served or even derived from divine purpose). Such an accommodation appears easy enough to forge in the realm of public opinion (see Room, "Sociological Aspects of the Disease Concept") because one gets the "disease," after all, only by repeatedly engaging in what for some people is discrediting behavior. Thus MADD did not have to invent a new ideology in order to claim that drinking-driving stems from free will. For a general discussion of the vicissitudes of medicalization, see Conrad and Schneider, *Deviance and Medicalization*.

44 This is not meant to imply that MADD has been sole or even senior author of this shift. The convergence of broader trends in alcohol production and consumption and in state policies across several nations led Makela et al. to the following conclusion before MADD was organized: "There is a growing conflict between increased concern about alcohol problems and the economic interests of the alcohol trade that is exacerbated by static or declining markets. In a situation of increased acceptance of drinking in everyday life [in the 1950–1975 period], policies may tend even more toward individual control of deviant drinkers. In an era of contracting public-welfare resources, this tendency may be expressed more in punitive than in treatment-oriented measures." K. Makela et al., *Alcohol, Society,*

and the State: A Comparative Study of Alcohol Control (Toronto: Addiction Research Foundation, 1981), 111.

[45] Although the deductibility of alcoholic beverages as "business expenses" has been narrowed by the 1987 tax reforms, the tacit subsidy continues on a reduced scale.

[46] Gusfield, *The Culture of Public Problems*, 148.

[47] Drinking drivers were not generally taken as people having alcohol problems per se, but rather as routine or "folk" criminals; see ibid. They therefore did not often come within the welfare state sphere. Moreover, the U.S. welfare state, in this area as in most others, was and is quite stingy relative to those of other developed capitalist democracies. "Drunks," for example, still cannot get disability benefits despite the disease status of alcoholism. I offer this note only to qualify the more general point about the broader direction of social policy in the post-World War II period, which allowed "drunks" to be conceptualized in other than merely moral terms.

[48] Gusfield, "Alcohol Problems—An Interactionist View," 79.

[49] See R. Goldstein, "The New Sobriety: What We Risk When We Just Say No." *Village Voice* (Dec. 30, 1986), 23–28; H. Levine and C. Reinarman, "Abusing Drug Abuse: What's Behind 'Jar Wars,'" *The Nation* (Mar. 28, 1987), 388–90. On the expanding panoply of social controls on youth, see T. G. Carpenter, "The New Anti-Youth Movement," *The Nation* (Jan. 19, 1985), 39–41.

10

"Road Warriors" on "Hair-Trigger Highways"

Cultural Resources and the Media's Construction of the 1987 Freeway Shootings Problem

Joel Best

Theories of social problems construction argue that the concerns policymakers and the public have about particular social problems are not simply a reflection of objective facts about social conditions (Blumer 1971; Spector and Kitsuse 1977; Schneider 1985; Hilgartner and Bosk 1988). Rather, social problems emerge—become a focus for concern—through a process of claimsmaking. This process determines not only which phenomena come to be designated social problems but the characteristics ascribed to those problems. Problems can always be depicted in more than one way: rape as a sex crime or a crime of violence; marijuana as a cause of psychosis, a precursor to hard drugs, or a threat to economic productivity; and so on. Explaining how and why particular images of problems emerge has become a central task for constructionist analysts (Best 1989).

Typically, constructionist explanations examine the organization of the claimsmaking process, assuming that claims originate with activists, professionals, or others with vested interests in bringing attention to an issue and/or promoting a particular image of the problem. The news media then transform the primary claims of these individuals and relay the resulting secondary claims to the public (Fishman 1978; Fritz and

Source: *Sociological Inquiry*, Vol. 61, No. 3, August 1991, pp. 327–345. © 1991 by the University of Texas Press. Reprinted with permission.

Altheide 1987; Stallings 1990). According to this two-stage model, the resulting images of problems depend, in part, on the primary claims-makers' interests and ideology, the constraints imposed by the media's routines, and the rhetoric adopted in making both primary and secondary claims (Best 1990).

Although others' primary claims usually shape news coverage of social issues, the media's role need not be reactive; the press can act as primary claimsmaker, discovering and constructing social problems on its own. In such cases, there might seem to be few constraints on how the media characterize the problem. Yet in practice, the press usually presents these problems within familiar frameworks and describes them in familiar terms. Shootings on Los Angeles freeways offer an example: during the summer of 1987, the press discovered, promoted, and then dropped this problem. Examination of this coverage reveals conventional elements, common to discussions of many other social problems. The conventional nature of this coverage is this article's topic. Unconstrained by independent primary claimsmakers, the press might have characterized freeway violence in many different ways. In fact, the media's treatment of freeway violence resembles most other social problems coverage. What accounts for this standardized, taken-for-granted treatment?

Sociological studies of the news media suggest that the answer lies in the nature of news work: reporters and editors work within constraints (e.g., television news broadcast time limits) for which they develop routines (e.g., television news favors stories which can be illustrated with videotape) (cf. Gans 1979; Gitlin 1980; Tuchman 1978). No doubt such routines helped shape the media's treatment of freeway violence, but they alone cannot account for the particular way the problem was described.

The press's coverage also drew upon a fund of cultural resources. In constructing freeway violence as a social problem, the media adopted a familiar template of elements routinely used in social problems coverage, borrowed familiar cultural images, and otherwise located the problem within a taken-for-granted cultural framework. Examining the use of cultural resources in claimsmaking about freeway shootings reveals the role of cultural concerns in the larger process of social problems construction.

Methods

This article analyzes the imagery used to construct the 1987 freeway violence problem in three major news media: newspapers (including all relevant stories, editorials, columns, and cartoons from the *Los*

Angeles Times, Los Angeles Herald Examiner, San Francisco Chronicle, and New York Times as well as selected items from other papers and interviews with two reporters who wrote key stories); magazines (including all stories indexed in the Reader's Guide to Periodical Literature); and national television broadcasts (videotapes of all eleven network news stories indexed in Television News Index and Abstracts, as well as a printed transcript for ABC's Nightline [July 30]). While not a systematic sample of press coverage, the sources examined include many of the most significant treatments—both local and national—of the freeway violence problem.

This analysis does not try to contrast the media's construction with the "reality" of freeway shootings, if only because it is impossible to convincingly draw such a contrast. Media coverage is virtually the only source of information about freeway violence; the short-lived problem produced no official records, victimization surveys, or public opinion polls, and only a single social scientific study of the phenomenon.[1] In 1987, for instance, no agency kept official statistics on the incidence of freeway shootings, nor was there any way to determine whether the rate of incidents had changed from the preceding years. Reporters covering the story compiled their own lists of violent incidents and argued that these incidents reflected a new social trend. The issue is not whether this was a "real" trend—a largely unanswerable question—but how journalists used "trend" and other language to characterize freeway shootings.

Evaluation of the freeway violence problem begins by examining the template—the standard elements of description, explanation, and interpretation—used in new stories about social problems. Then the author considers three sorts of imagery—popular culture, humor, and random violence—used as cultural resources in constructing freeway violence as a social problem and suggests some circumstances which affect claimsmakers' choices of images. Finally, an explanation is offered for the emergence and disappearance of freeway shootings as a social problem.

Freeway Shootings and the Template for Social Problems Stories

The 1987 freeway shootings problem seems to have been discovered in a June 26 Los Angeles Times column, "No Shelter From Freeway Violence," which suggested "there is a malevolence loose on those roads . . ." (Sauter 1987a). A month later, freeway violence received nationwide notice: all three television networks broadcast stories on their evening news programs; all three major newsweeklies ran stories; and feature articles, columns, and editorial cartoons appeared in newspapers throughout the country (see Appendix). After about three weeks, the national media turned to new topics, although freeway shootings occasionally resurfaced, e.g., a November, 1987 *Glamour* self-help article ("How to Handle On-the-Road Hostility"), and a 1988 exploitation movie (*Freeway*).

While short-lived, the media's treatment of freeway violence resembled coverage of other, better-established social problems. The press described freeway shootings as a social phenomenon, offered explanations for the violence, and located the problem within familiar interpretive schemes. These elements—description, explanation, and interpretation—form a template for social problems coverage. Although most contemporary news stories about social problems fit this template, the emphasis on description, explanation, and interpretation is socially constructed. Different news templates occur in other times and places, such as framing news stories in moralistic or ideological terms (Hallin and Mancini 1984).

Describing the Problem

On June 24, the *Los Angeles Times* ran a brief story, "2nd Freeway Shooting Incident Is Investigated," noting that there had been two apparently unrelated shootings during the previous weekend (Stewart 1987). This story seems to have performed a central task in social problems construction: it established a new category (freeway shooting), thereby redefining the two *incidents* as *instances* of a new problem. In Fishman's (1978, p. 534) language, freeway violence became a "news theme," which "presents a specific news event, or a number of such events, in terms of some broader concept." The new category inspired the June 26 column which claimed there had been "four unrelated freeway shootings over the past 10 months" (Sauter 1987a). Sauter later explained that this column reflected "a desire to seize on a trendoid—the journalistic category reflecting something new, potentially interesting and possibly—just possibly—indicative of a trend" (1987b). *Times* reporters recall that they were now "watching for a trend." An editor assigned reporter Lonn Johnston to write a feature article on the topic. Completed after a few days, the story "was held [i.e., not published] for a couple weeks" (Bill Billiter and Lonn Johnston, telephone interviews, 1989).

Journalists have a rule of thumb: once a third thing happens, you have a trend. The July 20 *Times* news story—"Traffic Dispute Results in Third Freeway Shooting"—revived the concept (Billiter 1987). The next day, Johnston's feature article (amended with a "new top" referring to the newest incident) appeared, shifting the focus from news reports about particular incidents to a general analysis of the freeway violence problem ("a new kind of urban warfare") (Johnston 1987). The same day, the *Los Angeles Herald Examiner*'s (1987) editorial cartoon showed a motorist shopping for "the ultimate freeway defense vehicle"—a tank.

The category was now familiar. A July 26 story began: "While police searched for suspects in the latest highway shooting . . ." (Kendall 1987); it was the first of four front-page *Times* pieces over five days. (The *Herald Examiner* ran front-page freeway violence stories on twelve of the fourteen days from July 21 to August 3.) As the story received more attention, the freeway shootings category began showing elasticity: not all reported incidents occurred on freeways, and not all involved shooting. Some reporters began using broader terms to refer to the problem; e.g., "traffic-related shootings" or "roadway violence," and a variety of incidents were presented as instances of the category, including rocks thrown at windshields (ABC *Nightline*, July 30) and:

> . . . one copycat has moved from the freeways to the busy Southern California skyways. The pilot of a Cessna says he was threatened by the pilot of another plane, who flew close—alongside—and pointed a handgun (CBS, August 5).

Press reports described freeway shootings as a series of incidents—"sudden evolution," "trend," "wave," "spate," "spree," "upsurge," "fad," "rash"—an "epidemic," "plaguing Southern California," "reaching alarming proportions." However, some reporters acknowledged that it was impossible to document increasing freeway violence. The category had no official standing; no law enforcement agency kept records of freeway shootings as such, and the press had no way to measure shifts in incidence. Instead, reporters quoted officials to the effect that violence seemed more common and referred to a running total of incidents, usually beginning with shots fired at a motorcyclist on June 18 (a case not mentioned in any of the early *Times* stories). By August, the list included over forty incidents.

Descriptions of the shootings emphasized that they began with mundane traffic disputes, that they seemed random, without clear motive, irrational. CBS anchorperson Dan Rather noted, "authorities are dealing with, literally, murderous rage" (CBS, July 24), but other stories spoke of copycats and "triggermen out for a cruel joke" (NBC, July 29). The result, reporters suggested, was freeways becoming "shooting galleries," "scenes of combat," "war zones," or a "terror zone."

If freeway shootings were random and senseless, then their context was irrelevant. For instance, the first network news story about freeway violence featured a typifying example:

> REPORTER JERRY BOWEN: Nineteen-year-old Jiang Nan was shot by another motorist last month during a race for a freeway exit. [video: shots of Nan in hospital bed] (CBS, July 24)

Three nights later, Nan reappeared in a story on another network:

REPORTER KEN KASHUIHARA: Jiang Nan was shot in the arm because, he says, he honked his horn at another driver. [video: Nan walking, bandaged]

NAN: You can't go around people, shooting people because people just honk your horn. You know. That's not right. [video: close-up of Nan speaking, sitting in car's driver's seat, labeled "Jiang Nan—Victim"] (ABC, July 27).

CBS and ABC used Jiang Nan's experience to exemplify the randomness of freeway violence. In contrast, the *Los Angeles Times* story about the same incident offered more information about its context:

Alhambra Police Detective Jim Varga said Sunday's shooting occurred after two cars approached the New Avenue freeway on-ramp in Alhambra at about the same time, and the drivers "began jockeying for position to see who would get on first."

Once on the freeway, occupants of both cars threw paper cups and other items at each other, and the other driver tried to prevent Nan from changing lanes, Varga said. When Nan headed for the Atlantic Boulevard exit, the gunman opened fire, striking Nan in the arm. (Stewart 1987).

This description makes the shooting seem less random, less an irrational response ("shooting people because people just honk your horn"), and more like the escalating "character contests" which often precede interpersonal violence (Luckenbill 1984). While the press did not offer detailed accounts of every incident, other reports showed violence emerging from a context of conflict. For instance, the aerial gun-waving incident mentioned above involved rival planes engaged in fish-spotting (Trippett 1987). Some reporters seemed to restrict the concept of freeway shootings to random incidents: "investigators believe that as many as four of the recent shootings involved gang activity or narcotics and may not have been examples of random roadway violence" (Kendall and Jones 1987, p. 20). In other words, not all shootings on freeways were "freeway shootings." (In 1987, the media attributed five deaths to freeway violence, but the CDC researchers, after eliminating cases involving prior disputes, found only two [one on a freeway] [Onwuachi-Saunders, Chukwudi, Lambert, Marchbanks, O'Carroll and Mercy 1989].)

If freeway shootings were random and on the rise, then all motorists were potential victims. The media reported that fear was widespread, that some motorists were buying bulletproof windshields or arming themselves to fight back, and that there had been a "courtesy surge by drivers fearful of reprisals" (Dean 1987, Gest 1987).

In short, the media described freeway shootings as a growing problem, characterized by random violence and widespread fear. Without official statistics or public opinion polls bearing on the topic, reporters relied on interviews with their sources to support these claims. Thus, the eleven network news stories used thirty-eight clips from interviews:

eleven with law enforcement officials promising to take action or advising caution; thirteen victims describing their experiences; ten person-in-the-street interviews revealing public concern; and four experts offering explanations.

Explaining the Problem

Having discovered and described freeway violence, the press sought to explain this new social problem. These explanations came from interviews with experts, mostly psychiatrists and social scientists who offered some version of frustration-aggression theory (cf. Dollard, Miller, Doob, Mowrer, and Sears 1939):

> Maybe you have a short fuse. Maybe you have a gun in a car. You're wrapped in steel armor, plenty of power under your foot, but constantly boxed in by traffic. A feeling of impotence and anger, and then someone cuts you off. That, authorities say, is how the shootings began. Then perhaps some people began firing for fun (NBC, August 3)

In this view, driving in congested "creep-hour traffic" produced stress and frustration which, in turn, led to anger and escalated into shootings and other violent acts (Lobue 1987).[2] Almost all press reports offered some version of this explanation; some added secondary accounts. Several stories suggested that a car's anonymity made aggression less risky ("It's the private bubble that brings out Mr. Hyde" [Johnston 1987, p. 3]); others implied that media coverage encouraged copycat crimes. Still others alluded to the effects of summer heat, "increased levels of violent crime in general, the prevalence of violence on television, drug and alcohol abuse, and even the breakdown of the family" (Armstrong, 1987, p. 4).

Interpreting the Problem

If freeway violence was a social problem, what sort of problem was it? There were several answers to this question, examples of what Gamson and Modigliani (1989) call interpretive packages:

> A package has an internal structure. At its core is a central organizing idea, or *frame*, for making sense of relevant events, suggesting what is at issue. . . . Finally, a package offers a number of different condensing symbols that suggest the core frame and positions in short-hand, making it possible to display the package as a whole with a deft metaphor, catch-phrase, or other symbolic device. (Gamson and Modigliani 1989, p. 3—emphasis in original).

These interpretations offered different orientations to understanding freeway violence and had different implications for social policy.

Perhaps the most straightforward interpretation treated freeway shootings as a *crime problem*. Government and law enforcement officials emphasized this theme. One Highway Patrol officer declared:

"These are difficult crimes to try to stop for law enforcement. These are ty—, these are crimes of passion which are akin to the types of crime that occur, uh, between family members" (NBC, August 3). If freeway violence was a crime problem, then its solution lay in increased patrols, better investigations, and more effective prosecution. All three freeway-violence bills which became law fit this model: A.B. 2416 added officers to the Highway Patrol; A.B. 2142 forbade probation for convicted offenders; and S.B. 117 created an additional five-year penalty for persons convicted in freeway shootings (Gillam 1987).

Other analysts portrayed freeway violence as a *traffic problem*, a product of congested highways. While Los Angeles Police Chief Daryl Gates (1987) warned of a "breakdown in self-discipline," his op-ed piece concentrated on ways to improve traffic flow, e.g., closing rush-hour freeways to single-occupant cars. Interpreting freeway violence as a traffic problem implied a need for new freeways, mass transportation, or other means of reducing congestion, although such long-term solutions rarely received detailed discussion.

Still others treated freeway violence as a *gun problem*, one more consequence of the ready availability of firearms. Newspaper editorial pages favored this interpretation; the *Times* (1987a; 1987c) and *San Francisco Chronicle* (1987b) editorials on freeway shootings advocated gun control, and the *Washington Post* (1987) ran a Herblock cartoon, showing a roadside gun stand with signs reading "Last Chance to Reload Before Freeway" and "NRA Freeway Special."

Several commentators spoke of a *courtesy problem*; they viewed the violence as a product of aggressive, hurried, self-centered driving habits. One "recovering Type A" urged people to change their habits: "It takes self-confidence to be a freeway wimp" (Brenner 1987). The CDC researchers offered a *medical* interpretation: "the full public health impact of roadway violence has never been investigated. Roadway assaults could have an enormous emotional impact on drivers in Los Angeles County as well as throughout the United States" (Onwuachi-Saunders et al. 1989, p. 2264). Finally, there were suggestions that freeway shootings were really a *media problem*, "a combination of coincidence and media hype" (Royko 1987a). But even these critics seemed to agree that more than hype was at work; after describing the "media circus," *Newsweek* went on to discuss traffic congestion—"the real cause of L.A.'s sudden evolution from 'Have a Nice Day' to 'Make My Day'" (Kaus 1987).

The Template for Social Problems Coverage

In covering freeway violence, the press concentrated on description, explanation, and interpretation. These are, of course, standard elements for stories about social problems; they form a template for social problems coverage. Because the press places a premium on the novel and the exotic, description is central to the construction of new social problems. Explanation and interpretation offer accounts for these problems. Some analysts argue that, while the American press is overtly nonideological, its underlying message is hegemonic (Gitlin 1980). In this view, freeway violence would be an attractive candidate for press coverage, because it could be explained as a problem caused by the flawed characters of deviant individuals rather than by flawed social institutions.

The only unusual feature of the press coverage was the diversity of interpretive schemes presented. Stallings (1990, p. 90) argues that the media prefer noncausal explanations; while early press coverage may offer competing interpretations, "later accounts tend to converge on a single factor." This failed to happen in the case of freeway violence, probably because the media continued to play the role of primary claimsmaker. Most social problems coverage follows the lead of the independent primary claimsmakers who promote a particular interpretation. Because the press discovered freeway violence, there was no single authoritative interpretation, commentators adapted several familiar interpretive packages, albeit from within a limited ideological range. Thus, interpretations of the problem came from both conservatives (crime problem) and liberals (gun problem), but there was no radical critique, challenging important institutional arrangements. Moreover, there were no parties who chose to make the issue their own, who made determined efforts to promote their interpretation over rival viewpoints.

Culture and Claims

Constructionist analysts suggest that it is easier to promote claims which "fit closely with broad cultural concerns" (Hilgartner and Bosk 1988, p. 64), which "resonate with larger cultural themes" (Gamson and Modigliani 1989, p. 5). The media's treatment of freeway shootings was noteworthy for the ease with which it incorporated imagery from other sources. Often, claimsmakers who presented different interpretations of freeway violence drew upon similar images.

Popular Culture

Discussions of freeway violence frequently borrowed images from violent films. Reporters invoked references to crime thrillers ("Make My Day"), action pictures set in post-Vietnam ("Freeway Rambos") or post-apocalyptic society ("Road Warriors," "A Mad Max mentality"), and Westerns ("hair-trigger impulses reminiscent of the frontier West" [Cummings 1987]). These images fit nicely with interpretations of freeway shootings as a crime or gun problem.

The importance of the film industry to Los Angeles no doubt encouraged these allusions to contemporary movies, and the frequent use of violent automotive chase scenes in action pictures must have helped forge the link between freeway shootings and movie imagery. But references to popular culture are not uncommon in constructions of social problems; most obviously, "Star Wars" has become a standard referent in defense policy debates.

Popular culture is a readily available cultural resource, offering a vast array of familiar images which are easily adapted to claimsmaking. There are advantages to using these images: they suggest that the claimsmaker is clever or up-to-date and they make claims more accessible or more interesting to a wider audience. But these advantages come at a cost. When popular cultural images typify a problem, they shape perceptions of it.

Thus, suggestions that freeway shootings somehow resembled the extraordinary violence in formula films implied an ambivalence toward violence, since popular culture simultaneously celebrates and deplores violence. And, since U.S. popular culture tends to locate good and evil within individual heros and villains, the movie imagery may have helped define freeway shootings in terms of deviant individuals. Finally, likening brief incidents of freeway violence to the prolonged, dramatic violence found in films implied a level of violence far greater than that found in press reports of particular freeway shootings. Although the references to Mad Max and Rambo were playful, they exaggerated the problem's seriousness.

Humor

Reports of freeway violence also inspired cartoonists and humor columnists. Most often, their work used exaggeration to make the problem seem ridiculous. Instead of depicting freeways as scenes of criminal violence, cartoonists militarized the problem (e.g., depicting a middle-class couple in a car, with the middle-aged female passenger wearing a Rambo-style headband and aiming a rocket launcher [Los Angeles Times 1987b], or showing a traffic reporter's helicopter under fire [San Francisco Chronicle 1987a]). Playing on reporters' references to war zones and Rambo, these cartoons extended the problem to a ridiculous extreme, showing ordinary people taking extraordinary violence for granted. Other cartoons contrasted freeway violence with earthquakes and drunk driving (Los Angeles Times 1987d, 1987e), suggesting that shootings were just one added problem faced by long-suffering urbanites. The humor lay in the implication that freeway shootings were mundane, not at all extraordinary, that random danger is simply another hazard of urban life. (Compare the analogous cartoons about nineteenth-century English crime waves in Pearson [1983]).

Other humor depended on freeway shootings having emerged in Los Angeles, notorious for its heavy, fast-moving freeway traffic. Thus, a CBS (July 24) story began: "It's always been crazy on the Southern California freeways—a real zoo—but these days the animals are armed and dangerous," while columnist Lewis Grizzard (1987) noted, ". . . there are more crazy people in Los Angeles than anywhere else in the country." Here, stereotypes of Southern California provided a cultural resource for the humorists. Other humorists warned that the roots of freeway violence were mundane, that aggressive driving was widespread, and that it was only a small step from everyday hostility to extraordinary violence (cf. Royko 1987b). Thus, all parties—and the larger culture—were to blame when incidents escalated to violence. As these examples suggest, claimsmakers incorporated humor into almost all of the competing interpretations of freeway violence.

Random Violence

The humorists' treatments of freeway shootings, like the reporters' references to Rambo, suggest a failure to take the problem completely seriously. However, most of the humor was not pointed; it made fun of the phenomenon, rather than the people involved. At the same time, press reports emphasized the random, senseless qualities of freeway violence, warning that ordinary drivers, going about their everyday business, were potential victims. This drew upon a more general, contemporary concern with irrational, capricious villains. The 1980s saw the construction of other villains said to strike at random, including serial murderers, strangers abducting children, and product-tampering copycats. (The movie *Freeway* illustrates the ease with which these typifications can be blended: its villain is an ex-priest, ex-mental-patient serial killer who shoots other motorists while talking to a radio psychiatrist on a car phone. The film was previewed under the title *Drive-By* [an allusion to the "wave" of "drive-by shootings" linked to Los Angeles gangs—another problem defined in terms of random violence]).

In the 1960s and 1970s, asserting randomness became a standard tactic for claimsmakers seeking to raise social concern; defining all children as potential child-abuse victims or all women as potential rape victims gave the widest possible audience an interest in confronting these problems. But it is easy to move from saying "X happens to all sorts of people," to "X can happen to anyone," to "X occurs randomly." And defining events as random encourages people to ignore or deny patterns in social life. Thus, claims that freeway shootings were random linked this problem to those involving other menacing deviants, while discouraging critical analysis of the problem's nature.

Incorporating Cultural Images

Because there were no independent primary claimsmakers guiding the interpretation of freeway shootings, the media had a relatively free hand in constructing the problem. However, rather than treating freeway violence as a unique phenomenon, the press located the problem within a set of existing—and not necessarily consistent—cultural concerns. Freeway shootings were said to resemble violent elements in popular culture, to have humorous features, and to reflect the random impulses of violent criminals. Confronted with a "new" problem, the media borrowed established cultural images to discuss it, with advocates of very different interpretations adopting similar imagery.

The problem's Southern California setting explains the frequent references to the film industry, the Los Angeles freeways, and the character of Californians. Not surprisingly, a different imagery characterized media coverage of an earlier "outbreak" of freeway violence in Houston, Texas in 1982 (King 1982; Ivey 1983). In particular, there were references to the frontier West ("gunfighter," "posse"), while the most prominent explanation held that Houston's economic boom had attracted "Texas newcomers," producing a "clash of cultures on the highway." A 1987 *Houston Post* article ("Freeway free-for-all: Why on Los Angeles' highways and not Houston's?") argued that, while Houston led the nation in traffic congestion, the city's recent economic slowdown had reduced the influx of newcomers and slowed the "frantic pace of life," causing a decline in freeway shootings (Flood 1987).

The contrasting treatments of freeway violence in Los Angeles and Houston suggest that primary claimsmaking by the media will usually draw from a pool of available imagery. This resembles Swidler's (1986, p. 273) model of culture "as a 'tool kit' of symbols, stories, rituals, and worldviews, which people may use in varying configurations to solve different kinds of problems." In this view, "individuals select the meanings they need . . . from the limited but nonetheless varied cultural menu a given society provides" (Schudson 1989, p. 155). Thus, reporters covering the 1987 freeway shootings incorporated familiar images—references to recent films, expertise from psychiatrists and social scientists, humorous stereotypes about Californians and their freeways, and warnings about random violence. If nothing else, the time constraints of news work make this sort of borrowing likely.

The problem with this tool-kit model is that it does not help us predict which images will be used to construct which problems (Schudson 1989). But claims do not emerge in a vacuum; they have an organizational context which affects the choice of imagery in at least three stages of the claimsmaking process. First, primary claimsmakers have ideologies, professional training, perceived interests, and other concerns which shape their construction of social problems. Claimsmakers' identities affect their characterization of problems; where moralists see sin, medical authorities detect disease.

Second, primary claimsmakers find themselves competing with one another for media attention. Not all claims receive coverage, and the press favors those which are dramatic, sponsored by powerful groups, and "relate to deep mythic themes" (Hilgartner and Bosk 1988, p. 64). Thus, bigots, political radicals, religious fundamentalists, and others outside the political and cultural mainstream have trouble getting the press to listen to their claims and often complain that the coverage they do receive distorts what they have to say. The media's role as a filter is less obvious when (as in the case of freeway violence) they act as primary claimsmakers. Here, reporters have insiders' knowledge of what makes a good story; they understand the template for social problems stories and shape their reports to fit.

In turn, media coverage shapes the reactions of policymakers and the public. Gamson and Modigliani (1989) discuss this third stage, arguing that the impact of claims depends upon the rhetoric and activities of primary and secondary claimsmakers and upon whether the claims have "cultural resonance." Claims presented in terms which are unfamiliar or ill-matched to the larger culture's concerns have little impact.

In short, while primary claimsmakers may seem to have a great deal of freedom in composing claims, they are in practice constrained by their own perceptions of the problem, the expectations of the press, and the concerns of policymakers and the public. Even so, the language and imagery used by independent primary claimsmakers is likely to be more diverse than the rhetoric adopted when the press serves as primary claimsmaker. When not prompted by outside claimsmakers, reporters and editors construct social problems within the familiar limits of news-work conventions. These constraints help explain why, in the case of freeway violence, the media adapted familiar explanations, interpretations, and images in their presentation of the problem. Still, the impact of those claims depended on a set of contingencies which shaped the rise—and fall—of the freeway shootings problem.

The Natural History of a Short-Lived Social Problem

Three contingencies accounted for the emergence of freeway violence as a social problem. First, the "freeway violence" category had to be discovered; someone had to define separate incidents as part of a larger pattern. The resulting category had its own appeal: it offered both drama (as a violent crime) and immediacy (i.e., most people were part of freeway traffic and therefore at risk). Yet freeway violence was not controversial; the media's construction of the problem did not threaten any powerful interest. And television had little difficulty illustrating the problems with videotape of dense traffic, bulletholes in cars, and interviews with victims. Once discovered, freeway violence fit several of the media's requirements for a good social problems story.

Still, these features alone cannot explain freeway violence becoming a focus for national attention. Most crime waves attract only local news coverage (Fishman 1978). Other outbreaks of freeway shootings—in California in 1977 (*Los Angeles Times* 1987a), Detroit in 1989 (*New York Times* 1989), and Houston in 1982—failed to attract as much national attention as the 1987 Los Angeles incidents.

This suggests the importance of a second contingency: the *Los Angeles Times* discovered freeway shootings. As the most authoritative newspaper in its state and region, it sets the agenda for Southern California print and electronic news coverage; a story treated seriously by the *Times* is likely to be picked up by radio and television stations, as well as other newspapers (Best 1986). (The fact that Van Gordon Sauter, the author of the first *Times* column on freeway shootings, was a former president of CBS News may have given the story additional authority.) Moreover, as a major metropolitan region and the center for the entertainment industry, Los Angeles has more than its share of reporters. Major newsmagazines and newspapers station correspondents there. All three television networks own and operate affiliates in Los Angeles, and the network news programs favor reports from owned and operated stations (Epstein 1973). Moreover, the widespread perception that Southern California often sets styles for the rest of the country makes it more likely that a Los Angeles "trend" will receive coverage in the national press.

Third, timing may have been important. There seem to have been relatively few stories competing for media attention. Journalistic folklore speaks of summer "dog days" and the "silly season" when news is slow, reporters must look harder for stories, and marginal stories are more likely to receive coverage. It may well be easier to gain coverage for social-problems claimsmaking during the summer. Consider the "crack epidemic" of 1986, freeway shootings in 1987, and the interest in polluted beaches in 1988. Claimsmakers must compete for media attention but, to the degree that this competition is seasonal, there may be periods when relatively weak claims can rise to visibility.

Taken together, these contingencies—the discovery of the category, by the *Los Angeles Times*, during a slow news season—help account for the rise of freeway violence to national prominence. Because the freeway shootings emanated from Southern California—often a source for new trends—the media anticipated that violence would spread. On CBS (August 5), Dan Rather asked: "Is it a local phenomenon, or does it indicate something in the country as a whole, something in society at large?"

Broadcasting from Chicago, ABC's (August 6) Peter Jennings noted, "There haven't been any incidents here in the Midwest. . . ." But the *Wall Street Journal* argued that the violence was nationwide: "the nation's freeways now resemble something out of the Wild West" (Gonzales 1987). In its August 17 issue, *Time* noted: "Highway officials in Arizona, Washington, Utah, and Northern California reported armed confrontations last week" (Trippett 1987); three months later, a short item reported freeway violence "appears to have faded on the West Coast but is all the rage in southern Illinois and is spreading to eastern Missouri" (*Time* 1987). However, these isolated reports were apparently insufficient to maintain media interest in freeway violence as a spreading problem.

The failure to document a dramatic spread in freeway shootings helps account for their disappearance as a social problem. Freeway violence both emerged and disappeared quickly. Why? The news media constructed the problem, but the story did not develop in any of the ways which might have let it remain visible. The light-hearted tone of some coverage may have discouraged people from taking the problem seriously. The press did not find sufficient cases to portray freeway violence as spreading throughout the country, nor did reporters find a growing number of incidents in Los Angeles; there was no dramatic new news to keep the story alive. Moreover, there were no independent primary claimsmakers interested in pursuing and promoting the story. The media brought freeway violence to public attention without prompting from outside claimsmakers. Once the problem achieved visibility, it might have been adopted by claimsmakers outside the press, but this did not happen, probably because the principal interpretations of the problem called for solutions which seemed unworkable. Whatever the arguments for expanded freeways, mass transportation, or other long-term solutions to Los Angeles traffic problems, few advocates expected progress, let alone solutions, in the near future. And defining freeway shootings as a gun problem offered little advantage; the tiny number of freeway homicides could not affect the entrenched debate over gun control. In other words, no constituency emerged to adopt the newly-constructed freeway shooting problem, to nurture it and help it develop into a well-established social problem.

Conclusion

Freeway violence offers an example of a short-lived social problem in which the media acted as primary claimsmakers. This problem was discovered and constructed by enterprising reporters and press commentators. In 1987, theirs were the only voices to be heard on the subject. Because they had a free hand in constructing this problem, we can view the result as a prototype of social-problems construction as practiced by the media. Most striking are the similarities between the construction of freeway shootings and the media's treatment of other social problems. The press framed its coverage within a standard structure, using a template of elements—description, explanation, and interpretation—usually found in contemporary social-problems stories. Moreover, the media adapted a variety of cultural resources, such as references to popular culture and random violence, to depict freeway shootings. The particular construction which emerged—a frightening yet funny spectacle of Los Angelinos, pushed beyond endurance by the frustrations of freeway driving, turning to random shootings and somehow incorporating this violence into their everyday lives—was engaging enough (and the immediate competition for media attention weak enough) to catapult freeway violence into national visibility. However, there was little to sustain the media's interest, and the attention soon faded.

By mid-August, 1987, freeway violence had disappeared from national news coverage. Still, the problem retains some familiarity and remains the subject of occasional asides (e.g., an article describes how Japanese drivers respond to a traffic jam, then notes: "this passivity is better than gunning other motorists down, as in Los Angeles" [Fallows 1989, p. 52]). Freeway shootings, then, have become a cultural resource in their own right, available for use in the construction of other social problems.

Appendix

Chronology of Principal 1987 Coverage of Freeway Violence
(June 24–August 11)

Wed., June 24 —*L.A. Times* story about "2nd Freeway Shooting"

Fri., June 26 —*L.A. Times* column about "freeway violence"

Mon., July 20 —*L.A. Times* story about "Third Freeway Shooting"

Tue., July 21 —*L.A. Times* feature article on "War Out There"

Fri., July 24 —CBS story (2:10)

Sat., July 25 —ABC story (2:00)

Sun., July 26 —NBC story (:20); *S.F. Examiner* front-page feature article on "Road Warriors"; *L.A. Herald Examiner* front-page feature article on "Hair-Trigger Highways"

Mon., July 27 —ABC story (2:40); *N.Y. Times* article

Wed., July 29 —NBC story (2:20)

Thu., July 30 —ABC *Nightline* episode

Fri., July 31 —*L.A. Times* front-page feature article on "Coping with Violence"; *L.A. Herald Examiner* front-page feature article "Shedding Light on Dark Side of L.A. Drivers"

Sun., August 2 —ABC story (1:40); NBC story (:30); *S.F. Examiner* feature article on "Freeway 'Rambos'"

Mon., August 3 —NBC story (1:50); *Christian Science Monitor* and *Wall Street Journal* articles

Tue., August 4 —*Newsweek* article—"Gunplay on the Freeway"; *U.S. News* article—"Rambo's Brothers Cruise Clogged Expressways"

Wed., August 5 —CBS story (2:40)

Thu., August 6 —ABC story (2:00); NBC story (:20)

Tue., August 11—*Time* article—"Highway to Homicide"

Notes

[1] Researchers from the Centers for Disease Control (CDC) compared summertime "roadway firearm assaults" in Los Angeles, 1985–87. They searched law enforcement records for reported incidents involving "the shooting or brandishing of a firearm at occupants of a moving vehicle on any freeway, highway, or surface street," then eliminated cases deemed gang-related or "the result of preexisting domestic quarrels" (Onwuachi-Saunders et al. 1989, p. 2262). They found 137 incidents in 1987 (49 on freeways)—an increase over 1985 (32 incidents, 4 on freeways) and 1986 (91 incidents, 15 on freeways).

[2] Novaco (1987) noted an important flaw in this explanation: "The road assaults are not being done by commuters. . . ." Many incidents occurred, not during heavily-congested rush hours, but at night or on weekends—a pattern common to other violent crimes. For instance, four of the five fatalities attributed to freeway violence occurred on weekend nights, two in a single incident at an intersection with a stop sign (i.e., not on a freeway). The CDC researchers note that "more than two-thirds (69%) of the 1987 assaults occurred outside of the hours of peak traffic flow," although they "found a positive association between freeway congestion and freeway firearm assaults" (Onwuachi-Saunders et al. 1989, p. 2264).

References

Armstrong, Scott. 1987. "Southern California Freeway Shootings Test Drivers, Police." *Christian Science Monitor* (August 3):3.

Best, Joel. 1986. "Famous for Fifteen Minutes." *Qualitative Sociology* 9:372–82.

_____. 1989. *Images of Issues*, edited by Joel Best. New York: Aldine de Gruyter.

_____. 1990. *Threatened Children*. Chicago: University of Chicago Press.

Billiter, Bill. 1987. "Traffic Dispute Results in Third Freeway Shooting." *Los Angeles Times* (July 20):13.

Blumer, Herbert. 1971. "Social Problems as Collective Behavior." *Social Problems* 18:298–306.

Brenner, Martin. 1987. "Power to the Freeway Wimps." *Los Angeles Times* (August 5): 117.

Cummings, Judith. 1987. "On Congested Highways, California Motorists Turn to Violence." *New York Times* (July 28): I10.

Dean, Paul. 1987. "Defensive Driving." *Los Angeles Times* (August 5): V1.

Dollard, J., N. E. Miller, L. W. Doob, O. H. Mowrer, and R. R. Sears. 1939. *Frustration and Aggression*. New Haven: Yale University Press.

Epstein, Edward Jay. 1973. *News from Nowhere*. New York: Random House.

Fallows, James. 1989. "Containing Japan." *Atlantic Monthly* 263 (May): 40–54.

Fishman, Mark. 1978. "Crime Waves as Ideology." *Social Problems* 25:531–43.

Flood, Mary. 1987. "Freeway Free-for-All." *Houston Post* (August 9): 1A, 20A.

Fritz, Noah J., and David L. Altheide. 1987. "The Mass Media and the Social Construction of the Missing Children Problem." *Sociological Quarterly* 28:473 92.

Gamson, William, and Andre Modigliani. 1989. "Media Discourse and Public Opinion on Nuclear Power." *American Journal of Sociology* 95:1–37.

Gans, Herbert J. 1979. *Deciding What's News*. New York: Pantheon.

Gates, Daryl F. 1987. "Highway Hostility Must Be Stopped." *Los Angeles Times* (August 23): V5.

Gest, Ted. 1987. "Rambo's Brothers Cruise Clogged Expressways." *U.S. News and World Report* 103 (August 10): 6.

Gillam, Jerry. 1987. "Bills Signed to Combat Violence on the Freeways." *Los Angeles Times* (September 27): I21.

Gitlin, Todd. 1980. *The Whole World Is Watching*. Berkeley: University of California Press.

Gonzales, Monica. 1987. "Motorist Mayhem." *Wall Street Journal* (August 3): 1, 14.

Grizzard, Lewis. 1987. "How to Avoid Getting Shot." *Atlanta Constitution* (August 2): B1.

Hallin, Daniel C., and Palolo Mancini. 1984. "Speaking of the President." *Theory and Society* 13:829–50.

Hilgartner, Stephen, and Charles L. Bosk. 1988. "The Rise and Fall of Social Problems." *American Journal of Sociology* 94:53–78.

Ivey, Mark. 1983. "Where the Commuter Is A Gunfighter." *Business Week* (May 1): 20A, B.

Johnston, Lonn. 1987. "Stress on Freeways Sparks 'War Out There'." *Los Angeles Times* (July 21): I3.

Kaus, Mickey. 1987. "Gunplay on the Freeway." *Newsweek* 110 (August 10): 18.

Kendall, John. 1987. "Death Raises Level of Fear on Highways." *Los Angeles Times* (July 26): I1.

Kendall, John, and Jack Jones. 1987. "4 Men, Woman Held in Highway Shooting Death." *Los Angeles Times* (July 29): I1, 20.

King, Wayne. 1982. "'Unfriendly Driving' Explodes into Violence on Texas Freeways." *New York Times* (December 17): A16.

Lobue, Ange. 1987. "Mayhem on the Freeways." *U.S. News and World Report* 103 (September 28): 9.

Los Angeles Herald Examiner. 1987. Editorial cartoon (July 21): A14.

Los Angeles Times. 1987a. "Guns and Tire Irons" (editorial). (August 6): I10.

_____. 1987b. Editorial cartoon. (August 8): I12.

Los Angeles Times. 1987c. "Guns in Cars" (editorial). (August 23): I14.

_____. 1987d. Editorial cartoon. (August 23): V5.

_____. 1987e. Editorial cartoon. (October 10): II9.

Luckenbill, David F. 1984. "Character Coercion, Instrumental Coercion, and Gun Control." *Journal of Applied Behavioral Science* 20:181–92.

New York Times. 1989. "Outbreak of Road Shootings Plagues Detroit." (February 12): 27.

Novaco, Raymond W. 1987. "Highway Violence Has Numerous Triggers." *Los Angeles Times* (August 2): V5.

Onwuachi-Saunders, E. Chukwudi, Deborah A. Lambert, Polly A. Marchbanks, Patrick W. O'Carroll, and James A. Mercy. 1989. "Firearm-Related Assaults on Los Angeles Roadways." *Journal of the American Medical Association* 262:2262–2264.

Pearson, Geoffrey. 1983. *Hooligan.* New York: Schocken.

Royko, Mike. 1987a. "California 'Trend' Strictly a Misfire." *Chicago Tribune* (August 4): 3.

_____. 1987b. "Were They Cruising for a Shooting?" *Chicago Tribune* (August 10): 3.

San Francisco Chronicle. 1987a. Editorial cartoon. (August 10): 54.

_____. 1987b. "Limiting Guns in Motor Vehicles" (editorial). (August 21): 72.

Sauter, Van Gordon. 1987a. "No Shelter from Freeway Violence." *Los Angeles Times* (June 26): V1.

_____. 1987b. "Too Much Ado about Freeway Shootings." *Los Angeles Times* (August 3): I15.

Schneider, Joseph W. 1985. "Social Problems Theory." *Annual Review of Soci-*

ology 11:209–29.

Schudson, Michael. 1989. "How Culture Works." *Theory and Society* 18:153–80.

Spector, Malcolm, and John I. Kitsuse. 1977. *Constructing Social Problems.* Menlo Park, CA: Cummings.

Stallings, Robert A. 1990. "Media Discourse and the Social Construction of Risk." *Social Problems* 37:80–95.

Stewart, Jill. 1987. "2nd Freeway Shooting Incident Is Investigated." *Los Angeles Times* (June 24): II1.

Swidler, Ann. 1986. "Culture in Action." *American Sociological Review* 51:273–86.

Time. 1987. "Homicide on the Highway." 130 (November 23): 31.

Trippett, Frank. 1987. "Highway to Homicide." *Time* 130 (August 17): 18.

Tuchman, Gaye. 1978. *Making News.* New York: Free Press.

Washington Post. 1987. Editorial cartoon. (August 3): A14.

11

Constructing "Crime"
Media Coverage of Individual and Organizational Wrongdoing

William S. Lofquist

Media coverage of crime is a matter of growing academic interest, and criticism of this coverage is widespread. In covering traditional or street crimes, media are accused of focusing on sensational cases (Barlow, Barlow, and Chiricos 1995b; Benedict 1992; Chermak 1994; Kappeler, Blumberg, and Potter 1996), overrepresentation of minorities as offenders (Sheley and Ashkins 1981; Smith 1984), emphasizing socially favored victims (Benedict 1992; Fishman 1978; Graber 1980), decontextualizing crime (Barlow et al. 1995a, 1995b; Garofalo 1981; Humphries 1981; Sherizen 1978), misrepresenting the extent and types of crime (Barlow et al. 1995b; Garofalo 1981; Reiman 1995; Sherizen 1978), misportraying the operations of the criminal justice system (Gorelick 1989), and exaggerating the incidence of stranger-based crimes (Chermak 1994; Kappeler et al. 1996; Tunnell 1992). All of these themes come together most clearly in media coverage of several recent prominent cases: the Charles Stuart murder case in Boston, the Susan Smith murder case in South Carolina, and the O.J. Simpson murder case in California.

Coverage of corporate crime has received much less academic attention. In this type of coverage, media are accused of minimizing corporate liability (Morash and Hale 1987; Wright, Cullen and Blankenship 1995), minimizing attention to causes of outcomes in favor of attention

Source: *Justice Quarterly*, Vol. 14, No. 2, June 1997, pp. 243–263. © 1997 Academy of Criminal Justice Sciences. Reprinted with permission.

to consequences (Wright et al. 1995), ignoring or underestimating the costs of corporate crime (Hills 1987; Kappeler et al. 1996; Reiman 1995), reluctance to use the term *crime* to describe this misbehavior (Bohm 1993; Lynch, Nalla, and Miller 1989; Wright et al. 1995), attaching blame to secondary or spurious causes (Wright et al. 1995), and inadequately understanding the complexity of corporate crime (Levi 1994; Randall 1987; Randall, Lee-Sammons, and Hagner 1988). These charges are illustrated clearly by several prominent cases of corporate wrongdoing including the General Motors pickup truck cases, the Ford Pinto case, the Kentucky school bus case (see Kunen 1994), and the Imperial Food Products case.

Though these inadequacies and biases are numerous and wide ranging, it can be argued that media coverage of these very different types of crime is unified by reliance on a hegemonic narrative (Ewick and Silbey 1995; also see Gamson et al. 1992).[1] Whatever the type of crime and whatever the fact scenario, media coverage tends to follow and reproduce a narrative composed of traditional, system-legitimizing assumptions and assertions (Bohm 1986; Tunnell 1992). When crime is restricted to interpersonal relationships and is portrayed as largely the result of pathological individual actions (Kappeler et al. 1996) unrelated to the conditions or actions of dominant institutions such as the family, business, or politics, or race, class, or gender relations, these institutions and the criminogenic inequalities within them are reproduced. Alternatively, a subversive narrative about crime challenges these institutions and relations, implicating them as important, even central in understanding the occurrence of crime.

In this article I present the results of content analyses of newspaper coverage of two widely reported "crimes" that occurred in the Rochester, New York area in 1994.[2] The analyses relied on local newspaper coverage, though each case also generated some regional and national coverage. The first case is the disappearance of Kali Ann Poulton, a four-year-old girl, from the street in front of her home in May 1994. Throughout the period of this study, Kali Ann had not been found and her disappearance had not been explained. The second case is the collapse and gradual flooding, in March 1994, of a large salt mine owned by Akzo Nobel Salt, a multinational conglomerate based in Holland.

These cases differ in that one deals with an individual as the central figure while the other focuses on a business. In many other respects, however, these cases are remarkably similar and thus provide a fortuitous research opportunity. Both occurred in the same year and in the same area. Both were subject to numerous possible explanations ranging from accident to crime. Both were investigated carefully. Both were unresolved at the time of the research in that the cause had not been determined. Holding these factors constant provides an opportunity to examine media coverage of two very different types of behaviors, each of which is potentially definable as crime. The unresolved nature of these cases allows us to examine whether hegemonic assumptions are used to "fill in the blanks" left by the incomplete fact scenarios.

Missing Children: A Hegemonic Project

Katherine Beckett (1994) makes the argument that the intensity and patterning of the War on Drugs are so far out of proportion to the extent and patterning of drug use that its continuation represents a hegemonic project (also see Chambliss 1994; Currie 1993; D. Gordon 1994; Reinarman 1996; Tonry 1994). In avoiding evidence for the ineffectiveness of a supply-side, deterrence-based strategy and for the macro-level causes of drug use and the associated crime, policy makers are engaged in an ideologically based effort to undermine the welfare state, and liberalism more generally, by fostering an image of the drug user as undeserving (Gans 1995; Katz 1989; Kleiniewski 1995).

A similar argument can be made about missing children. We have strong evidence that missing children are largely runaways or (less often) are abducted by family members or acquaintances. Thus the enormous attention focused on abductions by strangers raises questions about the entire project of publicizing missing children. A substantial social scientific literature has developed, which analyzes this moral panic (see Best 1987, 1990; Forst and Blomquist 1991; Kappeler et al. 1996). Its primary point is that abductions of children by strangers are exceedingly rare, accounting for far less than 1 percent of all missing children. Public, political, and media portrayals of this issue, however, focus disproportionately on these rare cases, implying that most missing children were abducted by strangers.[3] This conclusion has been strengthened by irresponsible claims by politicians, such as Rep. (later Senator) Paul Simon's (D-IL) assertion that at least 50,000 children are abducted each year by strangers (U.S. House 1981; also see Thornton 1983).

Public and media perceptions of missing children have also been shaped by the public forum provided for claims of stranger abduction through frequent congressional hearings and interest group initiatives, particularly in the 1980s. The extensive attention given to these rare but tragic cases has brought widespread visibility and influence to the Adam Walsh Foundation, the National Center for Missing and Exploited Children, Marc Klass (the father of stranger-abducted and murdered Polly Klass), and other activists, and has fostered the perception that the problem of missing children is largely synonymous with the problem of stranger abductions. Another component of this construction is the view of the offender as irrational, disturbed, or pathological (Best 1987)—a pedophile or a childless woman. Such a construction is hegemonic in that it calls forth more social control, as in the increasingly punitive law-making associated with crimes against children. A family-based or cul-ture-based construction of missing children would focus on the overwhelming class- and race-based pattern of runaways and abduc-tions by acquaintances, as well as on the physical and sexual abuse that is often a precipitating factor (Currie 1985; Forst and Blomquist 1991). Such a construction is more likely to suggest redistributive (and there-fore subversive) social welfare policies.

Corporate Crime: A Project Suggesting Hegemony by Neglect

In a 1993 cover story, *U.S. News & World Report* detailed the enor-mous costs of crime to Americans. Criminal justice system expendi-tures, medical costs, lost productivity, and other costs were all included in a price tag of $674 billion. In this putatively comprehensive analysis, however, the harms and costs of corporate crimes were not considered. A more recent, academic consideration of the costs of crime placed the price at $450 billion (Butterfield 1996); again, though media reports of this research did not specify the omission, the researchers excluded cor-porate crime from consideration. This inattention to corporate crime suggests hegemony by neglect.

Research on corporate crime further supports this view. Direct financial costs of corporate crime are frequently estimated at $200 billion[4] (Clinard and Yeager 1980; Kappeler et al. 1996; Reiman 1995; Simon and Eitzen 1993); human costs in terms of injuries and deaths, though not subject to precise measurement, are widely held to be greater than those associated with street crime (Beirne and Messerschmidt 1991; Clinard and Yeager 1980; Frank and Lynch 1992; Kappeler et al. 1996; Michalowski 1985; Reiman 1995). Thus corporate crime inargu-ably represents a serious social harm and legal problem.

At the same time, however, corporate crime has a low political, media, criminal justice, and public profile. Congressional hearings on the subject are few. The seemingly endless parade of crime bills gives no attention to corporate crime. Corporate misdeeds are rarely defined publicly or legally as crime. Further, as suggested by recent research on the savings and loan crisis (Calavita and Pontell 1994), it is those cor-porate crimes that threaten business and business confidence in the economy, not those that threaten consumers, employees, the environ-ment, or other stakeholders, that receive media and enforcement atten-tion.

Methodology

Sample

The articles used in this research were taken from the Rochester *Democrat and Chronicle,* the major daily newspaper for the Rochester and western Finger Lakes region. The only other daily paper in the region is the *Times Union,* the afternoon sister paper to the *Democrat and Chronicle;* both are Gannett publications. The same stories are often carried in both papers. I chose to examine the *Democrat and Chronicle* because it is the only print media outlet that gave sustained, detailed daily coverage to each of these stories.

I conducted content analyses on every relevant story published in the three-month period following each event. I developed story lists by contacting the newspaper, which provided a computer printout of all relevant headlines. I decided on a three-month period because it seemed to provide ample time for developments in each story and for consideration of their causes. Also, three months represents a natural point after which coverage diminished; after that period, relevant stories appeared only sporadically. This is particularly true in the Kali Ann Poulton case: the absence of new information led to a substantial decrease in coverage after one month, and to a further decrease after three months.

Content Categories

Borrowing substantially from the content analysis by Wright et al. (1995) of media coverage of the Imperial Food Products fire, I used three major content categories (cause, harm, and responsibility) as the basis of this analysis. Then I examined each story for some reference to each category and for the nature of that reference. Within each content category, I developed several subcategories to account for the various narratives available to tell each story. Because of this methodology, some content categories might not appear in a particular article or multiple subcategories might be mentioned in a particular article. Expanding on the methodology of Wright et al. (1995), I included two additional content categories (focus and sources) to provide additional insights into the construction of each case.

Cause. The cause of each of these events can be understood in several ways. The first is as an accident—an event beyond the control of, or unforeseeable by, any individual or group of individuals. Kali Ann Poulton, for example, could have wandered off and become involved in an accident that reduced her ability to return or be found. The Akzo mine collapse could have been the result of an earthquake, as initially reported, or of some other unforeseeable and uncontrollable situation such as the anomalous geological formations, the explanation preferred by Akzo (Bellaby 1995a, 1995c). Each outcome also can be understood as negligence: the result of inadequate parental or community supervision in the Poulton case, or of inadequate managerial or labor supervision of mining conditions or practices in the Akzo case. Finally, each outcome may be portrayed as a crime. Kali Ann Poulton's disappearance could be explained as a kidnapping. The mine collapse could be explained as the result of criminal negligence or wrongdoing on the part of Akzo management, the miners, or some outside party.

Harm. Each of these events caused an array of harms to a variety of parties. By identifying the harms that are featured in media coverage, one gains insight into the larger narrative into which each story was fitted. For example, as noted by Swigert and Farrell (1980–81), discussion of the harms to consumers in cases of corporate wrongdoing accompanies portrayals of those wrongdoings as criminal. The underlying logic is that a narrative or vocabulary of crime is more likely to be adopted, insofar as corporate wrongdoings resemble traditional violent crimes. In this study I analyzed each article for references to three different types of harm. *Direct harm* refers to harm experienced by the immediate parties to the events. In the Poulton case, direct harm refers to those harms experienced by Kali Ann. In the Akzo case, harms experienced by the corporation, its management, and its employees were identified as direct. *Residual harm* refers to harms experienced by these parties' families. *Community harm* refers, in the Poulton case, to insecurity, anxiety, or strain experienced by members of the Rochester community. In the Akzo case, community harms are those experienced by local property owners, business persons, other community members, and the natural environment.

Responsibility. In the three causal scenarios identified above, responsibility may be located in different places. As a result, attention to responsibility clarifies the details of narrative construction. I identified three levels of responsibility to facilitate this analysis. *Primary responsibility* is located in those parties closest to the event; Kali Ann Poulton's family and close friends and Akzo management were primary actors. *Secondary responsibility* focuses on nonsupervisory parties; in the Poulton case, any stranger is a secondary party, while laborers are secondary in the Akzo case. *Tertiary responsibility* refers to official regulatory agents, as in articles that identify regulatory inadequacy—whether insufficient police presence or lax or "captured" mine regulatory officials—as responsible to some extent for either outcome.

Focus. I use an additional content category, developed for this analysis, to examine the narrative focus of each article. Preliminary analysis revealed that much of the coverage of the Kali Ann Poulton case in particular did not focus on the events of the case or provide news about the progress of the investigation but concentrated on tangential issues, such as the picnic held to help relieve the searchers' stress. Therefore I developed a content category distinguishing between articles with a primary and a secondary focus. *Primary focus* refers to articles in which the case is in the foreground: the discussion advances the reader's understanding of the case and related developments. In articles with a *secondary focus*, the case is merely the backdrop for events generated by the extent and character of news coverage and public interest regarding the story. The number of secondary stories suggests the value of the case as a media phenomenon beyond its value as a news story.

Sources. The sources used in constructing a narrative are important in shaping and revealing that narrative. Because of the magnitude of the events discussed here, the media had access to a broad range of sources in researching and writing their accounts. Therefore it is important to examine the types of sources used in the articles and the extent of reliance on these sources. I identified seven types of sources. *Party* refers to those directly involved in the case, including members of the Poulton family and Akzo management and miners. *Community* includes any person identified as living in the affected area and not identified as belonging to any organization of stakeholders. *Regulatory* sources are official state sources such as police officers, mine safety or environmental officials, or local lawmakers.[5] *Activists* are persons identified as belonging to a nonstate organization active in promoting a particular set of interests affected by the case, such as members of the Adam Walsh Foundation in the Poulton case, or members of local environmental organizations in the Akzo case. *Experts* are individuals with credentials suggesting technical competence in the issues relevant in the case, who are not identified as affiliated with regulatory or activist organizations. These individuals usually occupy academic positions. *Business* sources refer to members of the community identified as business persons and speaking in that capacity. Finally, *media* sources are media professionals.

In addition to these substantive categories, the form of presentation of the stories was subject to quantitative analysis. I collected data regarding the frequency of coverage, as measured by the number of distinct stories with a substantial focus on the event in question.[6] I also analyzed the location of each story in the paper. Whether the story began on the front page, the editorial page, the front page of a section, or an interior page signifies the emphasis placed on the story by the newspaper. Front-page and editorial-page stories signify greatest importance, followed respectively by sectional front-page and interior-page coverage. Also, I measured the length of each story by counting the number of lines of coverage. Finally, to examine trends in coverage over time, I divided each story into three one-month periods for further analyses.

Findings

Form of Coverage

As shown in table 11.1, the Kali Ann Poulton case received somewhat more coverage than the Akzo case. As measured by story placement, the Poulton case was also given a higher priority: 43.5 percent of the articles were placed on the front page or the editorial page, compared with 36.6 percent in the Akzo case. The trends in coverage, however (see table 11.2) reveal a somewhat different picture. Table 11.2 makes clear that coverage of the Poulton case was skewed dramatically toward the first month after the event. During this period, 73 articles were published, sometimes three or four in a single day. Coverage declined dramatically after the one-month anniversary of the case. In contrast, the Akzo case received more consistent coverage over time; coverage declined steadily from Period 1 to Period 3. Also interesting in the Akzo case is the change of placement in the paper: during Period 1, front-page articles predominated; in Period 2, most articles appeared on the front page of the Region section; by Period 3, the story had moved to the inside of the paper.

Table 11.1 Form Analyses of Kali Ann Poulton and Akzo Stories

	Kali Ann Poulton		Akzo	
	N	%	N	%
Placement				
Front page	32	37.6	25	35.2
Regional front page	12	14.1	22	31
Editorial page	5	5.9	1	1.4
Other inside page	36	42.4	23	32.4
Total	85	100	71	100
Length				
Number of lines	9,577		6,238	
Mean	111.5		87.9	
Median	95		80	

These trends in coverage reflect differences in the development of each case more strongly than the interest of the media in covering the cases. The Poulton case was characterized by a frustrating lack of new information; apart from a serious hoax and a number of unsubstantiated sightings, the media reported no important clues or progress at any point. As a result, the media could not sustain the story despite considerable efforts through reliance on secondary articles. In contrast, the Akzo case continued to present new developments over the course of this analysis. The mine collapse caused an aquifer to drain into the mine, slowly flooding it. This event generated considerable news: Akzo endeavored to stop the flooding, local wells dried up as a result of aquifer drainage, and the movement of water through the mine eroded salt pillars, causing sinkholes and property damage.

Table 11.2 Form Analysis of Kali Ann Poulton and Akzo Stories, by Period

	Period 1		Period 2		Period 3	
	N	%	N	%	N	%
Kali Ann Poulton Story Placement						
Front page	30	41.1	2	33.3	0	0
Regional front page	7	9.6	0	0	5	83.3
Editorial page	5	6.8	0	0	0	0
Other inside page	31	42.5	4	66.7	1	16.7
Total	73	100	6	100	6	100
Length						
Number of lines	8,309		755		413	
Mean	113.8		125.8		68.8	
Median	102		139		61	
Akzo Story Placement						
Front page	20	57.1	4	17.4	1	7.7
Regional front page	5	14.3	13	56.5	4	30.8
Editorial page	1	2.9	0	0	0	0
Other inside page	9	25.7	6	26.1	8	61.5
Total	35	100	23	100	13	100
Length						
Number of lines	3,812		1.674		752	
Mean	108.9		72.8		57.8	
Median	114		69		68	

Although these stories developed differently over time, the Poulton case received more attention per article than the Akzo case throughout the period of this research. Overall, mean and median story lengths were 15 or more lines greater than in the Akzo case. Further, table 11.2 shows that although few Poulton stories were printed after the first month, mean and median story lengths remained longer for the Poulton case than for Akzo, particularly during the second month of each story.

Content of Coverage

Cause. In the content of media coverage, as summarized in table 11.3, several notable points emerge. In regard to cause, the two narratives contrast sharply. The Kali Ann Poulton story was constructed quickly and strongly as a crime. Within hours, the media were portraying Kali Ann's disappearance not only as a crime but as a crime committed by a stranger. Quoting "an unnamed source close to the investigation," the *Democrat and Chronicle* reported on May 25, 1994, "I think we might have the worst-case scenario, an abduction by a stranger" (Finnerty et al. 1994:1A). Alternative causes received no print coverage at this early point, and were mentioned only briefly in later months.

Table 11.3 Content Analyses of Kali Ann Poulton and Akzo Stories

	Kali Ann Poulton			Akzo		
	Story %	Category %	N	Story %	Category %	N
Cause						
Accident	1.2	1.5	1	100	89.9	71
Negligence	1.2	1.5	1	11.3	10.1	8
Crime	76.5	97	65	0	0	0
Harm						
Direct	100	79.4	85	26.8	21.3	19
Residual	12.9	10.3	11	1.4	1.1	1
Community	12.9	10.3	11	97.2	77.5	69
Responsibility						
Primary	7	12.5	6	11.3	80	8
Secondary	49.4	87.5	42	0	0	0
Tertiary	0	0	0	2.8	20	2
Focus						
Primary	37.6		32	94.4		67
Secondary	62.4		53	5.6		4

The Akzo story, on the other hand, was constructed immediately and almost unvaryingly as an accident; this construction appeared in every story on the case, though it was accompanied by suggestion of negligence in 11.3 percent of all stories. It was never suggested that a crime may have occurred when the mine collapsed. The "accident" narrative remained resistant to change in the following months, even as the fact scenario changed. This version of events was aided initially by reports that an earthquake caused the collapse. This explanation, however, was dismissed within five days in favor of the universally accepted view that the collapse caused the appearance of an earthquake. Yet even as this latter view emerged, media coverage still was dominated by the view that the collapse was itself the product of an accident. In a particularly interesting feat of obfuscation, the story line that emerged was that the collapse caused the problems in the mine; little independent consideration was given to the cause of the collapse.

Harm. Examination of the harm category reveals another interesting pattern. In the Poulton case, the dominant harm was to Kali Ann herself. Harms experienced by her family and by the surrounding community were each mentioned in 12.9 percent of all stories, seemingly little attention for such an intensively examined event.

In the Akzo case, on the other hand, emphasis was placed on the harm experienced by the mine and, in a related vein, by the natural environment. Harms experienced by Akzo management and miners were mentioned in 26.8 percent of stories; harms experienced by their families were mentioned in only 1.4 percent of the articles. Harms experienced by members of the community, though included in the community subcategory, received much less attention than harms to the environment. This pattern of coverage is instructive in light of Swigert and Farrell's research (1980–81) on the identification of corporate wrongdoing as crime. They argued that corporate wrongdoing comes to be publicly and legally defined as crime insofar as the harms associated with it resemble the harms associated with street crime. By giving little attention to the property damage, declining property values, and community stress and incivility associated with the mine collapse (harms also associated with street crime), the media weakened the relationship between this event and crime.

Responsibility. Media coverage of responsibility for these two events provides the key component of the larger narrative construction of these cases. In the Poulton case, in the 49.4 percent (42) of all the stories in which responsibility for Kali Ann's disappearance was discussed, that responsibility was placed on a stranger. In six of these 42 stories it was suggested that a member of her family might be responsible, though this was never the dominant implication of an article. Viewed in conjunction with the cause category, the Poulton case clearly was very quickly constructed to fit the "stranger abduction" narrative. This occurred even in the absence of any publicly disclosed evidence privileging this explanation or precluding alternative explanations.

Because the Akzo case was framed primarily as an accident, responsibility received little attention: it was mentioned in only 11.3 percent (8) of all the stories. In these eight stories, responsibility was focused on Akzo management; regulatory failure was also suggested in two of these stories. Rather than focusing on responsibility, media attention was focused on the consequences of the collapse, a hegemonic approach in that it reinforced the accident scenario and drew attention away from corporate responsibility.

Focus. Confirming the impression gained in my preliminary analysis, most of the coverage of the Poulton case (62.4% of the articles) focused on secondary events and issues. The limited progress made in the investigation provided little news, but the very high public consciousness of this case, aided strongly by the intense media coverage in the first few weeks after the disappearance, created a large volume of secondary stories. Thus the story was kept in the news even when the case itself provided nothing new to report. In this way the extent of secondary coverage becomes a means by which the newsworthiness of a story, in terms of its amenability to hegemonic interests, can be maintained and measured. The Akzo case generated only four secondary stories (5.6 percent of all articles); though this story is also hegemonic, the construction of the case as an accident gives it little news value beyond the occurrence of new developments. The Poulton case, on the other hand, fits into one of the most powerful and most pervasive hegemonic narratives of recent years: innocent, law-abiding individuals, particularly children, as the prey of pathological strangers.

Sources. The Poulton and the Akzo case are remarkably similar in the extent of their reliance on sources: An average of 3.53 different sources was cited in each Poulton article and an average of 3.51 in each Akzo article (see table 11.4). This general similarity masks the substantial and revealing differences in the types of sources used in constructing each narrative. Most notably, the Poulton narrative relies much more strongly on activists—in this case hegemonic activists, particularly those associated with the Adam Walsh Center. These sources strongly supported the "stranger abduction" narrative and quickly coupled this case with well-known actual and alleged stranger abductions such as the cases of Polly Klass, Adam Walsh, and Sara Anne Wood.[7] I also found a much greater reliance on community members, who shared the sense of threat and loss communicated in the hegemonic narrative, and much less reliance on parties than in the Akzo case.

In the Akzo narrative, the dominant sources of information (68.8 percent of the total) are "official" sources from Akzo or from relevant regulatory agencies. These sources overwhelmingly support hegemonic interests in their orientation toward the events; the absence of a regulatory agency concerned with mining techniques limited the likelihood that Akzo would encounter regulatory opposition and allowed Akzo to be characterized favorably by regulatory officials.[8] Activists in the Akzo case received much less attention than in the Poulton case[9] and were primarily subversive environmental groups and community members; many of the latter included adversely affected property owners. These patterns suggest that in each case, the media preferred predictable, hegemonic voices.

Table 11.4 Sources Used by Media

Source	Kali Ann Poulton Case		Akzo Case	
	N	%	N	%
Party	17	5.6	74	29.8
Community	96	32	34	13.7
Regulatory	110	36.8	97	39
Activist	42	14	7	2.8
Expert	17	5.6	31	12.3
Business	12	4	5	2
Media	6	2	1	.4
Total	300	100	249	100
Avg. Sources/Story	3.53		3.51	

Discussion and Conclusions

In a series of essays on Darwin's theory of evolution, Stephen Jay Gould (1980) points out that the substantial gaps in the fossil record of human evolution were "filled in" by Darwin and others with a linear trajectory suggesting steady evolutionary progress. More recent research suggests that these gaps cannot properly be connected by a straight line; rather, evolutionary progress is uneven, disrupted, even revolutionary. Darwin, Gould argues, filled the gaps in the fossil record in a hegemonic fashion; in the absence of evidence he favored order and predictability over disorder and revolution. The results of the present research suggest a similar conclusion: media create and reproduce hegemonic understandings of events. In the case of substantial uncertainty about the causes of two dramatic events in the Rochester area, the media framed these events in a manner consistent with established interests.

The most interesting aspect of these cases is that in each the hegemonic narrative runs contrary to the most likely fact scenario; that is, maintaining that narrative requires considerable effort. In the Poulton case, the statistical evidence is quite clear that Kali Ann was most likely abducted by a family member or acquaintance. Nothing in the evidence released to the community counters this scenario. In fact, maintaining the hegemonic narrative also required minimizing or ignoring the efforts of police and others to suggest the subversive narrative. Somewhat contrary to earlier research which suggests that crime reporters rely heavily on police sources and reproduce the police views of crime (Benedict 1992; Best 1990; Chermak 1994; Sheley and Ashkins 1981; Sherizen 1978), the present research suggests that the media will maintain the hegemonic narrative even when police do not support it.[10]

Four early articles are relevant in this regard. In an article offering expert advice to parents in helping their children deal with the Poulton case (McNamara 1994), pediatricians and child psychologists advised parents that children must be taught to have a "reasonable wariness" of strangers. They implied that Kali's disappearance was the result of an abduction by a stranger, even while they also mentioned that children are "overwhelmingly more likely" to be endangered by someone they know. The message of the story is that stranger abductions are a serious concern, and that the Poulton case, though rare, is an example. In an editorial appearing on the same day (Democrat and Chronicle 1994b), statistics on missing children showed that stranger abductions are a small percentage of all cases; nonetheless, the editorial concluded that "knowing the statistics doesn't help us deal with cases like that of . . . Kali Poulton." Again it is clearly implied that the rare event occurred in this case. Two days later, in a story that had little impact on the overall tone of coverage of the story, an expert was quoted as stating that "the information sheriff's investigators have released so far points to an abduction by someone who knew Kali" (Sopko and Smith 1994). On the same day, another article offered parents further expert advice on helping their children to be cautious around strangers (Democrat and Chronicle 1994c).

The Akzo case contains abundant evidence for inappropriate mining practices including the unprecedented size of the collapse, the miners' well-known objections to working in the area before the collapse, the closing of the area just before the collapse, subsequent expert findings relating to the mining methods used in the area, and Akzo's previous knowledge of the dangers of these methods (Bellaby 1995c; Petersen 1993).[11] Instead of developing this subversive counternarrative, the media presented the collapse as the cause of the mine disaster without considering the causes of the collapse itself. After the initial observation that "what caused the collapse is unknown" and that this knowledge was essential to stopping mine flooding (Democrat and Chronicle 1994a), coverage focused heavily on efforts to stop the flooding. In the face of continuing uncertainty about the cause of the collapse, the story line that emerged and was sustained throughout the 90-day period of this research was that the collapse was the precipitating event. In a manner typical of the coverage of this event, one reporter (Orman 1994) stated that "the leak was triggered by the March 12 mine collapse." This account is hegemonic in communicating that the collapse was an unforeseen and unforeseeable natural occurrence; Akzo fostered and favored precisely this version of events, which allowed attention to focus on the consequences of the collapse.

The media, rather than focusing on the background of the collapse, emphasized the consequences; this explains the frequency of articles that mention neither cause nor responsibility. Within two days of the collapse, the dominant story line was the flooding of the mine and the efforts to stop the flooding. This focus portrayed Akzo management as a victim of events beyond its control, much like the American media portrayal of Union Carbide in the aftermath of the Bhopal disaster (Lynch et al. 1989). This approach also casts Akzo as part of an aggressive but ultimately futile effort to save the mine. This version of events can be found in an article that depicts Akzo as fighting a battle to "survive a March 12 collapse" through a "step-by-step" process requiring the corporation to "win" approval from regulators (Rosenberg 1994).

Stories do not tell themselves. Rather, the aftermath of unanticipated events includes a period in which the definition of the situation is fluid. During this period, efforts at social construction are most active, entailing aggressive attempts to apply a stable and favorable understanding to the event in question. James Kunen (1994) illustrates this process in considerable detail in examining the efforts of different interests to construct the Kentucky school bus crash as the result of drunk driving or an unsafe bus. After initial media attention to the unsafe features of the bus, corporate, governmental regulatory and investigatory, media, religious, and community groups worked aggressively to fit the crash into the drunk-driving narrative that prevailed at the time (see Gusfield 1981; Ross 1984). In the present research I argue that this process also occurred in the Akzo and Poulton cases; media treatment of these events located them within dominant narratives about children and business, making it possible to tell these stories and to reproduce elite interests through their telling.

The swift emergence of stabilized, ratified, hegemonic understandings of the Kali Ann Poulton and Akzo cases testifies to the power and influence of their larger narratives. The 1980s and 1990s have been characterized by substantial national concern about children's well-being, evidenced most prominently by the attention to missing children. Children represent vulnerability and the future (Best 1990); our concern that they may be threatened expresses our concern about the society we have created. Representing the pathological individual as the specific threat—in this society but not of it—provides for a recognition and admission of threat, and allows media and other interests to be responsive to public concerns. At the same time, however, policy initiatives pursuant to this construction are limited to system-legitimizing efforts such as incarceration, "stranger danger" education, and public awareness programs. Broader, well-documented threats to children, such as poverty, illiteracy, infant mortality, educational inequality, and inaccessibility of health care, receive far less public and media attention. These threats, a product of social rather than interpersonal relations, are thus not amenable to a vocabulary of crime (Bohm 1993). They are ignored because of their subversive potential or are recast hegemonically as products of irresponsible parents and larger subcultural values.

The last two decades also have seen tremendous growth in the power, status, and profitability of corporations, accompanied by increasing security and declining wages for workers (D. M. Gordon 1996; Schor 1992). As more intense public and public policy scrutiny has been directed toward individuals, attention has been turned away from corporations. Explanations for declining wages, increasing debt, and lost leisure time focus on consumers' choices and on the putatively inevitable process of globalization rather than on the anti-union and low-wage strategies of corporations. Record corporate profits and executive salaries are hardly scrutinized; the media pass over their relationship to layoffs and declining wages in favor of concern about an "overheated economy," associated fears of inflation, and unrelenting attention to fluctuations in the stock market. A more clearly hegemonic framing of economic news is difficult to imagine. In a related area, deregulation of corporate conduct has been substantial. Because of increasingly conservative political administrations and growing economic concerns, the state today is more openly solicitous and supportive of corporations than in the recent past. In this context, organizational wrongdoing is obscured; the weakness of regulation and of media scrutiny limits the likelihood of "naming and blaming," and allows a vocabulary of accident to prevail.

Epilogue

On August 9, 1996 Mark David Christie apparently confessed to police that he had kidnapped and killed Kali Ann Poulton. Her body was found on August 10, in a large liquid storage tank where Christie formerly was employed.[12] He lived next door to the Poultons at the time of the kidnapping. According to police, Christie disclosed that he killed her within minutes of kidnapping her and managed to remove her body from the scene in the hours immediately following her disappearance.

He confessed to the police after first confessing to his wife and his employer, who turned him in.

By the time Kali Ann Poulton was found, media coverage had lessened substantially; stories appeared only to mark the anniversary of the case. The one-year anniversary was marked by the publication of a long article describing the futility of the investigation and the suffering experienced by the family. Accompanying the text was a picture of the most recent poster detailing the case, headlined "Stranger Abducted Child." This and other posters identifying Kali Ann as missing and stranger-abducted were common throughout the area until she was found. It was hardly noted that this case, in its ultimate tragic conclusion, did not fit the narrative into which it was so assiduously placed.

The Akzo mine collapse is also understood more fully, though organizational cases generally lack the neat resolutions provided by the arrest of an offender. In the summer of 1995, the federal Mine Safety and Health Administration released the findings of its investigation of the causes. A banner headline at the top of the front page stated "Akzo declared blameless" (Bellaby 1995a). The article made clear that Akzo was blameless in the sense that it "followed proper steps to ensure that no miners were injured"; workers' safety is the concern of this regulatory agency. However, because "we don't have a standard that says you can't lose your own mine" (p. A1), no federal or state regulatory agency explored the propriety of the mining methods used by Akzo. Subsurface mining techniques are unregulated; only workers' health and safety are subject to regulation.

Several weeks later, a report prepared for the New York Department of Environmental Conservation by a private consultant was released to the public. According to another front-page article, under the headline "Study faults Akzo method," the small-pillar mining technique used by Akzo contributed to the collapse (Bellaby 1995b). Akzo disputed this conclusion, arguing that anomalous geologic conditions were responsible. (Interpretations still differ.) The mine was fully flooded and closed by early September 1995.

In 1996, after making considerable progress in gaining permission to open a new mine several miles away, and after receiving more than $50 million in local and state subsidies to do so, Akzo announced that it was ceasing all mining operations in the area.

Notes

[1] An alternative and perhaps complementary critique of media reporting practices emphasizes how the production of news is influenced by features of media organizations, including race and gender compositions of newsrooms, financial constraints, and deadline pressures (see Benedict 1992; Gans 1979; Tuchman

1978). This meso-level approach specifies the organizational means by which macro-level elite interests are reproduced.

2 In view of evidence that newspaper coverage of crime correlates more strongly with public perceptions of crime than does coverage by other media (Sheley and Ashkins 1981), the coverage examined here probably approximates closely the public perceptions of these events.

3 See Forst and Blomquist (1991) and Best (1990) for extended discussions about estimates of the size of the missing children problem and the politics accompanying these estimates.

4 This figure represents direct costs to consumers. It does not include the secondary costs, such as law enforcement and other protective measures, cited by *U.S. News & World Report* in its estimate of the costs of crime. Also excluded are the substantial but not easily quantified environmental costs and the costs associated with loss of public and consumers' confidence.

5 New York State lacks any regulation of subsurface mining techniques, precisely the issue in the Akzo case. Instead the state's mining regulation focuses on workers' safety and health, which were not major issues in the Akzo case.

6 This step required some judgment calls, particularly in the Kali Ann Poulton case. Because of the prominence of this case, it quickly became a focal point of community concern and therefore a reference point in community discussions of crime, threats to children, and related issues. The several stories that made only passing reference to the case were excluded from this analysis.

7 The Sara Anne Wood case is well known in the New York area and the Northeast. Sara Anne Wood, a 12-year-old girl, was last seen riding her bike near her rural upstate New York home in August 1993. She is believed to have been abducted and killed by a stranger.

8 On August 10, 1995, as its lead story at the top of the front page, the *Democrat and Chronicle* ran as its headline "Akzo declared blameless: U.S. says owner of collapsed mine upheld safety rules." As pointed out in the story, however, workers' safety was never the major issue in the collapse. Highlighting the regulatory lacuna, Mine Safety and Health Administration official David Park is quoted as saying: "We don't have a standard that says you can't lose your own mine. . . . You just can't hurt any miners when you do it" (Bellaby 1995a).

9 Two local environmental groups were promoting subversive understandings of the mine collapse and other Akzo-related issues and were readily available for comment. In addition, members of the local college faculty were available to comment on the mine collapse from their various disciplinary perspectives. The absence of these generally subversive voices from media coverage suggests that organizational explanations relating to time and resource constraints on media are inadequate in explaining the construction of the Akzo story.

10 The subversive narrative of a family abduction of Kali Ann Poulton was not prominent in police accounts of this event, though when this narrative was mentioned, it was usually the police who mentioned it. Activists, readily available to the media through the Adam Walsh Center, provided regular and consistent support for the stranger abduction narrative.

11 Reports available to Akzo before the collapse (Petersen 1993) and reports released well after the event (Bellaby 1995b, 1995c) make it clear that the danger of a collapse had been well known to Akzo before it occurred.

12 All of the research and most of the writing for this article were completed before Kali Ann Poulton's body was discovered.

References

Barlow, M H., D. E. Barlow, and T. G. Chiricos. 1995a. "Economic Conditions and Ideologies of Crime in the Media: A Content Analysis of Crime News." *Crime and Delinquency* 41:3–19.

_____. 1995b. "Mobilizing Support for Social Control in a Declining Economy: Exploring Ideologies of Crime within Crime News." *Crime and Delinquency* 41:191–204.

Beckett, K. 1994. "Setting the Public Agenda: 'Street Crime' and Drug Use in American Politics." *Social Problems* 41:425–47.

Beirne, P. and J. Messerschmidt. 1991. *Criminology.* New York: Harcourt Brace Jovanovich.

Bellaby, M. D. 1995a. "Akzo Declared Blameless." *Democrat and Chronicle,* August 10, p. A1.

_____. 1995b. "Study Faults Akzo Method." *Democrat and Chronicle,* August 26, pp. 1A, 5A.

_____.1995c. "Akzo Collapse Scrutinized." *Democrat and Chronicle,* October 16, p. B1.

Benedict, H. 1992. *Virgin or Vamp: How the Press Covers Sex Crimes.* New York: Oxford University Press.

Best, J. 1987. "Rhetoric in Claims-Making: Constructing the Missing Children Problem." *Social Problems* 34:101–21.

_____. 1990. *Threatened Children: Rhetoric and Concern about Child Victims.* Chicago: University of Chicago Press.

Bohm, R. 1986. "Crime, Criminal and Crime Control Policy Myths." *Justice Quarterly,* 3:193–214.

_____. 1993. "Social Relationships That Arguably Should Be Criminal Although They Are Not: On the Political Economy of Crime." Pp. 3–29 in *Political Crime in Contemporary America,* edited by K. D. Tunnell. New York: Garland.

Butterfield, F. 1996. "Survey Finds That Crime Costs $450 Billion a Year." *New York Times,* April 22, p. A1.

Calavita, K and H. N. Pontell. 1994. "The State and White-Collar Crime: Saving the Savings and Loans." *Law and Society Review* 28:297–324.

Chambliss, W. J. 1994. "Policing the Ghetto Underclass: The Politics of Law and Law Enforcement." *Social Problems* 41:177–94.

Chermak, S. M. 1994. "Body Count News: How Crime Is Presented in the News Media." *Justice Quarterly* 11:561–82.

Clinard, M. B. and P. C. Yeager. 1980. *Corporate Crime.* New York: Free Press.

Currie, E. 1985. *Confronting Crime: An American Challenge.* New York: Pantheon.

_____. 1993. *Reckoning: Drugs, the Cities, and the American Future.* New York: Hill and Wang.

Democrat and *Chronicle.* 1994a. "Just Hope Experts Can Contain Damage at Akzo." March 23, p. 10A.

_____. 1994b. "A Little Girl Is Missing and a Community Rallies." May 26, p. 12A.

_____. 1994c. "Experts Help Parents Deal with Anxieties." May 28, p. 11A.

Ewick, P. and S. S. Silbey. 1995. "Subversive Stories and Hegemonic Tales: Toward a Sociology of Narrative." *Law and Society Review* 29:197–226.

Finnerty, B., G. Livadas, S. McNamara, and A. Morrell. 1994. "Authorities Voice Fear Girl Was Abducted." *Democrat and Chronicle*, May 25, pp. 1A, 5A.

Fishman, M. 1978. "Crime Waves as Ideology." *Social Problems* 25:531–43.

Forst, M. L. and M. E. Blomquist. 1991. *Missing Children: Rhetoric and Reality.* New York: Lexington.

Frank, N. K. and M. J. Lynch. 1992. *Corporate Crime, Corporate Violence.* New York: Harrow and Heston.

Gamson, W. A., D. Croteau, W. Hoynes, and T. Sasson. 1992. "Media Images and the Social Construction of Reality." *Annual Review of Sociology* 18:373–93.

Gans, H. J. 1979. *Deciding What's News: A Study of CBS Evening News, Newsweek and Time.* New York: Pantheon.

_____. 1995. *The War against the Poor: The Underclass and Antipoverty Policy.* New York: Basic Books.

Garofalo, J. 1981. "Crime and the News Media: A Selective Review of Research." *Journal of Research in Crime and Delinquency* 18:319–50.

Gordon, D. 1994. *The Dangerous Classes.* New York: Norton.

Gordon, D. M. 1996. *Fat and Mean.* New York: Free Press.

Gorelick, S. 1989. "'Join Our War': The Construction of Ideology in a Newspaper Crimefighting Campaign." *Crime and Delinquency* 35:421–36.

Gould, S. J. 1980. *The Panda's Thumb: More Reflections on Natural History.* New York: Norton.

Graber, D. A. 1980. *Crime News and the Public.* New York: Praeger.

Gusfield, J. R. 1981. *The Culture of Public Problems: Drinking-Driving and the Symbolic Order.* Chicago: University of Chicago Press.

Hills, S., ed. 1987. *Corporate Violence.* Totowa, NJ: Rowman and Littlefield.

Humphries, D. 1981. "Serious Crime, News Coverage, and Ideology: A Content Analysis of Crime Coverage in a Metropolitan Newspaper." *Crime and Delinquency* 27:191–205.

Kappeler, V., M. Blumberg, and G. W. Potter. 1996. *The Mythology of Crime and Criminal Justice.* 2nd ed. Prospect Heights, IL: Waveland.

Katz, M. 1989. *The Underserving Poor.* New York: Pantheon.

Kleniewski, N. 1995. "The War against Welfare Moves to the States." *Research in Politics and Society* 5:193–215.

Kunen, J. S. 1994. *Reckless Disregard: Corporate Greed, Government Indifference, and the Kentucky School Bus Crash.* New York: Simon and Schuster.

Levi, M. 1994. "The Media and White-Collar Crime." Presented at the annual meetings of the American Society of Criminology, Miami.

Lynch, M. J., M. K. Nalla, and K. W. Miller. 1989. "Cross-Cultural Perceptions of Deviance: The Case of Bhopal." *Journal of Research in Crime and Delinquency* 26:7–35.

McNamara, S. 1994. "What Do You Tell Kids?" *Democrat and Chronicle*, May 26, p. 10A.

Michalowski, R. J. 1985. *Order, Law, and Crime.* New York: Random House.

Morash, M. and D. Hale. 1987. "Unusual Crime or Crime as Unusual? Images of Corruption at the Interstate Commerce Commission." Pp. 129–49 in *Organized Crime in America: Concepts and Controversies*, edited by T. S. Bynum. Monsey, NY: Criminal Justice Press.

Orman, D. 1994. "Akzo Can Continue Drilling at Mine." *Democrat and Chronicle*, March 27, p. 1A.

Petersen, G. 1993. Letter to Kurt Kiser, Superintendent, AKZO, from Rock Mechanics Assist, Nov. 22.

Randall, D. M. 1987. "The Portrayal of Business Malfeasance in the Elite and General Public Media." *Social Science Quarterly* 68:281–93.

Randall, D. M., L. Lee-Sammons, and P. R. Hagner. 1988. "Common versus Elite Crime Coverage in Network News." *Social Science Quarterly* 69:910–29.

Reiman, J. 1995. *The Rich Get Richer and the Poor Get Prison: Ideology, Crime, and Criminal Justice*. Boston: Allyn and Bacon.

Reinarman, C. 1996. "The Social Construction of Drug Scares." Pp. 224–34 in *Social Deviance*, edited by E. Goode. Boston: Allyn and Bacon.

Rosenberg, E. 1994. "Akzo Salt Gets OK to Build a Pump Station." *Democrat and Chronicle*, April 3, p. 3B.

Ross, H. L. 1984. *Deterring the Drunk Driver*. Lexington, MA: Lexington Books.

Schor, J. B. 1992. *The Overworked American*. New York: Basic Books.

Sheley, J. F. and C. D. Ashkins. 1981. "Crime, Crime News, and Crime Views." *Public Opinion Quarterly* 45:492–506.

Sherizen, S. 1978. "Social Creation of Crime News: All the News Fitted to Print." Pp. 203–24 in *Deviance and Mass Media*, edited by C. Winick. Beverly Hills: Sage.

Simon, D. R. and D. S. Eitzen. 1993. *Elite Deviance*. 4th ed. Boston: Allyn and Bacon.

Smith, S. J. 1984. "Crime in the News." *British Journal of Criminology* 24:289–95.

Sopko, J. L. and V. Smith. 1994. "Police Usually Mum about High-Profile Cases." *Democrat and Chronicle*, May 28, p. 10A.

Swigert, V. L. and R. A. Farrell. 1980–81. "Corporate Homicide: Definitional Processes in the Creation of Deviance." *Law and Society Review* 15:161–82.

Thornton, J. 1983. "The Tragedy of America's Missing Children." *U.S. News & World Report*, October 24, pp. 63–64.

Tonry, M. 1994. *Malign Neglect*. New York: Oxford University Press.

Tuchman, G. 1978. *Making News: A Study in the Construction of Reality*. New York. Free Press.

Tunnell, K. 1992. "Film at Eleven: Recent Developments in the Commodification of Crime." *Sociological Spectrum* 12:293–313.

U.S. House of Representatives. 1981. "Missing Children's Act." Hearings before the Subcommittee on Civil and Constitutional Rights, Committee on the Judiciary, November 18, 30.

Wright, J. P., F. T. Cullen, and M. B. Blankenship. 1995. "The Social Construction of Corporate Violence: Media Coverage of the Imperial Food Products Fire." *Crime and Delinquency* 41:20–36.

Part III

EFFECTS OF CONSTRUCTING CRIME

12

A Serendipitous Finding of a News Media History Effect

Ray Surette

On January 16, 1989, a Hispanic Miami police officer shot and killed a black motorcyclist in a predominantly black section of Miami. A passenger on the motorcycle died later from injuries sustained in the subsequent crash. The officer was not involved in the initial chase, but was speaking with a citizen at the side of the street when he reportedly heard the radio transmission of the chase in progress and saw the motorcycle approaching at high speed. According to several witnesses, he stepped into the middle of the street and assumed a combat stance with his service pistol drawn. As the motorcycle passed, the officer fired one shot, striking and killing the driver. A crowd of about 30 community residents swelled to several hundred soon after the killing. Three days of civil violence followed.

On January 23, the officer was arrested and charged with two counts of manslaughter with a firearm.[1] During the following week, the shooting and its aftermath were the focus of 53 stories in the local newspaper, and received extensive television and radio coverage. Some of this coverage dealt with the poor relations between Hispanic police officers and the black community and with a perception, in the black community, of police misuse of force. Other stories reported on the perception that the police officer was prosecuted only because he was Hispanic. The shooting and the subsequent coverage came to be the best explanation

Justice Quarterly, Vol. 12, No. 2, June 1995, pp. 355–364. © 1995 Academy of Criminal Justice Sciences. Reprinted with permission.

of a change in attitude about police officers' use of weapons among the Hispanic recruits at the local police academy.

Validity of findings, as opposed to validity of measures, is not discussed commonly by criminal justice researchers.[2] Validity is seldom considered except in regard to measurement. Yet because of its public and political interest and the frequency of high-profile cases, criminal justice research is also sensitive to threats to the validity of its findings. In one such type of threat, an observed effect is due to an unplanned event external to the research design, which occurs between pretest and posttest data collection. This is commonly termed a *history effect* (Cook and Campbell 1979:51). The mass media, especially the news media, are prolific sources of history effects (Dye and Zeigler 1986; Surette forthcoming). Perhaps because history effects (media-generated or otherwise) are not often reported in the literature, their risk in criminal justice research has not received the attention they deserved. Although the mass media are commonly acknowledged as a major influence on the criminal justice system, few studies have examined expressly for confounding effects of the media. In an effort to encourage the routine consideration of media-based history effects, the chance discovery of an effect is described.

An understanding of media history effects derives from a "social construction of reality" perspective. In this perspective, individuals construct their social reality from the information and images they obtain from the media-dominated symbolic reality of their culture and from their personal social networks.[3] The assembled information constructs reality in each individual's mind and is used to direct and interpret social behavior. In modern societies, the media often play a more crucial role than personal social networks in constructing reality because knowledge of many social phenomena is obtained solely from the media. Because few people have direct experience with crime and because the media are a primary source of crime-related information, the process of social construction of reality and the role of the media have been proposed as particularly important for crime and justice.[4] Along these lines, the news media have been criticized as misleading sources of information about police work, although their impact on the police remains largely unexplored.[5] Because police recruits are in the formative stage, the construction of their crime and justice reality and the information sources they employ are particularly interesting.

Methods: Noting the Effect

A serendipitous finding of a history effect was made within a larger study of the relationship between police and correctional recruits' expectations about work and their consumption of media (Surette 1991). As part of this larger study, police academy trainees were surveyed before and after their academy training.[6] During initial exploratory analysis, pre- and posttraining stepwise regressions were run on a number of dependent variables. A history effect emerged in one set of these regressions.

In the regression runs of interest, expectation of weapon use by police recruits' was regressed on a set of independent variables. Predictor variables included a set of demographic items: age, sex, education, income, black, Hispanic, victimization history, criminal justice experience, and membership in a family with criminal justice employers. Also included were variables concerning media use: the number of daily newspapers read per week, the number of hours of television watched per day, and the number of hours of television news watched per day. Finally two indexes were created: the perception of the reality of television crime programs and a preference for crime programs. Expecting that the most accurate predictor of expectations at the end of training would be a recruit's expectations at the beginning of training, the posttraining regression included the pretraining expectation of weapon use as an additional predictor variable.

The results of the two regressions are reported in table 12.1. These results reflect an overall weak relationship between expectation of weapon use and the total set of predictor variables as well as revealing a potential problem with subject mortality.

The regression results reported in table 12.1 show a reversal in the beta sign for the Hispanic variable (a dummy variable reflecting the effect of being Hispanic). The resulting pre- and posttraining betas for Hispan-

Table 12.1 Exploratory Step-Wise Regression Dependent Variable Response to Likert Question: Most police can expect to fire their weapon often in the line of duty during their career.*

Dependent Variables	N	Adjusted R2	Significant Independent Variables	Beta	T. Sig. of Beta	F	Sig. of F
Pre Training Weapon Use Expectation	(179)	.08	TV Reality	.26	.000	8.90	.000
			Hispanic	-.14	.048		
Post Training Weapon Use Expectation	(120)	.16	Weapon (tl)	.33	.000	8.45	.000
			Hispanic	.21	.016		
			TV Reality	.18	.040		

*(Response Range: 1 "Strongly Agree" to 5 "Strongly Disagree")

ics reflect that before their training, Hispanic recruits' expectations regarding the use of weapons by police officers appear to be significantly less than those of non-Hispanic recruits (as signified by the significant negative betas). After training, the same variables are shown as significant. Surprisingly, however, Hispanic recruits now are more likely than non-Hispanics to expect that police will fire their weapons. Subsequent regression runs corrected for subject mortality show the same reversal of beta sign for Hispanics.[7]

A paired t-test analysis conducted on the Hispanic and the non-Hispanic groups confirmed this unexpected reversal in perception as unique to the Hispanic Recruits.[8] As shown in table 12.2, non-Hispanic recruits did not change from pre- to posttraining in regard to expectation of police weapon use, but Hispanic recruits changed significantly.

Paired t-test analyses also revealed the specificity of the effect on Hispanics. In addition to the item regarding expected weapon use, the pre- and posttraining surveys included sets of multiquestion Likert attitude scales measuring political cynicism, support for civil liberties, trust in people, and concern about crime. The survey also included a Likert item regarding the perception of the news media as fair. In all of these factors, recruits' attitudes changed significantly between pre- and posttraining survey measures. At the end of their academy training, both Hispanics and non-Hispanics had become significantly more cynical, believed significantly that the media reported less fairly about law enforcement, had significantly less trust in people, had significantly more concern about crime, and had significantly less support for civil liberties. The Hispanic and the non-Hispanic recruits similarly did not change along other dimensions such as support for the legal system, the view that police officers were guilty of discrimination, or the perception of criminals as inherently violent.[9] The pattern of change among both Hispanic and non-Hispanic recruits was identical along all dimensions examined except the single attitude regarding expected gun use. This

Table 12.2   Changes in Perceptions of Weapon Use from Pretraining (T1) to Posttraining (T2) for Hispanic and Non-Hispanic Recruits (Paired T-Tests)*

	Pretraining	Posttraining	T Value	DF	2-Tail Probability
Hispanic Recruits	3.98	3.54	2.70	56	.009
Non-Hispanic Recruits	3.92	3.93	-.06	144	.949

*Lower scores reflect greater expectation of weapon use.

expectation of gun use by police officers emerges as the sole distinguishing factor.

Findings: Testing the Effect Empirically

Suspecting that something strange had occurred in regard to expectations of police officers' weapon use, a search for the source of this reversal in perception began. The content of the training was a standard police academy curriculum; it included no components that should affect one ethnic group selectively.[10] The staff is trained not to send messages denoting gender, ethnic, or other social status differences. An examination of the Hispanic recruits' demographic composition revealed some minor differences from the non-Hispanic recruits, but none of these factors readily explained this particular difference.[11] More significantly, at the beginning of their training the two groups did not differ regarding expectation of officers' gun use, as would be expected if demographic factors were the source of the difference. A group t-test comparison shows that at their entry into the academy, Hispanics averaged a score of 3.98 on the gun use item, while non-Hispanics averaged 3.92.[12] In the posttraining surveys, however, the two groups differed significantly. The Hispanic recruits' average expectation of weapon use had fallen to 3.54, compared with the non-Hispanics' average score of 3.93.[13]

Because neither the recruits' training nor their characteristics offered plausible explanations for a difference affecting only one attitude among the Hispanic recruits, the search shifted to external sources. It was noted that during the data-collection period, a Miami Police Department officer had been involved in a publicized shooting incident in which the officer's ethnicity became a central issue. Follow-up discussions with academy staff members suggested that the incident was a topic of interest among the recruits and that the Hispanic recruits seemed particularly interested. The likelihood that this event had exerted a powerful but focused history effect on the Hispanic subset of recruits was explored; a final analysis supported the idea that this event and its news coverage were a media-generated history effect.[14]

If the apparent history effect of the shooting incident is a valid explanation of the observed change in Hispanic recruits' expectation of gun use, two additional empirical results can be hypothesized. First, one would expect the effect to diminish progressively after the date of the shooting. That is, one would expect the magnitude of change in recruits' perceptions of officers' gun use to decline over time. Second, one would expect to find this decline only among the Hispanic recruits.

Two variables were computed to test these hypotheses. The first, Change, is a measure of the magnitude of each recruit's attitude change regarding weapon use. This was computed by subtracting a recruit's pretraining score from his or her posttraining score. The second variable, Time, is the number of days between the shooting incident and the beginning of a recruit's academy training. If a history effect is operating, one would expect the Change variable to have larger positive values closer to the date of the incident; conversely, the greater the time since the shooting, the smaller the change in attitude. Therefore recruits beginning their training soon after the shooting should show the greatest attitude change. Empirical support for the proposed history effect would be shown by a negative correlation between Change and Time. Table 12.3 displays the one-tailed Pearson correlations between Change and Time for Hispanic and non-Hispanic recruits.

Table 12.3 shows an insignificant relationship between Change and Time for non-Hispanic recruits. For Hispanic recruits, however, we find a significant correlation (-.32) between the magnitude of attitude change regarding gun use and how long after the shooting incident they began training. In addition, the correlation is negative, as one would expect from a history effect: the greater the time since the shooting, the smaller the attitude change. Hispanic recruits who entered the academy closer to the date of the shooting show significantly stronger attitude change regarding gun use than Hispanic recruits who entered training later. As hypothesized, evidence of a history effect holds true only for the Hispanic recruits.[15]

Table 12.3   Pearson Correlations between Changes and Time for Hispanic and non-Hispanic Recruits

	Hispanic Recruits	Non-Hispanic Recruits]
Pearson's R	-.32	-.04
N	54	136
Significance	.009	.309

Discussion

This article offers an empirically supported case study of a news media-generated history effect and demonstrates that criminal justice researchers need to routinely check for such effects. High public and media interest in criminal justice activities places criminal justice research especially at risk for media-generated history effects; thus, as the news media have become more pervasive and more intrusive, a check for possible history effects has become more important. External, confounding history events are likely in the contemporary media atmosphere; when they are present, researchers must consider various causal models and make difficult decisions in ascribing cause.[16] The fortuitous finding of an effect regarding police recruits' perceptions of gun use argues that researchers should conduct a content review of local news media during data collection in criminal justice attitude studies. Program evaluations and policy studies depending on field data are also prone to these external media-generated influences. In sum, in an active news media environment, the criminal justice researcher will find it difficult to distinguish causal effects from external events and their coverage, and from the effects of internal processes such as training or new policies.

This case study also demonstrates the social construction of reality in operation. Although the effect reported here is somewhat narrow and limited, its discovery suggests the strength and importance of the media in influencing crime and justice, even for groups who have alternative sources of information. Police recruits presumably have greater interest and knowledge regarding criminal justice than most citizens. Therefore the fact that a media history effect appears among police recruits implies that the media have a stronger influence on the construction of crime and justice reality than reported previously. For the Hispanic recruits, media information dominated information from other sources, including the formal police academy training. Most prior research focused on broad media content and public perceptions; additional studies of the dynamics of small-scale, specific interactions, such as those reported here, would increase the general understanding of the social construction of reality.

Finally—an important policy implication of this analysis—police recruits are affected selectively by the news media in their work expectations. It is disturbing that the recruits' expectation of future gun use is revealed as highly volatile and subject to somewhat capricious external influences. I believe that the Hispanic recruits affected in this episode are by no means unique. There is no reason to conclude that other sets of recruits exposed to various news media do not undergo similar perceptual changes.

In addition to undermining scholarly research, lack of sensitivity to media-generated reality-constructing processes has serious real-world implications. In this case, the reality that the Hispanic recruits are led to expect is that of more frequent encounters involving officers' gunplay and violent encounters between police and offenders. These recruits subsequently are armed and sent forth into society; thus the concern is whether this expectation persists into their postacademy law enforcement careers and whether it influences their actions as police officers. With the expectation that they will do so, do they use their guns more often than their colleagues? Such questions will remain unanswered until the media and their history effects are taken into account more often.

Notes

[1] The officer initially was found guilty. He appealed, and his conviction was overturned. His retrial was moved numerous times within the State of Florida; eventually it was held in Orlando, where he was found not guilty in May 1994.

[2] The better-known arguments regarding validity involve measurement issues such as the measurement of victimization, fear of crime, and the meaning and usefulness of official police statistics. See McClintock (1970); Wilson (1968).

[3] See Adoni and Mane (1984); Cohen, Adoni, and Bantz (1990); Schneider (1985). Barak (1994), Cohen and Young (1981), and Ericson, Baranek, and Chan (1991) provide excellent overviews and introductions to the social construction of literature as applied to crime and justice.

[4] See Barrile (1984); Best (1989); Carlson (1985); Cohen et al. (1990), Hawkins and Pingree (1982); Surette (1992).

[5] See Culver and Knight (1979); Estep and MacDonald (1984); Thomas and Hyman (1977).

[6] The premise of the original study was that insofar as the media emphasize violent crimes and criminals and violent police-criminal encounters and arrests, the attitudes and perceptions of recruits who are heavy consumers of media should reflect this violent content and should contain associated violent expectations of police work. The overall analysis of this study showed that media consumption (particularly a perception that television programs are realistic) is related significantly to recruits' work expectations. A preference for crime shows was also found to be related, but less consistently than a belief in the reality of television programs.

[7] A comparable stepwise regression corrected for subject mortality ($N=121$ for both pretraining and posttraining regressions) yielded an adjusted R^2 of .11 for pretraining in which TV Reality (beta .33), Male (beta -.18), and Hispanic (beta .17) emerged as significant. At posttraining, the result was an adjusted R^2 of .13 in which Weapon Expectation at pretraining (beta .35), Hispanic (beta -.19), and TV Reality (beta .17) were significant. As discovered in the original stepwise regression, the beta for Hispanic is significant in both pre- and posttraining regressions but reverses in sign from Time 1 to Time 2.

[8] For readers who do not favor the use of a Pearson's t-test analysis with Likert survey items, all t-test analyses were conducted using Spearman's rank order tests with equivalent results. All analyses also distinguished between white and black recruits, but without any effect on results; nor did any history effect appear within these groups.

[9] Support for the legal system remained equally high after their training, few recruits viewed police officers as guilty of discrimination, and perceptions of criminals' violence remained neutral.

[10] The recruits' training lasts approximately 800 hours and is spread over 4-1/2 months. The major training categories are law, criminal investigation, patrol procedures, traffic and accident investigations, report writing, first response, interpersonal skills, firearms, defensive tactics, driving, conditioning, and inspections.

[11] Hispanic recruits are slightly younger (average age 25) than non-Hispanics (average age 27), report slightly lower family incomes ($37,000 per year compared with $43,000), and include a greater percentage of males (87% to 74%). Both groups averaged 13 years of formal education.

[12] Group t-test results before academy training: t=1.34, df=334, two-tailed sig.=.181.

[13] Group t-test results at the end of academy training: t=-2.08, df=200, two-tailed sig.=.039.

[14] The following analysis excludes an academy class that had finished its training just before the shooting incident; as a result, the incident could not have affected their attitudes. This class contained 15 students, with three Hispanics. All of the analyses discussed earlier were also re-run without this class, and no differences in the results were found.

[15] In addition, Hispanics and non-Hispanics do not differ significantly on the time variable (how many days after the shooting, on average, they entered training). This lack of significant difference rules out the possibility that more Hispanics were in training closer to the shooting date, if that had been the case, one could have explained the effect not as concentrated among Hispanics but as a result of the fact that Hispanics coincidentally were more likely to be in training at the time of the shooting. T-test comparison of Hispanics with non-Hispanics on Time shows that Hispanics' average days after shooting for beginning training = 128; non-Hispanics' average days after shooting for beginning training = 146, t= -1.37, df=155, probability= . 172.

[16] In situations dealing with news media coverage, researchers are faced with four possible effects. First, neither the media coverage nor the external event may have an effect. Second, the media coverage may be the sole cause of change. Third, an external event may be the cause of an observed change, even though the media have covered the event simultaneously, they play no causal role. Fourth, both the media coverage of an external event and the event itself may cause the observed change.

References

Adoni, H. and S. Mane (1984) "Media and the Social Construction of Reality." *Communication Research* 11:(3): 323–40.

Altheide, D. and R. Snow (1991) *Media Worlds in the Postjournalism Era.* New York: Aldine.

Barak, G. (1994) *Media, Process, and the Social Construction of Crime: Studies in Newsmaking Criminology.* New York: Garland.

Barrile, L. (1984) "Television and Attitudes about Crime: Do Heavy Viewers Distort Criminality and Support Retributive Justice?" in R. Surette (ed.), *Justice and the Media,* pp. 141–58. Springfield, IL: Thomas.

Best, J., ed. (1989) *Images of Issues: Typifying Contemporary Social Problems.* New York: Aldine.

Carlson, J. (1985) *Prime Time Law Enforcement.* New York: Praeger.

Cohen, A., T. Adoni, and C. Bantz (1990) *Social Conflict and Television News.* Newbury Park, CA: Sage.

Cohen, S. and J. Young (1981) *The Manufacture of News: Social Problems, Deviance, and the Mass Media.* London: Constable.

Cook, T. and D. Campbell (1979) *Quasi-Experimentation.* Boston: Houghton Mifflin.

Culver, J. and K. Knight (1979) "Evaluating TV Impressions of Law-Enforcement Roles." In R. Baker and F. Mayer (eds.), *Evaluating Alternative Law Enforcement Policies* pp. 201–12. Lexington, MA: Lexington Books.

Dye, T. and H. Zeigler (1986) *American Politics in the Media Age.* Pacific Grove, CA: Brooks/Cole.

Ericson, R., P. Baranek, and J. Chan (1991) *Representing Order: Crime, Law, and Justice in the News Media.* Toronto: University of Toronto Press.

Estep, R. and P. MacDonald (1984) "How Prime-Time Crime Evolved on TV, 1976 to 1983." In R. Surette (ed.), *Justice and the Media,* pp. 110–23. Springfield, IL: Thomas.

Hawkins, R. and S. Pingree (1982) "Television's Influence on Social Realty." In D. Pearl, L. Bouthilet, and J. Lazar (eds.), *Television and Behavior: Ten Years of Scientific Progress and Implications for the Eighties,* Vol. 2: *Technical Reviews,* pp. 224–47. Washington, DC: U.S. Government Printing Office.

McClintock, F. H. (1970) "The Dark Figure" [No edition for Council of Europe work]. *Collected Studies in Criminological Research,* pp. 13–34. Hague: Council of Europe.

Meyrowitz, J. (1985) *No Sense of Place.* New York: Oxford University Press.

Schneider, J. (1985) "Social Problems Theory: The Constructionist View." *Annual Review of Sociology* 11:209–29.

Surette, R. (1991) "The Relationship between Media Use, Training and Attitudes for Correctional and Law Enforcement Recruits at the Southeast Florida Institute of Criminal Justice." Report to the Southeast Florida Institute of Criminal Justice, Miami.

_____ (1992) *Media Crime and Criminal Justice: Images and Realities.* Pacific Grove, CA: Brooks/Cole.

_____ (forthcoming) "The Media and Criminal Justice Policy." *Criminal Justice Policy Review.*

Thomas, C. and J. Hyman (1977) "Perceptions of Crime, Fear of Victimization, and Public Perceptions of Police Performance." *Journal of Police Science and Administrations* 5:305–17.

Wilson J. (1968) *Varieties of Police Behavior.* Cambridge: Harvard University Press.

13

Measuring the Scope of Social Problems
Apparent Inconsistencies across Estimates of Family Abductions

Joel Best and Tracy Memoree Thibodeau

Justice policy derives from shared conceptions of social problems; conditions must be identified, named, and defined as problematic and demanding official attention. Criminologists traditionally approach this process in terms of criminalization, examining how the law creates new crimes (e.g., Hollinger and Lanza-Kaduce 1988). In contrast, recent sociological research focuses on the construction of social problems; constructionist studies examine how and why particular issues become the focus of public concern. Such a process may or may not lead to new laws or other official action (Best 1995; Holstein and Miller 1993; Spector and Kitsuse 1977). Claims that particular conditions should be considered social problems compete for the attention of the press, the public, and policy makers, and struggle to be heard over other claims. Thus claims of social problems can be analyzed as rhetoric intended to persuade others of the seriousness of a problem (Best 1990; Hilgartner and Bosk 1988). What makes claims convincing varies across time and cultures. In the contemporary United States, because science and rationality are important standards for designing and assessing policy, statistics often occupy a prominent place in social problem claims (Alonso and Starr 1987).

Source: *Justice Quarterly*, Vol. 14, No. 4, December 1997, pp. 719–737. © 1997 Academy of Criminal Justice Sciences. Reprinted with permission.

The most common claimsmaking statistics describe the size of social problems; claims that a problem is common or widespread usually receive more attention than others. Initially, claimsmakers often seek to draw attention to what they argue are neglected social problems. One symptom of this alleged neglect is a scarcity of reliable statistics, which leads claimsmakers to offer *estimates* of the problem's scope.

Once attention begins to focus on the problem, two other sorts of data can become available. First, agencies charged with addressing the problem begin to keep records of their activities; these records can be compiled in bureaucratic or *official statistics* (for example, UCR crime rates are compiled from crime reports to law enforcement agencies) (Kitsuse and Cicourel 1963). Second, special *statistical research* projects may measure features of the problem; such research can be conducted by official agencies (e.g., the National Crime Victimization Surveys) or by individuals or nongovernment organizations (who may have government funding via grants or contracts). Because these different methods of producing statistics have well-known strengths and weaknesses, statistics about social problems often become subjects of debates in which contending parties challenge one another's numbers.

In this article we offer a case study of conflicting statistical claims. We examine statistics about missing children, and particularly about the incidence of family abductions. During the 1980s, family abductions became the subject of activists' estimates, official statistics, and statistical research. These different sources for statistics produced markedly different numbers; those numbers have played distinctive roles in discussions of the missing children problem and the appropriate response by the justice system.

Activists' Estimates regarding Missing Children

"Missing children" emerged as a prominent social problem in 1981, when activists successfully promoted the term as a label encompassing runaways (relatively common), abductions by strangers (relatively rare but including some horrific crimes that could be used as typifying examples), and family abductions (a matter of direct concern to many activists) (Best 1990). The missing-children movement initially estimated that there were 1.8 to 2 million missing children each year, including 50,000 children kidnapped by strangers and 100,000 children abducted by noncustodial parents and other family members; runaways accounted for the remaining cases (U.S. House 1981). These claims about the victimization of large numbers of children inspired widespread concern: The press gave the issue considerable attention, legislators promised action, pictures of missing children received wide circulation, and parents were encouraged to fingerprint their children and take other protective measures.

By the mid-1980s, a contentious debate had emerged over the number of missing children. In particular, the estimate for stranger abductions was attacked by journalists and social scientists, who charged that the 50,000 figure was inflated and that the actual number was more likely to be between 70 and 600 per year. The *Denver Post* won a Pulitzer Prize for its stories exposing this "numbers gap" (Griego and Kilzer 1985).

The debate over missing-children statistics was not unprecedented. Claimsmakers routinely offer numeric estimates for the extent of a social problem, its rate of growth, the cost of combating it, and so on. Because claimsmaking is a form of persuasion, these estimates tend to be generous: Big numbers indicate a big problem, one that demands attention (Best 1990). Moreover, because claimsmakers often seek to draw attention to neglected problems, theirs may be the only available numbers; when there are no official statistics for a problem's magnitude, claimsmakers' guesstimates and ballpark figures, by default, may become the only (and therefore the most authoritative) available statistics. Once in circulation, these numbers can take on a life of their own, repeated without reservation in press reports, government documents, and even scholarly analyses.

Claimsmakers can produce exaggerated estimates of a social problem's magnitude in at least two ways. Some claimsmakers have no firm foundation for their statistics; they respond with educated guesses when asked about the size of the problem. Mitch Snyder, a prominent advocate for the homeless, explained how he produced his estimate of 2 to 3 million homeless persons:

> Everybody demanded it. Everybody said we want a number. . . . We got on the phone, we made a lot of calls, we talked to a lot of people, and we said, "Okay, here are some numbers." They have no meaning, no value. (quoted in Jencks 1994:2)

In other cases, claimsmakers may begin with more or less reliable data, but may interpret those data so as to produce inflated estimates. As Jenkins (1994:60–70) suggests, for example, claims that serial murderers killed 4,000 to 5,000 victims a year began with a misinterpretation of FBI Supplementary Homicide Reports which assumed that all unknown offenders were serial killers.

Critiques of claimsmakers' estimates have become more common in both investigative journalism and constructionist analyses of claimsmaking. These critics usually argue that claimsmakers' statistics exaggerate the magnitude of the problem in question. Examples include critiques of inflated statistics about missing children (Best 1990), drug abuse (Orcutt and Turner 1993), elder abuse (Crystal 1987), abuse by clergy (Jenkins 1996), homelessness (Jencks 1994), workplace violence (Larson 1994), sexual assault (Gilbert 1994), and serial murder (Jenkins 1994). Taken together, these analyses suggest that claimsmakers tend to exaggerate the scope of the problems addressed by their claims. This exaggeration need not be intentional or cynical. Claimsmakers are often intensely involved in social networks centered around the problem that concerns them; they may be sincere in their belief that a problem is widespread and convicted that their estimates are correct. Even so, exaggeration makes claims more persuasive, and because few statistical claims receive critical examination, there is much to be gained and little to be lost in erring on the side of overestimation.

Official Statistics about Missing Children

The debate over the number of stranger abductions reinforced the missing-children movement's calls for more thorough reporting and record keeping by official agencies. Activists complained that police often refused to begin searching until a child had been missing 24 to 72 hours, that there was no central register for missing-children reports, and that reports given to one local law enforcement agency were not necessarily disseminated to other agencies. These criticisms led to several reforms.

In response to the movement's charges that missing-children cases too often fell into the cracks between law enforcement jurisdictions, most states established statewide clearinghouses for missing-children reports. The structure and activities of these clearinghouses vary considerably, but some also became central record-keeping agencies for their states (Girdner 1994). In New York State, for example, "law enforcement agencies are required by law to report missing children cases to the statewide Register upon receiving missing children complaints." The clearinghouse, in turn, shares those reports with other agencies and publishes an annual statistical summary of the reports it receives (New York Division of Criminal Justice Services 1991:1).

At the federal level, the Missing Children's Act of 1982 encouraged law enforcement agencies to report missing-children cases to the FBI's National Crime Information Center (NCIC). The National Child Search Assistance Act of 1990 mandated that states receiving federal missing-children funds require local agencies to promptly report missing children to the NCIC (Forst and Blomquist 1991).[1] With the Missing Children's Assistance Act of 1984, Congress also began funding the National Center for Missing and Exploited Children (NCMEC). Individuals and agencies could report cases to the NCMEC, which, in turn, assisted in search efforts (for example, by disseminating children's photographs) (Jackson 1995). These various efforts were attempts to make reporting and searching for missing children easier and more efficient, but advocates recognized that none of these measures would produce accurate, national official statistics for the numbers of missing children. Therefore the federal government also sponsored the first large-scale statistical research to accurately measure the scope of the missing children problem: the National Incidence Studies of Missing, Abducted, Runaway, and Thrownaway Children (NISMART) (Finkelhor, Hotaling, and Sedlak 1990).

Statistical Research: NISMART's Findings

NISMART sought to resolve the debate about the number of missing children through an elaborate research design. For this research, conducted in 1988–1989, NISMART incorporated several sources of data including a telephone survey of households, an analysis of records from a sample of 83 law enforcement agencies, a secondary analysis of FBI homicide data, and surveys of juvenile residential facilities, returned runaways, and agencies in contact with children who might be abandoned. NISMART used different data sets to measure the incidence of different types of missing children. In an apparent effort to placate both activists (who preferred to define categories of missing children broadly) and their critics (who tended to favor narrower definitions), NISMART offered estimates based on both broad ("broad scope") and narrow ("policy focal") definitions:

> "Broad Scope" generally defines the problem the way the affected families might define it. It includes both serious and also more minor episodes that may nonetheless be alarming to the participants. By contrast, "Policy Focal" generally defines the problem from the point of view of the police or other social agencies. It is restricted to episodes of a more serious nature, where children are at risk and there is a need for immediate intervention. (Finkelhor et al. 1990:viii–ix)[2]

The NISMART report, once issued, achieved widespread acceptance; this is understandable, given the absence of authoritative national official statistics. Post-NISMART discussions of missing children by social scientists, journalists, and government officials routinely used NISMART's figures to estimate the scope of the problem.

Table 13.1 contrasts NISMART's findings with the early estimates of missing-children activists. NISMART's findings regarding stranger (nonfamily) abductions and runaways support the general rule that claimsmakers usually overestimate the magnitude of social problems. NISMART concluded that serious cases of stranger abduction number 200 to 300 annually, about .5 percent of the 50,000 figure promoted by activists and roughly what the movement's critics had predicted. Similarly, even NISMART's broad definition of runaways led to an estimate roughly one-quarter of that offered by the activists.

Table 13.1 Estimates by Activists and NISMART for the Annual Incidence of Three Types of Missing Children

Type of Missing Children	Activists' Estimates	NISMART Estimates	
		Broad Definition	Narrow Definition
Nonfamily Abductions	50,000	3,200–4,600	200–300
Family Abductions	100,000	354,100	163,200
Runaways	1,650,000–1,850,000	450,700	133,500

NISMART's third estimate—for the incidence of family abductions—deserves our attention. Even by NISMART's narrow definition, activists apparently underestimated the incidence of family abductions by more than 60 percent; NISMART found 163,200 cases, whereas activists had estimated only 100,000 cases per year. NISMART's broad definition led to an estimate more than 3 1/2 times as great as the movement's.[3] In other words, this result runs counter to the constructionist generalization that claimsmakers overestimate the scope of social problems; in the case of family abductions, missing-children activists apparently promoted statistical estimates that were too low. How can we account for this apparent anomaly?

Two possible explanations suggest themselves: Perhaps the activists underestimated the incidence of family abductions, or perhaps NISMART overestimated the extent of the problem. Unfortunately, no other reliable national data exist that might serve as a basis for measuring family abductions. The NCIC's missing-persons file does not distinguish types of missing children, and the great majority of missing-children cases are never reported to the NCMEC. Some statewide clearinghouses, however, compile records complete enough to be used as a benchmark for assessing the NISMART findings.

Family Abductions Reported to State Clearinghouses

After acquiring a list of state clearinghouses from the NCMEC we wrote to each, requesting a copy of the most recent annual statistical summary. Not all states had clearinghouses, not all clearinghouses issued statistics or responded to our request, and not all the statistical reports we received distinguished family abductions from other miss-ing-children cases. The analysis that follows draws on the eight state reports we received that presented usable data on family abductions (California, Colorado, Florida, Illinois, Indiana, Maryland, New York, and North Carolina).

Consider New York State's report. As noted above, New York law enforcement agencies are required by law to report missing-children cases to the state's clearinghouse; since the mid-1980s, that clearing-house has published annual statistical summaries. For 1993 New York reported 5 stranger abductions, 29 acquaintance abductions, 241 fam-ily abductions, and 27,756 runaways (New York Division of Criminal Justice Services 1994).[4] In 1993 6.66 percent of the U.S. under-18 pop-ulation lived in New York State (U.S. Bureau of the Census 1994:32). Thus we can extrapolate national estimates for the incidence of various types of missing children from the New York data. This step produces estimates of 75 stranger abductions (or, when we include acquaintance abductions, 511 nonfamily abductions) nationwide, 3,619 family abduc-tions, and 416,756 runaways (see table 13.2).

Table 13.2 Extrapolations from 1993 State Clearinghouse Statistics for the National Annual Incidence of Three Types of Missing Children

State Clearinghouse	Extrapolations		
	Nonfamily Abductions	Family Abductions	Runaways
California	609	16,867	623,242
Colorado	3,357	5,143	1,249,000
Florida	NA	8,072	1,079,300
Illinois	NA	3,567	NA
Indiana	183	4,338	199,269
Maryland	270	1,405	NA
New York	511	3,619	416,756
N. Carolina	157	1,654	191,535
Total	627	8,658	610,983
NISMART Estimates			
Narrow definition	200–300	163,200	133,500
Broad definition	3,200–4,600	354,100	450,700

Note: Extrapolations were calculated by dividing the number of cases reported in 1993 by the state's missing-children clearinghouse by the state's proportion of 1993 under-18 popu-lation. Extrapolations in "Total" row were calculated by adding cases from states with avail-able data, then dividing by those states' proportion of the under-18 population. Categories and definitions used in clearinghouse reports varied.

How do these New York estimates compare with those developed by NISMART? The estimates for nonfamily abductions and runaways fit NISMART fairly well: NISMART estimated 200 to 300 serious (i.e., narrowly defined) cases of nonfamily abduction per year or, under their broad definition, 3,200 to 4,600 cases. The extrapolation from the New York report leads to a number (511) in that range, and reasonably close to NISMART's narrow-definition estimate. Similarly, New York's reported runaways produce an extrapolation consistent with NISMART's estimate: NISMART's narrow definition leads to an estimate of 133,500 runaways, while its broader definition produces an estimate of 450,700. This latter figure is near the figure extrapolated from New York: 416,756. The great majority of New York cases are closed, usually when the child returns voluntarily. This suggests that the New York clearinghouse works fairly efficiently in that it records large numbers of reports of short-term runaways—the sort of cases included under NISMART's broad definition.

Whereas the extrapolations from New York's data for both nonfamily abductions and runaways are generally consistent with NISMART's findings, this is not the case for family abductions. The extrapolation from the New York data produces a national estimate of 3,619 family abductions, far fewer than the 163,200 cases derived from NISMART's narrow definition.

By using this process to extrapolate from 1993 data reported by the eight state clearinghouses, we produce a consistent pattern: an estimate for nonfamily abductions roughly comparable to NISMART's, but a figure for family abductions much lower than that based on even NISMART's narrow definition (see table 13.2).[5] In 1993 these eight states accounted for a substantial portion (36.7 percent) of the nation's under-18 population. They include four of the five states with the largest juvenile populations, all heavily urbanized states that might be expected to have above-average rates of crime and childhood victimization. Table 13.2 also presents extrapolations based on totals from the states for which clearinghouse data were available; again, the nonfamily abduction and runaway figures seem fairly consistent with NISMART's estimates, but the extrapolation for family abductions amounts to only 5 percent of NISMART's narrow-definition estimate. Of the right states, California yields by far the highest family-abduction estimate, and this is an order of magnitude lower than NISMART's narrow-definition estimate.[6]

These data from state clearinghouse reports create a new anomaly. NISMART's findings suggest, counter to what constructionists would predict, that missing-children activists underestimated the number of family abductions. The state clearinghouse data, however, are inconsistent with NISMART's findings: The clearinghouses receive far fewer reports than either the activists or NISMART would predict.

How NISMART Estimated Family Abductions

The NISMART researchers began with data from a well-designed, large-scale national household survey. A sample of 60,000 telephone numbers yielded 10,367 interviews with caretakers who had children in their households; and 104 of these caretakers reported episodes involving 142 children that the researchers coded as family abductions:

> Under our broad-scope definition, a family abduction occurs (a) when a family member takes a child in violation of a custody agreement or decree; or (b) when a family member in violation of a custody agreement or decree fails to return or give over a child at the end of a legal or agreed-upon visit, and the child is away at least overnight. (Finkelhor et al. 1991:808)

The researchers also applied a narrower definition to identify a subset of 59 more serious, "policy-focal" cases:

> [These cases] met one of three other conditions: (a) an attempt was made to conceal the taking or the whereabouts of the child and to prevent contact with the child; or (b) the child was transported out of state; or (c) there was evidence that the abductor had intended to keep the child indefinitely or permanently affect custodial privileges.[7] (Finkelhor et al. 1991:808)

Respondents to the household survey answered a set of screening questions. After a lead-in ("In the past 12 months, did *any* family member outside of your household, such as an ex-spouse, brother, sister, parent, or in-law, or someone acting for them, do any of the following things . . . ?"), the principal screening questions regarding family abductions were "Did any family member or someone acting for them *take or try to take* (this child/any of these children) in violation of a custody order, agreement, or other child living arrangement?" and "Did any family member outside of your household *keep or try to keep* (this child/any of these children) from you when you were supposed to have (him/her/them), even if for just a day or weekend?" (Sedlak, Mohadjer, and Hudock 1990:A8–9).[8]

These questions intentionally cast a broad net. When respondents gave an affirmative answer to a screening question, further questions followed. Presumably some episodes were discarded at this stage, while others were coded as family abductions. Even so, the final NISMART definitions remained broad: "For purposes of this study, 'taken' meant that the child was actually moved or transported at least 20 feet or into a vehicle or a building. Note that taking could have occur [sic] with the full voluntary cooperation of the child . . ." (Sedlack et al. 1990:7–36). (Note, too, that no minimal time was required for a child to be defined as "taken.")

The NISMART researchers subjected a subset of 36 family-abduction cases to reliability tests. In 7 cases they found disagreements on the evaluative coding for "taken/attempt"; in 4 cases they found disagreements on "not returned" (Sedlak et al. 1990:B9). (Presumably these disagreements involved different cases because episodes involved either "taking" or "keeping" children, although the researchers calculated reliability scores for the individual items.) This suggests a rather high level of coding disagreements: nearly one-third of the cases. We are not told how these disagreements were resolved, or how many of the cases ultimately coded as family abductions involved such disagreements.

Still, the findings give several clues that NISMART interpreted the respondents' answers so as to maximize the number of events coded as family abductions. The researchers observe that respondents did not always define as a serious offense what the researchers considered a codable event: "Respondents may not have stored this episode in their memories as a 'kidnapping' or even the 'taking' of a child" (Finkelhor et al. 1991:807). They acknowledge that their survey ignored the "abductors'" perspective: "In some cases, what were perceived by our respondents as 'violations' may have been honest disagreements (or misunderstandings) about the terms of a custody order or understanding" (Finkelhor et al. 1991:812). Remarkably, they found no differences in the length of the child's absence between the presumably more serious policy-focal cases (32 percent lasted 24 hours or less; 77 percent lasted a week or less) and the nonpolicy-focal cases (32 percent, 24 hours or less; 75 percent, a week or less) (Finkelhor et al. 1991:813).

In most cases, the respondent knew the child's whereabouts:

> Forty-eight percent in the broad-scope cases and 34% in the policy-focal cases said they knew the whereabouts "most of the time." The number who did not know where their children were at all was only 17% for broad-scope and 22% for policy-focal cases. This illustrates that family abduction is not primarily a problem of "missing children" but is rather a problem of children who are not where they are supposed to be. (Finkelhor et al. 1991:814)[9]

Caretakers reported only 39 percent of the episodes to the police (Plass, Finkelhor, and Hotaling 1995:209). Respondents in the policy-focal cases generally denied the occurrence of sexual abuse (no, 94%; don't know [DK], 6%,), physical abuse (no, 87%; DK, 8%), injury (no, 89%; DK/NA, 3%), or severe mental harm (mild/minor, 35%, no, 41%, DK, 7%) (Finkelhor et al. 1991:814).

Secondary analysis of the NISMART data raises further questions. Although the researchers describe policy-focal cases as "more serious . . . where children are at risk and there is a need for immediate intervention," we see indications that respondents did not always define the episodes as crises. Respondents in the policy-focal cases reported contacting the police only 59 percent of the time, and they said they considered the event a kidnapping in only 53 percent of the cases. (Only 41 percent of the policy-focal cases involved respondents who both contacted the police and considered the event a kidnapping.) In 56 percent of the policy-focal cases, the respondents acknowledged that the "abductor" claimed to justify the episode.

The portrait of family abductions derived from the NISMART data hardly resembles the way the study's results have been interpreted by officials, missing-children advocates, and journalists. According to a book co-authored by a New York legislator, "90 percent of parents who take their own children illegally are emotionally unstable or abusive, with approximately one-half having criminal records. . . . Children often live under cruel circumstances, almost paralleling the life of a fugitive, with frequent changes of residences and names" (Tedisco and Paludi 1996:18). Similarly, the U.S. Office of Juvenile Justice and Delinquency Prevention recently reviewed legal policies toward parental abductions—the authors begin by citing NISMART's (broad-scope) estimate. Then they state:

> Often people do not think of parental abductions as harmful. Yet many of these children already have lived through their parents' stormy relationship, failed marriage and difficult divorce. They are taken from the other parent and uprooted from their home, school, and community—possibly living on the run—changing names, schools, and homes. The lack of stability and continuity can have lasting detrimental effects on their development. They are children at risk. (Girdner and Hoff 1994:Exec. Summ. 1; also see Hoff 1985:vii)

Interpreting NISMART's findings, the NCMEC president writes:

> Over 354 family abductions occurred in 1988—far exceeding earlier annual estimates of 25,000 to 100,000. . . . in 80 percent of the cases, anger or the desire to cause emotional pain motivated the abducting parent. As a result, approximately 75,000 children suffer serious injuries—whether mental or physical—in this type of case each year. [NISMART] indicates that the number of child abductions by family members continues to grow at an alarming rate. (Allen 1992:18)

In the same spirit, a recent newsmagazine story began: "More than 350,000 children are 'kidnapped' by a parent each year in divorce custody disputes." The bulk of the story consisted of accounts of five cases: one in which the kidnapping parent murdered the child, three in which the abduction lasted at least five years (including one case involving long-term sexual abuse), and a year-long abduction to another country (Kearns 1995:69). In other words, claimsmakers illustrate the problem of family abductions with cases involving lengthy, often abusive separations of children from at least one parent. To couple these horror stories to NISMART's broad-scope estimate—or even to its policy-focal estimate—distorts both how NISMART defined family abductions and what the study found.

Can Underreporting Explain the Discrepancy?

The central problem with most criminal justice incidence statistics is underreporting—the so-called "dark figure." NISMART asked respondents whether they had reported the incident to the police; as noted above, 59 percent of the policy-focal cases and 39 percent of the broad-scope cases were reported. If we extrapolate (39 percent of NISMART's broad-scope estimate of 354,100 cases), the NISMART findings predict roughly 138,100 family-abduction reports per year. This figure is nearly 16 times greater than 8,658, the estimate based on the combined clearinghouse reports (see table 13.2).

This discrepancy compares two figures for reports to the police: Neither the NISMART figure of 138,100 nor the clearinghouse extrapolation of 8,658 includes unreported cases. Moreover, NISMART's methods would predict an even higher level of reporting. Multiple episodes of abduction occur in some families; for example, a noncustodial parent may repeatedly violate the terms of a custody agreement by taking a child without authorization or failing to return a child when agreed. NISMART avoided double counting by including only a household's most serious episode in its sample: If a respondent reported two or more family abductions of the same child during the year covered by the NISMART survey, only the instance considered most serious was included in the analysis. The estimate of 138,100 reported cases is based on the assumption that no child is abducted more than one per year; insofar as caretakers report multiple abductions of the same children, the NISMART estimate would seem to be too low.

Another possibility is that police underreport cases to the state clearinghouses. Table 13.2, however, suggests two problems with this explanation. First, the clearinghouse and the NISMART estimates for both nonfamily abductions and runaways coincide fairly closely. Therefore, if police are underreporting, they must be singling out family abductions and failing to process only those reports. Even the law enforcement agencies in states such as Colorado and Florida, which process runaway reports at very high rates, must be massively underreporting family abductions to state clearinghouses. Second, all eight state clearinghouses report levels of family abduction much lower than those projected by NISMART. These eight states presumably are governed by somewhat different laws and different organizational practices. Thus we must presume that police in these varied jurisdictions all underreport the great majority of family abductions. Why, in view of the prolonged, highly publicized campaign of the missing-children movement and the passage of numerous federal and state laws designed to improve reporting practices, would underreporting continue to be the norm in each state?

The Politics of Statistical Research

NISMART reminds us of the significance—often forgotten—of methodological decisions. The study's researchers had to create operational definitions for family abductions; this must have been a difficult task because any definition runs the risk of making two potential errors. On the one hand, an excessively narrow definition might lead researchers to exclude cases from analysis that ought to be considered: in effect, labeling false negatives, or making the equivalent of statisticians' Type I errors. If, for example, the researchers had set the minimum time for a policy-focal family abduction at three months (instead of setting no minimum time for "taking," and a minimum of overnight for "keeping" a child), their decision not only would have reduced the estimate dramatically. It also might have excluded from analysis some obviously serious cases: for example, a noncustodial parent who kidnapped a child by force and fled to another state with the intent of keeping the child, only to be located and arrested after 10 weeks. On the other hand, an excessively broad definition might cause the researchers to include minor cases that perhaps ought not be considered: in effect, identifying false positives, or making Type II errors.

NISMART's design and results suggest that the researchers feared false negatives far more than false positives. They devised and applied a broad, inclusive definition, one unlikely to be criticized for excluding any serious incidents. This choice, however, ensured that the study would count substantial numbers of less serious episodes. The criteria for identifying policy-focal family abductions led the researchers to include short-lived cases, cases in which no one was harmed, cases that neither parent considered abductions, and cases that were not reported to the police.

It is easy to understand this choice. The missing children movement had drawn national attention to what it claimed was a widespread, long-neglected problem. Calls for a fuller accounting of missing children—not only from the movement but also from the media, politicians, and official agencies—demanded statistical research that would not overlook or ignore serious cases, research that could not be criticized for further neglecting the plight of missing children. Considerable pressure was exerted to make the research inclusive enough to measure the full extent of the problem; it had to acknowledge the importance of, and to count, all types of missing children.

In contrast, although critics had accused the movement of propagating wildly exaggerated estimates, no organized forces were pressing the NISMART researchers to apply narrow definitions. When the report was released, no objections were raised. The critics seemed to be satisfied by NISMART's distinction between broadscope and policy-focal definitions. Moreover, criticism had focused on estimates of stranger abductions; those findings could expect to receive close scrutiny, but NISMART's other findings were less likely to attract close, critical attention, and did not do so. By arguing that the policy-focal category was "restricted to episodes of a more serious nature, where children are at risk and there is a need for immediate intervention" (Finkelhor et al. 1990:ix), the researchers suggested that they had addressed any reservations on the part of potential critics. Also, because there was no readily available benchmark against which the NISMART results might be compared, the study's findings achieved widespread acceptance.

Sociologists and criminologists sometimes scrutinize activists' estimates and official statistics (Alonso and Starr 1987; Kitsuse and Cicourel 1963), but critical analyses of the politics of statistical research have been less common. Social scientists argue that many social problems, especially those victimizing women and children, traditionally have been undercounted in official statistics and statistical research. If anything, they advocate designing research projects using broad definitions that will avoid the risk of false negatives and thereby will produce larger numbers (e.g., Smith 1994). NISMART seems to fit this model of inclusive statistical research.

Implications of an Anomaly

"Family abduction" is a socially constructed category, created and used by activists, social scientists, and criminal justice professionals. Calculation of the number of family abductions depends on how the term is defined and applied. We have shown that NISMART produced a large estimate for family abductions—even higher than the figure offered by missing-children activists—but that state clearinghouses have received far fewer reports of family abductions than NISMART would lead us to expect.

The missing-children movement must have been highly satisfied with the NISMART findings about family abduction. Although stranger abductions attracted most of the media attention, many activists entered the missing-children movement through their own experience and concern with family abductions (Best 1990). Many prominent child-search organizations, such as Child Find, began as efforts to locate children taken in family abductions. During the 1970s they tried (with limited success) to persuade authorities to treat family abductions as serious offenses (Hegar 1990; Spangler 1982). In the early 1980s, the leaders of these child-search organizations provided a cadre of knowledgeable, committed activists. These individuals led new efforts to promote the issue, now renamed "missing children" to encompass stranger abductions (which allowed the movement to point to horrific examples) and runaways (which enabled the movement to describe the problem in terms of very large numbers such as 2 million missing children per year). For these activists, NISMART's determination that the movement had overestimated stranger abductions and runaways may have been less significant than its finding that family abductions were more common than imagined.

Certainly NISMART's design produced a generous estimate for family abductions. It defined family abduction broadly, and applied even the more serious "policy-focal" designation to numerous short-term episodes, to episodes in which the child's location was known, and to events that respondents did not bother reporting to the police and did not consider kidnappings. NISMART's portrait of policy-focal cases hardly matches the claims that family abductions typically are long-term kidnappings involving violence and sexual abuse.

It is certainly possible that local police underreport family abduction cases. We can imagine officers deciding not to process some reports of brief episodes, particularly when the child's location is known. NISMART's estimate is generous, but the clearinghouse reports may well underestimate the number of family abductions.

Still, the gap between the two sets of figures seems too large to be explained by systematic underreporting. Police may underreport some cases, but to provide an explanation for the anomalous findings they would have to fail to report 15 of every 16 cases that came to their attention. This seems unlikely, given the continuing prominence of missing children as an issue.

Why, then, do NISMART's findings diverge so far from the clearinghouse data? Absent the discovery of some fundamental flaw in NISMART's research design, it seems likely that the researchers' decision to adopt a broad, inclusive definition accounts for much of the difference.

Statistics—especially statistics gathered through social research—play an important role in policy debates because they tend to be treated not only as the best available information but also as indisputable facts. The operational definitions, coding practices, and other methodological choices that underlie every social statistic tend to be ignored; they are overlooked as thoroughly as any forgotten victims of neglected social problems. The general, uncritical acceptance of the NIS-MART findings by the press and the policy makers illustrates the limitations of our society's mechanisms for critically assessing social statistics. Obviously these limitations extend far beyond statistics on family abductions.

Notes

[1] Although reports to NCIC presumably increased as a result of these laws, this change did not lead to a usable, authoritative official statistic for missing children. NCIC's system for classifying missing persons did not distinguish children from adults, nor did it use categories compatible with the missing-children movement's classification of stranger abduction, family abduction, and runaway.

[2] In classifying nonfamily abductions, NISMART gave these categories different labels: "The Legal Definition of Abduction corresponds to the crime of abduction as it is specified in the criminal law of many States and includes the short-term, coercive movement entailed in many rapes and assaults. Stereotypical Kidnappings, by contrast, reflect more closely the popular stereotype of a kidnapping, as a long-term, long-distance, or fatal episode" (Finkelhor et al. 1990:ix).

[3] In an early attempt to estimate the number of family abductions, Gelles (1984) reported that three national Harris polls asked: "Do you know of an instance of parental child snatching which occurred in your family or a family of someone you personally know in the last twelve months?" He acknowledged that "households other than [those of the] 'snatcher' and 'snatchee' may be involved. These could include grandparents, uncles, aunts, other in-laws, professionals (e.g., lawyers, judges, police officers, social workers, teachers . . .) or other friends or accomplices . . ." (p. 737). Nevertheless he derived estimates based on the assumption that the number of households reporting knowledge of each incident would be between two (626,000 cases per year) and four (313,000 cases). Gelles also stated, "A substantial number of the parental child snatchings reported in this survey could well have been of short duration" (p. 738). Perhaps because of these methodological limitations, this study was rarely cited in the missing-children debate.

[4] New York's clearinghouse reports are more elaborate than those prepared by other states: They are printed pamphlets, whereas many other states' reports consist of a few photocopied pages stapled together. Also, the numbers of reported cases have remained fairly stable from one annual report to the next, which suggests that the data are reliable (see Best 1990:54).

[5] The extrapolations for runaways vary a good deal; this variation probably reflects differences in the states' definitions and reporting practices. For example, Colorado, which yields the highest extrapolated estimate for runaways, reported locating 27 percent of missing children in less than 24 hours (Colorado Bureau of Investigation 1994:12). Since even NISMART's broad definition requires that runaways be absent overnight, this figure suggests that some state clearinghouses may define runaways even more broadly than NISMART.

[6] Although we compare NISMART's data collected in 1988–1989 with clearinghouse reports for 1993, we know of no reason to attribute the differences in the estimates to shifts in the incidence of family abductions. Certainly missing-children advocates do not argue that family abductions have declined markedly. Also,

where state clearinghouse data are available for 1988–1989, as in New York (see footnote 4 above), they are comparable to the 1993 reports.

Other estimates also seem to be inconsistent with NISMART's figures. Although reports to the NCMEC are unsystematic and incomplete, the Center handled only 4,979 reports of family abductions between January 1990 and March 1995 (Jackson 1995). Canadians reported 394 parental abductions during 1994 (Driedger et al. 1995:42), and "an estimate of parental kidnappings in the United Kingdom places the number at approximately 500 annually" (Greif and Hegar 1993:4).

[7] Reanalysis of the data show that among the 83 cases coded as nonpolicy-focal, 9 included efforts to conceal the child, 19 involved prevention of contacts between the child and the respondent, 5 involved removing the child out of state, and 19 involved efforts to permanently affect custody. (Some cases may have had more than one of these features.) We do not have enough information to know why these cases were not coded as policy-focal. We thank Professor Peggy S. Plass for sharing a copy of the 142-case NISMART family-abduction data set.

[8] Other screening questions (e.g., "Was there any time when anyone *tried to take* (this child/any of these children) away against your wishes?") also could cause episodes to be classified as family abductions, once subsequent questions identified the perpetrator as a family member (Sedlak et al. 1990). The NISMART documentation does not reveal which screening questions received the most positive responses.

[9] The codes for this variable include categories labeled both "most of the time" and " > half of the time." If we combine these categories, then respondents in 39 percent of the policy-focal cases and 59 percent of the broad-scope cases said they knew the child's location more than half of the time.

References

Allen, E. 1992. "The Crisis of Family Abductions in America." *FBI Law Enforcement Bulletin* 61 (August): 18–19.

Alonso, W. and P. Starr, eds. 1987. *The Politics of Numbers.* New York: Russell Sage Foundation.

Best, J. 1990. *Threatened Children.* Chicago: University of Chicago Press.

———, ed. 1995. *Images of Issues.* 2nd ed. Hawthorne, NY: Aldine.

Colorado Bureau of Investigation. 1994. *Missing Children Project: Annual Report to the Colorado General Assembly, 1993.* Denver: Colorado Department of Public Safety.

Crystal, S. 1987. "Elder Abuse: The Latest 'Crisis.'" *The Public Interest* 88:56–66.

Driedger, S. D., C. Du Gray, M. McDonald, and P. Chisholm. 1995. "Perils of Home: Abductions by Parents Far Outstrip Those by Strangers." *Maclean's,* July 24, p. 42.

Finkelhor, D., G. Hotaling, and A. Sedlak. 1990. *Missing, Abducted, Runaway, and Thrownaway Children in America.* Washington, DC: U.S. Office of Juvenile Justice and Delinquency Prevention.

Finkelhor, D., G. Hotaling, and A. Sedlak. 1991. "Children Abducted by Family Members: A National Household Survey of Incidence and Episode Characteristics." *Journal of Marriage and the Family* 53:805–17.

Forst, M. L. and M. Blomquist. 1991. *Missing Children: Rhetoric and Reality.* New York: Lexington Books.

Gelles, R. J. 1984. "Parental Child Snatching: A Preliminary Estimate of the National Incidence." *Journal of Marriage and the Family* 46:735–39.

Gilbert, N. 1994. "Miscounting Social Ills." *Society* 31 (March):18–26.

Girdner, L. K. 1994. "The View from State Missing Children Clearinghouses." Chapter 9 in *Obstacles to the Recovery and Return of Parentally Abducted Children,* edited by L. K. Girdner and P. M. Hoff. Washington, DC: U.S. Office of Juvenile Justice and Delinquency Prevention.

Girdner, L. K. and P. M. Hoff, eds. 1994. *Obstacles to the Recovery and Return of Parentally Abducted Children.* Washington, DC: U.S. Office of Juvenile Justice and Delinquency Prevention.

Greif, G. L. and R. L. Hegar. 1993. *When Parents Kidnap: The Families behind the Headlines.* New York: Free Press.

Griego, D. and L. Kilzer. 1985. "Truth about Missing Kids: Exaggerated Statistics Stir National Paranoia." *Denver Post,* May 12, pp. 1A, 12A.

Hegar, R. L. 1990. "Parental Kidnapping and U.S. Social Policy." *Social Service Review* 64:407–21.

Hilgartner, S. and C. L. Bosk. 1988. "The Rise and Fall of Social Problems." *American Journal of Sociology* 94:53–78.

Hoff, P. M. 1985. *Parental Kidnapping: How to Prevent an Abduction and What to Do If Your Child Is Abducted.* 2nd ed. Washington, DC: National Center for Missing and Exploited Children.

Hollinger, R. C. and L. Lanza-Kaduce. 1988. "The Process of Criminalization." *Criminology* 26:101–26.

Holstein, J. A. and G. Miller, eds. 1993. *Reconsidering Social Constructionism.* Hawthorne, NY: Aldine.

Jackson, D. D. 1995. "'I Lost a *Baby,* and When I Got Him Back He Was a Toddler." *Smithsonian,* October, pp. 70–74, 76, 78, 80.

Jencks, C. 1994. *The Homeless.* Cambridge, MA: Harvard University Press.

Jenkins, P. 1994. *Using Murder. The Social Construction of Serial Homicide.* Hawthorne, NY: Aldine.

———. 1996. *Pedophiles and Priests.* New York: Oxford University Press.

Kearns, S. 1995. "Parents Who 'Kidnap'." *U.S. News & World Report,* March 20, pp. 69–71, 73, 76.

Kitsuse, J. I. and A. Cicourel. 1963. "A Note on the Use of Official Statistics." *Social Problems* 11:131–39.

Larson, E. 1994. "A False Crisis: How Workplace Violence Became a Hot Issue." *Wall Street Journal,* October 13, A1.

New York Division of Criminal Justice Services. 1991. *Reported Missing Children in New York State—1990.* New York: State of New York.

———. 1994. *Reported Missing Children in New York State—1993.* New York: State of New York.

Orcutt, J. D. and J. B. Turner. 1993. "Shocking Numbers and Graphic Accounts: Quantified Images of Drug Problems in the Print Media." *Social Problems* 40:190–206.

Plass, P. S., D. Finkelhor, and G. T. Hotaling. 1995. "Police Response to Family Abduction Episodes." *Crime and Delinquency* 41:205–18.

Sedlak, A. J., L. Mohadjer, and V. Hudock. 1990. *National Incidence Studies of Missing, Abducted, Runaway, and Thrownaway Children (NISMART): Household Survey Methodology.* Rockville, MD: Westat, Inc.

Smith, M. D. 1994. "Enhancing the Quality of Survey Data on Violence against Women: A Feminist Approach." *Gender and Society* 8:109–27.

Spangler, S. E. 1982. "Snatching Legislative Power: The Justice Department's Refusal to Enforce the Parental Kidnapping Prevention Act." *Journal of Criminal Law and Criminology* 73:1176–1203.

Spector, M. and J. I. Kitsuse. 1977. *Constructing Social Problems.* Menlo Park, CA: Cummings.

Tedisco, J. N. and M. A. Paludi. 1996. *Missing Children.* Albany: SUNY Press.

U.S. Bureau of the Census. 1994. *Statistical Abstract of the United States, 1994.* 114th ed. Washington, DC: U.S. Government Printing Office.

U.S. House of Representatives. 1981. "Missing Children's Act." Hearings held by the Subcommittee on Civil and Constitutional Rights, Committee on the Judiciary, November 18, 30.

14

Crime, News and Fear of Crime
Toward an Identification of Audience Effects

Ted Chiricos, Sarah Eschholz, and Marc Gertz

In July, 1993 two teenaged girls in Houston took a shortcut home through a wooded area, crossed paths with six gang members to whom "life means nothing," and were raped and brutally murdered (*Newsweek*, 1993a). Two weeks later, the national newsmagazines ran cover stories on violent crime, and a media feeding frenzy was underway. Typical stories included: "Teen Violence: Wild in the Streets" (*Newsweek*, 1993b); "Danger in the Safety Zone" (*Time*, 1993a); "In a State of Terror" (*Newsweek*, 1993c); "Taming the Killers" (*Time*, 1993b), and "Florida: State of Rage" (*U.S. News*, 1993a).

The explosion of attention to this issue extended to other news outlets as well. Television and newspaper stories about violent crime and juvenile violence increased more than 400 percent between June and November of 1993 (figure 14.1). In the wake of this extraordinary burst of media coverage, public concern about crime rose dramatically. Americans ranking crime or violence as the nation's foremost problem jumped from 9 percent to 49 percent between January 1993 and January 1994 (Gallup 1994:6). Politicians at every level rose to the "challenge" of keeping up with public opinion. Proposals to stem the seeming "epidemic" of violence included everything from castration to caning, from fingerprinting school children to incorporating military technology

Source: *Social Problems*, Vol. 44, No. 3, August 1997, pp. 342–357. © 1997 by the Society for the Study of Social Problems. Reprinted with permission.

in the latest "war on crime." That levels of violent crime actually were declining was apparently irrelevant.

In this article, we examine relationships between fear of crime (FEAR) and the news consumption reported by 2,092 persons living in a state capital who were randomly sampled at the peak of the media frenzy about violent crime. We consider four sources of news: television, radio, newspapers, and weekly newsmagazines. We examine the relationship between news consumption and FEAR, controlling for age, gender, race, victim experience, and other crime perceptions, including the perception of risk. That perception is often misinterpreted as fear itself (Ferraro 1995).

Figure 14.1 Violent Crime and Media Coverage of Violent Crime

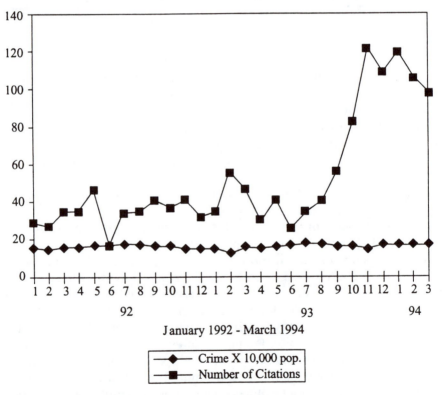

Values on the vertical axis show the combined total of newspaper and television stories involving violent crime or juvenile violence and the rate of UCR violent crime per *10,000* population.

Sources: U.S. Department of Justice (1993,1994,1995) for Violent Crime. Dialog Information Service (1994) for coverage of 26 major newspapers. Burelle's Transcripts (1994) for coverage of CBS, NBC, and FOX networks.

Most importantly, we explore the possibility that relationships between fear of crime and news consumption vary in ways that reflect socially patterned differences among respondents. In the manner of "reception research" (Dahlgren 1988) we assume that meaning does not reside entirely in media messages; rather, it is variably received and interpreted by audiences in distinctive social situations. Young African-American women likely bring a different set of experiences and interests to the construction of media meaning about crime than, for example, older white men. We assume that diverse categories of social existence frame orientations to media messages, and as Fiske (1986:405) noted, "contradictions in society reproduce themselves in subjectivities" (1986:405).

When patterned "subjectivities" coalesce around issues like crime and fear, they may form what some have termed "interpretive communities" (Jensen 1990; Lindlof 1988). The latter affirms "the complexity and variability of audience responses to media messages" and situates the "individual reader or viewer within broader social and cultural contexts" (Carragee 1990:86). In contrast with more structural interpretations of media effects (Gitlin 1979), this approach posits an active audience and, if not polysemic media messages (Fiske 1986), then at least polyvalent (Condit 1989) interpretations of them.

It has yet to be established that shared experiences of gender, race, age, income, and fear are sufficient to constitute "interpretive communities." Even so, if the relationship between fear and news consumption is patterned by gender, race, age, etc., we may begin to understand how news consumers "actively produce meaning from . . . within the context of their everyday lives" (Dahlgren 1988:289–90). In this article we examine whether "fear" is differentially produced by consumers of news who are distinguished by gender, race, age, income, and victim experience.

Prior Research: Media, Audiences and Fear of Crime

A recent review of "mass media and fear of crime" research by Heath and Gilbert concludes that the relationship is contingent on "characteristics of the message, of the audience, and of the dependent measure" (1996:384). Relevant message characteristics include the proportion of a newspaper devoted to crime (Gordon and Heath 1981), whether the crime is local versus distant (Heath 1984), whether the crime is random or is the subject of sensational crime reports (Heath 1984; Liska and Baccaglini 1990; Williams and Dickinson 1993) and whether there is "just" closure of a crime on television drama (Wakshlag 1983). Concerning dependent measures, Heath and Gilbert (1996: 380–384) report stronger links between media and fear when the issue is "societal concern" as opposed to personal fear (Tyler and Cook 1984) for apprehension about "the world out there" versus the immediate neighborhood (Heath and Petraitis 1987) and for urban as opposed to rural settings (Zillman and Wakshlag 1985).

Audience characteristics are the focus of this study. On this issue, Heath and Gilbert conclude that: ". . . belief in the reality of television drama (Potter 1986) and viewer apprehension about crime victimization (Tamborini et al. 1984; Wakshlag 1983; Zillman and Wakshlag 1985) affect the relationship with fear of crime" (1996:384). These are the only audience traits discussed by Heath and Gilbert. The remainder of this review examines other audience attributes that appear relevant in prior assessments of media relationships to FEAR. It should be noted that several of the best studies of crime news and fear (Heath 1984; O'Keefe 1984; O'Keefe and Reid-Nash 1987; Williams and Dickinson 1993) are not concerned with audience characteristics *per se*, while several studies of TV drama do raise issues of variable audience reception that warrant attention.

One potentially salient factor in the reception of media crime messages is whether audience members have direct victim experience or share characteristics making them more likely crime victims. Gunter argues that indirect sources of information, such as media accounts, will be more consequential "when direct experience is lacking" (1987:61). Though limited to 108 university students, Weaver and Wakshlag's (1985) study of crime-related television watching and "crime-related anxiety" demonstrated precisely that point.

Similarly, Liska and Baccaglini hypothesized that newspaper crime stories will have their strongest fear effects for those "least likely to experience victimization" such as "whites, the elderly and females" (1990:363). Their content analysis of newspapers and 1974–75 NCVS fear measures (perceived safety) for twenty-six cities, showed FEAR related only to local homicide stories in the first part of the paper. While this finding held for diverse demographic groups, the media influence was "weakest for those statuses [non-whites, young, males] most likely to experience victimization" (Liska and Baccaglini 1990:372).

Doob and Macdonald's (1979) frequently cited research comes to a different conclusion about the relationship between victim likelihood and media influence. Their interviews with 300 Toronto residents established the number and type of television programs watched in the previous week, as well as perceived chances of victimization (called fear). Overall, when age, sex, and neighborhood type were controlled, there was no relationship between television watching and "fear." However, in urban "high crime" neighborhoods, "fear" was significantly higher for those who watched the most television and significantly lower for those who read newspapers. No such relationships were found in "low crime" neighborhoods; people outside high crime urban neighborhoods "do not feel that the violence on television has any relevance for them . . ." (1979:177).

This is what Gerbner et al. (1980) termed "resonance" in their studies of television's ability to "cultivate" a violent and threatening view of the world. Much of their early work (e.g. Gerbner et al. 1978) argued for "across the board" consequences—with "heavy" television viewers more likely to describe a violent and fearsome world. Later, apparently in response to Doob and Macdonald (1979), Gerbner et al. hypothesized that when a particular television audience receives messages "congruent with everyday reality (or even perceived reality), the combination may result in a . . . powerful 'double dose' of the television message . . ." (1980:15). In short, media effects should be stronger when they "resonate" real life experience.

Gerbner et al. (1980) used their findings from a national survey (N=3903) to illustrate the "resonance" hypothesis. They noted that "city dwellers . . . show the strongest association" between amount of television viewing and FEAR. However, their data also showed that watching television makes a bigger difference for women and whites (who have low victim risk) than it does for men and non-whites. In fact, for non-whites and those with the lowest incomes (and higher victim risk) the relationship between FEAR and total television watching was actually *negative,* though not significant (Gerbner et al. 1980:21).

Another possibility raised by Gerbner and his associates could be described as audience "affinity." This approach posits that "we may be especially receptive to seeing how characters like ourselves . . . fare in the world of television" (1978:186). Since Gerbner's (1978) analyses of programs in the 1970s showed women, older women, and blacks (men and women) to be most victimized in television drama, Hirsch (1980) hypothesized that heavy television viewing should cultivate the greatest fear among these groups. Yet, his analysis of 1502 respondents to a national survey in 1977 revealed that "none of the expected . . . effects obtains in any of these groups" (12).

Skogan and Maxfield suggested that "vulnerability" to attack—as opposed to victim risk *per se*—could make some audiences "more sensitive to messages" that others discount. They hypothesized that "women and the elderly . . . would be more responsive to personal or media messages about crime." Their 1977 telephone survey (N=1389) of San Francisco, Chicago, and Philadelphia residents "failed to find any support for this notion" since the relationship between fear and ability to recall a recent crime story (television or newspaper) "was constant among more vulnerable and less vulnerable groups" (1981:179).

Finally, Heath and Petraitis (1987) conducted telephone interviews with 372 respondents in twenty-six medium sized U.S. cities. They found that total TV viewing increased respondents' fear of distant, urban settings—but only among *males*. Viewing crime drama increased the perceived likelihood of victimization in New York City and in one's own neighborhood—again, only for *males* (105–109). They suggested that the absence of a media relationship for women could be due to their consistently high fear levels and a kind of "ceiling effect" that mitigates additional influences. They also raise the prospect that "affinity" is a plausible interpretation for their findings (121).

From the foregoing, five audience circumstances can be identified with potential to influence the media/FEAR relationship. They are listed here with examples of the kinds of people who were (or could be) expected to experience those circumstances.

Substitution: Lacks victim experience or has reduced victim likelihood: (Women, elderly, whites, non-victims)

Resonance: Has victim experience or higher victim likelihood: (Urban, high-crime neighborhood residents, males, young, blacks)

Vulnerability: Less able to defend against attack: (Women, elderly)

Affinity: Shares characteristics of more likely media victims: (Women, older women, black women, victims)

Ceiling Effect: Has such high fear that media can have little influence: (Women, blacks)

Depending on the rationale employed, one could *expect* stronger media/FOC relationships for women, men, young, old, victims, non-victims, blacks, or whites. As we have seen, the *evidence*, though limited, is only slightly less equivocal than theoretical expectations.

More surprising than the inconsistency of theory and evidence on this issue, is the paucity of research dealing directly with audience traits, *news* consumption, and fear of crime. Only Doob and Macdonald (1979) and Liska and Baccaglini (1990) are relevant in this regard. Both use data from the 1970s. But, only Doob and Macdonald connect the specific news consumption of individuals to *their* fear. Liska and Baccaglini linked NCVS rates of "fear" (perceived safety) in twenty-six cities to newspaper content in those communities. While useful, such data cannot tell us whether those most fearful even read newspapers. In short, only one study relating *news* consumption by *individuals* to *their* fear uses audience characteristics to specify that relationship. That study was done in Canada almost twenty years ago (Doob and Macdonald, 1979). The audience trait at issue was living in an "urban high crime neighborhood" (N=83) or not.

Methods

Between January and March, 1994, we surveyed 2,092 adults in Tallahassee, the state capital of Florida—a state featured prominently in the frenzy of news accounts of violent crime noted above. Respondents were randomly chosen from adults (18 years or older) having the most recent birthday in households accessed by random digit dialing.[1] The sampling frame—the county where the city is located (1994 population: 212,107)—was stratified by telephone trunk numbers to insure proportional representation from all community areas. The demographics of the sample and sampling frame (in parentheses) are: female 55 percent (52%); African-American 18 percent (24%); median age: 37 (29) years; median household income $30,000 ($30,512) per year. The slight over-representation of women, white, and older respondents is not unusual in telephone surveys (Lavrakas 1987).

Dependent Variable: Fear of Crime

As recommended by Ferraro (1995), Ferraro and LaGrange (1987), Warr (1990) and others, we operationalize FEAR in a manner that is direct and crime specific. Respondents were asked:

> On a scale of one to ten, with ten representing the most fear and one representing the least fear, how much do you fear being robbed by someone who has a gun or knife . . . (someone breaking into your house to steal things; someone stealing your car; someone attacking you physically?)

Responses for auto theft did not correlate well with the other offenses and so the remaining crimes (robbery, assault, and burglary) were combined into a FEAR index with an alpha of .81 which is employed as our measure of crime fear.

Independent Variables

There are six measures of news consumption employed here. The first three use "a typical week" as a frame of reference: PAPER indicates the number of days a respondent reads a newspaper in a typical week. TVNEWS is the number of days that news is watched on television; and RADIO is the number of days the respondent listened to radio news. A fourth news variable, MAGAZINE, asks how often in a "typical month" a respondent reads a "national newsmagazine like *Time, Newsweek* or *U.S. News and World Report*?" Responses of "weekly," "a couple times a month," "less frequently" and "never" were coded from three to zero.

A fifth news measure, DETAIL, addresses how much information could be recalled about three highly publicized, seemingly random, *inter*racial crimes. The questions asked were: Have you read, seen or heard anything about . . .(1) "the attack on the truck driver in Los Angeles?" (2) ". . . the murder of tourists in Florida?" (3) ". . . people being shot on a train?" The first referenced the assault on Reginald Denny during the riot following the acquittal of policemen accused of beating Rodney King.[2] The second could have referred to the murder of a German tourist in Fort Lauderdale or the murder of a British tourist at a rest stop on I-10 in northern Florida. The third referenced the so-called "Massacre on the Long Island Railroad" (*Newsweek* 1993d) in which a gunman killed five people and wounded eighteen. For each incident, if respondents indicated awareness, they were asked what details they remembered. Up to six details were recorded for each incident and scores on this variable ranged from zero to 18.

The final news variable, LOCALTV, is dichotomous and reflects persons who say they *only* watch local television news (score = 1) and those who *only* watch national television news (score = 0). There are only 397 of these "exclusive" TV news watchers, since most (N=1573) say they watch both and are treated as missing cases. While the (N) limits the use of this variable in specifying audience subsamples, its relevance is well established and warrants attention (Heath 1994; Liska and Baccaglini 1990).

Other independent variables initially used to model FEAR in this study include FEMALE (male = 0), AGE, BLACK (white = 0), INCOME, and whether a member of the respondent's household has been a crime VICTIM in the past six months (yes = 1). FEMALE is the individual trait most consistently related to fear of crime in existing research (Bankston and Thompson 1989; Ferraro and LaGrange 1992). Regarding AGE, older persons *had* been reported most fearful (Clemente and Kleiman 1976; Jaycox 1978) but recent assessments question that understanding (Bankston and Thompson 1989; Ferarro 1995).

It is often found that FEAR is greater for blacks than for whites (Skogan and Maxfield 1981; Parker and Ray 1990). This is attributed either to victimization risk (actual or perceived) or the presence of "incivilities" in predominantly black or poor neighborhoods (Covington and Taylor 1991; LaGrange et al. 1992). For similar reasons, we include INCOME (self-reported for household) in our models.

On the premise that *cognitive* judgments relating to risk (Ferraro 1995; Ferraro and LaGrange 1987) could influence the *affective* state of fear, we include several judgments in our models. The first, SAFE, is operationalized with two questions: "How safe would you say you feel being out alone in your neighborhood at night? . . . (home alone at night?)" Responses from these two questions ranging from 'very safe' to "not at all safe" were combined in an index (alpha = .70). Values on SAFE ranged from 2 (most safe) to 6 (least safe). Ferraro (1995) among others, argues that assessments of safety or risk are distinct from the *affect* of fear, but play an important role in predicting fear. Other judgments include estimates of whether crime in the neighborhood (CRIMEN) and in the county (CRIMEC) has increased (yes = 1) in the past year.

Research Findings

Ordinary least squares regression is used to estimate the net relationship between news consumption and fear of crime. Residual plots indicate no violations of the assumption of homoskedasticity. Bi-variate correlations among independent variables show none in the full model higher than .27 and, with tolerance levels in excess of .86, there is no apparent problem of multicollinearity. Except for media variables, only those predictors with significant coefficients are included in these equations. It is particularly notable that INCOME and VICTIM dropped out of almost all estimates of FEAR. In tables 14.1–3, unstandardized (b) and standardized (Beta) coefficients are shown, with corresponding levels of significance.

Table 14.1 reports seven estimates of FEAR.[3] The first six introduce individual news measures separately, and for each equation the distinctive media variable is listed at the top of the relevant column. The seventh estimate combines RADIO and TVNEWS and that model (FINAL) is used in subsequent efforts to identity "media effects" for diversely constituted audiences.

Looking first at non-media control variables, AGE has a significant *negative* relationship with FEAR in every equation. The fact that older respondents report lower fear is consistent with recent findings questioning the presumption that older people fear crime most (Bankston and Thompson 1989; Ferraro 1995). Women and African Americans are significantly more fearful than men and whites respectively and FEAR is consistently elevated for those who feel less SAFE or perceive crime to be increasing in their neighborhood (CRIMEN) or in the county (CRIMEC).

More importantly, table 14.1 shows that when AGE, FEMALE, BLACK, and several cognitive perceptions of crime are controlled, both RADIO and TVNEWS have a significant independent effect on crime fear. That is, people who more often listen to radio news or watch television news express significantly higher levels of FEAR. The same effect appears for LOCALTV. The fact that people who *only* watch local television news have higher fear lends support to patterns established in the work of Heath (1984) and Liska and Baccaglini (1990).

In contrast, the frequency of *reading* newspapers or newsmagazines has no apparent relationship to FEAR. This is consistent with Doob and Macdonald's (1979) finding that reading newspapers lowered crime fear for residents of high crime areas but was not significant when age and gender were controlled. Finally, table 14.1 shows that attention to DETAIL in relation to several highly publicized, non-local, "random" violent crimes has no bearing on crime fear.

Table 14.1 **Regression of Crime Fear on News Media Variables and Other Controls**

Variable	(1) Paper b (Beta)	(2) Radio b (Beta)	(3) TV News b (Beta)	(4) Magazine b (Beta)	(5) Detail b (Beta)	(6) Local TV b (Beta)	(7) Final b (Beta)
Age	−.064** (−.147)	−.064** (−.146)	−.066** (−.150)	−.061** (−.139)	−.060** (.138)	−.106** (−.202)	−.069** (−.158)
Female	2.12** (.145)	2.10** (.144)	2.14** (.146)	2.07** (.141)	2.08** (.142)		2.17** (.149)
Black	1.19** (.064)	1.48** (.079)	1.16** (.063)	1.26** (.068)	1.27** (.068)		1.37** (.074)
Crimen	1.54** (.086)	1.60** (.089)	1.57** (.087)	1.58** (.088)	1.59** (.089)		1.58** (.088)
Crimec	1.81** (.106)	1.89** (.111)	1.76** (.103)	1.83** (.107)	1.84** (.107)	1.56** (.100)	1.82** (.106)
Safe	2.35** (.375)	2.31** (.368)	2.32* (.371)	2.34** (.373)	2.34** (.373)	2.29** (.375)	2.29** (.366)
Paper	.077 (.028)						
Radio		.115* (.045)					.102* (.040)
TV News			.138* (.042)				.135˙ (.041)
Magazine				.089 (.014)			
Detail					.008 (.003)		
Local TV						1.47* (.103)	
R²	.265	.267	.266	.262	.263	.233	.270
(N)	1914	1897	1919	1932	1935	382	1881

Note:
  * $p < .05$ ** $p < .01$ ˙$p = .052$

Disaggregating Audiences

In the following sections, we examine a variety of contexts to assess whether there are discernible social patterns to the news/FEAR relationship. These analyses seek to determine whether audiences of disparate social composition find meaning in news media reports about crime. Equation (7) had the highest R^2 value in table 14.1 and it is used in estimates for the disaggregated subsamples in the remaining tables. In table 14.2, estimates are done separately for women and men, blacks and whites, and respondents from three age groups. Despite its theoretical relevance and significance in table 14.1, LOCALTV had too many missing values to be useful in these analyses. To provide comparability across audience subsamples, variables are included in estimates for a particular category (e.g. gender) only if they are significant for one of its subsamples (e.g. male or female).

The frequency of watching television news is significantly related to *higher* FEAR levels for women, whites, and respondents between the ages of 30–54. Though not significant, television news is associated with *lower* FEAR levels among men, blacks, and those under 30 and over 55. Tests of significance for the difference between subsample slopes[4] show that TVNEWS effects[5] are significantly different (p<.01) for men and women and for middle-aged (as opposed to younger) respondents. The difference between black and white respondents fails to achieve statistical significance—even though the TVNEWS and FEAR relationship is positive and significant for whites and negative and non-significant for blacks. The only significant relationship between FEAR and listening to RADIO news is reported for women.

Table 14.2 Regression of Crime Fear on Radio and TV News For Audience Subgroups

Variable	Male b (Beta)	Female b (Beta)	Black b (Beta)	White b (Beta)	Under 30 b (Beta)	30 to 54 b (Beta)	55+ b (Beta)
Age	−.053** (−.129)	−.081** (−.187)	−.054* (−.111)	−.071** (−.165)			
Female			2.15** (.140)	2.11** (.147)	2.23** (.162)	1.98** (.135)	2.21** (.139)
Black	1.17* (.066)	1.51** (.083)			.847 (.055)	1.36* (.067)	2.49* (.107)
Crimen	1.78** (.105)	1.51** (.086)	.110 (.006)	1.92** (.110)	.862 (.053)	1.84** (.098)	2.29* (.121)
Crimec	1.03* (.070)	2.45** (.135)	1.21 (.069)	1.89** (.113)	.661 (.043)	2.60** (.153)	1.58 (.069)
Safe	2.40** (.385)	2.21** (.349)	2.71** (.420)	2.22** (.357)	2.29** (.373)	2.52** (.395)	1.97** (.320)
Radio	.043 (.018)	.159* (.063)					
TV News	−.099 (−.032)	.305** (.093)	−.139 (−.036)	−.185* (.058)	−.057 (−.018)	.246** (.076)	−.063 (−.013)
P Level Slope Difference	.002		.057		.017	.111	
R^2	.224	.227	.218	.264	.223	.300	.204
(N)	819	1062	360	1559	684	879	356

Note:
  * p < .05   ** p < .01

Table 14.3 examines the relationship of television and radio news to fear of crime for audiences with disparate household incomes, crime victim experience, and neighborhood racial composition. Incomes are divided into less than $30,000; $30–50,000, and above $50,000. Victim experience refers to anyone in the respondent's household being victimized in the past six months. Neighborhood racial composition—which has been variably linked to FEAR (Covington and Taylor 1991; Liska et al. 1982)—is a *perceptual* measure that asks respondents to estimate the percentage of blacks among those living within a mile of their home.[6] Because blacks comprise 24 percent of the population in the community studied, audience members are divided into those living in neighborhoods perceived to be above or below this criterion.

Table 14.3 Regression of Crime Fear on Radio and TV News For Audience Subgroups

Variable	Victim b (Beta)	Non Victim b (Beta)	Black Low Pct b (Beta)	Black High Pct b (Beta)	Under $30,000 b (Beta)	$30,000 to $50,000 b (Beta)	Over $50,000 b (Beta)
Age	−.045 (−.092)	−.065** (−.149)	−.065** (−.154)	−.077** (−.162)	−.071** (−.173)	−.053** (−.113)	−.081 (−.147)
Female	1.93* (.132)	2.15** (.147)	2.21** (.156)	2.16** (.147)	1.85** (.126)	2.48** (.176)	2.22** (.156)
Black	−1.49 (−.074)	1.58** (.086)	1.99* (.071)	1.01* (.063)	1.39** (.088)	1.84* (.083)	−.205 (−.007)
Crimen	1.32 (.088)	1.54** (.082)	1.90** (.107)	1.48** (.084)	1.60** (.093)	2.41** (.135)	1.02 (.055)
Crimec	2.24* (.134)	1.68** (.098)	1.66** (.097)	1.92** (.113)	1.50** (.090)	2.11** (.125)	2.35** (.135)
Safe	2.83** (.443)	2.26** (.360)	2.26** (.363)	2.19** (.346)	2.23** (.357)	2.56** (.340)	2.70** (.416)
Radio			.053 (.021)	.169* (.068)	.067 (.027)	.292* (.111)	.008 (.003)
TV News	.454* (.146)	.077 (.023)	−.002 (−.000)	.271** (.081)	.201* (.061)	.039 (.012)	.148 (.045)
P Level Slope Difference	.023		.018		.171	.375	
R²	.337	.258	.272	.250	.237	.285	.309
(N)	246	1653	899	932	902	449	463

Note:
   * p < .05   ** p < .01

In table 14.3, TVNEWS is significantly related to FEAR for those *with* recent victim experience, a *low* household income, or living in neighborhoods perceived to be disproportionately *black*. Subsample slope differences in TVNEWS effects are significant for the victim, non-victim comparison (p<.05) and for the racial composition of neighborhood comparison (p<.02). Apparent differences for income subsamples are not significant. RADIO is also a predictor of FEAR in neighborhoods perceived to be disproportionately black and for audiences above the median income.[7]

To this point, significant TVNEWS effects are found for female, white, and middle age audiences and for those with recent victim experience, low income, and living in disproportionately black neighborhoods. But these audience traits are not mutually exclusive and audiences are not one-dimensional. To pursue a more complete identification of those for whom news/FEAR relationships may be significant, we next consider audience composition in multi-dimensional terms.

Table 14.4 displays the results of estimating the FEAR and TVNEWS relationship for gender/race specific groups, with a series of other characteristics taken one at a time. To illustrate: for black females, FEAR equations were estimated with subsamples further specified sequentially by categories of age, victim experience, perceived safety, income, and neighborhood racial composition. This was also done for white females, black males, and white males.

Table 14.4 Significant Relationships: Fear and TV News for Specified Audience Subgroups*

Variable	Black Females	White Females	Black Males	White Males
Under 30	YES (99)	no (263)	no (78)	no (227)
30 to 54	no (81)	YES (412)	no (50)	no (324)
55 and over	no (31)	no (176)	no (13)	no (127)
Victim	no (20)	YES (127)	no (15)	no (79)
Non-Victim	no (189)	YES (715)	no (123)	no (593)
Low Safety Perception	no (57)	YES (348)	no (77)	no (451)
High Safety Perception	no (154)	YES (503)	no (64)	no (227)
Less than $30,000	no (158)	YES (366)	no (106)	no (272)
$30,000 to $50,000	no (29)	no (213)	no (22)	no (185)
More than $50,000	no (15)	YES (237)	no (10)	no (201)
Low Percentage Black	no (39)	no (474)	no (21)	no (365)
High Percentage Black	no (164)	YES (359)	no (114)	no (295)

Note:
  * YES indicates positive and significant (p < .05) TVNEWS effect.
  ( ) N size.

Table 14.4 lists forty-eight audience subsamples and for each, indicates whether TVNEWS has a significant relationship with FEAR after controlling for other variables (using equation 7 from table 14.1). Because so many estimates are involved, we show only whether the FEAR coefficient is significant at p<.05 (YES) for each subsample. Full equations are available on request.

The first thing apparent in table 14.4 is that *all* television "news effects" are limited to *women*. There are no audience traits associated with males—black or white—for which TVNEWS has a significant relationship to FEAR. Moreover, almost all TVNEWS effects are limited to *white women*. (The only contrary instance—with a relatively small N (99)—involves *young* (<30) black women). In fact, among white women a significant link between FEAR and TVNEWS is sustained whether or not they have recent victim experience, whether or not they perceive their neighborhoods to be safe or have high or low incomes. The news/ FEAR relationship is concentrated, among *middle-aged* white women (30–54) and those living in disproportionately black neighborhoods.

Table 14.2 indicates that a positive relationship between TVNEWS and FEAR exists for whites, women, and middle-aged audiences. Table 14.4 shows that it exists specifically and *only* for white middle-aged women—and for no one else among whites and almost no one else among women. While table 14.3 indicates that the news/FEAR relationship is significant for those with victim experience, low income, and those living in disproportionately black neighborhoods; table 14.4 shows that it is *only* white women in those groups who manifest a "news effect."

These data clearly indicate that the relationship between television news and fear of crime is exclusive to women and almost entirely exclusive to white women. The question we address in the remainder of this article is: what explains this concentration of media effects?[8]

Discussion

Several ways that audience traits could inform construction of the media/FEAR relationship were discussed above. These included: (1) the "*resonance*" of personal experience with media messages which increases their salience (Doob and Macdonald 1979; Gerbner et al. 1980); (2) the lack of experience with crime or its immediate threat, which allows media messages to "*substitute*" as a prime information source (Gunter 1987; Liska and Baccaglini 1990; Weaver and Wakshlag 1986); (3) the "*affinity*" that may exist between audience members and the characteristics of victims portrayed by media (Gerbner 1978; Hirsch 1980); (4) the differential "*vulnerability*" to crime of some audience members which makes them "more sensitive" to media crime messages (Skogan and Maxfield 1981), and (5) a "*ceiling effect*" which leaves little room for media influence among audience types with already high levels of fear (Heath and Petraitis 1987).

At first glance, the pattern of current findings appears to rule out the relevance of "ceiling effects" (Heath and Petraitis 1987). Women in our sample have levels of FEAR (17.6) that are 25 percent higher than men (13.9) and still, all "news effects" involve women. Looking closer, it happens that white, middle-aged women—who manifest virtually all of the TVNEWS effects in this sample—have FEAR levels (16.5) lower than black women (19.6) and substantially lower than middle-aged black women (20.3). If "ceiling effects" are real, they may apply here to black women and may help to explain the lack of a news/FEAR relationship for that group.

The issue of "vulnerability" has had a prominent place in discussions of FEAR (Baumer 1985; Garofalo 1981). A presumption that women and the elderly can less well defend against attack is sometimes used to explain the "seeming paradox" of higher fear levels despite lower risk and experience of crime. It has also prompted the hypothesis that the most "vulnerable" will be most responsive to media messages (Skogan and Maxfield 1981). Even if the elderly and women are less able to ward off attacks—not altogether certain with increased gun ownership and "advances" in self-defense technology—this issue seems not to explain the pattern of TVNEWS effects reported here. White middle-aged women should be no *more* "vulnerable" than black middle-aged women or *older* women of either race. In fact, in terms of the ability to resist victimization, it is not certain that a thirty-five-year-old white woman would be more vulnerable than, for example, a seventy-year-old man of either race. In our sample, there are no TVNEWS effects for older females who presumably would feel the most vulnerable.

A concentration of TVNEWS effects among white middle-aged women is not entirely consistent with a "resonance" interpretation (Doob and Macdonald 1979; Gerbner et al. 1980). In general, white, middle-aged women have consistently low victim risk (U.S. Department of Justice 1996) and for most, media messages would not resonate their experience. Of course, there are some white middle-aged women with experience as victims. In this sample, TVNEWS is significantly related to FEAR among white women *with* recent victim experience, and for those with *low* income or living in disproportionately black neighborhoods—a pattern consistent with "resonance." This interpretation would have greater relevance if males and blacks with those same characteristics also had significant TVNEWS effects. They do not.

Since white women *without* recent victim experience and living in *high* income circumstances also show significant TVNEWS effects, it seems likely that for them, something other than resonance is at work. A possibility to explain news/FEAR relationships among these white women (high-income or no victim experience) is that media messages "substitute" for lived experience in the genesis of fear (Gunter 1987; Liska and Baccaglini 1990).

It may be plausible that "substitution" explains the news/FEAR relationship for some white women (high-income, no victim experience) and "resonance" explains it for other white women (low-income, victim experience). However, neither of these explanations account for the more basic fact that, except for white women, virtually no TVNEWS effects are found.

A final interpretation of these findings could be that an *affinity* exists between the audience for whom TVNEWS effects are found (white women) and the content of televised news messages. The rationale, as Gerbner et al. (1978:186) note in their discussion of the "cultivation" of fear, is that "we may be especially receptive to seeing how characters *like ourselves* . . . fare in the world of television" (original emphasis). Hirsch hypothesized that television "viewers from subgroups whose members are most often victimized or killed should appear more afraid" than others (1980:10).

We have additional data that may be relevant to this hypothesis. Eighteen months *after* the FEAR survey discussed here, we did a content analysis of televised evening news programs in Tallahassee. For nine weeks, three teams of three judges (graduate students) recorded various features of crime incidents reported on local and network news. A detailed study of those incidents in relation to a FEAR survey taken at the same time is underway. Assuming the demographics of TV news victims changed little in eighteen months, what we learned about their race and gender may help to explain the present findings. When both race and gender could be identified, the profile of TV news victims was: 32 percent—white female; 26 percent—white male; 12 percent—Hispanic female; 11 percent—black male; 6 percent—black female; 3 percent—Hispanic male; 10 percent—other.

The distribution of TVNEWS victims is consistent with an *affinity* interpretation of the relationship found in this study between TVNEWS and FEAR. The audience most likely to see itself victimized in the news—white women—is the only audience for which significant TVNEWS effects are found. This suggests that regardless of actual victim experience (table 14.4), seeing people like themselves victimized frequently in televised news may have substantially contributed to the fear of crime among white women.

The purpose of the present analysis has been to underscore the importance of attending to specific "audience effects." Without doing so, we may ask the wrong questions. The issue is not whether media accounts of crime increase fear, but which audiences, with which experiences and interests, construct which meanings from the messages received. We have found that the construction of fear from the messages of television news is limited to middle-aged white women. Since white women are most often shown as victims on the news in this television market, an "affinity" explanation for the relationship of media consumption to fear is supported. In their early studies of television and the "cultivation" of fear, Gerbner and his associates noted that "it is important who scares whom and who is 'trained' to be the victim" (1980:715). They further observed that televised violence in particular, demonstrates "the realities of social power . . . generates fear, insecurity and dependence and thus serves as an instrument of social control" (1980:715). In the present study, white women see victims "like themselves" on TVNEWS and are more fearful. It is for them that "the realities of social power"—implicit in crime—have the most salience. It is in them that "fear, insecurity and dependence" are cultivated, and it may be for them that TVNEWS serves as an instrument of social control (Gerbner et al. 1980:715).

Notes

[1] The survey was conducted by The Research Network, Inc., in Tallahassee, using a two-stage Mitofsky-Waksberg sampling design. Business, fax and disconnected numbers were eliminated and a response rate of 80 percent for those beginning the survey was realized.

[2] The attack took place in 1992, but the trial of alleged assailants was underway in the summer of 1993. Helicopter video of the attack was replayed almost nightly for several weeks.

[3] An eighth estimate combined five of the news variables (excluding LOCALTV). In this presumably misspecified model, none of the news variables achieved significance at $p < .05$.

[4] The conventional formula for assessing differences in regression coefficients across sub-groups takes into account the sample sizes of each of the sub-groups (Kleinbaum et al. 1988:266). With large samples this formula is shown to asymptotically converge to: $(b1-b2) / (se\ (b1)^2 + se\ (b2)^2)1/2$ (Kleinbaum & Kupper, 1978: 101). Given the magnitude of our sample sizes, it is appropriate to use this latter formula, and we have done so.

[5] It is possible that what we are calling TVNEWS effects are the *consequence* of FEAR, rather than its antecedent (Gunter, 1987; Sparks, 1992). That is, people who are more fearful (e.g. women) may watch more television. In the absence of panel data (O'Keefe and Reid-Nash 1987) this possibility cannot be tested.

[6] The rationale for including percent black is given by the extent to which popular rhetoric has typified the crime problem in racial terms (Anderson 1995). In 1992, for example, Senator Bill Bradley observed that "fear of black crime covers the streets like a sheet of ice" (Skogan, 1995: 60).

[7] The remaining discussion is limited to TVNEWS because its meaning is less ambiguous than RADIO. The latter may be a very different input, for example, to someone listening to NPR and someone listening to music with news briefings at the top of every hour.

[8] One explanation could be that men admit fear less often, which would truncate the distribution of their responses relative to women, thereby reducing the likelihood of significant relationships. Because differences in standard deviations on FEAR, however, range from 6.4 (white males) to 7.2 (white females), this is not a likely explanation for the observed pattern.

References

Anderson, David C. 1995. *Crime and the Politics of Hysteria*. New York City: Random House.

Bankston, William B., and Carol Y. Thompson. 1989. "Carrying firearms for protection: A causal model." *Sociological Inquiry* 59:75–87.

Baumer, Terry L. 1985. "Testing a general model of fear of crime: Data from a national sample." *Journal of Research in Crime and Delinquency* 22:239–55.

Burrelle's Transcripts. 1994. *Burrelle's Index of Broadcast Transcripts*, Annual Edition. Livingston, NJ: Burrelle's Information Services.

Carragee, Kevin M. 1990. "Interpretive media study and interpretive social science." *Critical Studies in Mass Communication* 7:81–95.

Chiricos, Ted. 1995. "Moral panic as ideology: Drugs, violence, race and punishment in America." In *Justice with Prejudice: Race and Criminal Justice in America*, Michael J. Lynch and E. Britt Patterson, (eds.), 19–48. New York: Harrow & Heston.

Clemente, Frank, and Michael Kleiman. 1976. "Fear of crime among the aged." *Gerontologist* 16:207–10.

Comstock, George, Steven Chaffee, Nathan Katzman, Maxwell McCombs, and Donald Roberts. 1978. *Television and Human Behavior*. New York: Columbia University Press.

Condit, Celeste M. 1989. "The rhetorical limits of polysemy." *Critical Studies in Mass Communication* 6:103–122.

Covington, Jeanette, and Ralph B. Taylor. 1991. "Fear of crime in urban residential neighborhoods: Implications of between- and within-neighborhood sources for current models." *The Sociological Quarterly* 32: 231–49.

Dahlgren, Peter. 1988. "What's the meaning of this?: Viewers plural sense-making of TV news." *Media, Culture & Society.* 10:285–301.

Dialog Information Service. 1994. Newspaper and Periodical Abstracts. [Online], January 1992–June 1994. Ann Arbor, MI: UMI. Available: DIALOG File: Newspaper and Periodical Abstracts (484).

Doob, Anthony N., and Glenn E. Macdonald. 1979. "Television viewing and fear of victimization: Is the relationship causal?" *Journal of Personality & Social Psychology* 37:170–79.

Ferraro, Kenneth A. 1995. "Fear of Crime: Interpreting Victimization Risk." Albany, NY: SUNY Press.

Ferraro, Kenneth A., and Randy LaGrange. 1987. "The measurement of fear of crime." *Sociological Inquiry* 57:70–101.

———. 1992. "Are older people afraid of crime?: Reconsidering age differences in fear of victimization." *Journal of Gerontology: Social Sciences* 47:233–44.

Fiske, John. 1986. "Television, polysemy and popularity." *Critical Studies in Mass Communication* 3:391–408.

Gallup, George Jr. 1994. *The Gallup Poll*, No. 341 (February). Wilmington, DE: Scholarly Resources.

Garofalo, James. 1979. "Victimization and the fear of crime." *Journal of*

Research in Crime and Delinquency 16:80–97.

_____. 1981. "The fear of crime: Causes & consequences." *Journal of Criminal Law and Criminology* 72:839–57.

Gerbner, George, Larry Gross, Marilyn Jackson-Beeck, Suzanne Jeffries-Fox, and Nancy Signorielli. 1978. "Cultural indicators: Violence profile No. 9." *Journal of Communication* 28:176–207.

Gerbner, George, Larry Gross, Michael Morgan, and Nancy Signorielli. 1980. "The 'mainstreaming' of America Violence profile No. 11." *Journal of Communication* 30:10–29.

Gitlin, Todd. 1979. "Prime time ideology: The hegemonic process in television entertainment." *Social Problems* 26:251–66.

Gordon, Margaret, and Linda Heath. 1981. "The news business, crime and fear." In *Reactions to Crime*, Dan Lewis, ed., 227–50. Beverly Hills: Sage.

Gunter, Barrie. 1987. *Television and the Fear of Crime*. London: John Libbey.

Gunter, Barrie, and J. Wakshlag. 1986. "Television viewing and perceptions of crime among London residents." Paper presented at the international Television Studies Conference, Institute of Education, London, July.

Hall, Stuart. 1981. "Notes on deconstructing the popular." In *People's History and Socialist Theory*, R. Samuel, (ed.), 227–39. London: Routledge and Kegan Paul.

Hall, Stuart, Chas Critcher, Tony Jefferson, John Clarke, and Brian Roberts. 1978. *Policing the Crisis: Mugging, the State and Law and Order*. London: MacMillan.

Heath, Linda. 1984. "Impact of newspaper crime reports on fear of crime: Multi methodological investigation." *Journal of Personality and Social Psychology* 47:263–76.

Heath, Linda, and John Petraitis. 1987. "Television viewing and fear of crime: Where is the mean world?" *Basic and Applied Social Psychology* 8:97–123.

Heath, Linda, and Kevin Gilbert. 1996. "Mass media and fear of crime." *American Behavioral Scientist* 39:379–86.

Hirsch, Paul M. 1980. "The 'scary world' of the nonviewer and other anomalies: A reanalysis of Gerbner et al.'s findings on cultivation analysis, part 1." *Communication Research* 7:403–56.

Hughes, Michael. 1980. "The fruits of cultivation analysis: A reexamination of some effects of television watching." *Public Opinion Quarterly* 44:287–302.

Jaycox, Victoria. 1978. "The elderly's fear of crime: Rational or irrational?" *Victimology* 3:329–34.

Jensen, Klaus B. 1990. "Television futures: A social action methodology for studying interpretive communities." *Critical Studies in Mass Communication* 7:129–46.

Kleinbaum, David G., and Lawrence L. Kupper. 1978. *Applied Regression Analysis and Other Multivariate Methods*. North Scituate, MA: Duxbury Press.

Kleinbaum, David G., Lawrence L. Kupper, and Keith E. Muller. 1988. *Applied Regression Analysis and Other Multivariate Methods*, second edition. Boston: PWS-KENT Publishing Company.

LaGrange, Randy, Kenneth F. Ferraro, and Michael Supanic. 1992. "Perceived risk and fear of crime: Role of social and physical incivilities." *Journal of Research in Crime and Delinquency* 29:311–34.

Lavrakas, Paul J. 1987. *Telephone Survey Methods*. Newbury Park, CA: Sage.

Lindlof, Thomas R. 1988. "Media audiences as interpretive communities." In *Communication Yearbook*, Jay Anderson, (ed.), 2:81–107. Newbury Park, CA: Sage.

Liska, Allen E., Joseph J. Lawrence, and Andrew Sanchirico. 1982. "Fear of crime as a social fact." *Social Forces* 60:761–70.

Liska, Allen E., and William Baccaglini. 1990. "Feeling safe by comparison: Crime in the newspapers." *Social Problems* 37:360–74.

O'Keefe, Garrett J. 1984. "Public views on crime: Television exposure and media credibility." In *Communication Yearbook*, R. Bostrom, (ed.), 8:514–35. Beverly Hills: Sage.

O'Keefe, Garrett J., and Kathaleen Reid-Nash. 1987. "Crime news and real-world blues: The effects of the media on social reality." *Communication Research* 14:147–63.

Newsweek. 1993a. "Life means nothing." (July 19):16–17.

_____. 1993b. "Wild in the streets." (August 2):40–47.

_____. 1993c. "In a state of terror." (September 27):40–41.

_____. 1993d. "Death ride: Massacre on the LIRR." (December 20):26–31.

Parker, Kenneth D., and Melvin C. Ray. 1990. "Fear of crime: An assessment of related factors." *Sociological Spectrum* 10:29–40.

Potter, W. James. 1986. "Perceived reality and the cultivation hypothesis." *Journal of Broadcasting and Electronic Media* 30:159–74.

Skogan, Wesley. 1995. "Crime and the racial fears of white Americans." *The Annals of the American Academy of Political and Social Science* 539:59–71.

Skogan, Wesley G., and Michael G. Maxfield. 1981. *Coping With Crime*. Beverly Hills, CA: Sage.

Sparks. 1992. *Television and the Drama of Crime*. Philadelphia, PA: Open University Press.

Tamborini, Ron, Dolf Zillman, and Jennings Bryant. 1984. "Fear and victimization: Exposure to television and perceptions of crime and fear." In *Communications Yearbook*, R. Bostrum. (ed.), 8:492–513. Beverly Hills: Sage.

Time. 1993a. "Danger in the safety zone." (August 23):29–32.

_____. 1993b. "Taming the killers." (October 11):58-59.

Tyler, Tom R., and Fay L. Cook. 1984. "The mass media and judgments of risk: Distinguishing impact on personal and societal level judgements." *Journal of Personality and Social Psychology* 47:693–708.

U.S. Department of Justice. 1993. *Crime in the United States—1992*. Washington, DC: U.S. Government Printing Office.

_____. 1994. *Crime in the United States—1993*. Washington, DC: U.S. Government Printing Office.

_____. 1995. *Crime in the United States—1994*. Washington, DC: U.S. Government Printing Office.

_____. 1996. *Criminal Victimization in the United States, 1993*. Washington, DC: Bureau of Justice Statistics.

U.S. News and World Report. 1993. "Florida: The state of rage." (October 11):40–44.

Wakshlag, Jacob. 1983. "Viewer apprehension about victimization and crime drama programs." *Communications Research,* 10:195–217.

Warr, Mark. 1990. "Dangerous situations: Social context and fear of victimization." *Social Forces* 68:891–907.

Weaver, James, and Jacob Wakshlag. 1986. "Perceived vulnerability to crime, criminal experience and television viewing." *Journal of Broadcasting and Electronic Media* 30:141–58.

Williams, Paul, and Julie Dickinson. 1993. "Fear of crime: Read all about it?" *British Journal of Criminology* 33:33–56.

Zillman, Dolf, and Jacob Wakshlag. 1985. "Fear of victimization and the appeal of crime drama." In *Selective Exposure to Communication,* Dolf Zillinan and Jennings Bryant (eds.), 141–56. Hillsdale, NJ: Lawrence Erlbaum.

15

Dominant Ideology and Drugs in the Media

Craig Reinarman and Ceres Duskin

"Jimmy is 8 years old and a third-generation heroin addict, a precious little boy with sandy hair, velvety brown eyes and needle marks freckling the baby smooth skin of his thin brown arms."

So began a front page feature in the *Washington Post* on Sunday, Sept. 28, 1980. The reporter, Janet Cooke, claimed that Jimmy had "been an addict since the age of five." She told of how Jimmy "doesn't usually go to school, preferring to instead to hang with older boys." When he did go, Cooke wrote, it was "to learn more about his favorite subject—math," which he planned to use in his drug dealing career. She noted the "cherubic expression" on Jimmy's face when he spoke about "hard drugs, fast money and the good life he believes both can bring." He sported "fancy running shoes" and an "Izod shirt." "Bad, ain't it, I got me six of these," the child reportedly told Cooke.

She described Jimmy's house in detail. There were addicts "casually" buying heroin everyday from Ron, Jimmy's mother's "live-in-lover," cooking it and then "firing up" in the bedrooms. "People of all shapes and sizes," a "human collage" including teenagers, "drift into the dwelling . . . some jittery, uptight and anxious for a fix, others calm and serene after they finally "get off." These things were, Cooke wrote, "normal occurrences in Jimmy's world."

Source: *International Journal on Drug Policy*, 1992, Vol. 3, No. 1, pp. 6–15.

"And every day, Ron or someone else fires up Jimmy, plunging a needle into his bony arm, sending the fourth grader into a hypnotic nod." Cooke then quoted Ron on how he first "turned Jimmy on": "He'd been buggin' me all the time about what the shots were and what people was doin' and one day he said, 'When can I get off?'" She described Ron as "leaning against the wall in a narcotic haze, his eyes half-closed, yet piercing," and quoted him as answering Jimmy, "'Well, s—, you can have some now.' I let him snort a little and, damn, the little dude really did get off."

"Six months later," Cooke wrote, the 5-year-old "was hooked." She quoted the boy as saying, "I felt like I was part of what was goin' down. . . . It (heroin) be real different from herb (marijuana). That's baby s—."

Cooke also quoted Jimmy's mother: "I don't really like to see him fire up. But, you know, I think he would have got into it one day, anyway. Everybody does. When you live in the ghetto, it's all a matter of survival. . . . Drugs and black folk been together for a very long time."

The mother had been routinely raped, Cooke wrote, by her mother's boyfriend, one such instance leading to Jimmy's birth and then to heroin use to blot out her growing pain. When her drug sources dried up after a bust, she turned to prostitution to support further heroin use. Cooke quoted the mother as saying that she wasn't alarmed by her son's dealing ambitions "because drugs are as much a part of her world as they are of her son's."

Cooke made the more general point that heroin use had "become part of life" among people in poor neighborhoods people who "feel cut off from the world around them"—often "filtering down to untold numbers of children like Jimmy who are bored with school and battered by life." Many kids "no older than 10," Cooke claimed, could "relate with uncanny accuracy" dealer names and drug nomenclature.

Cooke's story then offered a familiar litany of quotes to bolster and contextualize her story. Drug Enforcement Agency officials noted the influx of "Golden Crescent heroin." Local medical experts spoke of the "epidemic" of heroin deaths in Washington. Social workers observed how the lack of "male authority figures" and peer pressure combine to make such childhood tragedies common.

"At the end of an evening of strange questions about his life," Cooke concluded, "the calm and self-assured little man recedes" to reveal a "jittery and ill-behaved boy" who was "going into withdrawal." Ron then left the room, according to Cooke, and returned with "syringe in hand, and calls the little boy over to his chair." He grabbed Jimmy's "left arm just above the elbow, his massive hand tightly encircling the child's small limb. The needle slides into the boy's soft skin like a straw pushed into the center of a freshly baked cake. Liquid ebbs out of the syringe, replaced by bright red blood. The blood is then re-injected into the child." The final scene in Cooke's drama depicted little Jimmy "looking quickly around the room" and climbing into a rocking chair, "his head dipping and snapping upright again in what addicts call 'the nod.'"

The Story Becomes the Story

The Washington Post is not prepared to identify
young Jimmy; Mayor Barry orders a city-wide search.

Two days after Cooke's story appeared, the Washington Post ran a fascinating follow-up article entitled, "D.C. Authorities Seek Identity of Heroin Addict, 8." Such a tragic tale of young life lost to drugs, so compellingly conveyed by Cooke and so prominently published by the Post, led to hundreds of outraged calls and letters to the paper and to local officials.

The then Mayor Marion Barry was "incensed" by the story and assigned a task force of hundreds of police and social workers to find Jimmy. It was later learned that the police intensively combed the city for nearly three weeks. Teachers throughout Washington checked the arms of thousands of young students for needle marks. Citizens from housing projects called in offering to help. A $10,000 reward was offered. The police, supported by the Mayor and the U.S. Attorney, threatened to subpoena Cooke in an effort to find and "save" the boy. The *Post* refused to identify Jimmy, citing First Amendment rights to protect confidential sources (*New York Times*, 4/16/81, p. Al).

The *Post* assigned an 11-member reporting team to cover all this, six of whom were told to search for another Jimmy, "on the theory that if there is one, there must be others" (Green, 1981:A13). Cooke and one of her editors searched for Jimmy's house for seven hours. For some unexplained reason, they never found it. Neither the police nor anyone else found Jimmy either. And, neither the other *Post* reporters nor anyone else ever found any other child addict.

Meanwhile, *Post* publisher Donald Graham congratulated Cooke. Bob Woodward, a senior editor who eight years earlier had broken the Watergate scandal, promoted her. The *Post* went on with its normal coverage of drug issues.

Six months later, on April 13, 1981, "Jimmy's World" resurfaced in a ceremony at Columbia University in New York, where it was announced that Janet Cooke had won the Pulitzer Prize in Feature Writing for her story. The next day, the *Post* published a piece proudly announcing Cooke's prize and reprinted "Jimmy's World" in honor of the occasion. The story noted that "Jimmy's World" had first met with shock and disbelief. But despite the fact that none of the massive follow-up efforts had ever turned up Jimmy, or anyone like him, the *Post* asserted that experts had confirmed the fact that heroin addicts of Jimmy's age were common.

For any American reporter, winning a Pulitzer—the journalist's equivalent of a Nobel Prize—is as good as it gets. Such prizes make careers, catapult people out of the grind of routine reportage into prestigious positions, often to fame and fortune. Journalism students fantasize about such feats. Competitive cub reporters across the country covet chances for front-page stories that might get noticed and nominated. Janet Cooke should have been ecstatic. As the world would soon learn, she wasn't.

Two days later, on April 16, the *Washington Post* published another front-page piece on "Jimmy's World":

> The Pulitzer Prize Committee withdrew its feature-writing prize from *Washington Post* reporter Janet Cooke yesterday after she admitted that her award-winning story was a fabrication. . . . It was said to be based on interviews with the boy, his mother and his mother's boyfriend. Cooke now acknowledges that she never met or interviewed any of those people and that she made up the story of Jimmy. . . . .

The *Post* lead editorial that day, "The End of the 'Jimmy' Story," began with a phrase unusual for papers of the *Post's* stature: "We apologize." It went on to say that "This newspaper, which printed Janet Cooke's false account of a meeting with an 8-year-old heroin addict and his family, was itself the victim of a hoax—which we then passed along in a prominent page-one story taking in the readers as we ourselves had been taken in. How could this have happened?"

To find out, Executive Editor Ben Bradley invited the *Post's* ombudsman, Bill Green, to conduct an independent "full disclosure" investigation. Green learned that the *Post* had been running many more routine stories about drug problems in Washington, and that Cooke had been researching the local heroin problem for some time. She took extensive notes to City Editor Milton Coleman. In describing her material she mentioned in passing an 8-year-old addict. Recognizing the print media equivalent of "dramatic footage," Coleman stopped her right there and said, "That's the story. Go after it. It's a front-page story."

Green discovered that when Cooke followed Coleman's instructions she was unable to come up with the young addict. Coleman sent her back out to find him. Again she could not. A week later Cooke told him that she had found another 8-year-old addict, "Jimmy," by going to elementary school playgrounds and passing out her cards. She told her editor that one of her cards found its way to a mother, who called and angrily asked, "Why are you looking for my boy?".

Cooke then extracted promises of confidentiality for "Jimmy's" mother and told her editors that she had visited the child's home, according to Green's report. She soon turned in a 13-page draft of the story. She rendered the furnishings and other aspects of the home and "Jimmy's" life in such delicious detail, Green found, that no editor had ever asked for "Jimmy's" or his mother's identity. Editor Coleman later told Green that he went over the story carefully: "I wanted it to read like John Coltrane's music. Strong. It was a great story, and it never occurred to me that she could make it up. There was too much distance between Janet and the streets."[1]

Green came to feel that the *Post* had been blinded by its ambition for a dramatic feature and by the fine prose of a reporter who was black and thus assumed trustworthy on such matters. Editors dismissed doubts and decided to run "Jimmy's World." It was not until Cooke was awarded the Pulitzer that the story started to unravel. Even then, questions centered on her background, not her story.

The first clue emerged when Cooke's earlier employer, the *Toledo Blade*, wanted to run the prizewinning story. In setting up a sidebar on Cooke's Toledo roots, *Blade* editors discovered that the biographical information they had received over the Associated Press wire "did not jibe" with what they knew of Cooke's background. Her "official" resume—sent in by the *Post*, released by the Pulitzer Committee, and carried with the AP story—had Cooke graduating from Vassar magna cum laude, studying at the Sorbonne, earning a Masters degree from the University of Toledo, speaking four languages, and winning half a dozen Ohio newspaper awards.[2] When the editors at the *Blade* called AP to check on the discrepancies, AP editors began to ask questions of their own. They discovered other discrepancies. No Sorbonne. No masters degree. They called Cooke. She asserted that her official resume was correct. AP knew at this point, according to ombudsman Green's report, that "something was wrong."

Prompted by the AP inquiry, Green discovered, the *Post's* editors compared her personnel file and the Pulitzer biography form she filled out. After discovering that the two did not match in several respects, Bradley told Coleman to "take her to the woodshed." Coleman took Cooke for a walk and grilled her. Cooke eventually admitted she had not graduated from Vassar but continued to insist that everything else, especially the Jimmy story, was true.

Coleman phoned his superior with these answers, according to Green's report. Bradley told him to bring Cooke back to the *Post* via a side entrance "to avoid being conspicuous" and to sequester her in a vacant office three stories above the newsroom. Bradley came up and grilled her. He asked about the foreign language skills she had listed on her resume: "Say two words to me in Portuguese," Green quoted Bradley as saying. She couldn't. Her French wasn't much better. He asked about the journalism prizes. Her answers were inconclusive. Bradley said, "You're like Richard Nixon, you're trying to cover up."

In another office, Assistant Managing Editor Bob Woodward joined deputy Metro Editor David Maraniss, and another editor to go over the 145 pages of Cooke's notes and two hours of tape-recorded interviews. According to Green's report, they found "echoes" of the "Jimmy" story, but no evidence that she had actually spoken with a child addict.

Meanwhile, under pressure of intense questioning, Cooke gave Coleman what she claimed were the real names of Jimmy, his mother, and her boyfriend, as well as their address. Coleman and Cooke went there, but, as had been the case six months before, she somehow could not find the house. (Forgotten at this point in the investigation was the fact that in the immediate aftermath of her story, Cooke had been unable to find the house, returning the next day claiming to have found it but that the family had moved.)

It was nearly midnight when they got back to the *Post*. By this time, according to Green, each of the editors who had bought the story all along had become convinced that she was lying. Woodward then confronted Cooke: "It's all over. You've gotta come clean. The notes show us the story is wrong. We know it. We can show you point by point how you concocted it." Cooke continued to deny it. The more Woodward yelled, the more stubbornly she stuck to her story.

Exhausted from failed interrogations, they left Cooke in the room with only her closest colleague, Maraniss. Cooke knew that he knew, according to Green. They talked quietly for an hour about how tough it was to succeed at a national newspaper (Bradley called it "major-league journalism" or "hardball") and how far they had come. After she had tiptoed all around a confession, Maraniss gently pushed Cooke by asking her what he should tell the others.

She broke down. "Jimmy's World" was, she finally admitted, "a fabrication." "There was no Jimmy and no family. . . . I want to give the prize back," Green quoted her as saying. Maraniss told the others. Bradley asked him to get a written admission and a resignation. Cooke complied.

The Lessons Learned

Where does the blame lie: breakdown in editorial procedure, pathological ambition or systematic prejudice?

The ombudsman's report (Green, 1981) was the second longest article ever published in the Post. Its conclusions were that warning signals were ignored, that senior editors were uninformed, that competition for prizes had pushed an ambitious young reporter too hard, and that the result was "a temporary lapse." The majority of the Post editors and reporters interviewed agreed, interpreting this lapse in terms of ambition and competition.

The *Post* editorial accompanying the first admission of the fraud framed the whole affair in terms of the breakdown of normal journalistic editing procedures—"quality control," Green later dubbed it. The writers thus implied that this was the ultimate cause of the fraud and expressed the hope that it would be seen as the aberration it was, thereby leaving intact the *Post's* "prized credibility" (*Washington Post*, 4/16/81).

Other newspapers, of course, closely covered the scandal and offered similar interpretations. The *San Francisco Chronicle* (4/19/81) blamed the *Post* editors for trusting their reporters too much. The *Los Angeles Times* (4/19/81) blamed the fraud on the growing use of unnamed sources, a practice it claimed arose during the Vietnam and Watergate debacles. A few days later an *L.A. Times* columnist went further to opine that the lesson of the Cooke fraud was that the Watergate-era spirit of "gung-ho press investigators" needed to be reversed (4/23/81).

According to the *New York Times* (4/23/81, p. 16), the 600 editors who attended the annual convention of the American Society of Newspaper Editors a week after the scandal broke talked of little else. They expressed a variety of concerns about the "loss of credibility for all newspapers." But almost all supported the ombudsman's principal conclusions that the scandal stemmed from "internal pressures" to "produce sensational articles and to win prizes" and from the failure to use the editing and checking "system that should have detected the fraud." Some editors added that the scandal had "forced them to re-examine" the procedures for checking the background of new reporters and the use of unidentified sources.

The *Post* itself (4/18/81, p. A3) published a summary of what other papers said about the Cooke affair. The core themes were the same: failure to check confidential sources and the risks of putting sensationalism above editorial judgment. The *Post* story also quoted a *Wall Street Journal* piece which asked whether in all of these investigations "the hard questions" would be raised, but did not say what those questions were. The *Post's* summary closed with a *Chicago Tribune* editor's rotten apple theory—like many others, he blamed the whole affair on "one highly unethical person."

Strangely, none of these accounts mentioned anything about the media's general assumptions and beliefs about drugs and drug users, which ultimately allowed Cooke's concoction to slip into print. For us, this is the hardest question, and it was neither asked nor answered in any of the press post mortems.

What of the Pulitzer Prize jury? Surely if the *Post's* editors could suffer a "temporary lapse," at least one of the esteemed editors and journalists selected to serve on the prestigious Pulitzer jury should have detected some flaw in Cooke's story. As it turns out, a few of the jurors were concerned. One questioned Cooke's guarantee of confidentiality when a child's life seemed at stake. A second was troubled by the lack of attribution, but accepted Cooke's piece "on faith" because "it had gone through the editing process on a reputable newspaper." A third overcame her doubts because she felt the article "spoke to a very compelling problem of our time. We did not suspect that it was not what it seemed to be. *We had no reason to*" (*Washington Post*, 4/17/81, p.9; emphasis added).

Still other jurors expressed doubts after the fact, but these centered largely on the unusual procedure by which Cooke's article had won. The *Post* had submitted it in the "general local reporting" category. The local reporting jury picked "Jimmy's World" second. The Pulitzer Board agreed with the jury, awarding that prize to another reporter. However, several Board members felt that the Cooke piece belonged in the feature category. After discussion, board member Joseph Pulitzer suggested that it be re-considered later in that category (Green, 1981).

Meanwhile, the jury for the feature-writing prize had selected three finalists and submitted them to the Board. None had ever seen the Cooke article. When the Board discussed overruling the jury in favor of "Jimmy's World," some members raised the familiar questions about the article. Their opposition "evaporated," however, when one member, distinguished African-American journalist Roger Wilkins, "eloquently" argued "that he could easily find child addicts within 10 blocks" of where the Board was meeting at Columbia University (*Washington Post*, 4/17/81, p. 9). Just as no one at the *Post* had challenged an articulate African-American reporter six months earlier, no juror challenged Wilkins' assertions about addiction in the inner city. Whatever questions they may have had about "Jimmy's World" were dropped. The Board overruled the jury and unanimously awarded Janet Cooke the Pulitzer Prize in feature writing.[3]

The Lessons Not Learned

What happens to the editorial 'crap detector' when
newspaper editors are confronted with a drug story?

In all of this, no one ever turned up any concrete evidence that a child addict such as "Jimmy" existed. It is, of course, statistically possible that America's inner cities may somewhere contain a few 8-year-old addicts whose mothers' boyfriends shoot them full of heroin every day. But it is a virtual certainty that if such child addicts exist at all they are exceedingly rare. So for us, the most curious part of the Cooke scandal is that in the ensuing decade and throughout the dozens of press accounts we analyzed, no one has yet critically examined the underlying ideology that allowed her bizarre claim that such child addicts are common to pass unnoticed into publication and on to a Pulitzer.

No one doubts that Janet Cooke was a talented writer. No one disputes that the "Jimmy" story was compelling. And certainly no one questions that tragic drug problems persist across the USA, particularly in inner cities. Was it not reasonable, then, for the *Post*'s editors to have been "taken in," and for even the prestigious Pulitzer jury to have become "victims of a hoax"? Who could have seen through a fraud perpetrated by an otherwise fine reporter whose pathological ambition led her to such thorough deceit?

We wish to suggest that the "Jimmy" story was, in fact, rather unreasonable on its face, and that the media would not have been "taken in" by it had they not been blinded by bias. We think that the *Post* editors and Pulitzer jurors—and virtually all the others in the news business who interpreted the scandal—*missed the point.*

The "hoax" to which the American media became "victim" was one they played a central role in making. Drug scares have been a recurring feature of American history. From the early nineteenth century until Prohibition passed in 1919, many in the press were willing handmaidens to the zealous moral entrepreneurs in the Temperance crusade. Newspapers and magazines often uncritically repeated wild claims that alcohol was the direct cause of most of the crime, insanity, poverty, divorce, "illegitimacy," business failure, and virtually all other social problems afflicting America at the time of its industrialization (Levine, 1984).

Throughout the twentieth century the media helped foment a series of drug scares, each magnifying drug menaces well beyond their objective dimensions. From the turn of the century into the 1920s, the yellow journalism of the Hearst newspapers, for example, offered a steady stream of ruin and redemption melodramas. These depicted one or another chemical villain, typically in the hands of a "dangerous class" or racial minority, as responsible for the end of Western civilization (see Musto, 1973; Mark, 1975; Morgan, 1978). In the 1930s, newspapers repeated unsubstantiated claims that marijuana, "the killer weed," led users, Mexicans in particular, to violence (Becker, 1963). In the 1950s, the media spread a story of two teenagers in Colorado who had gotten high accidentally by inhaling model airplane glue. This led to nationwide hysteria, which in turn spread the practice of glue-sniffing (Brecher, 1972).

In the 1960s, the press somehow re-made "killer weed" into "the drop-out drug" (Himmelstein, 1983), and spread other misleading reports that LSD broke chromosomes and yielded two-headed babies (Becker, 1967; Well, 1972). The media that might have served as a source of credible warnings about the risks of drug abuse were dismissed with derision by the very users they needed to reach. In the 1970s, the press again falsely reported that "angel dust" or PCP gave users such superhuman strength that the police needed new stun guns to subdue them (Feldman et al., 1979). In 1986, the press and politicians once again joined forces on crack use among the black underclass. The drug was unknown outside of a few neighborhoods in a few cities until newspapers, magazines, and TV networks blanketed the nation with horror stories that described the crack high (Reinarman and Levine, 1989).

In each of these drug scares the media has consistently erred on the side of the sensational and dutifully repeated the self-serving scare stories of politicians in search of safe issues on which to take strong stands. And in each scare, including the current "war on drugs," reporters and editors have engaged in the *routinization of caricature*—rhetorically recrafting worst cases into typical cases, and profoundly distorting the nature of drug problems in the interest of dramatic stories.

A century from now historians may ponder this construction of drug demons just as they now ponder the burning of witches and heretics.[4] But what is already clear is that a century's worth of scapegoating chemical bogeymen left even the very best journalists quite prepared to believe the very worst about drug users, especially inner-city addicts. Given such a deep structure of bias prevailing within media institutions, it is little wonder that Janet Cooke's story elicited so little of the press's vaunted skepticism.

Thus, her immediate editor Milton Coleman told the *Post*'s investigating ombudsman that he "had no doubts" about "Jimmy's World" and that "it never occurred to me that she could make it up." Assistant managing editor and former Pulitzer winner Bob Woodward admitted similarly that "my skepticism left me," that his "alarm bells simply did not go off," and that "we never really debated whether or not it was true." The few doubts of the distinguished Pulitzer jury were washed away when one black voice asserted that "Jimmys" were everywhere in the ghetto. Even after the scandal broke wide open, ombudsman Green's thoroughly detailed report never really asked *why*, as he put it, "None of the *Post*'s senior editors subjected Cooke's story to close questioning."

These things were possible, we contend, precisely because America's guardians of truth had no touchstone of truth on drug problems apart from their own scare stories. In this the *Washington Post* was no worse than most media institutions in the USA. When seen as part of the historical pattern of news "coverage" of drug issues, the Pulitzer Prize-winning fraud was less a "lapse" than part of a long tradition. On almost any other subject, editors' "crap detectors" would have signaled that something was amiss.

The evidence for this contention oozed from every pore of Cooke's tale and was bolstered at every turn in the follow-up investigations. First, there were the shaky assumptions about addiction. Cooke alleged that "Jimmy" was "addicted" to heroin at age 5 and that he smoked marijuana before that. Children are curious creatures, so it is theoretically possible that a 4- to 5-year-old might push himself to learn to inhale foul-tasting smoke and hold it deep in his lungs repeatedly. It is even possible, although even less likely, that a 5-year-old could learn to enjoy snorting heroin powder into his nostrils day after day. What is hardly possible and highly unlikely is that a 5-year-old would ask to have a needle stuck into his "thin brown arms" more than once a day for the weeks it would take him to become addicted. One needn't be a drug expert for such claims to set off "alarm bells," one need only have seen a doctor try to vaccinate a child.

All this aside, if any journalists had checked, they would have found that most heroin users experience serious nausea the first few times they use. In addition to the difficulties posed by needles and nausea, a mildly skeptical editor easily could have discovered that drug effects are rarely unambiguously pleasurable early on. Drug "highs" are in many important respects acquired tastes that are teamed over time through processes that 5- or 8-year-olds are exceedingly unlikely to endure (Becker, 1953; Zinberg, 1984). Yet, after all of journalism had put this story-scandal under its microscopes, no one had even asked about such things.

Cooke's fiction contained a second set of what Green called "red flags," which had to do with assumptions about addicts. How moronic could addicts have to be (even crass "junkie" stereotypes depict them as shrewd) to allow a reporter from a top newspaper to witness them "firing up"? Even if criminalization had not made paranoia an occupational hazard of addicts, there is no evidence that they are proud of their habits. And in a home Cooke herself described as a dealing den and shooting gallery full of other addicts, no known drug is capable of inducing the magnitude of stupidity necessary for an adult addict to show a reporter how they inject heroin into their small child.

Let us leave this aside, too, and examine a third set of red flags. Neither *Post* editors nor Pulitzer jurors nor any of the other editors who both reprinted Cooke's article and later dissected the scandal ever seemed to question Cooke's claims that "Ron" routinely injected "Jimmy" and that his "mother" tacitly approved of this. Not even the tallest tales of Temperance crusaders gave us such villainous villains. What sort of people would knowingly and repeatedly inject heroin into a child that they clothed, fed and bathed?

There is nothing in the scientific literature to suggest that addicts recommend addiction to anyone, much less their own kids. The media apparently knew so little about heroin they could simply assume it induced depravity and transformed users into the sort of vile subhumans who think nothing of doing such things. Thus the media smuggled into their stories a simplistic sort of pharmacological determinism. Clearly heroin can be powerfully addicting, but even if it were capable of morally lobotomizing all addicts, why would such addicts give away the very expensive stuff for which they reputedly lie, cheat, and steal?[5]

Almost any street junkie could have served as an expert informant (a "Deep Throat," if you will) and saved the *Post* from scandal. If the editors had picked ten addicts at random and asked them if a junkie would give away precious junk to a child, nine would have thought it absurd, moral qualms aside. Asked to read the Cooke story, most addicts could have told the *Post* immediately that is was concocted. Even if one accepted all of the other demonstrably dubious assumptions upon which the story rested, it made no sense even according to the perverse logic attributed to addicts.

A final set of red flags shot up immediately after "Jimmy's World" was published. According to the *Post*'s own follow-up stories, hundreds of police officers and social workers scoured the city looking for "Jimmy." Elementary school teachers inspected thousands of small student arms. Aroused citizens from housing projects in neighborhoods like "Jimmy's" all over Washington hunted for him. As Green's (1981) report put it, "The intense police search continued for 17 days. The city had been finely combed. Nothing." Half a dozen *Post* reporters also searched in vain for any other child addict. Our point here is not merely that none of these myriad searches turned up so much as a clue as to "Jimmy's" specific whereabouts. More significant is that with everyone so certain that "untold numbers of children like Jimmy" existed, no one found any child addict—not an 8-year-old, not a 10-year-old, not a 12-year-old.

For some reason these journalistic findings were not considered newsworthy. Presented with the choice of publishing the recalcitrant facts uncovered by their reporters or what they wanted to believe, *Post* editors and their print brethren chose to print the more ideologically compliant assertion that 8-year-old heroin addicts are common in America's inner cities. The Cooke affair thus suggests that the *Post* had more in common with President Reagan than it liked to believe. Reagan was fond, for example, of attacking "welfare chiselers" for buying vodka with their food stamps. No matter how many times his own experts told him this was untrue due to food-stamp redemption rules, he continued to tell the tale because it suited his ideological purposes. Lies uttered as political demagogy are one thing, but we expect more from the great newspapers on which we rely to expose such lies. In continuing to insist that "Jimmys" were everywhere in the face of their own evidence to the contrary, the *Post* seemed to be saying, â la Reagan, that if "Jimmy's World" doesn't exist in reality, then it can be made to exist in ideology.

Unfortunately, the nonfictional lives of African Americans in our inner cities and of growing numbers of other poor Americans are sufficiently harsh that some of them seek solace, comfort and meaning in drugs. But editors seem to believe that readers don't like to be reminded that there is something fundamentally wrong with the social system from which most of them benefit. Editors and readers alike, it seems, feel more comfortable believing that the worsening horrors of our inner cities are caused by evil individuals from a different gene pool—"addicts." Thus, a story about how crushing poverty and racism give rise to despair that sometimes leads to drug use, abuse or addiction is not considered "newsworthy." Stories that simply depict addicts as complicated, troubled human beings would be neither comforting enough for readers nor dramatic enough for prizes. To us, this sin of omission is more the real pity of this story than Janet Cooke's sin of commission.

About a week after the story first appeared and months before the scandal broke, *Post* publisher Donald Graham sent Cooke a congratulatory note on her "very fine story" (Green, 1981). It said, in part, that "The *Post* has no more important and tougher job than explaining life in the black community in Washington." Here he was as close to the ideal of journalism as Cooke's tale was distant from it.

Graham went on to praise the struggle of "black reporters who try to see life through their own eyes instead of seeing it the way they're told they should." In calling attention to the importance of independent reporting, Graham again articulated an important ideal. Ironically, Cooke had so internalized the way reporters in general "are told they should" see drug users that she gave a whole new meaning to the idea of seeing things through her "own eyes."

Finally, Graham wrote of how Cooke's article displayed the "gift" of "explaining" how the world works. "If there's any long-term justification for what we do," he wrote, it is that "people will act a bit differently and think a bit differently if we help them understand the world even slightly better. Much of what we write fails that first test because we don't understand what we're writing about ourselves." Here Graham displayed unintended prescience. For what he took to be a grand exception turned out to be a glaring example of his rule.

Cooke's concoction led readers to misunderstand the lives of addicts "in the black community." But hers was only an egregious case of the press's cultivated incapacity for understanding drug problems. If the *Post* scandal has value, it inheres in the accidental glimpse it affords into the nominally hidden process by which media institutions force the untidy facts of social life through the sieve of dominant ideology (Molotch and Lester, 1974). We submit that it is this process that allowed Cooke's tale to sail undetected past *Post* editors, Pulitzer jurors, and the hundreds of other journalists who analyzed the fraud. And we suggest that this process continues to camouflage the ways our world produces drug problems in the first place, and thereby helps to forge a public prepared to swallow the next junkie stereotype and to enlist in the next drug war.

Notes

[1] By all accounts in Ombudsman Green's investigation, Janet Cooke was not street-wise. She was middle-class and upwardly mobile. Her immediate supervisor told Green that Cooke "was not really street-savvy—She was Gucci and Cardin and Yves St Laurent—she didn't know the kinds of people she was dealing with, but she was tenacious and talented" (Green, 1981:A12).

[2] The Vassar degree had caught Editor-in-Chief Ben Bradlee's eye, causing him to sift Cooke's resume from the hundreds he receives each week and to set in motion the hiring process which brought her to the *Post* (Green, 1981:A12).

[3] The Pulitzer Board drew its own lesson from the Cooke scandal. Seven months later it adopted new procedures to guard against such problems. Pulitzer juries would henceforth deliberate for two days instead of one *(New York Times,* 11/22/91).

[4] The authors are indebted to Dr. Peter Cohen for the analogy to witches and heretics. Personal communication, 1991.

[5] To be fair, we did find one article *(New York Times,* 4/16/81) that at least mentioned the idea that addicts might not want to give away their heroin, but this lead was not pursued. Also, Mayor Marion Barry told the *Post* after the city-wide search that he doubted "the mother or the pusher would allow a reporter to see them shoot up" (Green, 1981:A13).

References

Becker, Howard S. 1953. Becoming a marijuana user. *American Journal of Sociology,* 59:235–43.

Becker, Howard S. 1963. *Outsiders: Studies in the Sociology of Deviance.* New York: Free Press.

Becker, Howard S. 1967. History, culture, and subjective experience: An exploration of the social bases of drug-induced experiences. *Journal of Health and Social Behavior,* 8:162–76.

Brecher, Edward M. 1972. *Licit and Illicit Drugs.* Boston, MA: Little, Brown.

Cooke, Janet. 1980. Jimmy's World—8-year-old heroin addict lives for a fix. *Washington Post,* Sept. 28, A1.

Feldman, Harvey, Michael Agar, and George Beschener. 1979. *Angel Dust.* Lexington, MA: D.C. Heath.

Green, Bill. 1981. Janet's world—The story of a child who never existed—How and why it came to be published. *Washington Post,* April 19, Al.

Himmelstein, Jerome. 1983. *The Strange Career of Marihuana.* Westport, CT: Greenwood Press.

Levine, Harry Gene. 1984. The alcohol problem in America: From temperance to Prohibition. *British Journal of Addiction*, 79:109–19.

Los Angeles Times. 1981. Story that was fabricated found a friend on Pulitzer board. April 17, I, 9.

Los Angeles Times. 1981. A matter of confidence. April 19, IV, 5.

Los Angeles Times. 1981. Finally, the Watergate spirit is dead in America. April 23, II, 11.

Los Angeles Times. 1981. Pulitzer fiasco's ripples spread too far. April 24, II, 1.

Mark, Gregory. 1975. Racial, economic, and political factors in the development of America's first drug laws. *Issues in Criminology*, 10:56–75.

Molotch, Harvey and Marilyn Lester. 1974. News as purposive behavior: On the strategic uses of routine events, accidents, and scandals. *American Sociological Review*, 39:101–12.

Morgan, Patricia. 1978. The legislation of drug law. *Journal of Drug Issues*, 8:53–62.

Musto, David. 1973. *The American Disease: Origins of Narcotic Control*. New Haven, CT: Yale University Press.

New York Times. 1981. *Washington Post* gives up Pulitzer, calling article on addict, 8, fiction. April 16 A1.

New York Times. 1981. Paper's false article is a major topic at convention of newspaper editors. April 23, A16.

New York Times. 1981. Pulitzer prize board adopts new procedures. November 22, A38.

Reinarman, Craig and Harry Gene Levine. 1989. Crack in context: Politics and media in the making of a drug scare. *Contemporary Drug Problems*, 16:535–77.

San Francisco Chronicle. 1981. *Washington Post* blames its editors for Pulitzer fiasco. April 19, A6.

Washington Post. 1980. D.C. Authorities seek identity of heroin addict, 8. September 30, A11.

Washington Post. 1981. *Post* writer wins Pulitzer for story on child addict. April 14, A1.

Washington Post. 1981. The end of the "Jimmy" story. April 16, A18.

Washington Post. 1981. *Post* reporter's Pulitzer Prize is withdrawn. April 16, A1.

Washington Post. 1981. The district line: The problem is all too real. April 17, C13.

Washington Post. 1981. "Jimmy" episode evokes outrage, sadness. April 17, C13.

Washington Post. 1981. Nation's editors plumb "Jimmy's World." April 18, A3.

Washington Post. 1981. Putting the creator of "Jimmy's World" in context. April 19, D1.

Well, Andrew. 1972. *The Natural Mind: An Investigation of Drugs and the Higher Consciousness*. Boston, MA: Houghton Mifflin.

Zinberg, Norman. 1984. *Drug, Set and Setting: The Basis for Controlled Intoxicant Use*. New Haven: Yale University Press.

Epilogue

A potential pitfall of studying crime, particularly when its reality is forged through the media, is that some may get the impression that the complex processes leading to the construction of crime can be captured in formulaic fashion. It might seem that with enough careful scientific study, a matrix or model of media-crime construction will emerge. Working through the research can leave one with a sense that a significant scientific project is underway. Certainly scholarship on the media and crime has generated a detailed inventory of the practices, actors, and effects of crime construction. Because of the imagination and effort of many researchers, we can now list and describe media practices that contributed to the social construction of crime—the creation and spread of news "themes" and "crime waves" (Fishman, 1978), the use of "motifs" and "typifications" (Ibarra & Kitsuse, 1993; Best, 1990) to culturally situate crime and the media's over reliance on sources and practices closely tied to the crime control industry to generate a reality of crime (Kappeler, Blumberg & Potter, 1996; Welch, Fenwick & Roberts, 1998).

We can enumerate some of the many actors in the social production of crime—the press, politicians, law enforcement officials, action groups, activists, and individuals and mythic incidents that are transformed into "folk devils" and "urban legends" (Cohen, 1980; Fine, 1980, 1992). Likewise, we can recount and analyze the often complex effects of media-crime presentations—public fear, collective insecurity, changes in lifestyle, and support for a growing web of social control (Carlson, 1995; Gerbner, 1994; Liska & Baccaglini, 1990). Yet, this rich and detailed inventory cannot lead to a precise formula, comprehensive matrix, or conclusive scientific explanation for the social reality of crime (Kappeler, et al., 1996). We can use broader brushes to paint the media's reality of crime as "morality plays" or "crime dramas" (Cavender &

333

Bond-Maupin, 1993). Even so, these portraits only capture a limited view of the entire landscape of crime reality.

Unlike researchers, the media are not bounded by the logic of science. Media workers care little about the assumptions of linearity or temporal sequence, and they certainly are not concerned with selective observation or overgeneralization. In fact, these are some of the practices used to construct crime waves, moral panics, and epidemics. Mark Fishman (1978: 34) observes that "the crime wave dynamic is necessary for a theme to grow into a wave: There must be a continuous supply of crime incidents that can been seen as instances of a theme." Of course, justice officials provide the media with highly selective crime reports, and journalists arrange the spatial and temporal sequences of these incidents to match their themes.

For social researchers, however, even isolating a unit of study is a particularly vexing problem. Should researchers analyze national stories, regional news, or local broadcasts? If one of these levels is selected, how does one take into account interactive media constructions of crime that cross all of the levels? Not only do local newspapers and television stations repeat the stories selected by the Associated Press or the major networks, they resituate national problems in local contexts. That is, the local media introduce viewers and readers to a localized version of a crime problem or the local personification of some folk devil. Gray Cavender and Lisa Bond-Maupin (1993: 52) remark that, "Good storytellers localize their tales in time and place."

When focusing on media constructions of crime, should researchers isolate television from newspapers or advertisements from the news? Do we even know where the news ends and entertainment begins? The media are "embedded in a configuration of institutions" (Fishman, 1978: 25). The Walt Disney Corporation includes ABC and ESPN. Viacom is the parent company of Paramount Pictures, MTV, Nickelodeon, Nick at Nite, Comedy Central, Showtime, The Movie Channel, All News Channel, UPN and, Blockbuster. Simon and Schuster Publishing includes Prentice-Hall, Allyn and Bacon, and Macmillan Publishing. Similarly, media presentations utilize crime within broader patterns of production and consumption. Media constructions of crime, then, come at us from many directions and origins. Our most public images of crime are influenced reciprocally by media business practices and organization of information and by how our society organizes activities. To disentangle the modern web of media, crime, and society is more than a challenge.

Understanding the social construction of crime problems is perhaps even more problematic when researchers attempt to use tools designed for measuring the physical world. These tools are not always conducive to measuring changing social constructions. We know, for example, that the processes and techniques used by the media are not static and the consequences of these processes are less than predictable. Sometimes moral panics center around marginalized or unpopular groups, other times the media-amplified victimization of a celebrity causes a national panic. While physical objects wait for careful researchers to calibrate their measuring, media practices are constantly changing as fast as sound bites are produced.

Even media-generated moral panics defy uniformity. Some crime problems emerge, develop, hold public interest, have long lives, and result in social policy; others never fully mature. Occasionally, immature panics resurface in media loops. Road rage and the "ice" epidemic are two examples of immature crime problems that only occasionally resurface in the media. Likewise, as we prepare to make our measurements, the media can capriciously abandon a current panic to report on another newsworthy story—perhaps a celebrity trial, the death of a prominent person, or some "natural disaster." We know very little about the processes that displace or diffuse emerging crime panics. Attempting to map the terrain of the cause and effect relationships between media constructs and behavior or even making useful generalizations in a territory where the boundaries are constantly changing is problematic at best. Perhaps we can account for some of these contradictions by broadening the focus a bit beyond the media-crime landscape.

The Transformational Media and Commodified Society

The media are beset by transformational obsolescence. As soon as we became accustomed to visiting movie theaters, radio brought entertainment into the home. The social construction process now had two players capable of reaching mass audiences. The visual images of the movies were somewhat displaced by the more readily available audio messages. Television combined both and pervaded daily life. Even the hardware that disseminates media images and messages overlaps to make distinctions difficult. One can listen to radio broadcasts through television speakers and watch the news on a computer monitor. One can now interact with the media through computers and use this same hardware to see the reality produced through the mix of "live" participation with mediated images. The proliferation of technology combines all the modern communication sources into a multi-media "spectacle" where image, sound, and interactions are possible (Debord, 1970, 1990).

Mass communication makes it increasingly difficult to distinguish the viewer from the viewed. We watch ourselves entering department stores on large screen security cameras. At sporting events, student sections cheer wildly as soon as the red light indicates the television camera is panning the audience. Television and the media industry serve not as a "window on the world," but rather as a "mirrored looking glass"—allowing us to look out only to have our distorted image reflected back. The media selectively capture and frame what they see. In this process, the media transform viewers as well as the world around them. The media capture human desires for predictability, safety, order, security, and power; they also transform, frame, and make the foundation of these desires obsolete. The media estrange us from reality and treat us like commodities—producing and satisfying desires that no longer correspond with any underlying reality. The media, in this sense, create a phantom "public" where individuals and their desires are massified into a market conformity and uniformity of thought destroying "all personality" (Kierkegaard, 1978, 1982) in favor of a "marketable personality" (Fromm, 1947).

This of course is done in the mass-market place of production and consumption that generates "abstractions" from reality (Kierkegaard, 1978) and tends to erase difference and magnitude in favor of global appeal, intensity, and fantasy. Striving for universal appeal, the media erase distinctions between forms of reality and between social class, social groups, and political ideology in favor of composite abstractions. We can all go with Kathy Lee Gifford on a Caribbean cruise; we are all, along with our credit cards, "accepted wherever we go"; and we can all "rock the vote" with our participation. The media also introduce us to the universalized dangers of living. This seems particularly evident in the media construction of drug panics. "Drug scares typically link a scapegoat drug to a troubling subordinate group—working-class immigrants, racial, or ethnic minorities, or rebellious youth" (Reinarman & Levine, 1995: 147). Media reality extends the threat beyond these urban groups to suburban, white middle-class teenagers and women. This was certainly the case with the "ice danger" (Jenkins, 1994) and the now emerging concern with the use of heroin among affluent small-town teenagers. If media accounts are to be believed, the country stands at the edge of an epidemic of heroin use (Wolf, 1997). Heroin moves from inner-city shooting galleries to the pockets of suburban teenagers (Associated Press, 1997). To match the constructed market, the rhetoric describing the "new" forms of use throws the term "designer" into the mix.

In essence, just as advertisers use technology to blend race and ethnicity to construct human faces that have universal marketing appeal, the media now mix and blend behaviors, places, and populations into a composite danger. The media no longer need to instruct us about "urban danger," or specific "different ones." They create for us a symbolic "dangerous world" (Kappeler, et al., 1996; Cavender & Bond-Maupin, 1993) where the symbol is detached from its reality. Danger becomes global; differences and particularities are dissolved in abstraction. Because the desire for safety is universal, the new reality consumes us despite the absence of any anchors to individual reality. In these transformational processes, reality is erased as the desire for safety and predictability is assumed and magnified.

Of course the media instruct us where safety and predictability can be sought. FOX, for example, announces, "It's 10 o'clock. Do you know where your children are?" After a short pause the announcer states, "FOX—safe at home!" There is contradiction in the messages sent by the media. Previously that evening viewers might have watched a crime info-commercial that reenacted some criminal slaughter committed in someone's home (Cavender & Bond-Maupin, 1993). The media first project obscure and sensational incidents as universal dangers to attract attention and then calm the sensations aroused to retain their market—you're safe at home in front of the television. Both messages are, of course, absurd. The construction creeps into everyday life and common sense. The television industry has an economic interest in keeping people in their homes and in front of their television sets. The needs of the marketplace are transformed into the necessity of safeguarding one's family. The ritualistic enactment of prudent behaviors, the simulation of taking action (by not leaving home), and the domination of self are all intertwined. We are projected into the very spectacle we consume.

Technological changes, media constructions, and the processes of mass communication along patterns of directed production and consumption are fundamentally altering the process by which the reality of crime and everyday life is manufactured. The media comprise a cultural industry which blend production, information, and technology into complex forms of domination which remove us from reality. A few crime incidents are transformed into waves. The maxim that "once you have three things you have a trend" is minimized further by the spectacle of modern media (Best & Hutchinson, 1996: 192) The media can construct crime and social problems based on their own fabrications and abstractions. The urban legend or folk devil need not be featured; it is already embedded in the abstraction. We have consumed so many images of criminals and constructions of appropriate behavior in response that we no longer need the missing abstraction—we unconsciously supply it. Today, the media are both a part of the reality collected and the reality projected. The media become a source of "cultural stock" from which the industry draws to create the next abstraction.

Reproducing Crime in Everyday Life

The allure of the sensationalism that drives the media captures everyone, including those who study the media and crime. While the media's construction of gangs, drunk drivers, road warriors, and drug epidemics are important issues deserving both attention and debunking, we seem less attracted to how crime is folded into in everyday life. This is understandable given the richness and the sensational properties of media-based crime presentations—as well as our obsession with them. Yet, crime and the social order are reproduced in far more mundane occurrences. A less sensational example illustrates the pervasive effects. The following newspaper column appeared on the front page of a small-town newspaper.

> Christmas season is a time for joy, but it is also a time for car thefts and personal burglaries, police officials said. During the holiday season while Madison County residents are shopping, they need to take extra caution of where they put their packages, Richmond Police Officer David Pence said.
>
> While at malls and shopping centers, Pence said he recommends hiding Christmas packages either in the trunk or under blankets and locking vehicle doors. "It is too tempting (for the burglars)," Pence said. "We're not living in Mayberry society. You want to take care of your belongings. You don't want to make it so easy for people to take your stuff.
>
> "Think about personal safety. You want to make sure you don't give people the opportunity to rip you off."
>
> When approaching a vehicle that should be parked in a lighted area, Pence said the owner of the vehicle should scan under the vehicle and in the back seat to make sure no one is near their car.
>
> During this time of year, Pence said police also talk to businesses about anti-theft safety and do extra patrols of 24-hour convenience stores.
>
> Because the holiday times are also a time for depression and pressure for many people, Pence said robberies and burglaries tend to rise. Pence said he recommends businesses to not obscure their windows with decorations so police officers can see clearly if the clerk is safe (Gay, 1997: 1).

In these dozen sentences of general instructions, latent urban legends are invoked, legal misconstructions of criminality promote serious danger, media constructions of safe and fearful places are regenerated, and contemporary patterns of production and consumption are embedded. The journalist uses the holiday as a backdrop for official commentary on crime—the perfect "idiom for expressing urban fear and a corresponding sense of danger" (Cavender & Bond-Maupin, 1993: 46). The police officer uses the opportunity to transmit official beliefs and values and to legitimize himself as a source of knowledge about crime, prevention, and control. All the elements and linkages are present in their symbolic forms. "These links need not be made explicit; when experienced members of the culture make sense of a particular legend or news report . . ., they draw on their broader understandings of the nature of deviance and social problems" (Best & Hutchinson, 1996: 98).

The journalist conveys and transforms the law enforcement construction of a common event (located at the center of the modern spectacle of consumption, the shopping mall) into media reality that elicits fear with the predictable use of dark, isolated areas and menacing strangers. The thief, likely to steal your "stuff," merges with the armed robber. The latent legends of the "slasher" and the "killer in the backseat" reemerge without need of direct reference. This all, of course, takes place "in a parking lot, the hotbed of contemporary legend violence—the shopping mall" (see, Best & Hutchinson, 1996: 86-87). In the abstraction, the officer does not refer to a real small town as a basis of comparison; rather, he chooses a television reality—this is no "Mayberry."

This media abstraction needed no sensational incident, no repeated instances of behavior to create a crime wave, and no real town to reproduce a reality of crime in an everyday aspect of social life. The abstraction based on a generic dangerous world was sufficient. It is doubtful that the officer being interviewed ever encountered a real case of the urban legends he promotes—either "slasher" or "killer in the backseat." Even if shoppers faithfully adhere to the instructions to park in well lighted areas, what are the probabilities that a police cruiser will pass by at just the precise moment to thwart an attack? It is likewise doubtful that the dutiful shopkeepers who keep their windows unobstructed will be fortunate enough to avoid a random act of violence because the "extra patrol" passes by just in time. The officer is merely providing commonsense reality; the advice reproduces the abstraction forged from an ideology of crime long since divorced from the social circumstances that created it.

Abstract danger legitimizes public surveillance and regimented personal action by forging the spectacle between the media, the audience, and comprehensive social control. The real power to control crime pales in comparison to the illusion of control and the universalized desire to control the "evil" that is inscribed in even the most insipid media accounts of crime. These techo-cultural rituals reaffirm faith in control and the "administration" of justice. The perpetrator walk—marching the accused person in handcuffs before a crew of reporters and cameras—feeds the desire for justice. The criminal is reduced to the glare of publicity, caught by the system of control that protects all of us. It is a compelling drama for the media to project to an audience eager to believe that the system of control works. The spectacle of reality produced by mass-media images reduces life, justice, and the real crime that exist to something less than the abstraction.

Certainly we need to study the construction of crime waves and urban legends—and to unmask the organizational forces within the media industry that forge our common-sense notions of crime, but we must also begin to expand the landscape of crime construction beyond the manufacturing of sensational images projected on our television screens and the journalistic practices that create the words that appear in newspapers and magazines. We must begin to understand how crime plays a central role in the spectacle of social life as it reproduces patterns of behavior, production, and consumption in a society increasingly attracted to the abstraction of reality.

References

Associated Press (1997). Authorities fear growth of 'Special K' use in teens. *The Richmond Register,* 106(344): A9.

Best, J. (1990). *Threatened children.* Chicago: University of Chicago Press.

Best, J., & Hutchinson, M. M. (1996). The gang initiation rite as a motif in contemporary crime discourse. In this volume, pp. 113–135.

Carlson, J. (1995). *Prime time enforcement.* New York: Praeger.

Cavender, G. & Bond-Maupin, L. (1993). Fear and loathing on reality television: An analysis of America's most wanted and unsolved mysteries. In this volume, pp. 73–85.

Cohen, S. (1980). *Folk devils and moral panics: The creation of the Mods and Rockers.* New York: St. Martin's Press.

Debord, G. (1970). *The society of the spectacle.* Detroit, MI: Black and Red.

Debord, G. (1990). *Comments on the society of the spectacle.* New York: Verso.

Fine, G. A. (1980). The Kentucky fried rat: Legends and modern society. *Journal of Folklore Institute,* 17: 222–243.

Fine, G. A. (1992). *Manufacturing tales.* Knoxville: University of Tennessee Press.

Fishman, M. (1978). Crime waves as ideology. In this volume, pp. 53–71.

Fromm, E. (1947). *Man for himself.* New York: Holt, Rinehart and Winston.

Gay, T. (1997). Police urge safety techniques during holidays. *The Richmond Register,* 106 (328): 1.

Gerbner, G. (1994). Television violence: The art of asking the wrong question. *Currents in Media Thought,* (July): 385–397.

Goode, E., & Ben–Yehuda, N. (1994). *Moral panics.* Cambridge, MA: Blackwell.

Ibarra, P. R., & Kitsuse, J. I. (1993). "Vernacular constituents of moral discourse." In J. A. Holstein and G. Miller (eds.), *Reconsidering social constructionism,* pp. 25–58. New York: Aldine.

Jenkins, P. (1994). "The ice age": The social construction of a drug panic. In this volume, pp. 137–160.

Kappeler, V. E., Blumberg, M., Potter, G. W. (1996). *The mythology of crime and criminal justice* (2nd ed.). Prospect Heights, IL: Waveland Press.

Kierkegaard, S. (1978). *Two ages: The age of revolution and the present age.* Princeton: Princeton University Press.

Kierkegaard, S. (1982). *The corsair affair.* Princeton: Princeton University Press.

Liska, A., & Baccaglini, W. (1990). Feeling safe by comparison: Crime in the newspapers. *Social Problems,* 37, 360–374.

Reinarman, C., & Levine, H. G. (1995). The crack attack: America's latest drug scare, 1986–1992. In J. Best, (ed). *Images of issues: Typifying contemporary social problems*, pp. 147–190. New York: Aldine.

Sacco, V. F (1995). Media constructions of crime. In this volume, pp. 37–51.

Welch, M., Fenwick, M., & Roberts, M. (1998). State managers, intellectuals, and the media: A content analysis of ideology in experts' quotes in feature newspaper articles on crime. In this volume, pp. 87–110.

Wolf, R. (1997). Texas suburb's dark side: Heroin. *USA Today*, (Nov. 20): 3A.

Index